TIME LIFE BOOKS

Your Old House

GIVE NEW LIFE TO YOUR OLDER HOME

BY THE EDITORS OF TIME-LIFE BOOKS, ALEXANDRIA, VIRGINIA

ABOUT THIS BOOK

The information in this book will help you maintain, improve, and protect what is probably the biggest investment of your life—your house. Naturally you are concerned about maintaining the value of your investment, as well as its condition.

However, a house changes with time. No matter how substantial its original construction, over the years weather, constant use, and the normal aging of materials result in problems that need attention. Some of these are primarily matters of maintenance, others may call for making repairs or replacements to avoid more serious problems at a later time. The positive aspect of home maintenance and repair is that you can do a great deal yourself, at great savings.

In these pages, the editors of Time-Life and consulting experts have identified the most common problems and concerns in maintaining and improving old houses. They show you how to inspect and evaluate all aspects of the interior and exterior of your home; how to correct or repair any problems you find; and how to keep things in condition to minimize the need for future repairs. Each of the hundreds of projects is explained step by step, so you can do the work yourself or talk knowledgeably with any workers you hire. An appendix describes the many kinds of professional specialists you might turn to, and tells you how to select and deal with them.

Altogether, this book gives you a wealth of useful instruction and information to make it both easy and profitable to perform the maintenance and make the repairs that will keep your old house in excellent condition.

CONTENTS

MAINTAINING THE EXTERIOR

The exterior of your home is one of the most visible indications of your taste and life-style—so of course you want it to look its best. But taking care of the outside of your home is more than a matter of appearances.

A well-maintained exterior increases the market value of a house and helps keep the yearly expenses to a minimum. When taken care of immediately, maintenance is easy and repairs are inexpensive. If neglected, they rapidly become expensive and may cause interior problems as well.

You can do all the work yourself or have a specialist take care of some things (see pages 250–251). In either case, this chapter tells you how to inspect the exterior of your home, how to keep the roof in good condition, how to maintain and repair wood, brick, and stucco walls, and how to paint your whole house safely and efficiently. Remember, every bit of work you do not only gives you immediate comfort, security, and economy but also protects your investment for the future.

▷ *Right:* Stucco, widely used in some areas, weathers well. Painting can give it a new look and hide any repairs—it's easy to do with a deep-nap roller.

▽ *Below:* A white clapboard exterior is a classic American style. To preserve its beauty decade after decade, be sure joints are caulked, replace damaged sections promptly, and keep the weatherproof "skin" of paint intact.

△ *Above:* Wood elements such as window frames and shutters are especially vulnerable to the effects of weather, so it is important to check every year to see if they need repairs or a fresh coat of paint.

△ *Above:* Decorative wood trim gives charm to many old houses. Such details on porches, gables, and eaves often need maintenance attention more frequently than wood siding.

▷ *Right:* Combined brick and wood construction presents a variety of maintenance concerns. Keep brick faces clean and the joints filled with solid mortar. Repair and repaint wood trim at the first signs of deterioration.

INSPECTING THE OUTSIDE OF A HOUSE

Once a year, inspect the exterior of your house as carefully as if you were going to buy it. Late spring is best, so you will have plenty of time for any repairs or improvements that need to be done.

Water Damage: Examine the roof surface, gutters and downspouts *(opposite)*, and all areas vulnerable to leaks. Gutter runs longer than 40 feet should have two downspouts. If gutters and downspouts have deteriorated, masonry, wood-siding, and stucco walls may show signs of rot or crumbling *(pages 20–21)*.

Insect Damage: Before checking for infestation *(page 21)*, ask local exterminators about the most common insects in the area. An exterminator must be hired to eliminate termites, carpenter ants, and powder-post beetles—which can cause serious structural damage.

Surface Drainage: Make sure that the soil next to the foundation has been graded so it noticeably slopes away from the house for at least 6 feet. If the ground is level or slopes toward the foundation, look for signs of a wet basement and foundation damage *(pages 228–229)*. Improper grading can be corrected by filling around the foundation with earth.

Check walkways and driveways for cracks and sinking. Generally, pavement that has sunk more than 1 inch is hazardous and is best replaced. Low points in a driveway should have a functioning drain, particularly if the driveway slopes toward the house.

Retaining walls need weep holes near the bottom for drainage, so water will not back up against the house.

In the Garage: Check the structure inside and out. Make certain that garage doors work smoothly and that a door-opener reverses direction when it meets resistance. Check the condition of the floor. Be sure the door to an attached house is at least 4 inches above the garage floor to prevent gasoline fumes, which are heavier than air, from entering the house.

CAUTION

Safety Procedures for Lead Paint and Asbestos

Lead and asbestos, known health hazards, pervade houses constructed or remodeled before 1978. Whereas lead is found primarily in paint, potential asbestos locations include wallboard, joint compound, insulation, flooring and related adhesives, roofing felt, shingles, and flashing. A visual inspection cannot determine the presence of lead or asbestos, but you may ask that the seller get testing done. Depending on the terms of the sale, you may be responsible for removal, which can be costly. Hire a professional licensed in hazardous-substance removal for large jobs indoors or if you suffer from cardiac, respiratory, or heat-tolerance problems that may be triggered by the protective clothing and respirator you must wear to do the work yourself. Tackle a roof only if you are experienced working at heights, and remember that the respirator impairs vision. If you remove asbestos or lead yourself, follow these procedures:

- *Keep children, pregnant women, and pets away from the area.*
- *Indoors, seal off work area openings with 6-mil polyethylene sheeting and duct tape. Cover rugs and nonmovable furniture with more sheeting and tape. Turn off air conditioning and forced-air heating systems.*
- *When you finish indoor work, mop the area twice, then run a vacuum cleaner equipped with a high-efficiency particulate air (HEPA) filter.*
- *Cover the work area ground outside with 6-mil polyethylene sheeting. Never work in windy conditions.*
- *If you must use an electric sander on lead paint, get one equipped with a HEPA filter. Never sand asbestos-laden materials or cut them with power machinery. Instead, mist them with water and detergent, and remove them carefully with hand tools.*
- *On a roof, pry up shingles, misting as you go. Place all debris in a polyethylene bag; never throw roofing material containing asbestos to the ground.*
- *Always wear protective clothing (available from a safety equipment supply house or paint stores) and a dual-cartridge respirator. Remove the clothing, including shoes, before leaving the work area. Wash the clothing separately, and shower and wash your hair immediately.*
- *Dispose of the materials as recommended by your local health department or environmental protection office.*

START AT THE ROOF

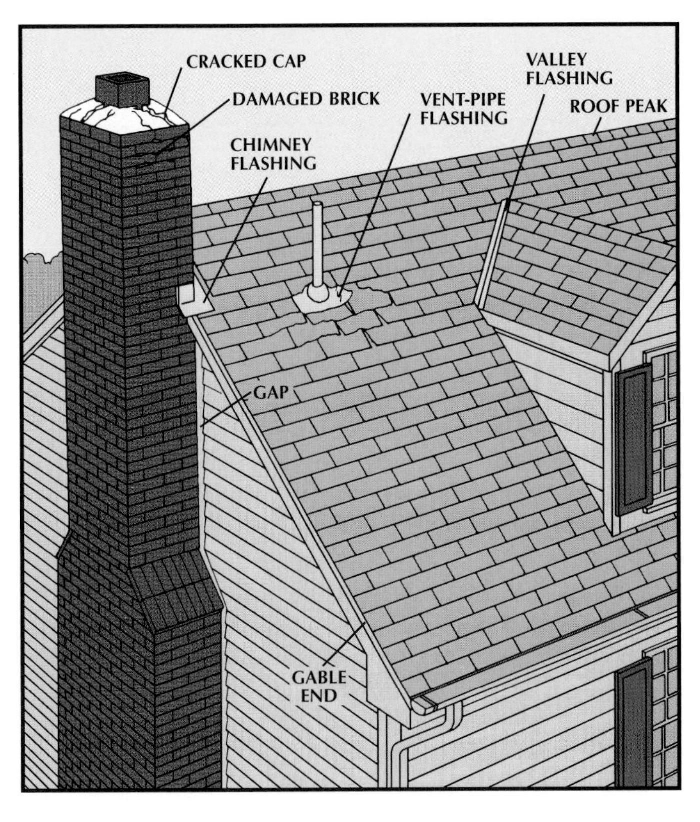

Critical areas on the roof.

◆ Use binoculars or get up on the roof safely *(page 14)* to check its condition. Compare its appearance with the photographs on the next page. Consult pages 15–19 if repairs are needed. Also look at the roof edge along the gable. If you can see more than one generation of shingles, they must all be removed if you need to replace all the roofing.

◆ Check for sags along the ridge.

◆ Inspect exposed flashing around the chimney, in roof valleys, and around any protruding pipes. Bent, rusted, or cracked flashing requires immediate attention; look for corresponding water damage inside.

◆ Inspect the joint between the side of the house and the chimney. A gap narrower than 3 inches at the top is caused by gradual settling and should be watched for any enlargement. A wider gap may mean that the footing under the chimney is failing; consult a foundation engineer.

◆ In both exterior and interior chimneys, look for loose or damaged bricks and gaps in mortar joints and for a cracked, chipped chimney cap. Such flaws admit water, which can further damage the masonry and constitute a fire hazard, since sparks may escape into wood framing. Remedy these defects before using the fireplace.

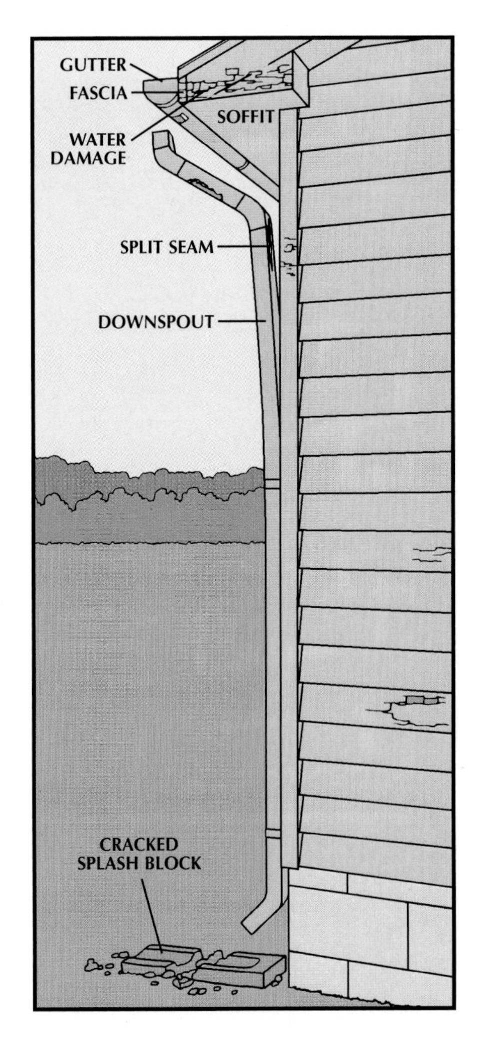

Faulty gutters and downspouts.

◆ Examine steel or copper gutters—a magnet sticks to steel—for signs of corrosion, especially at joints and along the bottoms, where leaves might collect.

◆ Check downspouts made of any material for a separated seam along the back, often caused by clogging and freezing.

◆ Step away from the house to confirm that no gutter has pulled away from the fascia and that each slopes along the fascia board toward its downspout.

◆ Look at the splash blocks or drainpipes at the ends of downspouts. Make sure they are in good condition and positioned to direct water away from the foundation. Confirm that drainpipes are not clogged.

Wherever you spot a fault in a gutter system, examine the nearby soffit and fascia board, the siding below, and the wood framing at ground level. Look for peeling paint, dark rot spots, or other signs of water damage.

ESTIMATING THE LIFE OF A ROOF

As illustrated by the pairs of photographs below—the left-hand picture shows a new roof, and the right-hand one shows an aging roof of the same material—you can tell a lot about the condition of a roof and its life expectancy just by looking at it.

When evaluating a roof, look most closely at the southern exposure of the house, if it has one. Also, distinguish between localized damage that can be repaired and widespread deterioration that only a new roof can correct.

Repairable problems include a few broken shingles, isolated shingle leaks, or leaks around flashing *(pages 15–16)*. However, if more than 25 percent of the shingles are broken or the roof looks substantially worse than the right-hand examples below, the house will need a new roof soon—as it will if you detect leaks in the flashing at valleys (where the roof of one part of the house meets the roof of another).

Asphalt shingles. The curling evident here signifies this roof is near the end of its 20- to 25-year life span. Rust stains *(above, right)* from old flashing are harmless to the shingles, but the flashing should be replaced.

Cedar shakes. Weathering soon turns cedar gray, so color is no indicator of age. But this roof, with almost every shake split and curling, is near the end of its 35-year life span. Cedar shingles, thinner than shakes, last 25 years at most.

Slate. More expensive than any other material, slate makes a roof that can last as long as a century. When slate surfaces flake, as these do, or show white stains, the roof is within about 10 years of requiring replacement.

Metal. With application of rustproofing, a metal roof may last 50 years or more. Though bare in spots and beginning to rust, this old roof has no broken seams. It can be saved by painting preceded by thorough preparation.

KEEPING A ROOF IN GOOD CONDITION

Roof leaks and gutter problems often start small, but they can cause major damage to the house if left uncorrected. Clean out the gutters at least twice a year, and at the same time check for flaws in gutters, roofing, and flashing. Some defects may not be noticed until water enters the house during a storm. In that case, catch the drips in buckets and wait for the rain to end—and the roof to dry—before getting up on the roof to begin repairs.

Patches for the Roofing: The simplest faults to detect and remedy are leaks in the broad expanse of the roof itself. Asphalt shingles may be torn, worn, or curled. Wood shingles can rot, and slates or tiles can crack. In some cases, shingles, slates, or tiles may be missing altogether. Unless the damage is so severe that complete reroofing is required, confine your repairs to a small area consisting of one or two damaged pieces. Trying to repair a larger expanse can disturb the overall pattern of the roofing and cause more problems than are solved.

Fixing Flaws in the Flashing: Somewhat harder to find and remedy are leaks under flashing—the metal strips that seal joints where roof slopes converge or where the roof meets a wall, chimney, or vent pipe. Examine flashing to see that it is unbroken and that the edges are sealed. If the house has an unfinished attic, you can check for leaks from inside: Look for daylight, and mark any opening by poking a wire through.

Flashing is available in copper, aluminum, zinc, or galvanized steel; when you must replace a section of flashing, match the metal you already have to avoid galvanic corrosion. Roofing cement seals flashing best on most roofs.

Gutter Repairs: After you clean the gutters, spray the roof with a hose and watch the gutters for pooling—a sign of sagging or other misalignment. Also inspect the gutter surfaces; vinyl, aluminum, and copper gutters rarely need maintenance, but rust may develop in steel gutters and rot in wood ones. You can patch small holes with fiberglass or other materials available at home centers; replace large sections that are damaged. Paint steel gutters every few years, and coat wood gutters with a preservative annually.

Strengthening the Roof: Although you should never try to reverse a sag in the roof, you can keep it from getting worse. Two bracing methods are shown on page 237; both are effective but can cause hairline cracks in plaster below. A third way to reinforce a roof is to install sister rafters and joists cut to the same size as the old counterparts and nailed to them.

CAUTION *Consult page 14 for precautions to take when you work on a roof. To avoid causing further damage, never walk on a slate, tile, or wood-shingle roof.*

TOOLS

- Hammer
- Roofer's mop or push broom
- Ball-peen hammer
- Cold chisel or brick set
- Slate ripper
- Hacksaw blade
- Electric drill
- Tin snips
- Plumb bob
- Mallet
- Carpenter's level

MATERIALS

- Roofing cement
- Galvanized roofing nails ($1\frac{1}{4}$")
- Flashing
- Fibrous aluminum roof coating
- Masonry nails ($\frac{3}{4}$")
- Slates
- Clay tiles
- Wood shingles
- Drip edge
- Gutter spike
- Ferrule
- Sheet-metal screws
- Lumber (2 x 4, 2 x 6, 4 x 4)
- Common nails ($2\frac{1}{2}$")

SAFETY TIPS

Wear soft-soled, slip-resistant shoes when working on a roof. When you clean gutters, gloves will protect against sharp metal edges and such debris as roofing nails and thorns. Goggles guard your eyes when you are hammering, and a hard hat is advisable in an unfinished attic.

WORKING SAFELY ON A ROOF

Safety is the paramount concern during roof work. While the slope of your roof is the main factor in determining whether you need to rent or buy special equipment, your personal tolerance for heights is also important. If you feel uncomfortable on a low-slope roof, take the same safety precautions that others might reserve for a steeper one, or consider hiring a professional to do the work for you.

If you do choose to work on a roof, exercise great care. In general, if the roof slopes less than 4 inches in 12, you can move about it in safety by observing common-sense precautions and wearing rubber-soled shoes. On a steeper roof use roof brackets *(below)* or ladder hooks *(bottom)*.
For your own protection and to avoid damage, never walk on a roof made of tile, slate, or wood shingles. Also never walk on a roof in cold weather. Asphalt materials can crack, and any surface—especially metal—can be dangerously slippery.

On steep-sloped asphalt roofs, metal supports called roof brackets *(above, left)*, along with a board, can provide a platform for a worker and up to 40 pounds of materials for every 4 feet of space *(above, right)*. Secure the brackets with $3\frac{1}{2}$-inch nails driven to leave the heads $\frac{1}{4}$ inch above the surface so you can easily pull them out later. You can lay the brackets entirely over the shingles and nail through as shown. However, it is better to carefully lift the shingle flaps and slip the ends of the brackets underneath so the nail holes will be covered later. Whichever way you secure the brackets, spot-patch the holes with roofing cement after you pull the nails to remove the brackets.

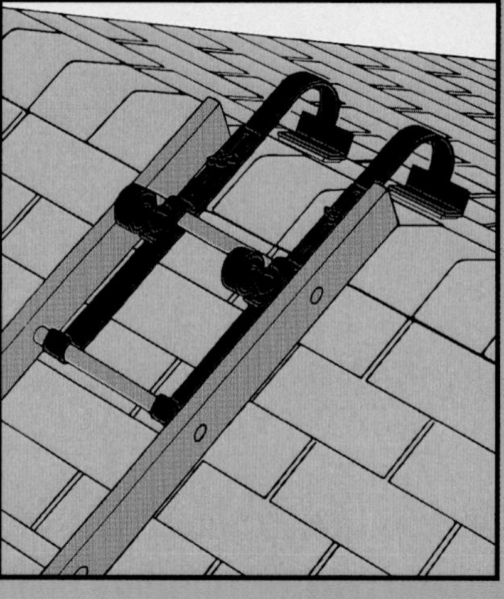

Another way to work on a steep slope is to hang a ladder from the ridge with ladder hooks *(above, left)*, which adjust to fit any extension ladder. Models with casters permit you to roll the hooks, with the ladder attached, up a finished roof without damaging it. Turn the ladder over for the hooks to grip the ridge *(above, right)*.

SMALL DO-IT-YOURSELF ROOF REPAIRS

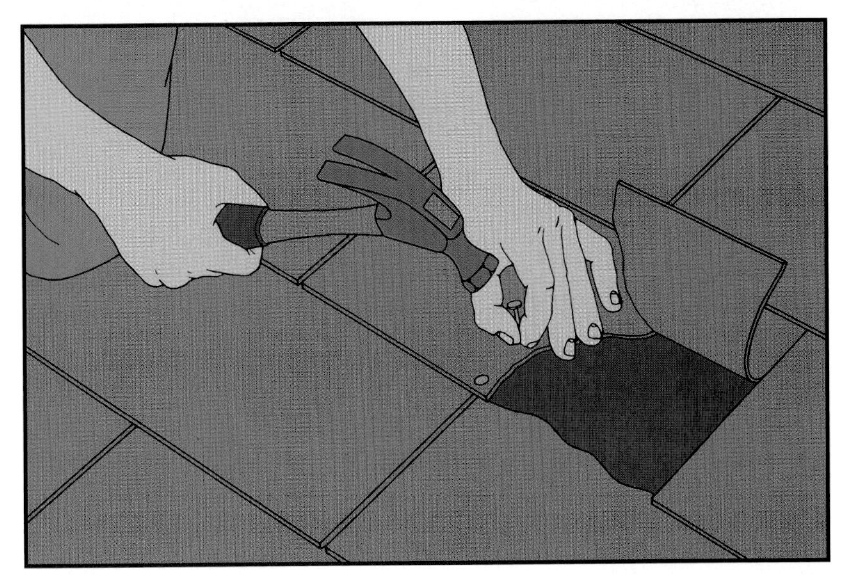

Mending a torn shingle.

◆ Spread a thin coating of roofing cement under a damaged asphalt shingle.

◆ Press the flaps flat and drive galvanized roofing nails along each side of the tear *(left)*.

◆ Cover the nailheads and the tear with roofing cement.

Patching a crack with metal.

◆ As a temporary measure to stop leaks through a cracked wood shingle or slate, cut a piece of metal flashing that is twice the width of and 3 inches longer than the exposed part of the damaged shingle.

◆ Spread roofing cement on one side of the flashing along what will be the upper edge. Insert that edge under the broken shingle and the adjacent shingles, with the cemented side down.

◆ Use a wood block and a hammer to tap the flashing in until its upper edge extends under the lower edges of the shingles in the course above *(right)*.

◆ For a more permanent repair, remove and replace the broken piece *(pages 16–18)*.

Coating pitted or pinholed metal.

You can extend the life of a pitted metal roof somewhat by applying fibrous aluminum roof coating with a roofer's mop or a stiff-bristled push broom *(left)*. Work the coating well into all valleys and joints. Most coatings last about a year; since a second layer is not recommended, plan to replace the roof within that time.

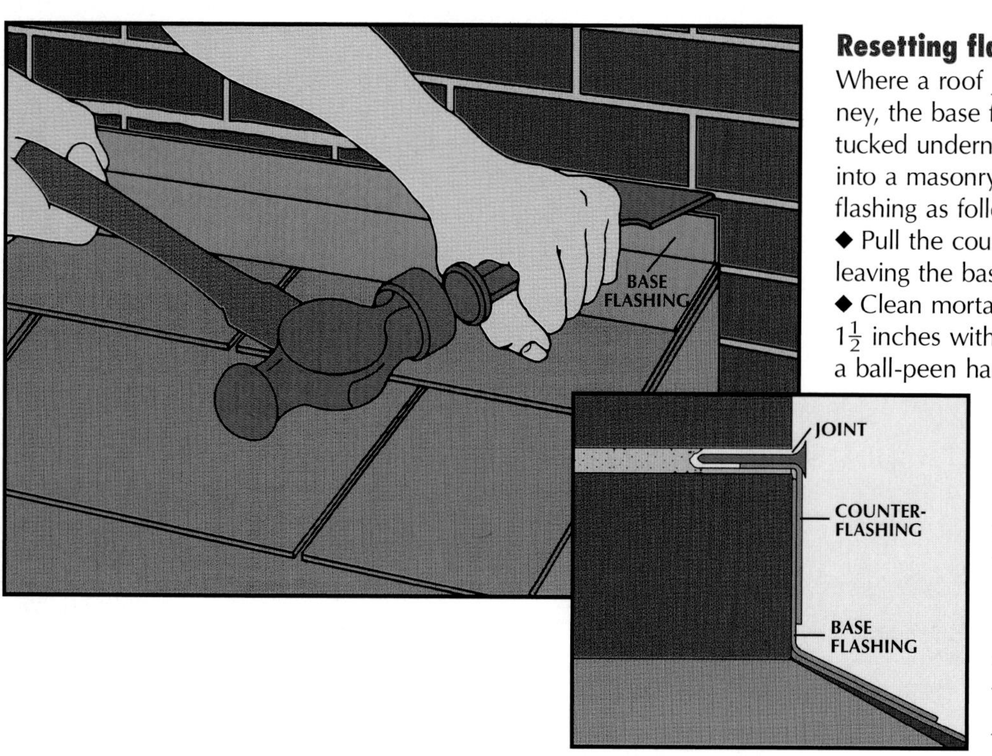

Resetting flashing in a mortar joint.
Where a roof joins a masonry wall or chimney, the base flashing on the roof is generally tucked underneath counterflashing inserted into a masonry joint. Reseat loose counterflashing as follows:

◆ Pull the counterflashing out of the way, leaving the base flashing in place.

◆ Clean mortar out of the joint to a depth of $1\frac{1}{2}$ inches with a cold chisel or brick set and a ball-peen hammer *(left).*

◆ Refill the joint with roofing cement, push in the lip of the counterflashing, and drive a masonry nail above it near the top of the joint so that it wedges the counterflashing in place without piercing it *(inset).* For a long section, place a masonry nail every 2 feet.

◆ Seal the metal-to-masonry joint with roofing cement.

REMOVING SLATES, TILES, OR WOOD SHINGLES

Extracting broken remnants.

◆ Slide the arrow-shaped head of a slate ripper *(below)*—a special-purpose tool available at roofing-supply stores—under a broken slate, wood shingle, or clay tile. Hook an end notch around a nail. The nails holding tiles are located along the flat section of the tile *(inset).*

◆ Cut the nail with a sharp blow on the raised handle of the slate ripper with a ball-peen hammer *(right).*

◆ After cutting the nails, slide out the broken piece without disturbing adjacent slates or tiles.

If you do not have a slate ripper, wrap one end of a long hacksaw blade with thick tape. Wearing work gloves, cut the nails with the other end.

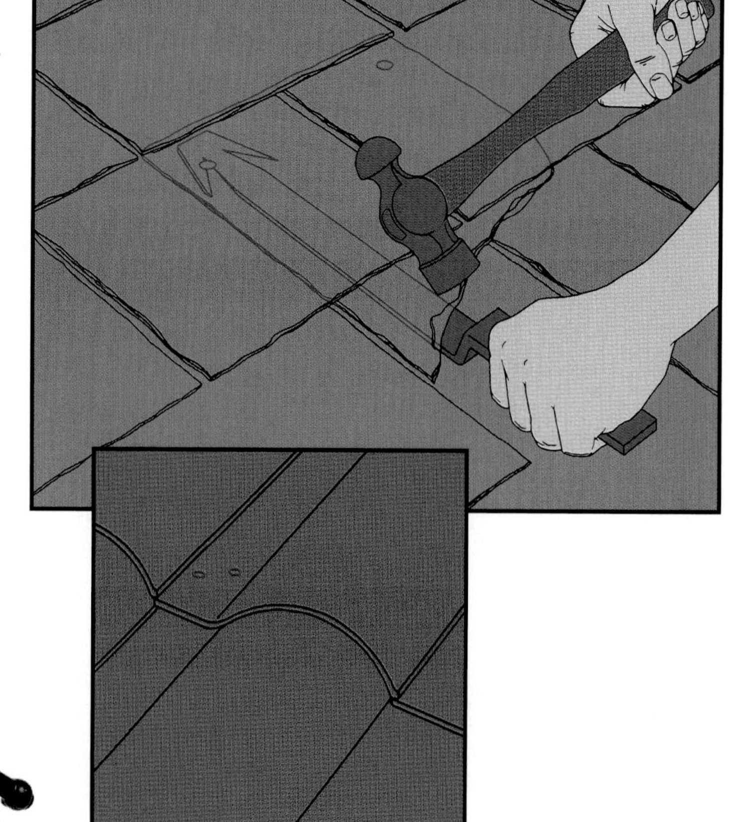

INSTALLING REPLACEMENTS

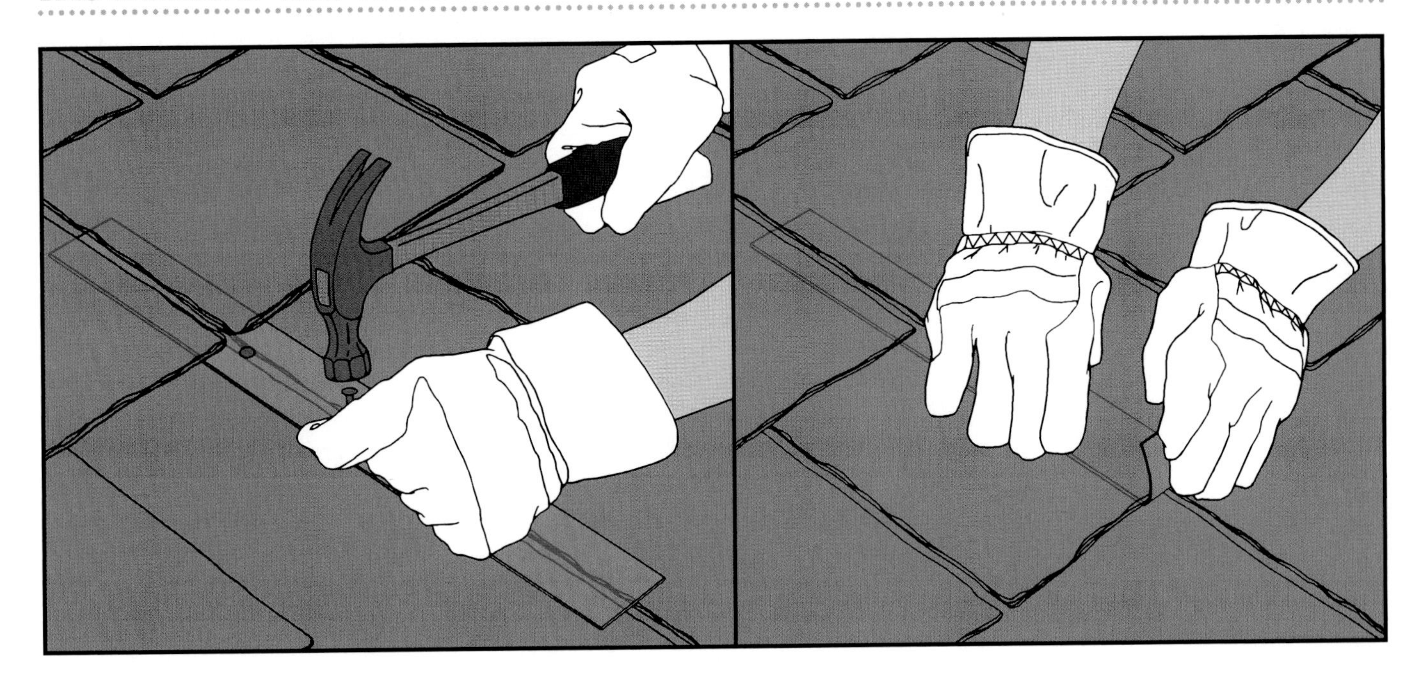

Securing a replacement slate.

◆ Cut a 2-inch-wide strip of metal flashing long enough to extend several inches under the course above the replacement slate and about an inch below it.

◆ Nail the strip to the roof through the joint in the course that underlies the replacement *(above, left)*. If necessary, seat each nail with a punch. Coat the nailheads with roofing cement.

◆ Slide the new slate into position and bend the projecting metal strip up and over the bottom edge of the new slate *(above, right)*. Seal it to the slate with roofing cement so that snow and ice do not dislodge it.

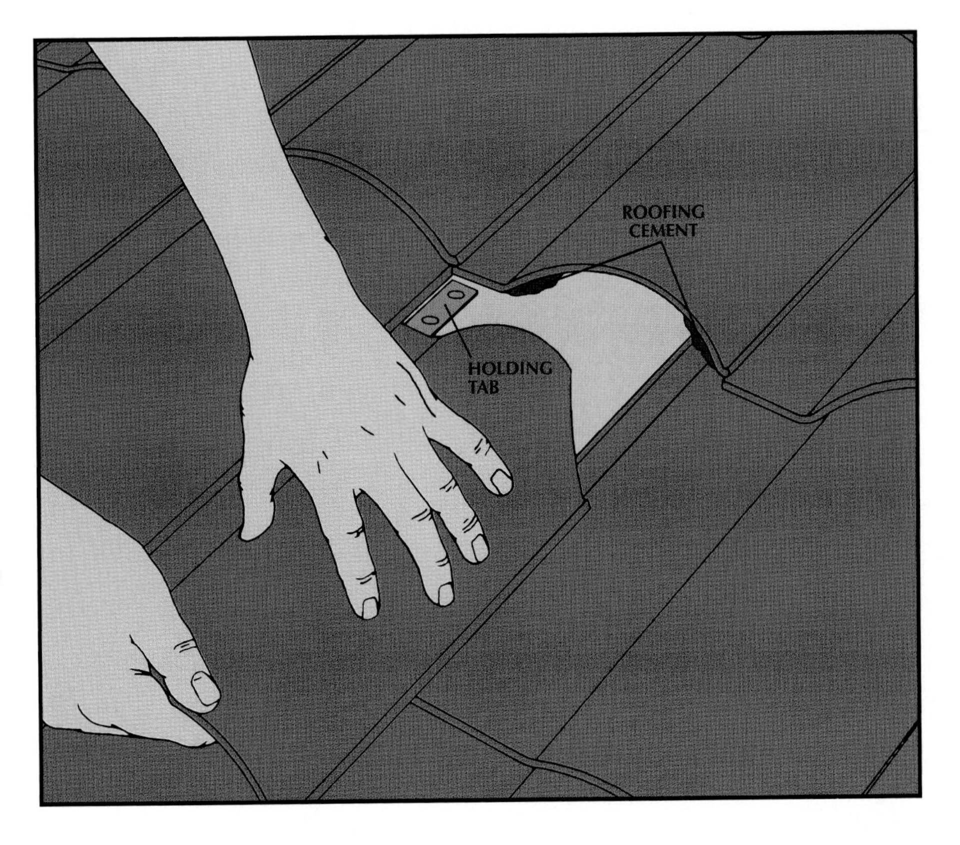

Replacing a tile.

◆ Nail a holding tab like the one used for a slate *(above)* to the roof where the flat part of the new tile will rest.

◆ Put dabs of roofing cement over the nailheads and underneath the tile in the overlying course, where the edges of the new tile will slide.

◆ Slide the new tile into position and bend the holding tab up and around its bottom edge. Seal the exposed tab in position with roofing cement.

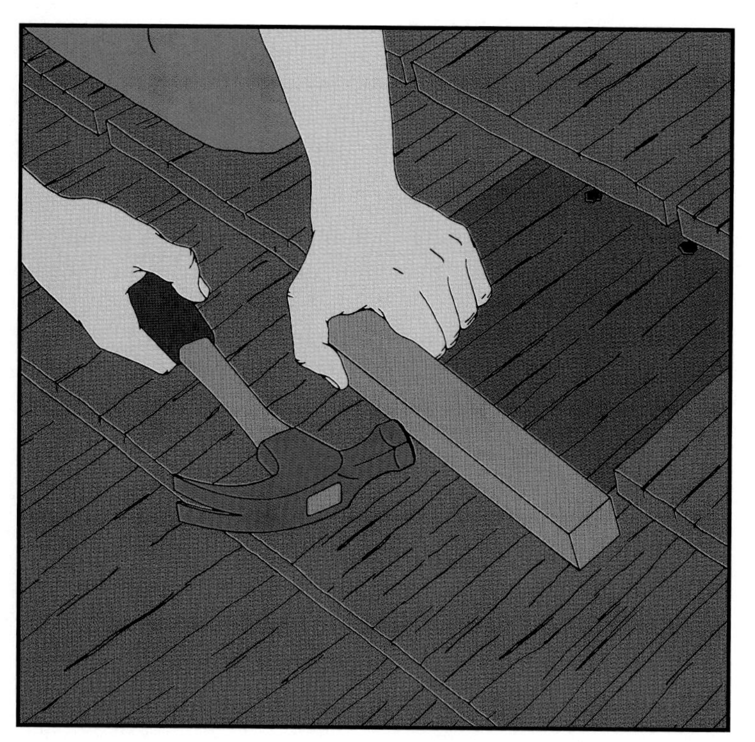

Replacing a wood shingle.

◆ Finish removing all the remnants of the damaged shingle, splitting it with a chisel if necessary.
◆ Cut the replacement shingle $\frac{1}{2}$ inch narrower than the space it will fill, to allow for expansion. If the shingle is too long, trim the excess length from the thin end.
◆ With a hammer and wood block, tap the shingle upward, but stop when the bottom edge is $\frac{1}{4}$ inch below the others in its course.
◆ Toenail two galvanized roofing nails just below the edge of the overlying course, making sure the nailheads are even with the shingle surface—not recessed into it, which can cause splitting. Dab roofing cement on the nailheads.
◆ Tap the shingle into place, so that the nailheads lie just under the edge of the overlapping shingles.

DRIP EDGES AND GUTTERS

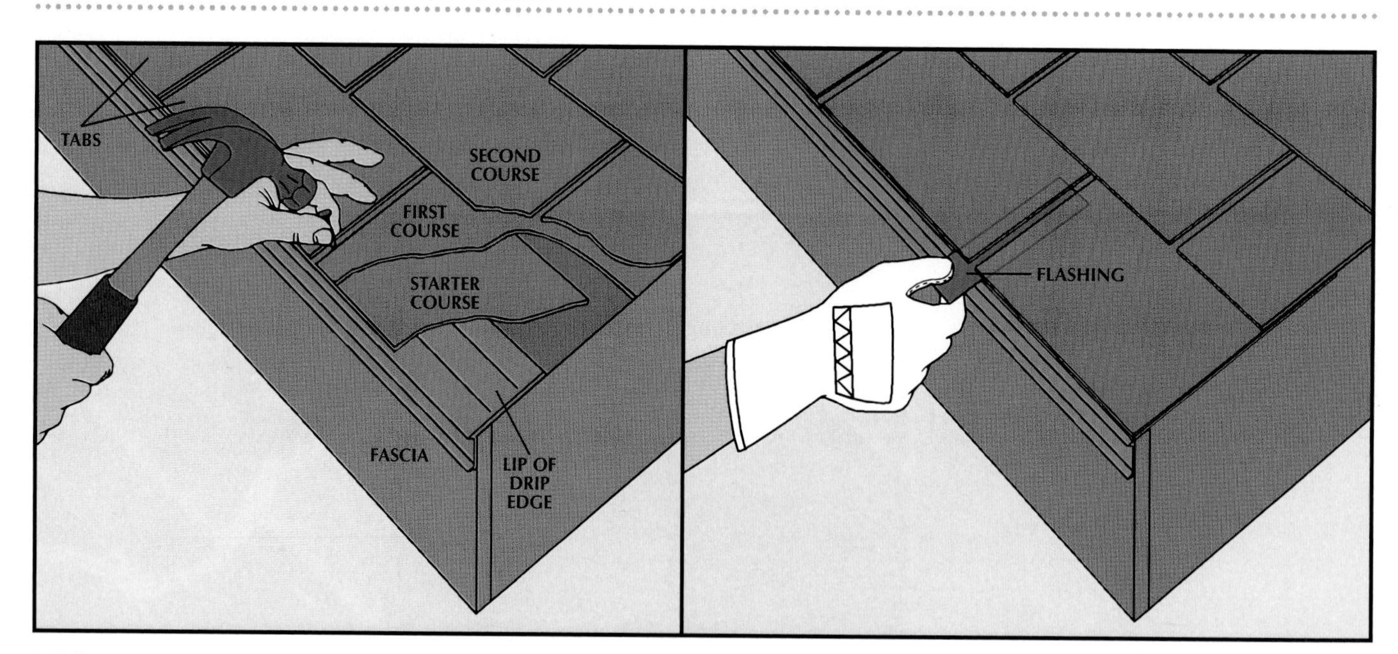

Adding a drip edge.

The fascia, a board running across the rafter ends at the eave, can rot if water soaks it. You can retrofit a metal drip edge to an asphalt-shingle roof by following these steps:
◆ Working on a warm day, when shingles are most pliable, slide the lip of a preformed metal drip edge under the shingles at the eave. The front panel of the drip edge should be about $\frac{1}{4}$ inch in front of the fascia board.
◆ Drive roofing nails between the tabs of the first course of shingles, through the underlying starter course and the drip edge, and into the sheathing *(above, left)*.
◆ Cover the nailheads with roofing cement. Slide a 2-inch-wide strip of flashing over them, under the first course of shingles and slightly under the second *(above, right)*.

If you then install a gutter as well, slide the upper part of the gutter's back edge behind the drip edge before securing the gutter in place.

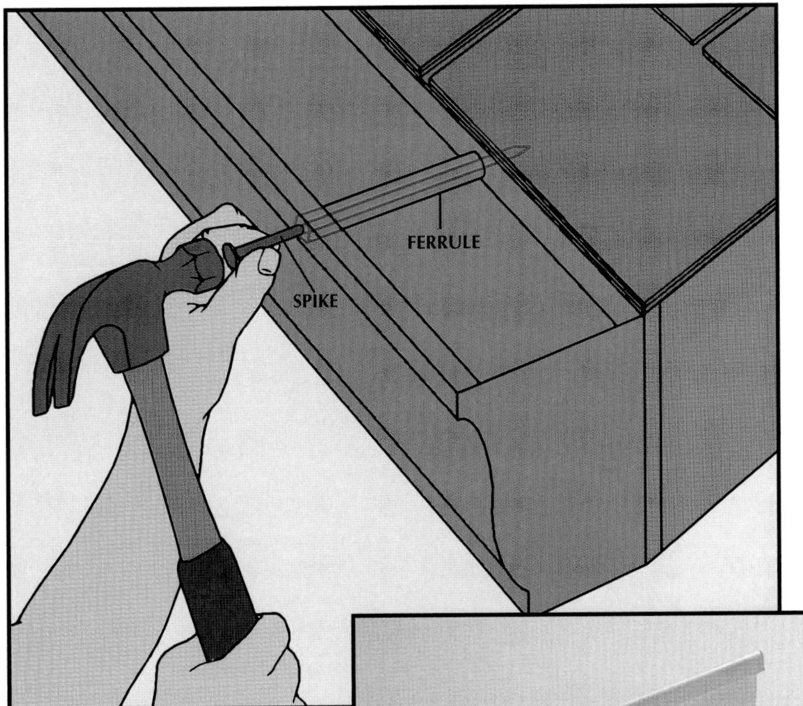

Taking the sag out of a gutter.

When pooling water indicates that a gutter has sagged out of alignment, adjust the gutter slope.

◆ Remove the hardware that supports the sagging portion.

◆ Reposition the gutter so it will drain; one rule of thumb is $\frac{1}{4}$ inch of incline for each 4 feet of run.

◆ Reattach the gutter. Secure metal gutters with spikes and ferrules (tubelike spacers) at the rafter ends, which are indicated by vertical lines of nailheads in the fascia; drive the spike through the gutter, then through the ferrule and into the rafter end *(left)*.

Vinyl gutters require mounting brackets *(photograph)*. Mark the new position, take down the gutter, install the brackets, and put the gutter in place.

Replacing a rusted section.

◆ Use a hacksaw to cut away a steel gutter section that has rusted through.

◆ Spread roofing cement inside the cut ends on each side of the opening.

◆ Slip in a new piece of gutter long enough to rest on the cut ends.

◆ Drill at least four holes through the overlapping ends of the old and new gutter sections *(right)*.

◆ Drive sheet-metal screws into the holes to secure the sections.

◆ If the crimped front edges of the old and new sections do not fit tightly, use tin snips to cut the crimp off the ends of the new section.

◆ Before painting the new section, etch the surface with a half-vinegar, half-water solution.

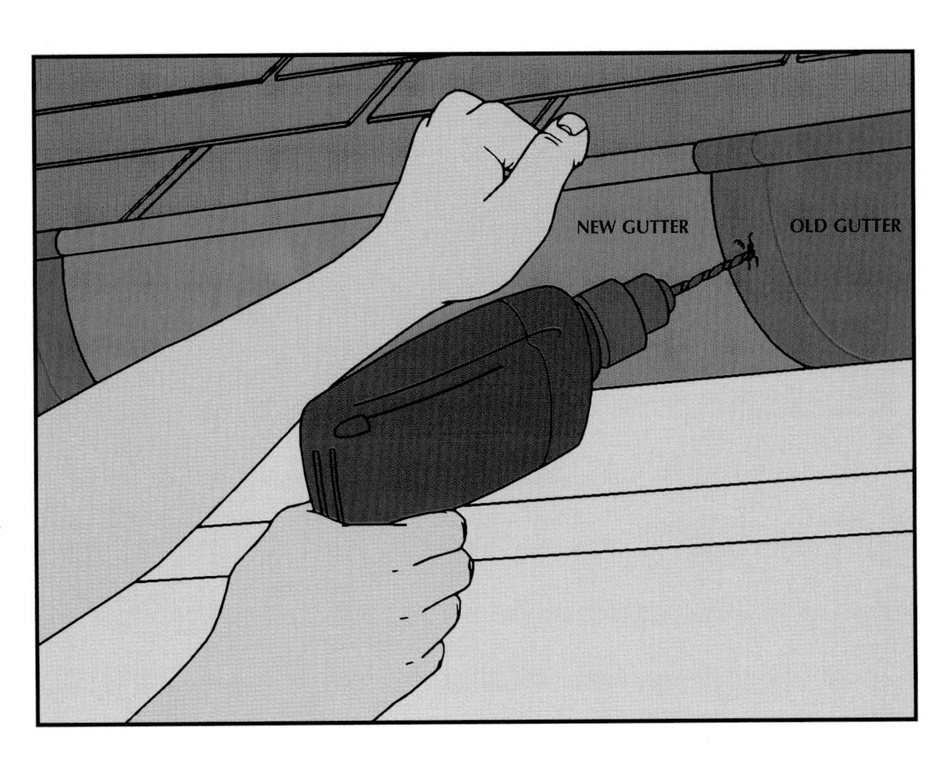

EVALUATING EXTERIOR WALLS

Scrutinizing wood siding.
From each corner of the house, look down the horizontal lines of the siding for any dip in the boards at the far corner. A noticeable dip indicates a sinking corner, often caused by rot or insect damage in the wood framing inside the wall or by a sinking foundation. This constitutes a serious structural problem and requires consultation with a structural engineer.

◆ Examine the siding boards for curling and cracking, and with an awl probe any rotted-looking areas *(left)*. If the awl penetrates easily more than $\frac{1}{2}$ inch, the rot needs repair. Slightly bowed boards can be nailed back in place and small areas of rot patched with fiberglass. But extensive rot or cracks all the way through the board along more than half its length call for new boards.

◆ Check the paint on the walls: The more layers, the harder it will be to achieve a smooth finish with new paint.

Spotting a faulty brick wall.
Examine the wall for bulging in the brick, especially near the bottom of the wall and midway up the wall near windows. Bulges indicate mortar failure in solid-masonry construction or deteriorated ties between brick veneer and the frame of a house. Such bulges rarely threaten the entire house but may require major work in a few years.

◆ Probe mortar joints with an awl *(right)*. If the mortar seems to be soft or sandy and falls out of the joints easily you must undertake the time-consuming job of repointing—scraping and refilling the joints *(page 38)*.

◆ Examine the mortar for gaps longer than 1 inch. A few spaces can be refilled, but many may require a mason to determine whether foundation settling may be threatening the entire house.

Evaluating bulges in stucco walls.

◆ To spot bulges, examine stucco walls at an oblique angle.

◆ By applying light pressure *(left),* check for resilience of small bulges—generally caused by localized separation between the stucco and underlying lath—and listen for a hollow sound when you tap them.

◆ If an entire wall bulges at the center, the house may have a major structural flaw—either undersized framing members that will require strengthening or uneven settlement of the foundation.

◆ All bulges and major cracks in stucco should be repaired as soon as possible, to prevent water damage inside the wall.

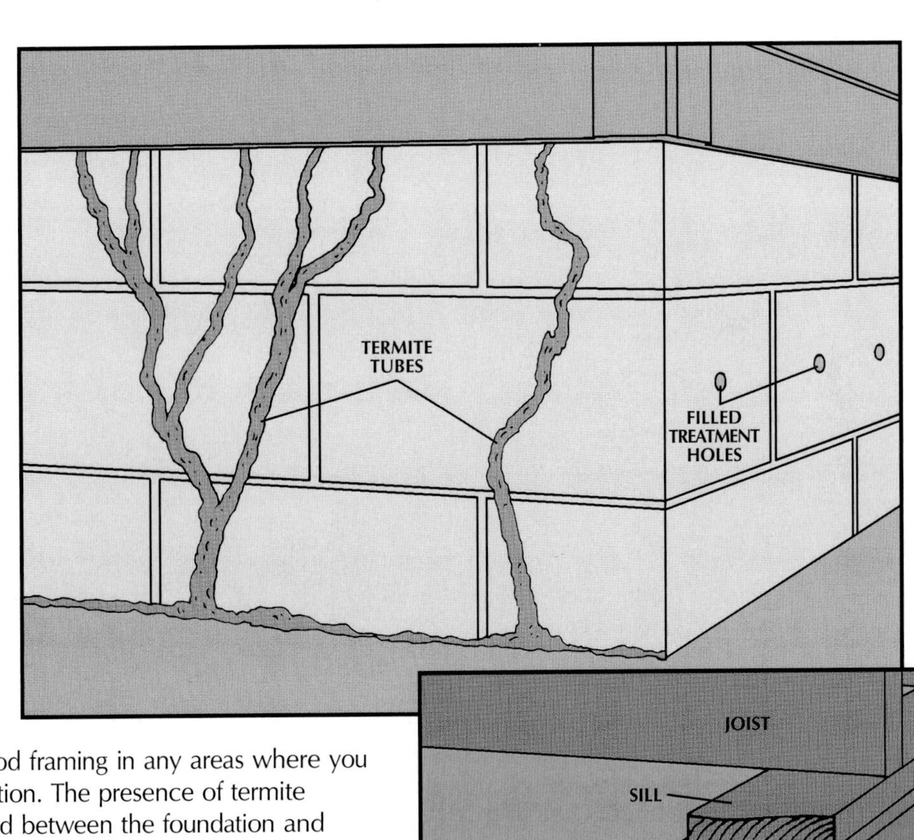

Detecting insect damage.

◆ Along foundation walls and wherever wood members are near the ground—as in a crawlspace with a dirt floor—look for termite tubes (mud tunnels built by these wood eaters) and small piles of fine sawdust signifying boring.

◆ With an awl, probe the wood framing in any areas where you suspect present or past infestation. The presence of termite shields—metal barriers installed between the foundation and framing *(inset)*—should not deter you from your inspection, since such shields are often ineffective.

◆ Note evidence of previous termite treatment: $\frac{3}{4}$-inch-diameter holes refilled with mortar in masonry walls or in the concrete floor of a basement. Prior treatment is not necessarily a bad sign, for it may have been done to forestall termites.

A TOOL KIT FOR EXTERIOR WORK

Preparing and painting the exterior of your house will require, in addition to a ladder *(pages 24–26)* and a caulking gun, at least some of the tools shown on these pages. All of them are available at your local hardware or home-supply store. Heat guns *(opposite)* and wire brushes in an electric drill *(below)* can cause serious injury; consult the manufacturer's instructions for precautions specific to each tool. In general, however, wear eye protection when using a maul and cold chisel, using a wire brush in an electric drill, and when painting overhead. A respirator reduces the amount of dust inhaled when sanding.

CAUTION *To reduce the chance of electric shock when working outdoors, plug power tools only into a receptacle protected by a ground-fault circuit interrupter (GFCI, page 213).*

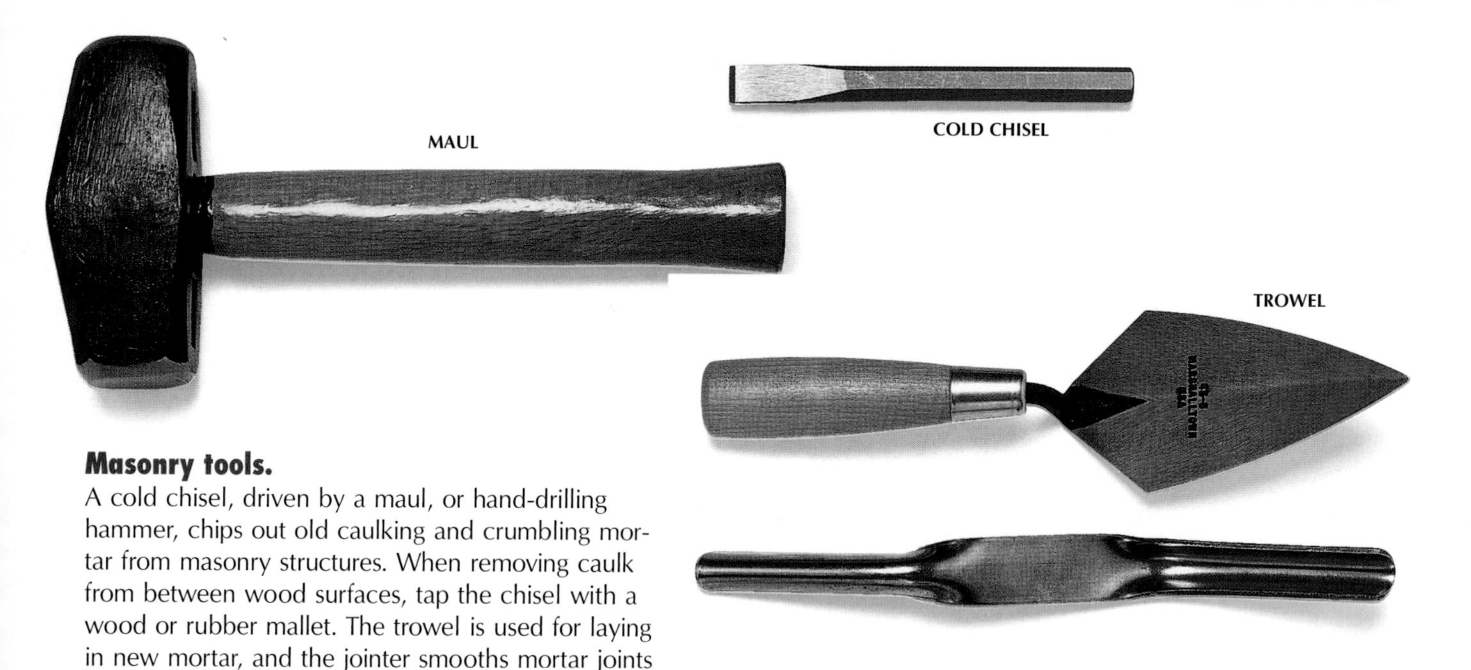

Masonry tools.
A cold chisel, driven by a maul, or hand-drilling hammer, chips out old caulking and crumbling mortar from masonry structures. When removing caulk from between wood surfaces, tap the chisel with a wood or rubber mallet. The trowel is used for laying in new mortar, and the jointer smooths mortar joints between bricks or concrete blocks.

DRILL WITH CUP BRUSH

DISK BRUSH

WIRE BRUSH

Metal-restoration tools.
Wire brushes, either the hand-held variety or those intended for use with an electric drill, remove paint and rust from metal. Brushes for the drill—available in both cup and disk varieties—work faster with less effort but have a limited reach. To scrape areas inaccessible with the drill, use the hand brush.

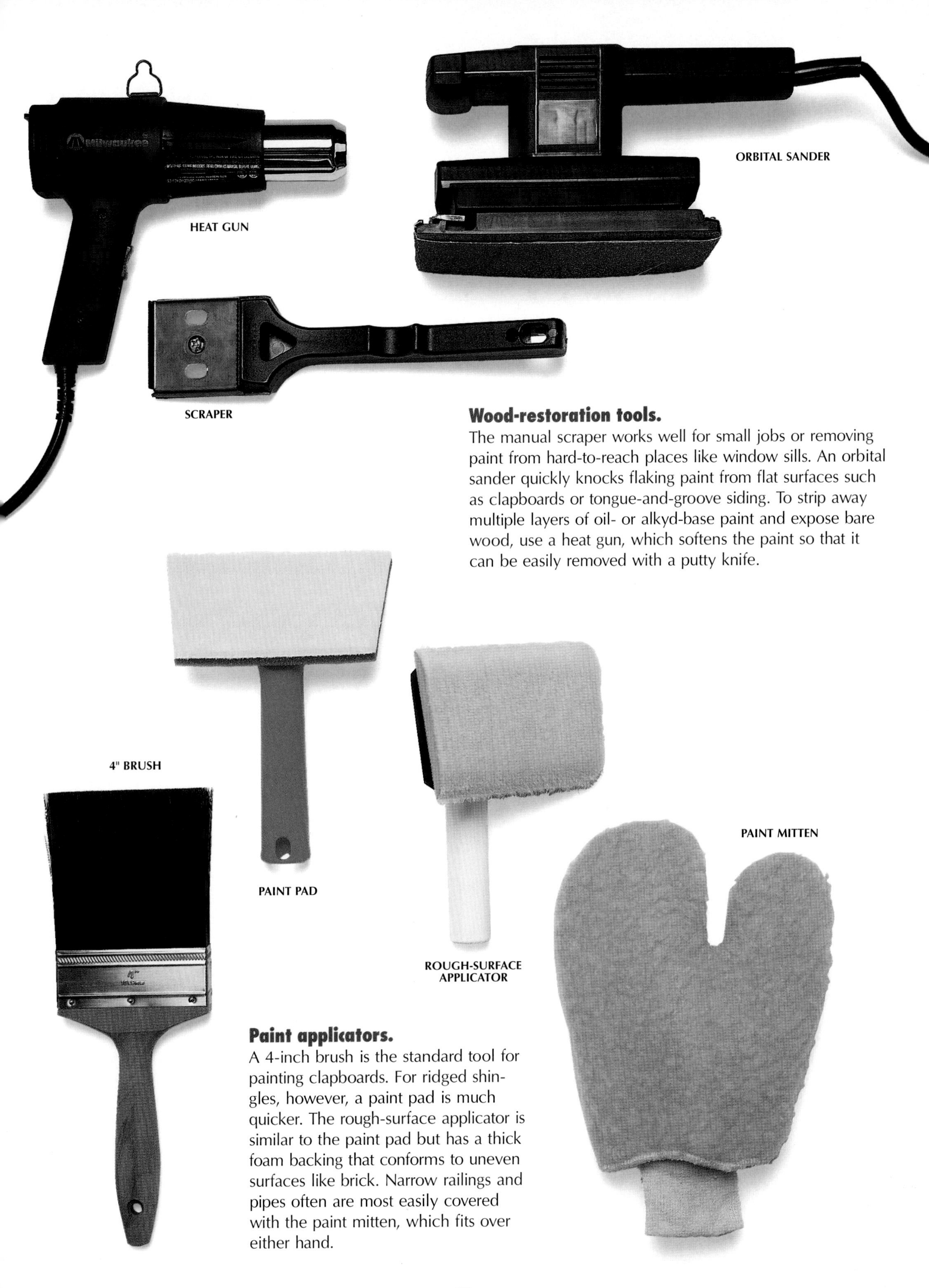

Wood-restoration tools.
The manual scraper works well for small jobs or removing paint from hard-to-reach places like window sills. An orbital sander quickly knocks flaking paint from flat surfaces such as clapboards or tongue-and-groove siding. To strip away multiple layers of oil- or alkyd-base paint and expose bare wood, use a heat gun, which softens the paint so that it can be easily removed with a putty knife.

Paint applicators.
A 4-inch brush is the standard tool for painting clapboards. For ridged shingles, however, a paint pad is much quicker. The rough-surface applicator is similar to the paint pad but has a thick foam backing that conforms to uneven surfaces like brick. Narrow railings and pipes often are most easily covered with the paint mitten, which fits over either hand.

CHOOSING AND USING A LADDER

For exterior work, especially painting, you will need at least one tall ladder—an extension ladder *(opposite)* is best—and a shorter one, a stepladder or folding sectional ladder *(below)*. Aluminum ladders cost no more than wood or fiberglass types, but weigh about 20 percent less, and are durable and easy to maintain. However, they conduct electricity. If you need to work near electrical cables, use a nonmetallic ladder instead.

Strength: A ladder's rating number indicates its strength. Type IA, the strongest, can bear up to 300 pounds. In order of decreasing strength are Type I, Type II, and Type III, which can support a load of 200 pounds. Look for an "ANSI" seal, which indicates approval by the American National Standards Institute.

Platforms and Scaffolds: Some exterior work is easier above level ground if you use ladder jacks to support a platform of planks from two extension ladders *(page 26)*. Use only specially fabricated planks available at scaffold and ladder suppliers. If the ground is uneven, or the house structure prevents setting up ladders within reach of the work, hire a professional to erect scaffolding.

Maintenance: Before climbing a ladder, inspect it for components that are cracked, twisted, jammed, or loose. If you find any defects, do not attempt repairs; buy or rent a new ladder. When you are not using a long ladder, store it horizontally on at least three large, strong hooks in a dry place. To ensure smooth operation, periodically lubricate all movable parts.

Some Ladder "Don'ts"

✔ Don't level a ladder by placing objects under the feet.
✔ Don't use a ladder in a high wind.
✔ Don't stand a ladder on ice, snow, or any other slippery surface.
✔ Don't lean the top of a ladder against a windowpane or screen.
✔ Don't link ladders to add height.
✔ Don't place a metal ladder near electrical wires.
✔ Don't step from one ladder to another.
✔ Don't carry tools in your hands or pockets while climbing. Set them on the shelf of a stepladder; on a tall ladder, place them in a bucket and hoist them up with a rope.
✔ Don't hold a paint bucket with one hand while painting. Instead, place it on the shelf of a stepladder or hang it from a rung of an extension ladder with a hook.
✔ Don't stand above the third-highest rung of an extension ladder or the second-highest step of a stepladder.
✔ Don't overreach to either side of the ladder.
✔ Don't take both hands off the ladder at once.

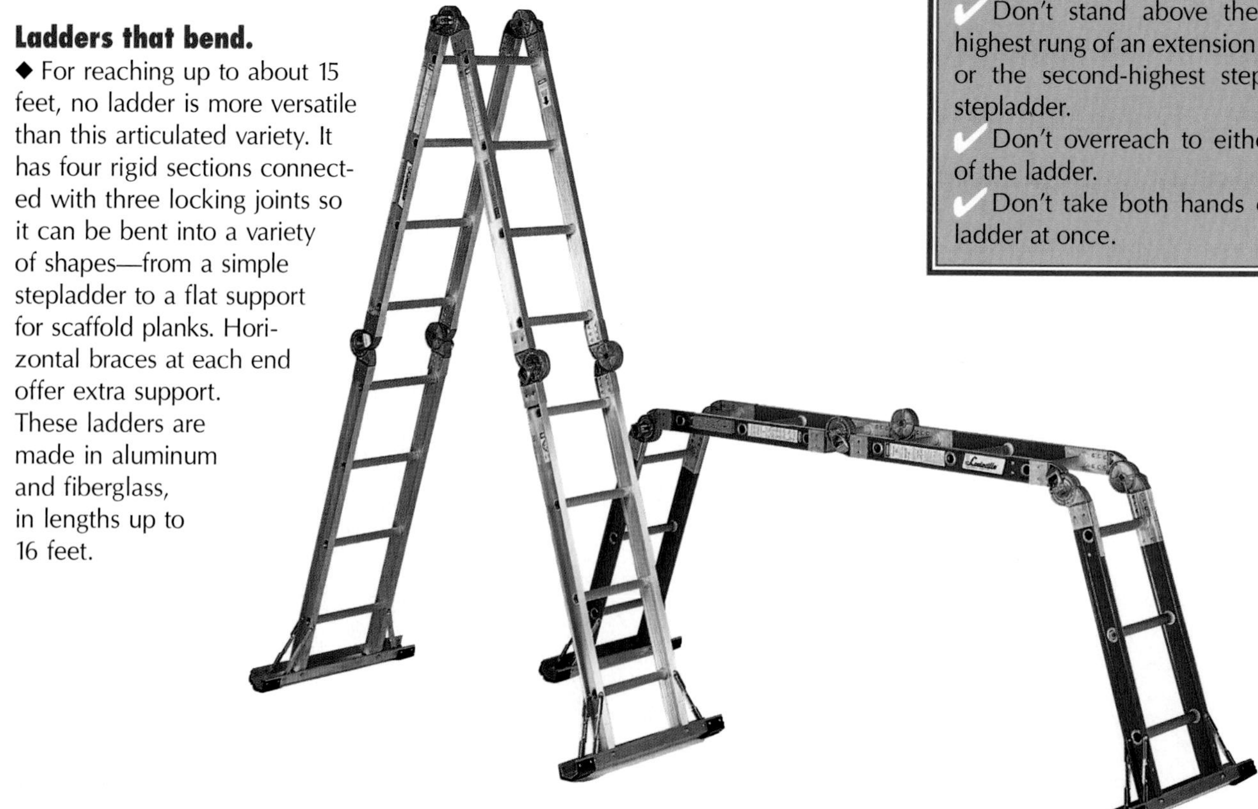

Ladders that bend.
◆ For reaching up to about 15 feet, no ladder is more versatile than this articulated variety. It has four rigid sections connected with three locking joints so it can be bent into a variety of shapes—from a simple stepladder to a flat support for scaffold planks. Horizontal braces at each end offer extra support. These ladders are made in aluminum and fiberglass, in lengths up to 16 feet.

Setting up an extension ladder.

◆ Place the ladder flat on the ground, with its feet a few inches from the vertical surface to be painted.

◆ Raise the top end. Then, grasping the rungs hand over hand, "walk" the ladder to a vertical position *(right)*.

◆ Lift the bottom slightly and shift the ladder outward so it leans firmly against the wall. You can compensate for uneven ground with leg levelers *(page 26)*.

TRICKS OF THE TRADE

The Right Angle for a Ladder

Use the following technique to set an extension ladder against a wall at a safe angle. After raising the ladder, move the base away from the wall so that your outstretched arms comfortably reach the rung nearest to shoulder height when you stand with your toes touching the ladder feet *(right)*.

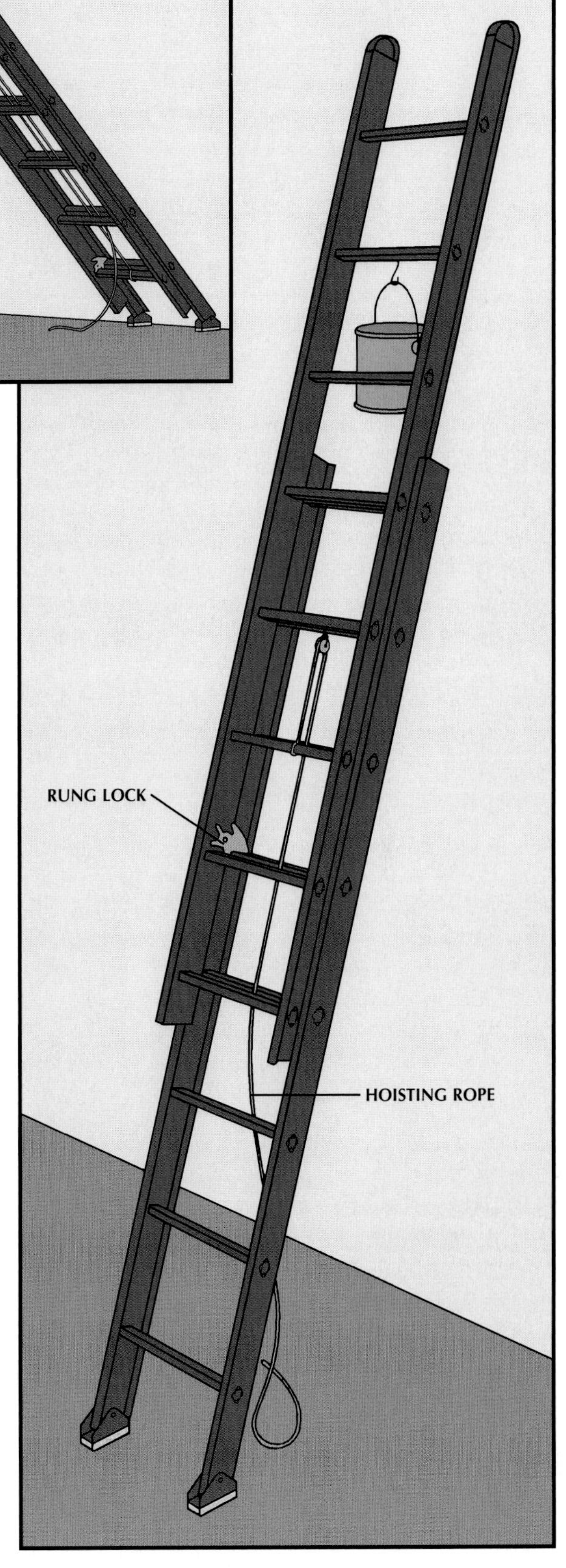

Extending the ladder.

◆ Pull the hoisting rope to raise the upper section to the desired height. Check to see that the rung locks on the upper section have fully engaged against the rungs on the lower section.

◆ Set the ladder at a safe angle against the wall using the procedure that is described above.

CAUTION *Make sure the upper section overlaps the lower one by at least 3 feet.*

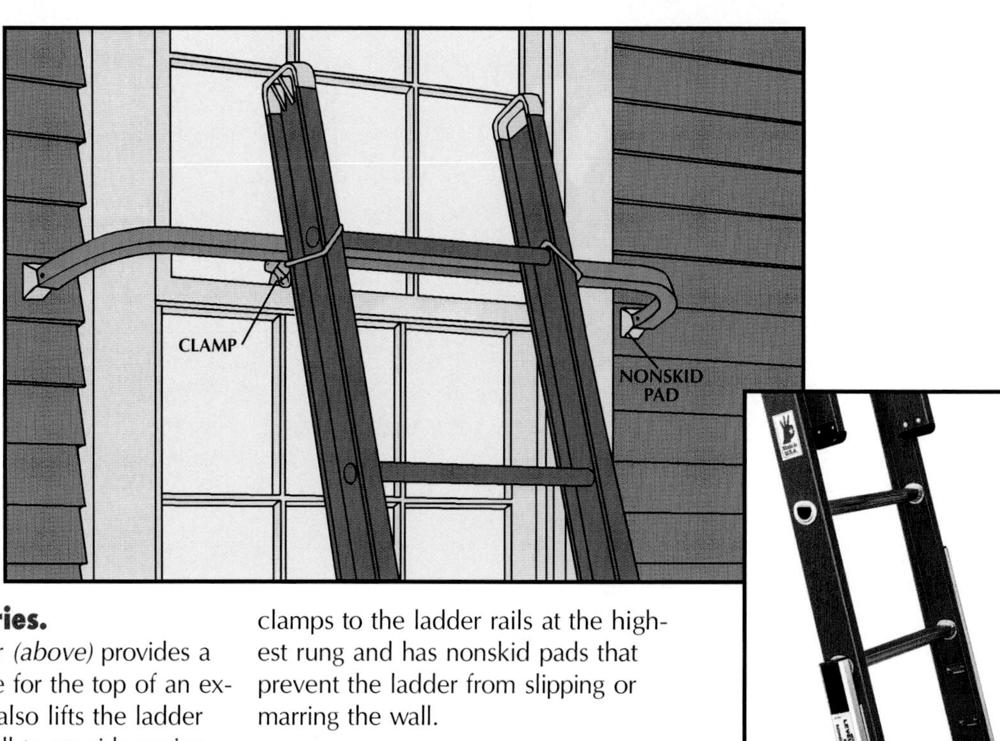

Ladder accessories.
A ladder stabilizer *(above)* provides a broad, sturdy base for the top of an extension ladder. It also lifts the ladder away from the wall to provide easier access to roof overhangs. Stabilizers are available in a variety of materials and designs; the one shown above is made of square aluminum tubing bent into a shallow U that is wide enough to bridge a window. The stabilizer clamps to the ladder rails at the highest rung and has nonskid pads that prevent the ladder from slipping or marring the wall.

Leg levelers *(right)* allow you to set a ladder on uneven surfaces. Fasten one to each rail of the ladder according to the manufacturer's instructions, then adjust them independently to make the rungs level.

Turning ladders into scaffolding.
Two Type I or IA extension ladders, two 2-by-10 scaffold planks 10 feet long, and a pair of ladder jacks like those at right are the ingredients for this one-person painting scaffold.

◆ Adjust the lengths of the ladders so that the rung at the height you wish to stand—no more than 20 feet—will lie about $2\frac{1}{2}$ feet from the wall ($3\frac{1}{2}$ feet for spraying).

◆ Lean the ladders against the wall no more than 8 feet apart and attach the ladder jacks to the rungs *(right)* or rails, depending on the model. Level the arm of each jack with its brace.

◆ With a helper, carry the planks one at a time up the ladders and lay them across the arms of the ladder jacks.

CAUTION *Be careful when working from this kind of platform; there are no handholds or safety rails to keep you from falling.*

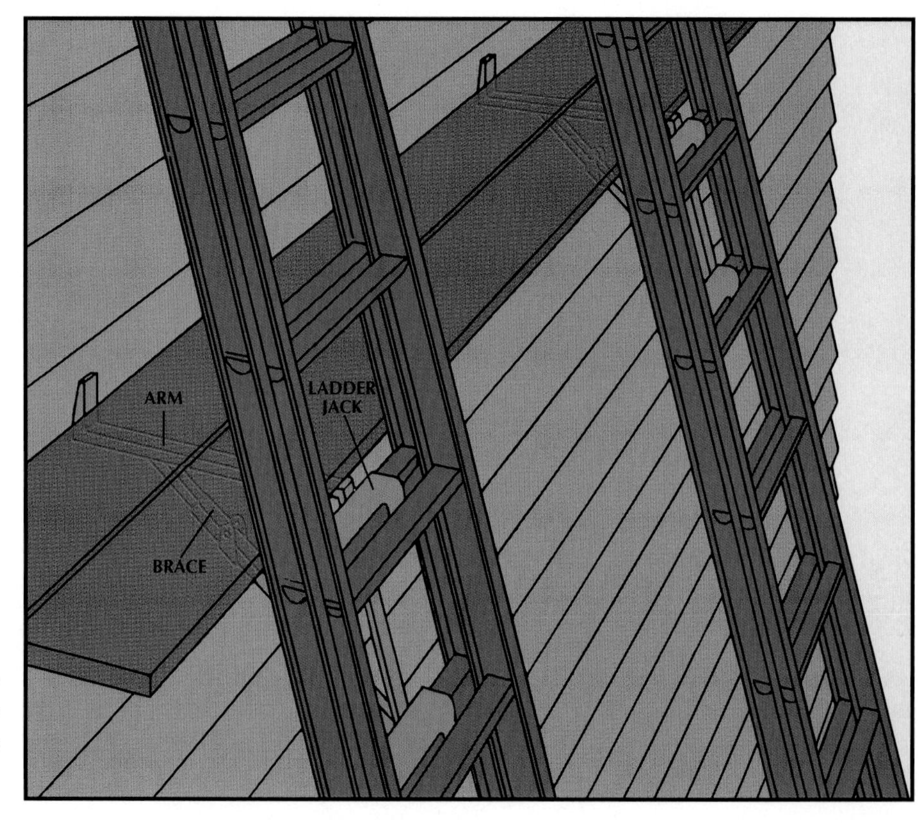

SHIELDS AGAINST MOISTURE AND DIRT

The exterior walls of a house, no less than the roof, must be kept in good condition to protect against the elements. Masonry walls—brick or stone—provide good weather protection but benefit from application of a waterproofing sealer. Wood sidings require more attention: Except for such naturally rot-resistant woods as cedar and redwood, they must be periodically repainted to repel water effectively.

Protecting Wood Exteriors: Once a year, and definitely before repainting a wood house *(pages 50–55)*, wash it with a garden hose, a mild detergent, and a scrub brush where needed. Scrape off loose or peeling paint, then examine the entire surface. Dark stains, blistering, cracking, and rust streaks around nailheads all indicate that moisture is getting into the wood. Unless the source is found and fixed, the new paint will not last.

Cracks and splits can be filled with caulk; large breaks may need to be packed with foam backer rods first *(page 28, top)*. A board with a slight degree of rot can be saved if you scrape it bare, let it dry for several days, and apply wood preservative. Any board with significant rot must be replaced *(page 35)*.

Dealing with Brick: Brick is a low-maintenance material. Unless brick walls have deteriorated badly, repointing is the only repair that they are likely to need *(page 38)*. Even cleaning is optional. Masons once believed that dirt and other pollutants gradually ate into the surface, but research suggests that in some cases grime can actually form a protective shell.

To clean fragile, old brick, try flushing it with a garden hose. Otherwise rent a pressure washer, which blasts off dirt with a high-velocity jet of water *(pages 29–31)*. A unit that generates a pressure of less than 1,500 pounds per square inch is preferable. If you can get only a higher-pressure machine, use the widest nozzle orifice that will work.

Brick walls that have been painted should be repainted—never sandblasted. Sandblasting would seriously damage the surface of the brick. Remove flaking paint from brick by hand, with a wire brush or paint remover.

CAUTION *Consult page 10 for advice on testing for and working with lead paint.*

CAUTION *Work carefully from a well-secured ladder. Place materials in a bucket, hung from a rung of an extension ladder with a hook.*

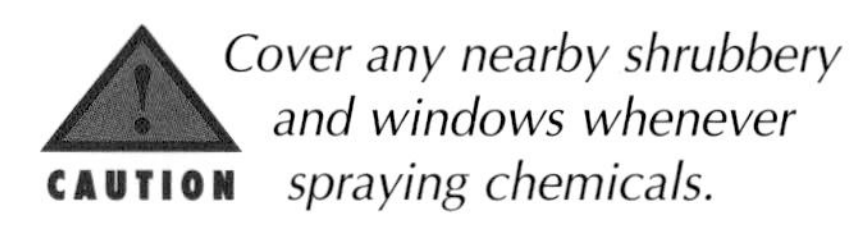
CAUTION *Cover any nearby shrubbery and windows whenever spraying chemicals.*

TOOLS

WOOD
- Replaceable-blade paint scraper
- Heat gun
- Wood chisel
- Caulking gun
- Paintbrush
- Stiff-bristled, nonmetallic brush

MASONRY
- Garden hose
- Pressure washer (gas-powered)
- Stiff-fiber brush
- Paintbrush
- Wire brush with scraper attachment
- Tank-type deck sprayer

MATERIALS

WOOD
- Backer rod
- Acrylic latex caulk (exterior-use)
- Stain killer (exterior-use, oil- or alcohol-based)
- Oxalic acid
- Medium-grade sandpaper or steel wool

MASONRY
- Detergent
- Paint remover
- Waterproofing sealer
- Turpentine

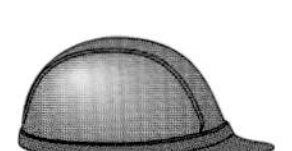
SAFETY TIPS

Protect your eyes with goggles when chipping old caulk. Wear goggles, a cap, and long sleeves when applying paint remover or spraying chemicals.

WORKING ON WOOD SIDING

Sealing cracks and joints in wood siding is essential before hosing and scrubbing the house and especially before using a high-pressure spray cleaner *(pages 29–30)*. Be sure to remove old flaking or powdering paint *(pages 40–43)* before doing any sealing. To choose the right kind of caulk for your house, see the chart on page 46.

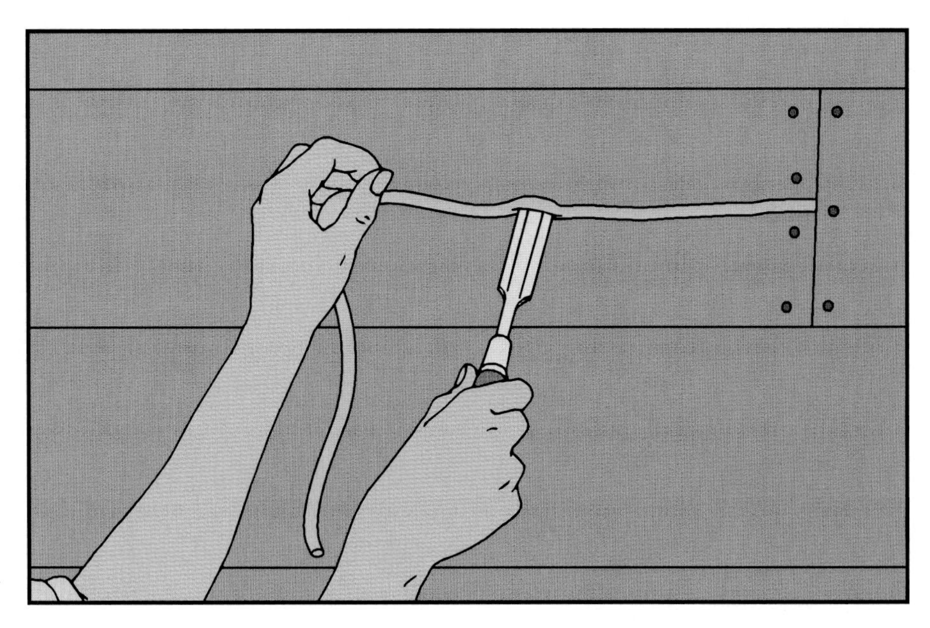

Filling cracks with backer rod.

◆ Insert one end of a strip of backer rod into the widest part of the crack. (Use additional rods as needed.)

◆ Working along the length of the crack, jam the backer rod tightly into the opening with a wood chisel *(left)*. Pack the crack to within $\frac{1}{2}$ inch of the surface.

◆ Cover the backer rod with acrylic latex caulk to create a smooth painting surface.

Caulking the joints.

◆ Put a tube of caulk into a caulking gun and slice off the tip of the tube to make an opening about $\frac{1}{4}$ inch in diameter.

◆ Starting in an unobtrusive spot (under a window sill or above a door), pull the trigger of the gun to about a 45-degree angle and drag the tip of the gun slowly along the joint so that the bead of caulk fills but does not overflow the joint. If the caulk does not flow smoothly, warm the tube slightly over a heat source.

◆ Release the trigger just before reaching the end of the seam.

◆ With a wet finger or a damp cloth, bed the caulking compound into the joint and give a slightly concave shape to its surface.

◆ Wipe off any excess caulking material with a wet cloth.

For more about using a caulking gun see page 47.

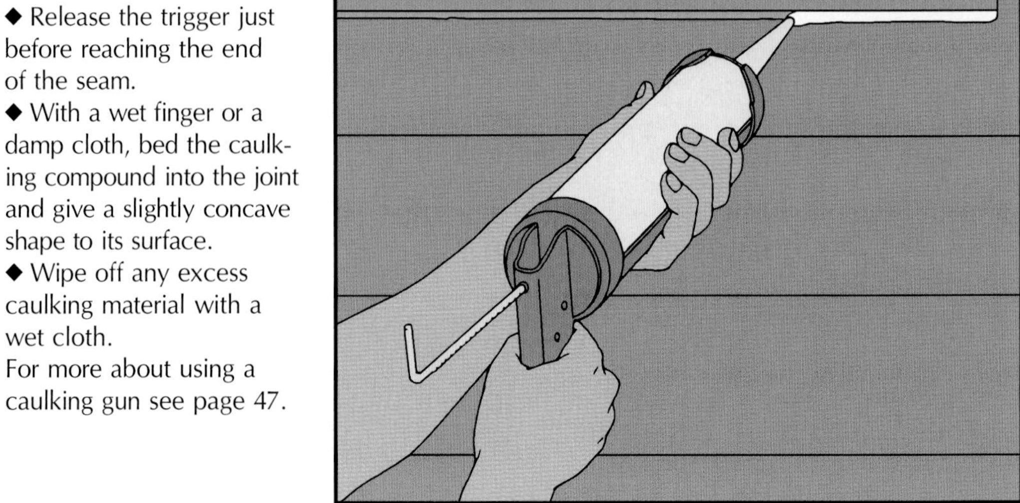

HIGH-POWERED HOUSE CLEANING

A high-pressure spray-cleaning device—which you can rent at many paint and hardware stores—reduces the labor of removing dirt, mildew, sea-spray salt, paint-chalk accumulations, or even peeling paint.

How a Spray Cleaner Works: A typical spray cleaner takes water from the supply system of the house or a barrel and pumps it out in a narrow jet at a pressure of 1,000 pounds per square inch or more, blasting off dirt and loose paint. The machine can also mix a variety of cleaning agents, stored in a reservoir on top of the pump housing, with the water for more efficient cleaning. Some models use only cold water, but others have a kerosene burner that heats the water for tough cleaning jobs.

SAFETY TIPS

Wear rubber gloves at all times when spraying. Add a hat, long sleeves, long pants, and goggles when spraying a solution that contains liquid household detergent, bleach, or trisodium phosphate.

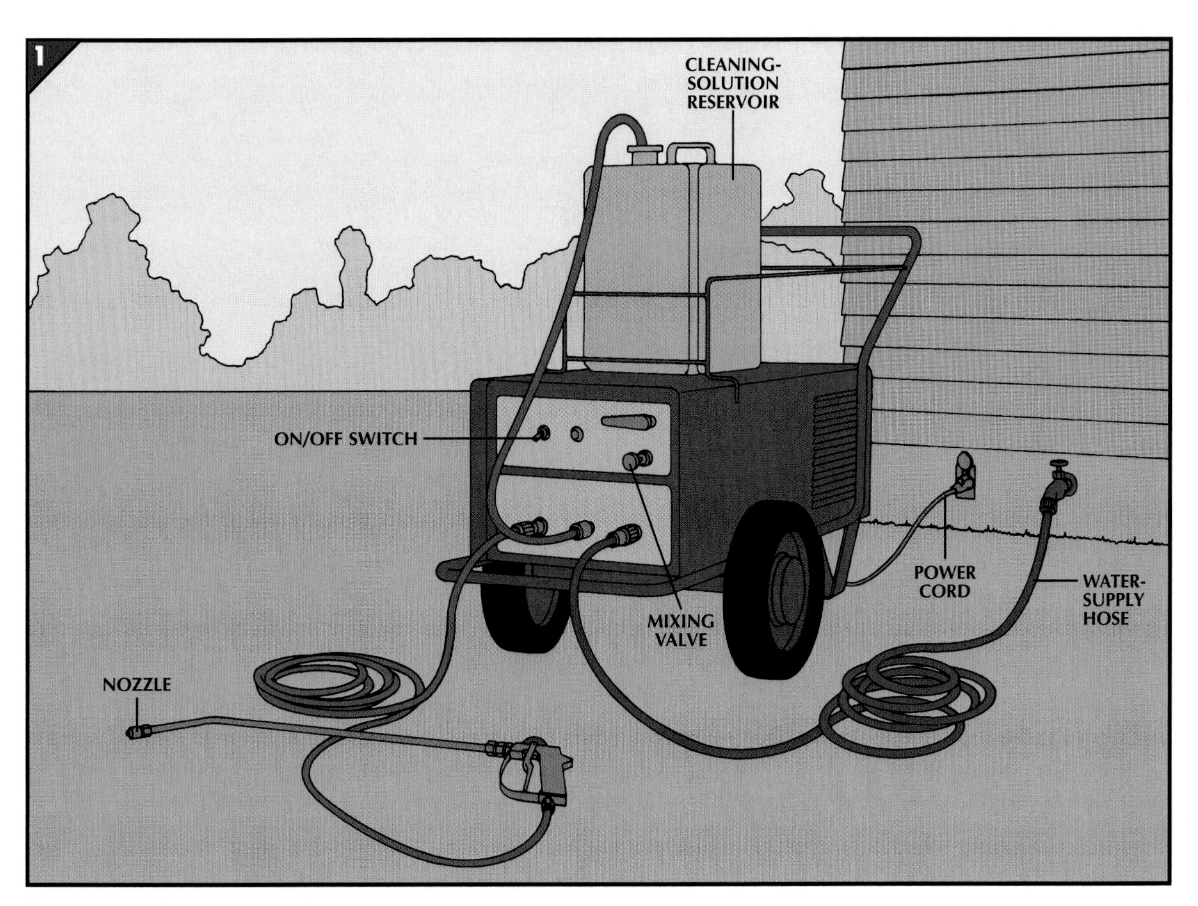

1. Making the connections.

◆ You must hook up three hoses to the spray cleaner before operating it: an ordinary $\frac{3}{4}$-inch garden hose to connect the spray cleaner with an outside faucet; a smaller hose, furnished with the unit, to couple the cleaning-solution container to the pump; and a third hose, also part of the equipment, to carry water and cleaning solution from the pump to the nozzle.

◆ Adjust the dilution of cleaner in the jet spray with a valve on the unit. Because powder granules may damage pump seals, use only heavy-duty liquid detergents for routine cleaning, or full-strength liquid chlorine bleach to remove mildew.

◆ Plug the unit into a receptacle that accepts a three-pronged plug and is protected by a ground-fault circuit interrupter. Heavy-duty extension cords equipped with this device are available for use with unprotected circuits.

2. Applying the cleaner.

◆ Fill the cleaning-solution reservoir and open the mixing valve to add cleaning solution to the water supply. For very grimy walls, turn on the heater, if your unit has one.

◆ Hold the nozzle 1 to 2 feet from the wall *(left)* and aim the stream parallel to the ground or slightly downward to avoid forcing water behind siding. Squeeze the trigger to spray, and beginning at the top of a section, sweep back and forth in 6- to 8-foot strokes. Continue working downward for about 10 minutes so the solution can loosen dirt and stains.

3. Rinsing off.

◆ Turn off the mixing valve in order to prevent cleaning agent from entering the rinse water.

◆ Start at the top of a section and hold the nozzle about 6 inches away from the surface and at a 45-degree angle in the direction you are moving. This allows the full force of the jet to shear off any loose paint chips.

◆ Spray across the section, from one side to the other. At the end of each sweep, reverse the direction of the 45-degree angle.

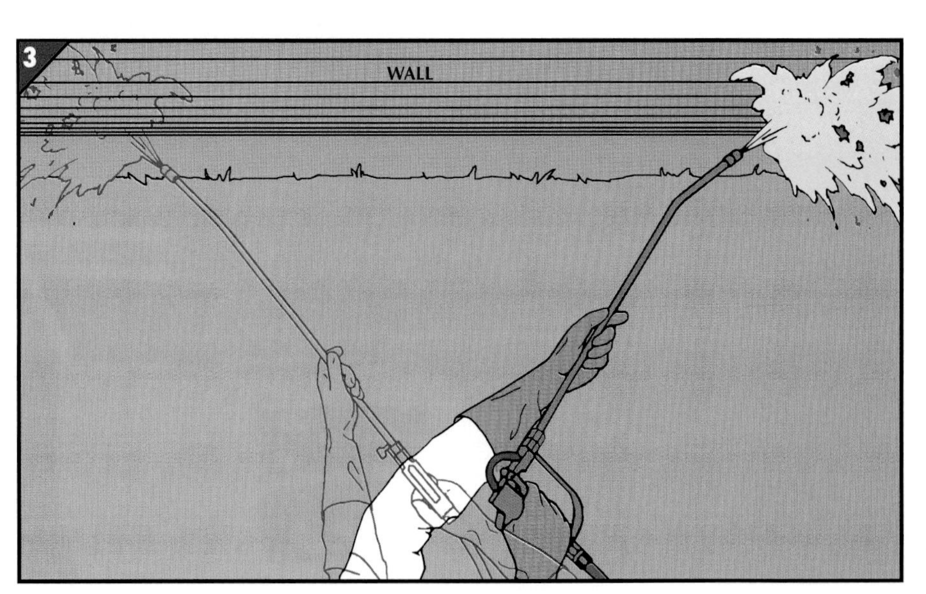

DOING AWAY WITH MILDEW

Mildew is a fungus that thrives on damp, shaded walls. Since it prevents new paint from adhering, you must remove it completely before painting. Scrubbing alone, however, is not sufficient to prevent regrowth; the spores embedded in the surface must be killed.

First, test stains that look as though they might have been caused by mildew. Apply full-strength liquid chlorine laundry bleach to the area with a rag. If the discoloration disappears in a few moments, it is caused by mildew. To remove it, make a cleaning solution of 1 to 2 quarts of bleach to 1 gallon of warm water. You can also make the solution with $\frac{1}{2}$ cup of an alkali detergent, such as trisodium phosphate (TSP)—if it is available in your community—dissolved in 2 gallons of water.

Remove any loose paint, then, for small patches, vigorously scrub the solution into the siding with a stiff-bristled brush. Tackle larger areas by spraying the solution from a high-pressure cleaner—preferably one that heats the water to 190°F. When the mildew is gone, flush the surface with water and let it dry before painting. Ask for paint containing a mildew-inhibiting agent, whether you use an alkyd- or water-base product.

SURFACE-CLEANING MASONRY

Operating a pressure washer.

◆ With a garden hose, connect the unit to your house cold-water supply.

◆ Determine the greatest distance from which dirt and pollutants can be removed: With brick that seems sturdy, begin by holding a 25-degree nozzle orifice attachment 3 feet away from the surface; if the masonry is fragile, start farther back, or use a wider nozzle at an indirect angle.

◆ For reaching under eaves, extension rods such as the one shown at right are available with some units.

CAUTION *Do not operate a pressure washer from a ladder.*

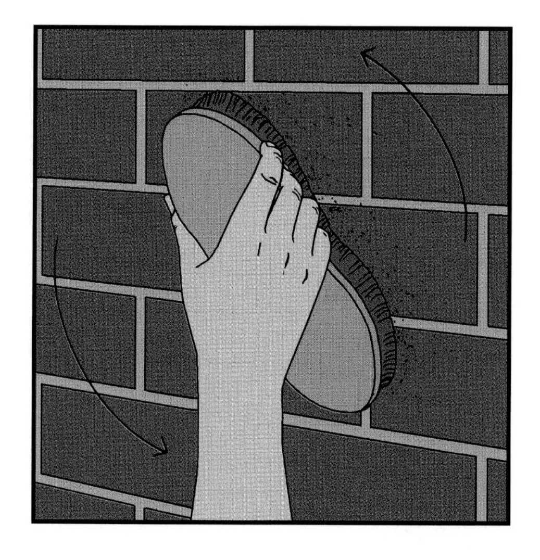

Scrubbing brick.

◆ Walls that are badly soiled with soot or other pollutants may need to be scrubbed. As a cleaning solution, use a handful of detergent in a bucket of cold water. With a stiff-fiber brush, scrub in a circular motion to avoid washing old, fragile mortar out of the joints between bricks; do not scrub back and forth along a mortar line. After the scrubbing, rinse the wall well with clean water.

Applying paint remover.

◆ After wetting the wall, brush on paint remover in one direction *(left).*

◆ Let the stripper work for 15 to 30 minutes.

◆ Rinse the stripper thoroughly with a garden hose—or, if necessary, a pressure washer.

Scraping and brushing.

◆ To remove spots of paint that dripped onto brick when wood trim above was painted, use a tool with a wire brush on one end and a scraper on the other. Flip the tool every few strokes, first brushing and then scraping; avoid the mortar joints. Even when used with care, the brush may leave the mortar joints with depressions that will need filling.

RESTORING OUTSIDE WALLS

Although bared to the elements, exterior walls are the least trouble-prone structural part of a house and can usually be kept sound with preventive maintenance. When water damage occurs, it is often caused by a roof or gutter leak that has allowed moisture to accumulate on the undersides of exterior boards. In such a case, find and patch the leak *(pages 17–19)* before you make wall repairs. Also check window sills: Water collecting on their horizontal surfaces can lead to rot.

Fixing a Damaged Sill: Correct minor defects in a window sill by scraping away damaged wood, soaking the boards with a wood preservative, and applying a fiberglass patch. For damage that is more extensive, cover the sill with aluminum sheathing as shown on pages 33 and 34, and then paint it to match the house. You may need to restore the original shape of the sill with wood putty before installing either type of patch.

Rotted Exterior Boards: Check for rot or other damage to wood siding as described on page 27. It is easy enough to replace a few small rotted sections of siding *(page 35)*. Overhang repairs are also straightforward *(pages 34–35)*, although you may need scaffolding to stand on if the overhangs are wide. Patch any holes in the fascia—the board that covers rafter ends—and in the soffit, the board on the underside of the overhang, if only to keep out birds and squirrels. Paint the backs of replacement boards to prevent future rot.

Repairs to Brick Walls: In a masonry wall, the most common failure is the deterioration of mortar. Chip decaying mortar out of the joints and refill them with new mortar *(page 38)*.

Crumbling mortar joints over a door or window opening can cause bricks to sag or even fall out of the wall. You can reinstall the bricks and strengthen the opening with a pair of L-shaped steel lintels. You may have to remove trim molding and knock out some plaster on the interior wall before you can replace interior courses of bricks. If you must use new bricks to replace broken or missing ones, try to match the old in size and color. When you finish the repair, scrub mortar stains from the bricks with muriatic acid.

TOOLS

SILL REPAIRS
Scissors
Tin snips
Caulking gun
Hammer
Rubber mallet
Paintbrush

OVERHANG AND SIDING REPAIRS
Electric drill with $\frac{1}{2}$" bit
Saber saw
Keyhole saw
Wood chisel
Backsaw
Hacksaw blade

MASONRY REPAIRS
Cold chisel or brick set
Maul (4-lb.)
Stiff wire brush
Trowel
Jointer
Bricklayer's hammer

MATERIALS

SILL REPAIRS
Heavy paper
Aluminum sheathing (0.019")
Butyl caulk
Roofing nails ($1\frac{1}{2}$")
Metal preparative
Paint

OVERHANG AND SIDING REPAIRS
Pressure-treated lumber
Galvanized screws
Wood strips (1 x 4)
Wood putty (exterior-grade)
Wedges
Wood blocks
Common nails
Wood siding

MASONRY REPAIRS
Steel lintels
Metal primer
Bricks
Mortar mix
Muriatic acid

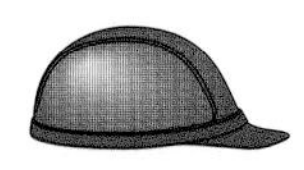

SAFETY TIPS

Protect your eyes with goggles when you hammer nails, saw into old wood, or cut a brick. When cutting pressure-treated lumber, wear a dust mask, and wash your hands thoroughly afterward. Don a hard hat if you are removing or installing bricks overhead. Always wear gloves and a long-sleeved shirt to protect your skin when working with mortar or any lime, and put on rubber gloves and goggles when you work with muriatic acid.

SHEATHING FOR A WOOD SILL

1. Making templates.

◆ With scissors and heavy paper, make a template to cover each end of a damaged window sill *(left)*, fitting the paper against the jamb and around that ear of the sill and reaching from the window stool to the underside of the sill.

◆ Unfold each template *(inset)*. Tape a rectangular piece between the two that establishes the correct distance between the jambs.

◆ Transfer the pattern of the assembled paper templates—including the interior cut made at each end—onto 0.019-inch aluminum sheathing. Cut the aluminum with tin snips and check the fit against the window.

2. Caulking the edges.

With a caulking gun, lay a bead of butyl caulk on and around the sill wherever the edges of the metal sheathing will lie—along the window stool, the jambs, the siding, and the underside of the sill.

3. Securing the sheathing.

◆ Position the metal sheathing on the sill and press it into the bead of caulk along the stool, the jambs, and the siding.

◆ Secure the sheathing with $1\frac{1}{2}$-inch roofing nails at 4-inch intervals along the joint of the window sill and stool *(left)*.

◆ Nail the metal in place along the jamb edges and the top of each ear.

4. Fitting the sheathing.

◆ Using a rubber mallet, bend the sheathing flaps down over the ears, with the tabs at the ends folded under the ears. Bend the sections produced by the interior cuts around the sill face and secure them with nails.
◆ Bend the long part of the sheathing over the face of the sill *(left),* then up under the bottom.
◆ Nail the folded-under edges to the bottom of the sill.
◆ Seal small gaps with caulk.
◆ Clean the aluminum with metal preparative (available in paint stores) and paint the sheathing with a paint recommended for use on aluminum.

REPAIRING ROTTED CORNICES

1. Cutting away damaged wood.

Replace a rotted section of a fascia or soffit as follows:
◆ Locate nearby rafter ends and lookouts *(below)* by the position of nailheads in the fascia and soffit. (Lookouts are not always present.)
◆ Avoiding rafters and lookouts, drill a $\frac{1}{2}$-inch pilot hole just beyond the area of damaged wood.
◆ Insert the blade of a saber saw or keyhole saw in the hole and cut through the board *(left).*
◆ Make a second saw cut on the other side of the damaged area.
◆ Use a chisel as necessary to complete the two cuts, then pry out the damaged section of board.

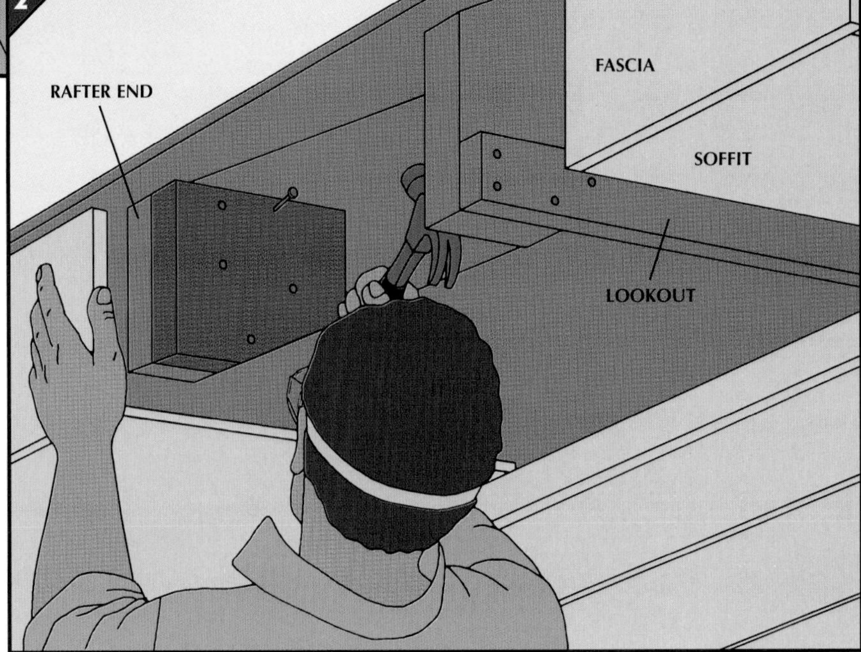

2. Doubling damaged rafter ends.

◆ Where a rafter end has rotted, cut a piece of pressure-treated lumber to match the shape of the end of the rafter, long enough to reach back to sound wood.
◆ Nail the new piece alongside the rotted end *(right).*

If a horizontal lookout board is in the way, remove it in order to nail on the new rafter end. Replace rotted lookouts with new lumber cut to the same dimensions.

3. Attaching new boards.

◆ Using galvanized screws, attach a 1-by-4 wood strip that will overlap the back of the new joint at each edge of the sound part of the fascia or soffit *(left).*
◆ Screw a replacement section to the strips and nail it to any rafter ends or lookouts that it crosses.
◆ Seal the joint at each end with exterior-grade wood putty before you paint.

REPLACING DAMAGED SECTIONS OF SIDING

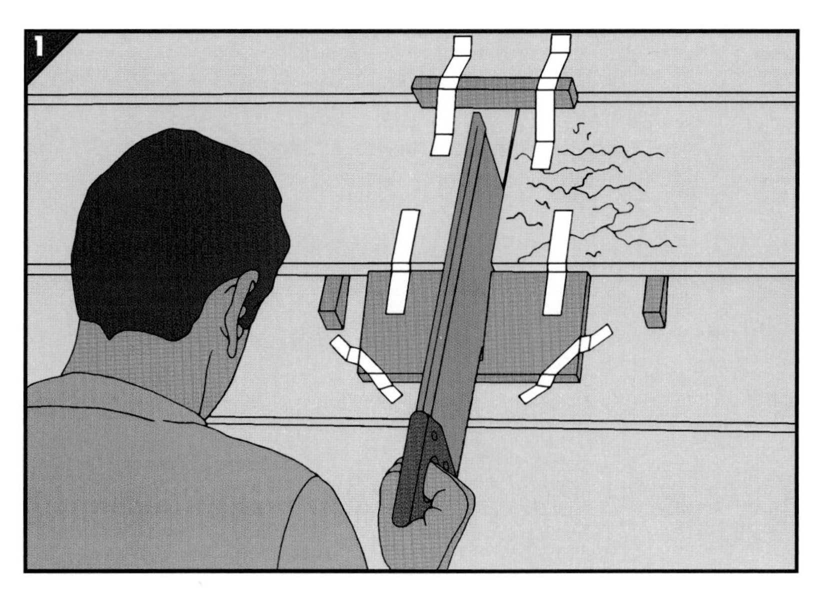

1. Cutting out damaged clapboards.

◆ Tap wedges under a damaged section of clapboard siding to separate it from the piece below.
◆ Tape wood blocks to the boards located above and below the damaged area to protect them as you saw.
◆ Cut through the damaged section with a backsaw *(left).*

If the siding is made of flush boards, cut out damaged wood with a hammer and chisel and replace it with new wood, using the techniques explained on pages 68 and 69 for repairing floorboards.

2. Finishing the cut.

◆ Move the wedges to the top of the damaged piece to raise the clapboard above.
◆ Finish the cuts, using a keyhole saw with the blade reversed *(right).*
◆ Wrap one end of a hacksaw blade with tape and use the other end to cut through any nails under the damaged piece.
◆ Remove the piece.
◆ Replace it with a new clapboard, driving nails through the lower part just above the top of the clapboard below.

If there is no sheathing beneath the siding, fasten new siding to old with the technique shown above for attaching a new fascia or soffit board.

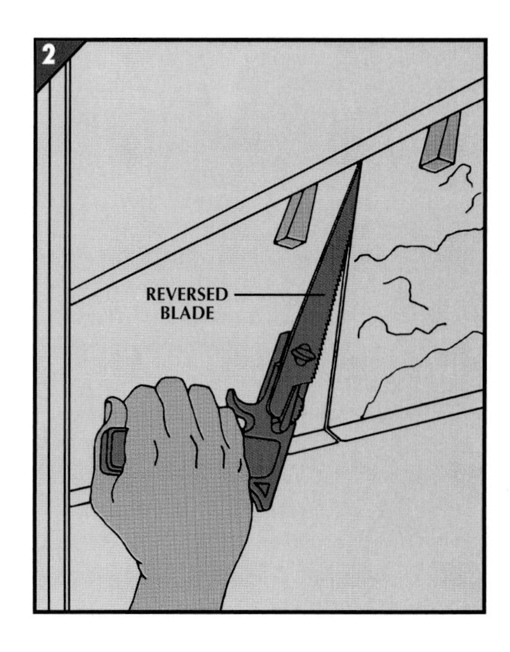

PATCHING HOLES IN STUCCO

Properly applied and cured, stucco is a nearly indestructible wall covering. It dries concrete hard and has no seams or joints to admit water. Over the years, however, stucco can develop small cracks or holes. Water entering through the damaged areas can then rot the supporting wood structure within. Patching such flaws in the stucco is straightforward, but it takes several days because of the required drying intervals.

For this type of small repair, buy stucco in ready-mixed dry form. Add just enough water to give it a uniform, plastic texture that leaves a fairly heavy residue on your glove but still holds together when it is picked up and squeezed. If the stucco mix begins to dry out as you work, chop it and mix it with a trowel to restore its proper consistency or mix a fresh batch. Do not add more water; that would weaken the mixture.

It is best to patch a stucco wall on a humid, overcast day, moderate in temperature. In any case, the night before you apply the stucco, wet down the area to be patched, and spray it again just before you begin.

TOOLS

- Trowel
- Old scrub brush
- Putty knife
- Garden hose

SAFETY TIPS

Wear goggles when you pour out the dry mix, which contains lime. Protect your hands with gloves as you work with wet stucco.

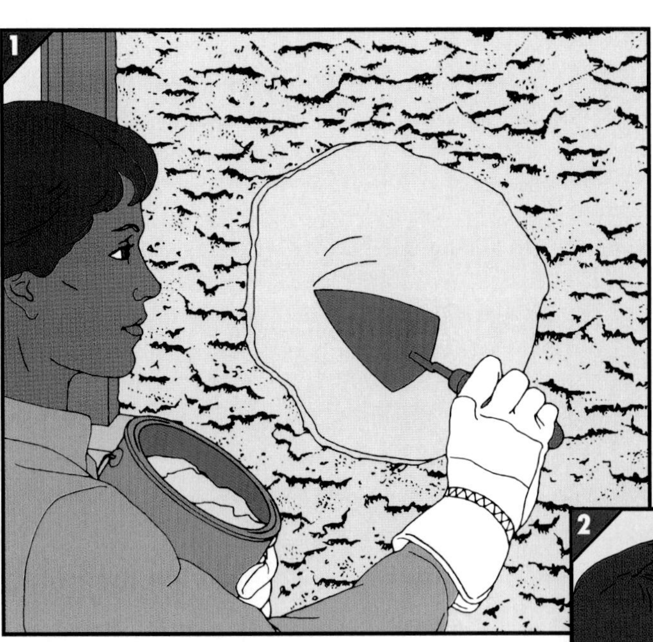

1. Filling a hole or crack.

◆ Clean away any loose debris with an old scrub brush. Widen narrow cracks to about an inch with a putty knife, taking care not to deepen the crack.

◆ Apply stucco with a trowel to within $\frac{1}{4}$ inch of the surface of the wall *(left)*. Tamp the stucco in firmly as you work.

If the wall has been exposed down to the lath, apply this level of the stucco in two layers, letting the first set overnight.

2. Smoothing the patch.

◆ An hour after completing the underlying stucco, smooth the surface with a small block of wood, using a circular motion *(right)*.

◆ Dampen the patch with light spray from a garden hose every 12 hours for the next 48 hours.

◆ Let the stucco dry completely before adding the finish coat; depending on the climate and the thickness of the patch, drying may take 2 to 5 days.

3. Applying the final coat.

◆ Dampen the wall.
◆ Trowel on a finish coat of stucco $\frac{1}{8}$ to $\frac{3}{4}$ inch thick, depending on the texture you must match.
◆ Let the stucco set until it just yields to finger pressure, then add the design. You can produce the basic English-cottage texture at left by applying thick blobs of stucco over a thin base, then using a twisting motion with a triangular trowel. For other styles, see the box below.

MATCHING THE STUCCO PATTERN

Three common alternatives to the stucco design shown above can also be produced with a minimum of equipment. To create the modern-American pattern *(below, left)*, scrape a block of wood downward over the damp surface of a thin coat of stucco. For a spattered effect *(below, center)*, fill a short broom or brush with stucco and hit it against a stick so that it sprays the stucco onto the wall. To make the travertine pattern, first jab a whisk broom repeatedly into a thick coat of stucco *(right, top)*, then smooth out the high points with a wood block or finishing trowel *(right, bottom)*.

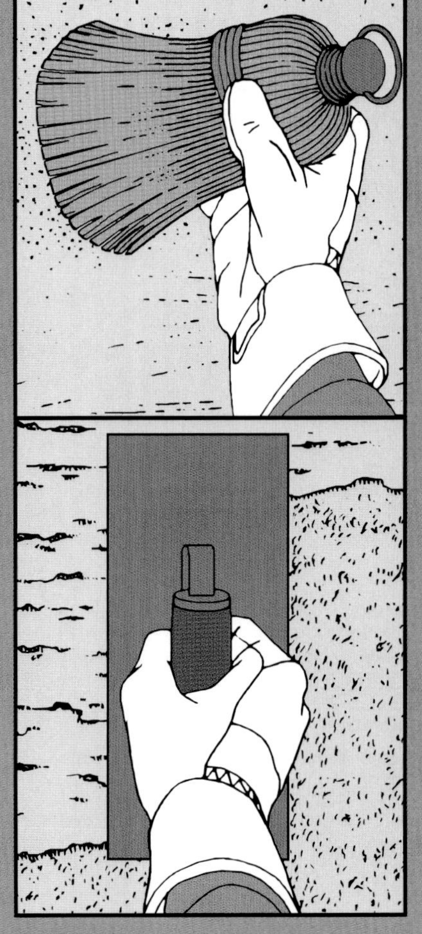

TRAVERTINE

MODERN-AMERICAN

SPATTERED

RESTORING BRICK

SAFETY TIPS

Work gloves and goggles offer protection when you are refurbishing brick. Switch to heavy-duty rubber gloves and add protective footgear and a respirator if you plan to work with acid solutions or concrete etchers.

1. Digging out broken mortar.

◆ Chip out loose and crumbling mortar from between bricks with a cold chisel and maul. Take out enough mortar to expose bare brick on at least one side of every joint you repair; new mortar must have brick to adhere to. Chip deeply into the joint as well; it is better to take out some solid mortar than to leave broken pieces behind.

◆ Clean the dust from the joint with a brush.

2. Laying in fresh mortar.

◆ Prepare a small batch of mortar from a packaged mix, adding water to make a mixture stiff enough not to run out of the joint.

◆ Brush water into the joint to wet the brick and prevent it from extracting moisture from the mortar. Do not use a hose; you may force water behind the bricks and damage the wall.

◆ Pile mortar on a hawk and press the mixture firmly into the joint with a trowel *(left).* As an alternative, you can buy a mortar bag—which is similar to a cake-frosting bag—to squeeze mortar into the joints.

3. Shaping the joint.

◆ Use a mason's tool called a jointer, or striker, to force the still-wet mortar between the bricks and to give a smooth, even finish to the surface.

◆ After the mortar has dried—3 or 4 days—neutralize the alkalis in it, which can damage paint *(box, opposite page).*

ELIMINATING EFFLORESCENCE

Efflorescence, a white, powdery crust often found on brick and concrete walls, is a major cause of peeling paint. It is caused when moisture in the masonry carries alkali compounds to the surface. As the water evaporates, the alkalis form crystals, causing paint to peel.

Efflorescence must be scrubbed away with a solution of 1 part muriatic acid to 10 parts water. If the deposits do not come off easily, make the solution stronger—1 part acid to 8 parts water.

After the masonry is clean, neutralize the acid by scrubbing with a solution of 1 part ammonia to 2 parts water. Then flush with a hose, working from the top of the wall downward.

Let the bricks and mortar dry for several days before painting. For best results on bare bricks, apply an undercoat of primer; otherwise the bricks may absorb paint unevenly, giving a mottled appearance.

CAUTION *To prevent dangerous splashes, always pour acid into water, never the reverse.*

TREATMENTS FOR CONCRETE

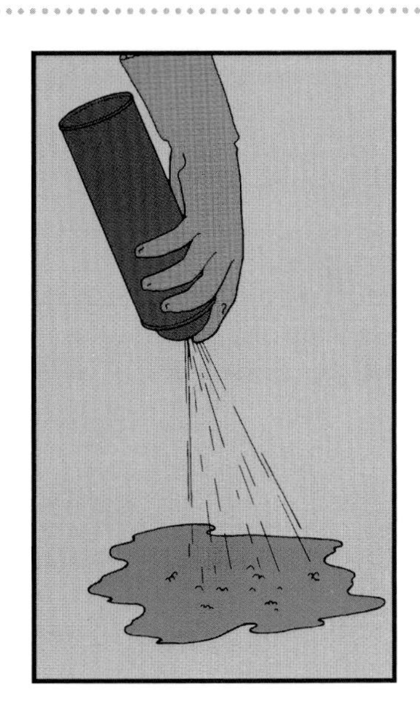

Using a degreaser.
Paint will not adhere to concrete surfaces that are slick with grease or oil. Spray a stain with an aerosol degreaser and let the solution stand for the time that is recommended by the manufacturer. Clean up and dispose of residue according to the manufacturer's recommendations; degreasers can harm grass or plants even if they are diluted by rinse water. Use a degreaser specifically labeled as safe for asphalt if you are working close to an asphalt surface. Let the surface dry completely before painting.

CAUTION *Vapors from these cleaners are flammable and toxic. Do not smoke while using them, and if you are working indoors, ventilate the area as thoroughly as possible.*

Etching concrete.
Before concrete is painted for the first time, etch it with a solution of 1 part muriatic acid to 5 parts water to neutralize the alkali in the concrete and roughen the surface to help the paint adhere. Scrub acid onto the concrete with a stiff-bristled brush. Once the solution stops bubbling on the concrete surface, mop it up and follow the manufacturer's recommendations for disposal.

CAUTION *Always pour acid into water, never the reverse.*

DIAGNOSING PAINT PROBLEMS

Before you repaint the outside of your house, inspect the walls carefully. If you notice any stains, cracks, blistering, peeling, or other faults in the existing paint, consult these and the following pages to identify the source of the problem and how to fix it. Address these flaws before repainting; otherwise, the blemishes are likely to reappear, and over time they can result in damage to the house.

How Paint Problems Arise: Very rarely is the culprit the paint itself. More often it is a defect such as faulty construction that traps moisture in the walls, incomplete surface preparation on the last paint job, incompatible paints, or careless application. Though the examples shown here are more common on exteriors because of their exposure to weather, many of them can also occur on interiors.

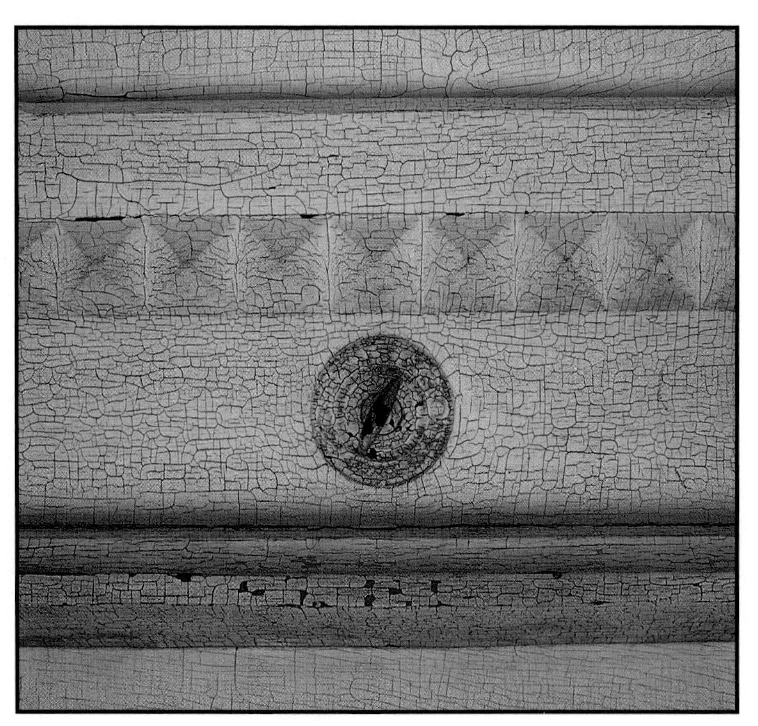

Alligatoring.
Scales like these result when the top coat of paint bonds poorly to the paint below it. The paints may not have been applied according to the manufacturer's instructions, or they may be incompatible with each other. Remove the cracked top layer and apply a new paint that is compatible with the surface.

Checking.
These short fractures along the grain of siding occur when paint loses its elasticity; as the surface expands and contracts with changes in the weather, the resulting stress causes the paint to break up. Remove the checked paint, as well as previous layers if there are more than two coats already on the surface. Prime the siding with a latex primer—it expands and contracts better than alkyd products—then repaint.

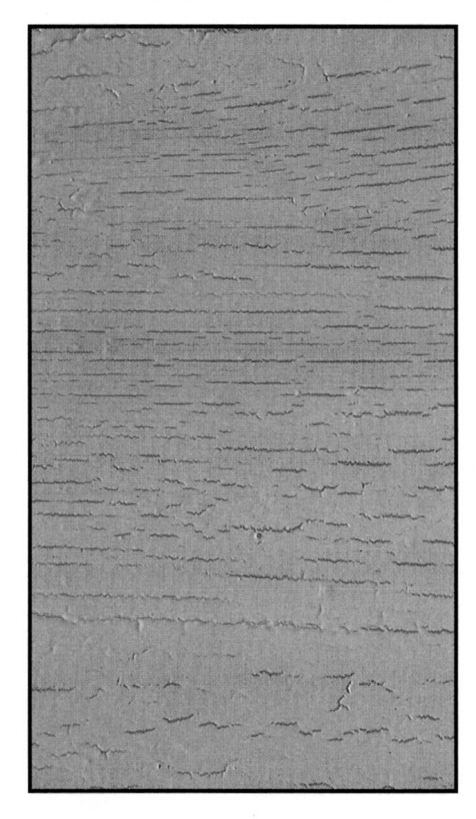

Flaking.
As checking or alligatoring becomes severe, paint begins to flake off between cracks. In advanced cases, the large gaps left behind by flaked paint allow water easy access to the bare wood, which ultimately rots. Scrape off the flaked paint and prime the wood with a latex primer before repainting.

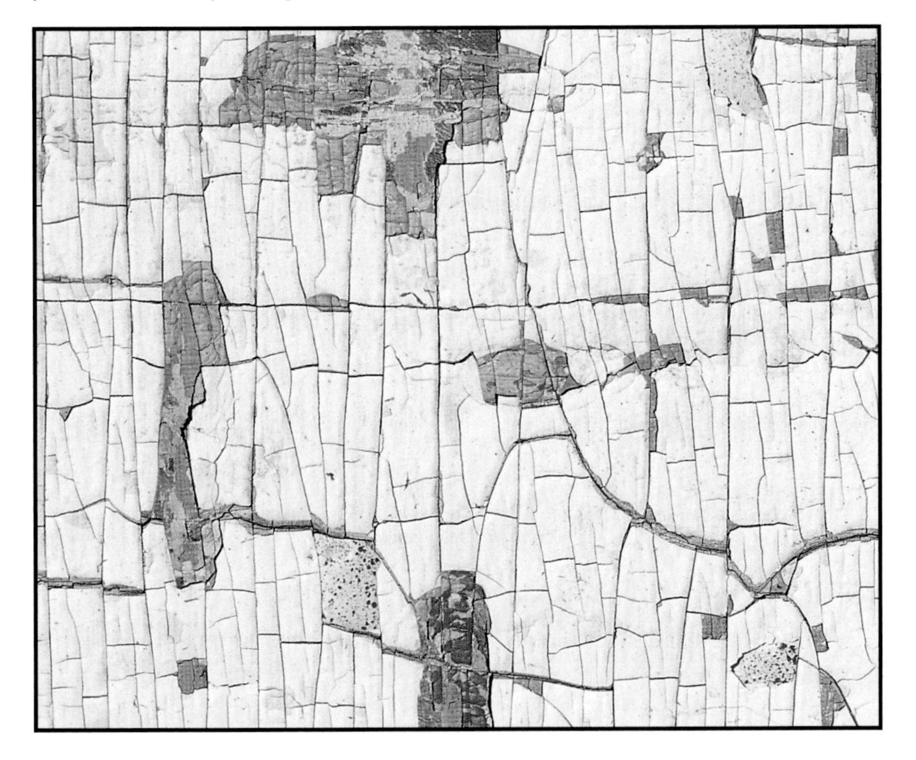

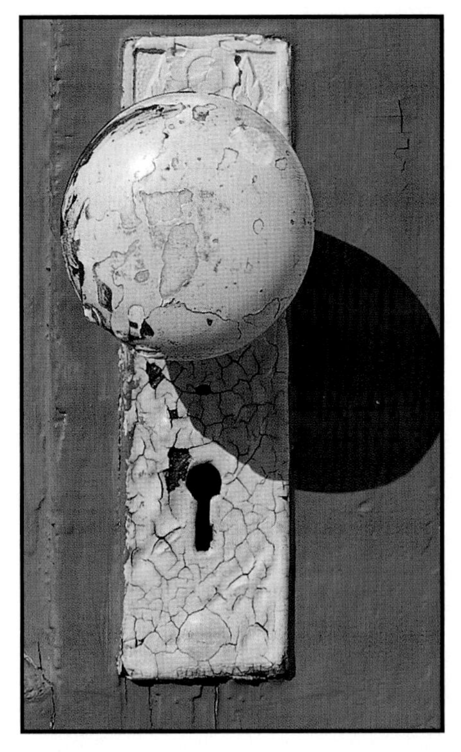

Flaking on metal.
If water penetrates the paint on a steel or iron fixture, the resulting rust can push the paint off the surface. Paint will also eventually flake if the fixture was not completely clean at the time of painting. Scrub the surface with a wire brush *(page 22),* arrest any rust as described on page 49, then apply a fresh coat of paint.

Blistering.
More common with alkyd-base paints than latex paints, blisters pop up for two reasons. One is water vapor trapped under the paint; with no place to go, it pushes out against the paint. The other is painting a wall or roof whose surface temperature is above about 75°F. In such heat, a skin forms that traps solvent vapor to form bubbles. Scrape or sand off the blistered paint, then eliminate any source of moisture in the walls. Repaint only when the air temperature is between 50 and 75°F and the surface is not bathed in sunshine.

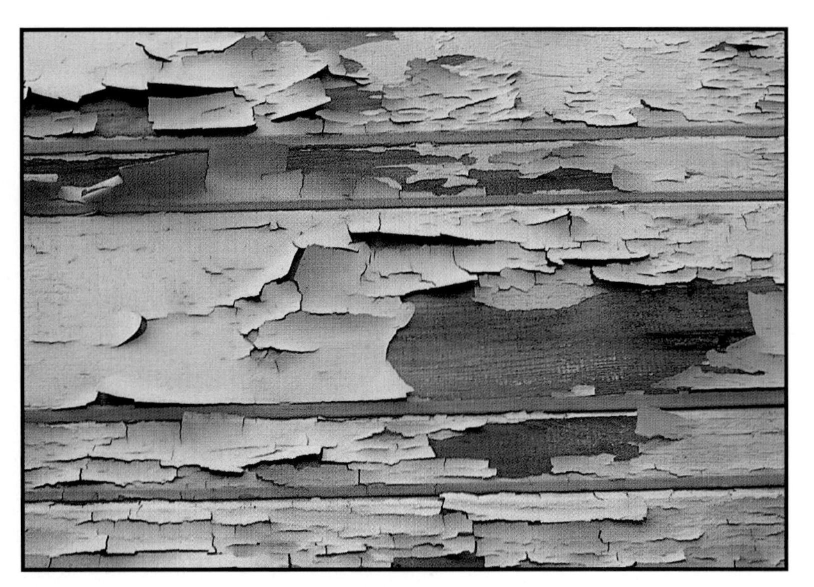

Peeling from wood.
This problem is often a consequence of blistering; as a blister grows, it tends to break loose from the wall. Peeling also occurs when paint is applied over dirt, grease, or loose paint. Scrape or sand off all loose paint and eliminate any sources of moisture in the wall. Repaint with latex primer and paint, since they are more permeable to water vapor than alkyds.

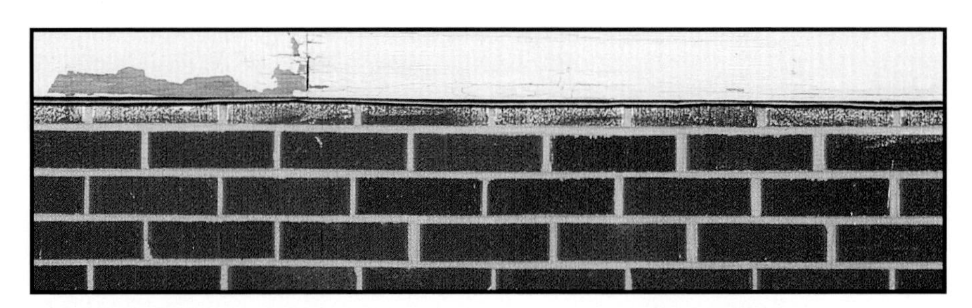

Chalk stains.
The brick wall above has been discolored by paint chalk that has washed down from the siding above it. Chalking paint helps keep the siding clean but should not be used where the chalk can streak areas below. The remedy for this situation is to wash the siding and repaint it with a nonchalking paint. Restore the brick by scrubbing it with detergent.

Rust stains.
Aluminum or stainless-steel nails and fixtures prevent this problem, which is caused by waterborne rust from iron or steel fixtures and nails that runs down the walls. Clean the rust from the metal, seal the metal with a rust-inhibiting coating, and scrub the stains from the walls.

Peeling from masonry.
Paint peels from masonry if it is applied to a heavily chalked or dirty surface. It also peels due to efflorescence, a process in which moisture drags salts within the masonry to the surface, where they crystallize and lift the paint from the wall. Strip the peeling paint, and check for sources of moisture; leaky pipes and gutters are often to blame. Follow the instructions in the box on page 39 to wash away any salt deposits.

Mildew.
The dark discolorations on this window frame inside a house are the result of mildew fungus growing on the paint. Kill the mildew with a fungicide such as chlorine bleach *(box, page 30)*. And since alkyd paints contain organic compounds on which mildew feeds, use only latex paint on mildew-prone areas. As an extra precaution, choose a paint containing a mildewcide or add one to the paint yourself.

Dye and resin stains.
Redwood *(above)*, along with woods like cypress and red cedar, contains natural dyes that can seep through a layer of paint. Use only alkyd primers and paints on such woods, as they cover dye stains more effectively than latex products.

The resin contained in wood knots often rises to the surface, where it can discolor the finish. Scrape the resin off the surface and seal the knots with shellac before applying new paint.

PREPARING THE SURFACE FOR PAINTING

After cleaning the exterior *(pages 29–30),* set to work removing various stains and making repairs to damaged brick, siding, and trim. Replace split shingles, cracked caulk around windows and doors, and loose mortar in brick walls.

Eliminating Stains: Rust and other metallic discolorations repel most paints, so these blemishes must be removed and prevented from recurring. If the stains are caused by leaks, stop them at the source: Seal joints *(pages 46–47),* fix broken downspouts and gutters, and repair damaged roofs.

Steel nails in clapboard or shingle siding are a common source of rust streaks. If screens or gutters are depositing metal stains, scrape the metal clean with a wire brush and then coat it with an appropriate paint. Clear acrylic varnish will seal copper screens and prevent stains from occurring.

Removing Unsound Paint: Paint in poor condition—examples of typical deterioration are illustrated on pages 40 through 43—that did not come off with power spraying *(pages 29–30)* must be removed by other means. Follow the safety precautions for lead paint and asbestos described on page 10.

There is no need to remove all the old paint. Where it still adheres well to the surface, sand the edges of the paint smooth to help the new coat of paint form a continuous film. Also, roughen the surface of glossy paint with sandpaper to provide "tooth" for the new coat.

Hand sanders and scrapers are good for removing small patches of damaged paint from clapboard siding *(opposite).* Where flaking is widespread, consider using an orbital power sander to speed the work. Hold the sander flat against the clapboard and keep the tool moving to avoid oversanding.

Around window trim and moldings, whose contours can make them difficult to scrape with a tool, chemical paint removers offer a working advantage.

While you are working on bare wood surfaces, seal any knots and oozing sap pores with shellac *(page 131).* Repair areas of rotted wood typically found on window sills and at the bottoms of door casings and support posts *(pages 48–49).* Most products for this task consist of a liquid wood hardener that solidifies and seals the wood and a two-part epoxy paste that fills in the damaged area. After drying, the filler is sanded and painted.

Peeling paint on metal and masonry surfaces usually comes off easily with a wire brush, although stubborn cases may have to be sandblasted by a professional. Chemical paint removers usually work well on metals but seldom work satisfactorily on masonry.

WOOD
Sanding block
Hammer
Nail set
Stiff-bristled nonmetallic brush
Paint scraper
Orbital sander
Heat gun
Flexible putty knife
Wood chisel
Hacksaw blade
Rasp

JOINTS
Cold chisel
Mallet
Caulking gun

METAL
Stiff-bristled wire brush
Electric drill with wire brush attachments

BRICK & CONCRETE
Cold chisel
Maul
Stiff-bristled brush
Mortar hawk
Trowel
Mortar jointer

WOOD
Sandpaper
Exterior-grade wood putty
Primer
Oxalic acid
Stainless-steel or aluminum nails
Wood hardener
Epoxy wood filler

JOINTS
Caulk

METAL
Rust-converting sealer

BRICK & CONCRETE
Mortar mix
Muriatic acid
Ammonia
Primer
Aerosol degreaser

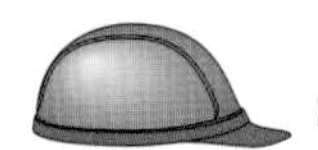

SAFETY TIPS

Heavy-duty rubber gloves and goggles are essential when you are working with corrosive agents such as oxalic acid. Work gloves protect your hands from hot flakes of paint when you are using a heat gun. Wear a dust mask when sanding old paint.

Eliminating rust stains. Lightly rub a surface rust stain on clapboard or other smooth siding with sandpaper *(far left),* then sand down to bright metal the rusty nailhead that caused the stain. Coat the broad head of a common nail with a rust-converting sealer. Do the same for the head of a finishing nail, but first drive the nail $\frac{1}{8}$ inch below the surface with a hammer and nail set. When the sealer dries, fill the nail hole with an exterior-grade wood putty, let it dry, and then coat it as well as any bare wood with primer *(near left).*

If rust has worked its way deeply into the wood, sanding alone would remove too much material. In such a case, try bleaching the stain with oxalic acid (available at paint stores) applied with a stiff-bristled nonmetallic brush. If the discoloration remains, scrape and seal the nailhead, then prime the shingle before painting it with the rest of the house.

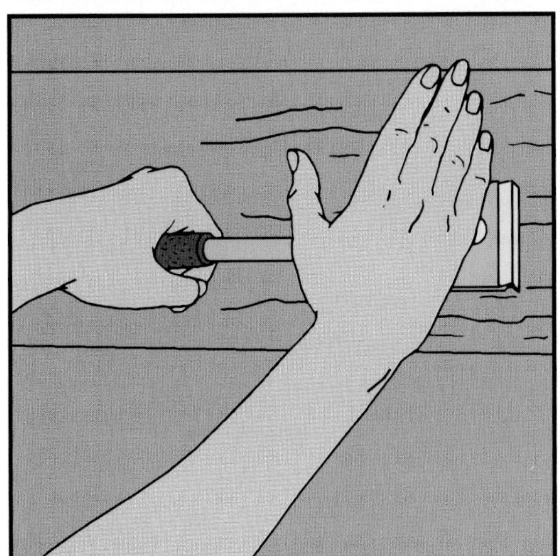

Scraping paint.
A rigid blade makes this scraper an efficient tool for removing small areas of flaking paint from house siding. Look for a scraper that also accepts a triangular blade, for working in corners, and a curved blade, for scraping concave shapes often found on door and window casings.

With any blade, experiment to find the minimum pressure needed to take the paint off without damaging the underlying wood. Apply pressure on the blade with the heel of one hand as you work, scraping in the direction of the wood's grain to remove loose or peeling paint. If the paint is resistant, you can speed the job with a heat gun *(below).*

Removing paint with heat.
Sanding is the only way to completely remove water-base paints from siding, but a heat gun is a faster alternative for oil- and alkyd-base paint. Set the temperature according to the manufacturer's recommendations, then hold the heat gun a few inches from the surface until the paint begins to bubble and wrinkle. Scrape away the softened paint with a flexible putty knife or scraper.

CAUTION *Never use a heat gun to remove paint that contains lead unless you wear a dust-and-fume respirator rated for that purpose. Additionally, keep the area where you are working free of paper, wood shavings, and solvent-soaked rags, which can be ignited by hot paint that falls to the ground.*

RESEALING JOINTS

SAFETY TIP

Goggles protect your eyes when you are chipping old caulk.

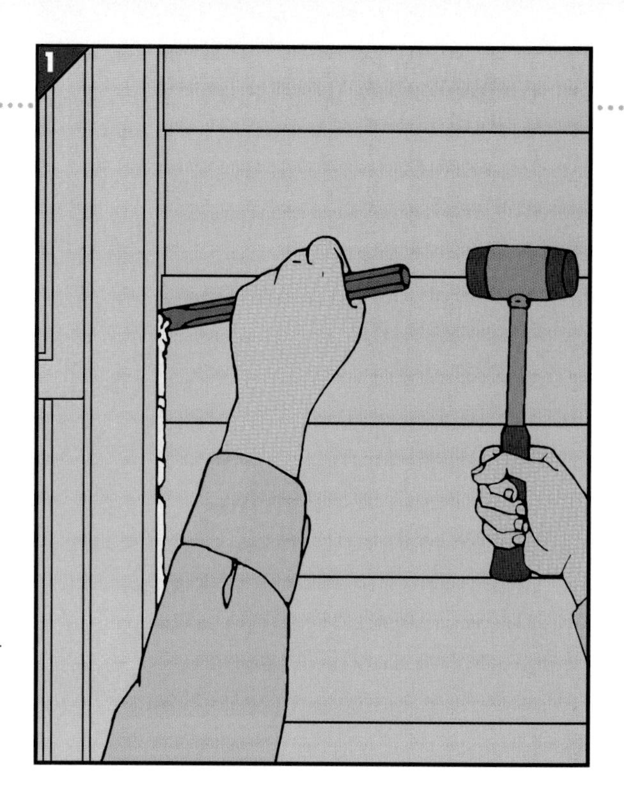

1. Removing old caulk.
Sealing with long-lasting butyl caulk requires joints that are completely free of old caulk. Use a cold chisel and mallet to remove it *(right),* then dust with a rag or brush. With other types of caulk, however, you need only clean loose pieces of deteriorated caulk from joints with a screwdriver or knife.

The Right Caulk for the Job

The chart below lists the five types of caulk most often used outdoors. Water-base latex caulks are easier to clean up than the silicone and butyl varieties but may not last as long. Check carefully that the caulk you buy is compatible with the surfaces that straddle the joint you wish to seal.

Type	Cleanup	Recommended Surfaces	Pros and Cons
Latex	Water	Glass, wood, metal	Paintable. Easy to apply and clean up. Available in colors. Apply in temperatures above 40°F. Limited flexibility, becomes brittle. Lifetime: 2–10 years.
Acrylic latex	Water	Glass, brick, wood, metal	Paintable. Easy to apply and clean up. Apply in temperatures above 40°F. Greater flexibility than latex caulk. Lifetime: 2–10 years.
Acrylic latex with silicone	Water	Glass, brick, wood, metal, concrete	Paintable. Available in colors, including clear. Apply in temperatures above 40°F. Stands up to weathering better than acrylic latex caulk. Lifetime: 5–15 years.
Silicone	Mineral spirits	Glass, wood, metal, concrete	Not paintable. Application temperatures vary by manufacturer. Excellent weathering characteristics. Fills large gaps better than latex caulks but tends to be more expensive. Lifetime: 10–50 years.
Butyl	Mineral spirits	Brick, wood, metal, concrete	Paintable. Inexpensive. Application temperatures vary by manufacturer. Good weathering characteristics, long-lasting. Ideal for joints subject to extremes of expansion and contraction and exposed to all weather conditions, such as for gutters and downspouts. Hard to clean up, slow curing time. Lifetime: 2–10 years.

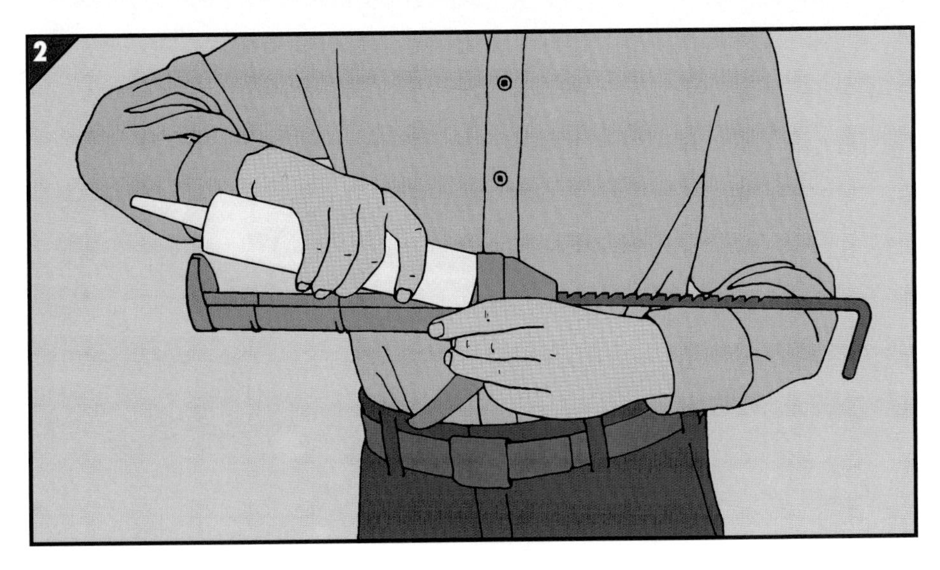

2. Loading a caulking gun.

◆ Turn the plunger rod until its teeth face up, then pull the rod back as far as it will go.

◆ Slip the cartridge into the gun, push the rod into the base of the cartridge, and turn the teeth facedown.

◆ Snip the plastic spout at a 45-degree angle to make an opening no more than $\frac{1}{4}$ inch wide.

◆ Silicone and butyl caulks are sealed. Insert a length of clothes-hanger wire into the spout to puncture the seal.

3. Applying caulk.

◆ Set the spout into the joint at an angle *(left)* and squeeze the trigger gently until the caulk begins to flow.

◆ Push the spout steadily forward along the joint while applying slow, consistent pressure to the trigger so the caulk fills the joint but does not overflow it.

◆ After filling the entire joint, run your finger or the bottom of a plastic spoon along the caulk to form it into a concave shape.

TRICKS OF THE TRADE

Caulking in Hard-to-Reach Spots

To reach joints that are all but inaccessible to a caulking gun—the top of a window frame on a house with a roof overhang, for example—jam a short length of vinyl tubing onto the spout. This flexible extension, affixed to the spout with duct tape if necessary, makes it possible to reach almost any joint.

REPLACING BROKEN SHINGLES

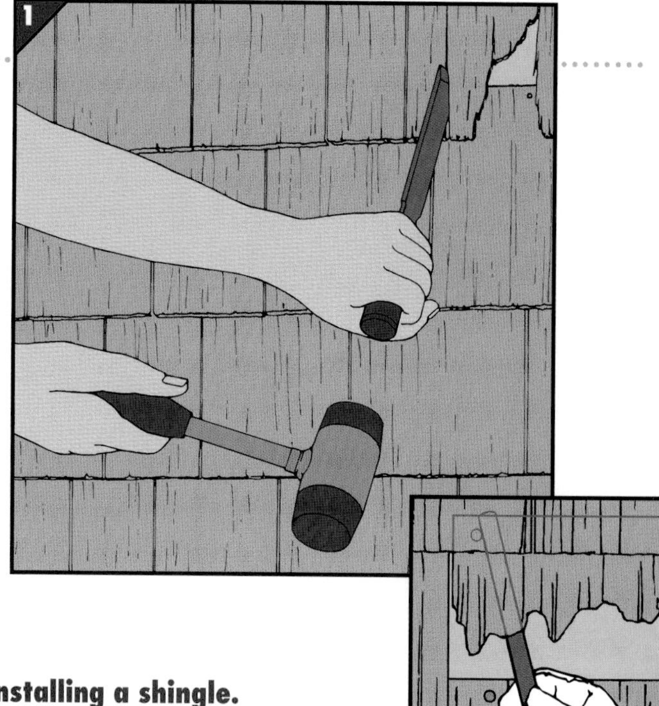

1. Removing a shingle.

Replace all broken or warped shingles before you repaint the house. Painting over bad shingles may disguise the damage but will also permit water to seep behind the good shingles and cause further deterioration.

◆ Split a shingle with a wood chisel along the grain, breaking it into narrow strips and slivers of wood.

◆ Wearing a glove to protect your hand, slip a hacksaw blade under the broken shingle and saw off the nails that hold it in place *(inset)*. Then pull out all the pieces of old shingle.

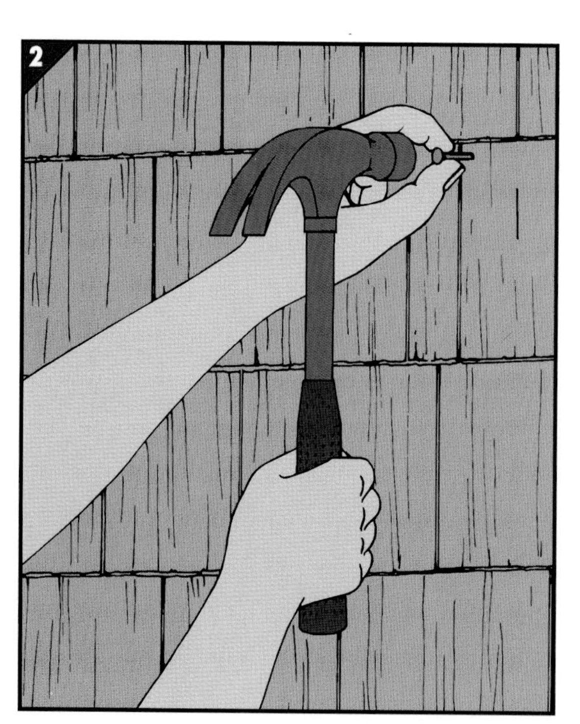

2. Installing a shingle.

◆ Slip the shingle under the course that is above and hold it in place.

◆ Drive two or three stainless-steel or aluminum nails through the new shingle just below the shingles that overlap it.

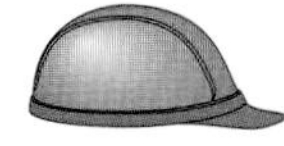

SAFETY TIP

Goggles protect your eyes from flying debris when you are splitting a shingle or stripping paint from metal with a wire brush or especially with a power drill.

REPAIRING ROTTED WOOD

1. Removing damaged wood.

Rotted wood is gray and spongy. When probed with a sharp tool such as an awl, it crumbles, whereas sound wood cracks or splinters.

◆ With a scraper or chisel, carve out the rotted area until you reach undamaged wood *(right)*. Be sure to remove all the rot, even if you have to cut slightly into good wood.

◆ Using a brush or a squeeze bottle, apply a generous coat of wood hardener to all surfaces of the cavity and let it dry.

2. Filling the cavity.

◆ Mix two-part epoxy wood filler following the manufacturer's directions. These mixtures cure rapidly, so mix no more than you can apply in about 5 minutes.

◆ With a flexible putty knife, fill the cavity with the paste, being sure to compress it into all voids and cracks. Overfill the hole slightly and let the paste cure.

◆ Once it has dried, smooth the overfilled paste—first with a rasp, then with sandpaper—until the surface of the repair is smooth and flush with the surrounding wood.

◆ Prime the repair, then paint.

PREPARING METAL SURFACES

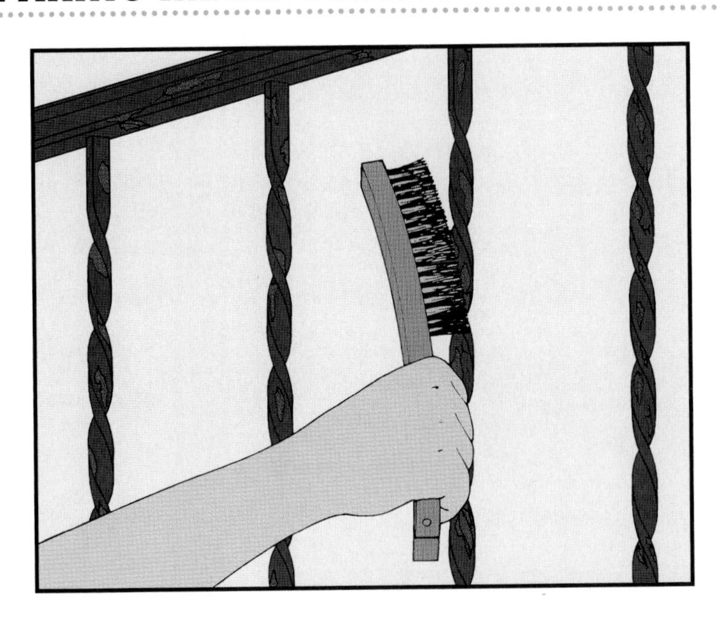

Preparing metal by hand.

◆ Remove any loose or peeling paint and corrosion from wrought iron and aluminum with a wire brush.

◆ Clean aluminum with a commercial solution that is specifically made for the purpose. Coat rusted wrought iron with a rust-converting sealer that chemically transforms the rust into a paintable surface.

Fast stripping with a power brush.
A wire brush attached to an electric drill shortens any metal cleaning task. A cup-shaped brush works best for broad surfaces like the face of a gutter *(right);* a wheel-shaped brush *(inset)* is better suited to corners and to smaller features such as gutter edges and wrought-iron railings. Always hold the drill so that debris from the brush flies away from you.

PAINTING A HOUSE IN LOGICAL ORDER

Painting the exterior of a house calls for the same top-to-bottom strategy—and many of the same tools and techniques—as painting the interior. Careful planning is a necessity, due to the variety of exterior construction details.

Be sure to cover shrubs with drop cloths in the work area and tie them back as necessary. Prune or tie back tree branches to get clear, safe access to the upper walls.

Working High above the Ground: One way the exterior differs from the interior is in its scale. Painting the upper reaches of the exterior is more perilous than any indoor job. Extension ladders can help you do the sides of the house *(pages 25–26)*, but many houses have dormers that can be painted only from a sloping roof. If you use a ladder that reaches at least 3 feet above the edge, you can step safely from it onto the roof without standing on the top two rungs of the ladder or climbing over the eaves. While on the roof wear shoes with nonslip soles, use a ladder equipped with a ladder hook for foot- and handholds, and sit down as much as possible.

Applying the Paint: An exterior paint job has two major stages—coating the sides of the house and then the trim. Avoid painting in direct sunlight; begin on the shady side and do dormers first, leaving the overhang, trim, and windows for later. Continue downward and coat the siding in horizontal strips, moving the ladder as needed.

Next, start on the trim. Again, begin with the dormers, then do the overhangs, gutters, and downspouts. Continue with the windows, shutters, and doors of the main part of the house. Paint door and window exteriors in the same way as their inside surfaces *(pages 137–139)*.

Finally, do the stair railings, stairs, and foundation. If stairs must be used before they dry, paint all the risers but only alternate treads, then do the rest after the first half has dried. Apply a coat of tough urethane varnish on wooden thresholds.

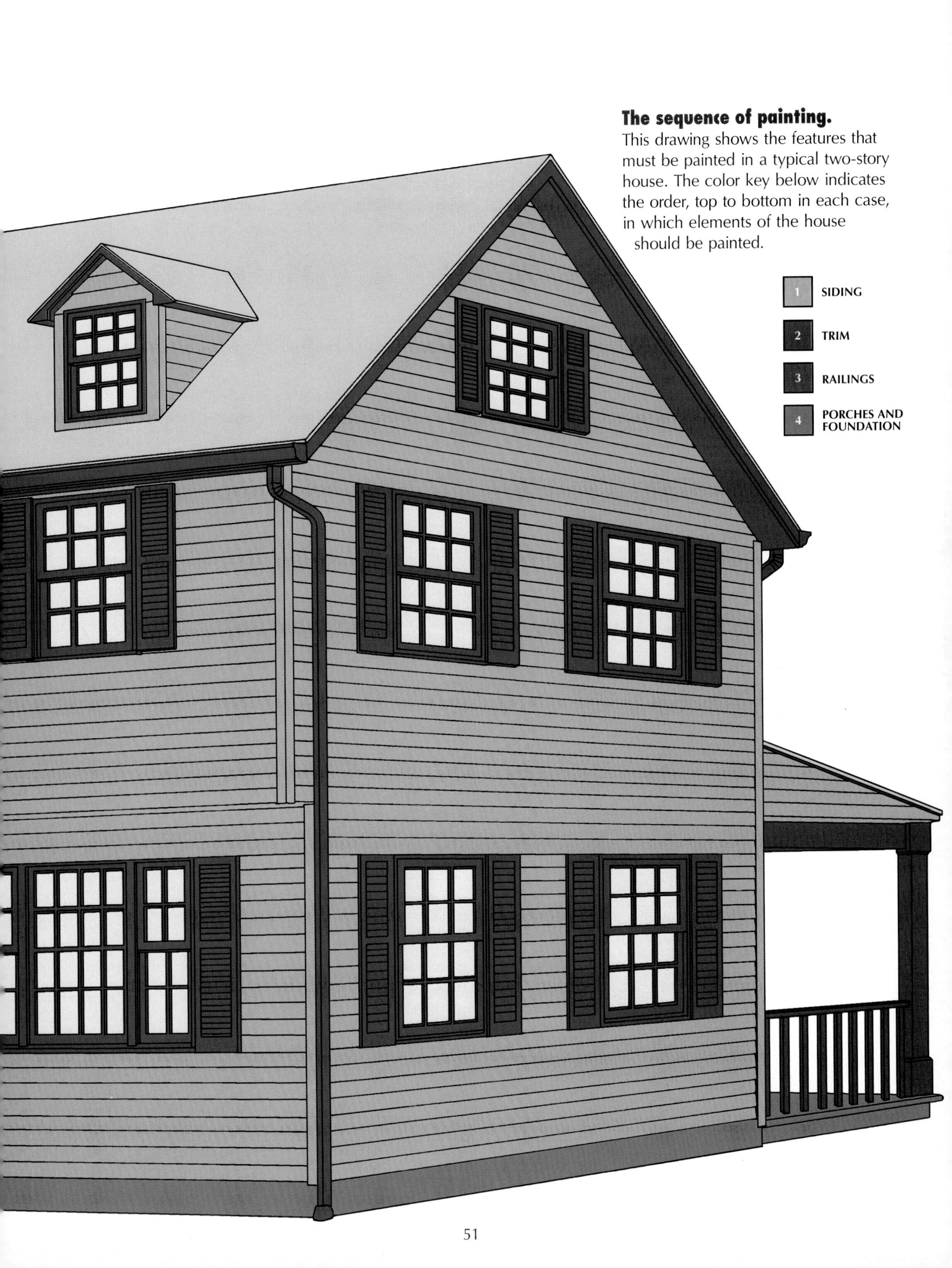

The sequence of painting. This drawing shows the features that must be painted in a typical two-story house. The color key below indicates the order, top to bottom in each case, in which elements of the house should be painted.

SPECIAL METHODS FOR THE OUTSIDE

Conventional brushes and rollers work fine on smooth exteriors like clapboard and siding. But there are some surfaces—such as cinder block, wood shingles, and narrow railings—that these ordinary applicators might not be able to handle. In such cases, the applicators and techniques shown on the following pages come in handy.

Spray-Painting: One option for outdoor work is to buy or rent an airless paint sprayer *(pages 54–55)*. The great advantage of this device is its speed—it can paint a house in just a fraction of the time it would take with brushes and rollers. Furthermore, sprayers can apply a thicker, more uniform coat of paint to the house than is possible with conventional applicators.

However, airless sprayers have their drawbacks. Because they operate under tremendous pressure, they can cause serious injury *(box, page 54)*. And because these sprayers produce a relatively coarse mist of paint, a chance breeze may blow paint in any direction. For that reason, some localities restrict the use of these paint sprayers and you must mask or move anything within a 10-foot radius of the sprayer that you do not want to be painted.

Using the Sprayer: Before starting work, read and understand the manufacturer's instructions for setting up, operating, and cleaning the sprayer. Also make sure the sprayer is equipped with the correct spray tip *(page 54)*. Thin liquids such as stains require a tip with a small opening; viscous fluids such as latex paint require a larger one. Generally, a tip that sprays a pattern about 8 inches high provides the best compromise between speed and ease of use.

To get the hang of spraying, first practice on a piece of cardboard or plywood. When you move to the house itself, start with an inconspicuous section, where mistakes can be corrected with a paintbrush.

TOOLS

Paintbrushes
Pad applicator
Rough-surface applicator
Paint mitten
Paint sprayer

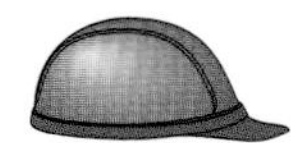

SAFETY TIP

Latex gloves protect your hands when you are working with alkyd-base paints and the solvents used to clean them from brushes and other applicators.

Painting clapboards with a brush.
Work in sections 3 feet wide and four or five clapboards high.
◆ Coat the bottom edge of each clapboard in a section *(left, top)*.
◆ Next, apply heavy dabs of paint along the face of one board *(left, middle)*.
◆ Then distribute the paint across the clapboard with horizontal brush strokes *(left, bottom)*.
◆ Finish the clapboard with a single horizontal stroke to minimize brush marks.
◆ Repeat the preceding steps for the next clapboard in the section.

Paint shingles in the same way you would clapboards, but cover their faces with vertical strokes, rather than horizontal ones, to follow the grain of the wood.

A pad applicator for shingles.
Consisting of a soft "rug" of short nylon bristles, the pad applicator works well on the uneven surfaces of shingles. As with clapboards, work in sections 3 feet long and four or five courses high.
◆ Apply the paint first to the shingle edges with the edge of the pad.
◆ Then paint each shingle face by pressing the entire pad firmly against the front of the shingle *(left)* and pulling downward with a single stroke.

A rough-surface applicator.
Similar to the pad used for shingles, the rough-surface applicator has a thick, spongy backing that conforms to the contours of brick and cinder block. Work the paint into the surface with a circular motion *(left),* then smooth it out with straight finishing strokes.

A paint mitten.
Faster than any brush for coating narrow pipes and railings, this applicator is a bulky mitten covered with lambs wool. Fit the mitten over either hand and dip it into a tray of paint. Lightly grip one end of the object to be painted with the mitten, then slide it toward the other end *(right).* When finished, clean the mitten as you would a roller.

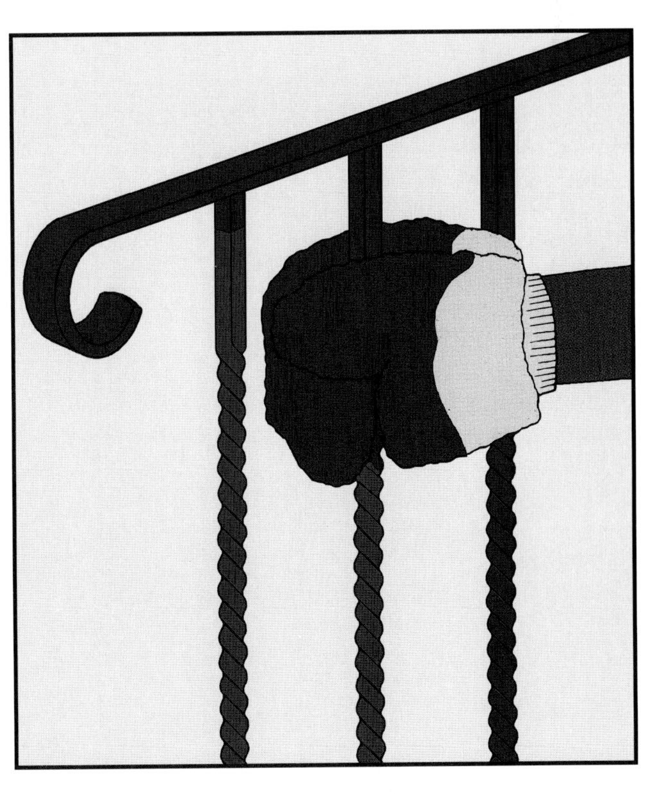

POWER SPRAYERS

How the sprayer works. At the heart of a paint sprayer is a pump run by a powerful electric motor. The pump draws in paint from a bucket through a pickup tube equipped with a coarse screen to trap foreign matter. The paint travels through a high-pressure hose, past a pressure regulator, and through a filter fine enough to capture particles that might clog the spray tip. An additional high-pressure hose carries the paint to the spray gun.

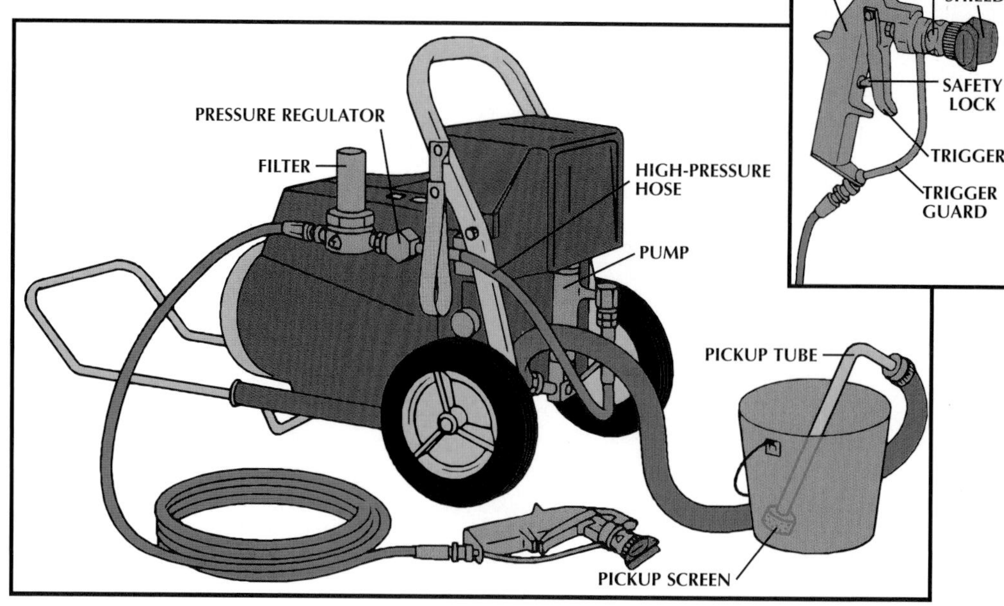

The gun itself *(inset)* is equipped with a trigger guard and a safety lock to prevent accidental discharge. A safety shield keeps fingers from getting too close to the spray tip.

A PORTABLE POWER SPRAYER

Instead of renting a commercial sprayer, you may wish to purchase a portable sprayer, available at home-supply stores. The smallest have 1-pint reservoirs that screw directly into the handle and are suitable for painting items like fences and lawn furniture. Larger models *(below)* are intended for larger jobs—like an entire house.

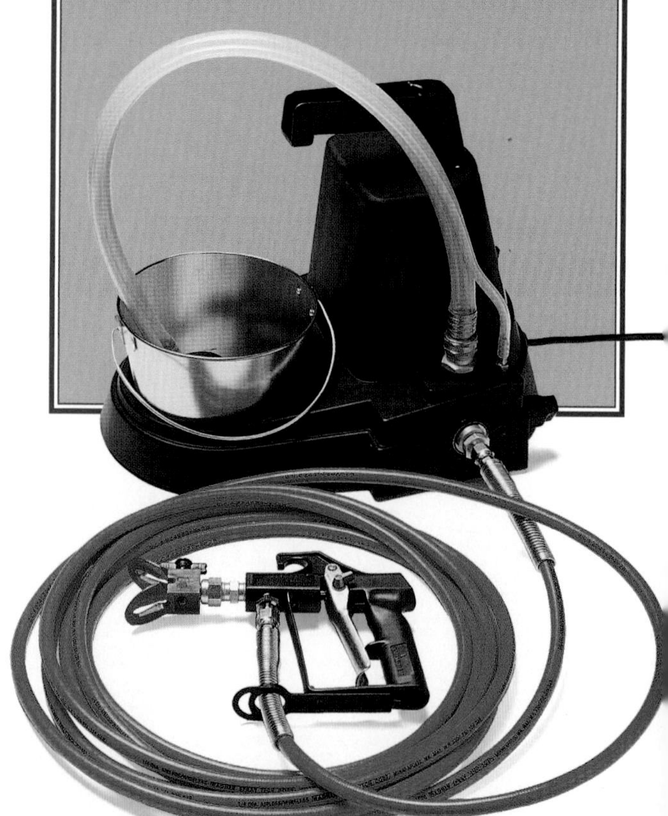

Handling Sprayers with Care

Airless sprayers push paint through the spray tip at pressures up to 3,000 pounds per square inch, enough to inject paint through skin. If any part of your body is hit at short range by an emerging jet of paint or solvent, seek immediate medical attention. A hospital emergency room is the best place to go; your family doctor may not know how to treat this special kind of wound effectively. To prevent accidents, follow these safety rules:

- ✔ Always wear eye protection and a cartridge-type respirator when spraying.
- ✔ Make sure the sprayer you rent or buy has a trigger guard, a safety lock, and a safety shield around the spray tip *(above)*. Keep the safety lock engaged when not actually spraying.
- ✔ Never point the gun at yourself or another person.
- ✔ Keep your fingers away from the spray tip. Never try to clear out the nozzle of a gun by pressing your finger against the spray tip while paint is being discharged.
- ✔ Do not disassemble the equipment for any reason without first turning it off, unplugging it, and then depressing the spray-gun trigger to release residual pressure in the hose.
- ✔ Keep children and pets away, and never leave the sprayer unattended.

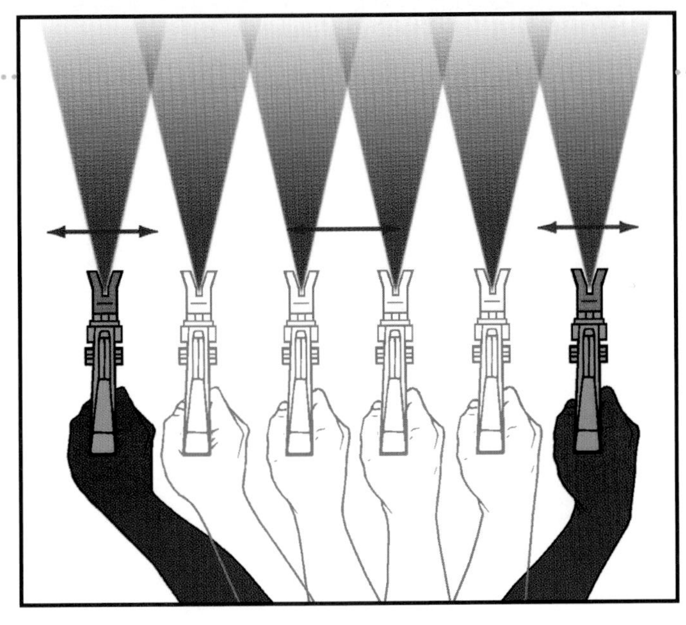

Gripping the spray gun.

The key to successful spray-painting is to hold the gun properly: perpendicular to the wall and 12 inches away. To maintain this constant angle and distance, crook your elbow slightly and bend your wrist *(above)*, so that you can move the gun in a line exactly parallel to the wall. For best results, do not spray a section wider than you can comfortably reach—about 36 inches for most people.

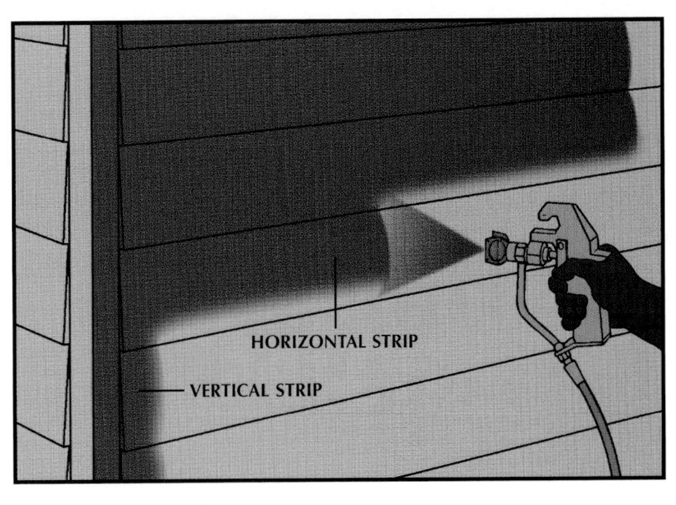

Covering a wall.

The best way to evenly coat a wall is to spray in a series of smooth, overlapping strips. Start the gun moving before depressing the trigger at the beginning of each stroke, and keep it moving after releasing the trigger at the end.

◆ First spray a vertical strip down the edge of the wall, releasing the trigger at the end of the stroke. This strip keeps you from spraying past the edge and wasting paint when applying horizontal strips.

◆ Then make a series of horizontal passes across the wall. Each pass should overlap the previous strip and the vertical strip by about an inch to compensate for the thin coating at the ends of the spray pattern.

DIAGNOSING SPRAYING PROBLEMS

The paint patterns illustrated at right are a tip-off that you are either holding or moving the spray gun incorrectly.

An hourglass-shaped pattern *(right, top)* results if you move the spray gun back and forth without bending your wrist to keep the sprayer the correct 12-inch distance from the wall. As the gun arcs past the wall, it first moves closer to the wall and then farther away, leaving a wide thin coat at the ends of the strip and a narrow thick coat at the center.

Tilting the gun while spraying causes a different kind of unevenness *(right, bottom)*. If the gun is pointed slightly downward, the resulting layer of paint will be denser at the top of the spray pattern than it is at the bottom. The reverse occurs when the gun is pointed upward.

CHAPTER 2

FLOORS AND STAIRS

Among the attractions of many old houses are handsome floors and graceful, spacious stairways. Even houses that are only moderately old are likely to have floors and stairs that are of better quality and that were built or installed with more care than those in most contemporary houses.

But floors and stairs must absorb the heaviest wear of any part of a home. For that reason, they ought to be kept in good condition, and not just on the surface. Often, a squeak or noticeable springiness underfoot is the first sign that the underlying structure needs some attention. Taking care of such problems promptly makes it easy to keep floors and stairs in excellent condition and looking their best.

This chapter tells you how to inspect floors and stairs, how to deal with underlying problems, and how to repair, maintain, or replace finish flooring, whether it is wood, vinyl tile, or resilient vinyl sheet flooring. It also shows you how to deal with loose and squeaky stair treads, and how to repair stairway handrails, called balustrades.

△ *Above:* A balustrade is a safety feature as well as a decorative element on a stairway. Replace missing or cracked balusters and make sure the newel post, the railing, and the balusters are all securely mounted.

△ *Above and right:* Stairway styles in old houses range from grand Victorian to functional simplicity. Most are built in the same way and therefore call for the same techniques to fix common old-house stairway problems such as squeaky treads and loose balusters.

◁ *Left:* Traditional wood strip flooring is one of the most beautiful features in older homes. Repair, sanding, and refinishing can make damaged or worn flooring look like new.

▽ *Below:* Inlaid wood borders, seldom installed today, are found in many old houses. They can be repaired and refinished with the same techniques used for parquet flooring.

▷ *Right:* Durable, easy-to-clean resilient flooring is excellent for high-traffic areas of a house. Repair is easy if needed: Individual tiles can be replaced and sheet flooring often can be patched invisibly.

EVALUATING FLOORS

Floors receive the hardest use of any part of a house. The finished surface receives the direct wear of traffic every day, while the subfloor and supporting structure *(below)* must constantly absorb the weight and impact of every step. After several years, a floor may have surface damage, it may sag or tilt, or it may flex and squeak as you walk across it. The following pages tell you how to deal with these problems.

Testing Floors: Squeaks are usually caused by subflooring that is no longer firmly attached to the joists. They may also result from the rubbing of finish floorboards that have worked loose from the subfloor. Squeaks can be eliminated in a number of ways *(pages 61–62)*.

To detect tilt or sag in a floor, drop a marble or small rubber ball. If it rolls repeatedly and quickly in one direction, indicating sag, add support to the underlying framing as necessary *(page 63)*.

Walk across the floor in several different directions to check for squeaks, springiness, or window rattling. These are usually signs of loosened subflooring or poor joist support. An overall bounciness may indicate a lack of diagonal bridging between joists, needed for any joist span of 8 feet or more. Check from below. Refasten any loose bridging. If there is none, install prefabricated steel bridging, available at home centers, lumberyards, and construction suppliers.

Surface Defects: Stains and burns that start to lift out when you test the area with a wood scraper can be removed quickly by sanding. Replace split or ruined wood flooring *(pages 67–69)* and vinyl tiles *(page 76)*; patch damaged sections of vinyl sheet flooring *(page 77)*. Wherever you remove finish flooring, check the underlayment or subfloor; if there is decay, you may have to replace that first.

Ceramic tiles can be replaced indetectably if you can match the color accurately—not always easy to do in a floor several years old. Score the surface with a glass cutter, then pry the pieces loose with a hammer and cold chisel (wear safety goggles). Scrape the underlayment clean and install new tiles with mastic or mortar; fill the joints with grout.

TOOLS

- Hammer
- Stud finder
- Electric drill
- Nail set
- Screwdriver
- Putty knife
- Mallet
- Wood chisel
- Pry bar

MATERIALS

- Construction adhesive
- Finishing nails or trim head screws (3")
- Wood shingles
- Screws and washers
- Glazier's points
- Steel bridging
- Replacement boards
- Flooring nails (3")

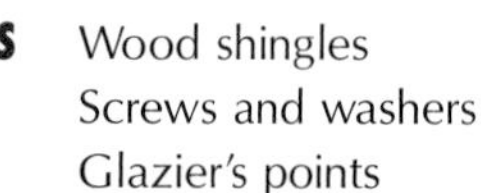

SAFETY TIP

When hammering nails, wear safety goggles to protect your eyes from flying debris.

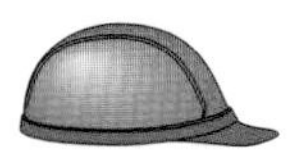

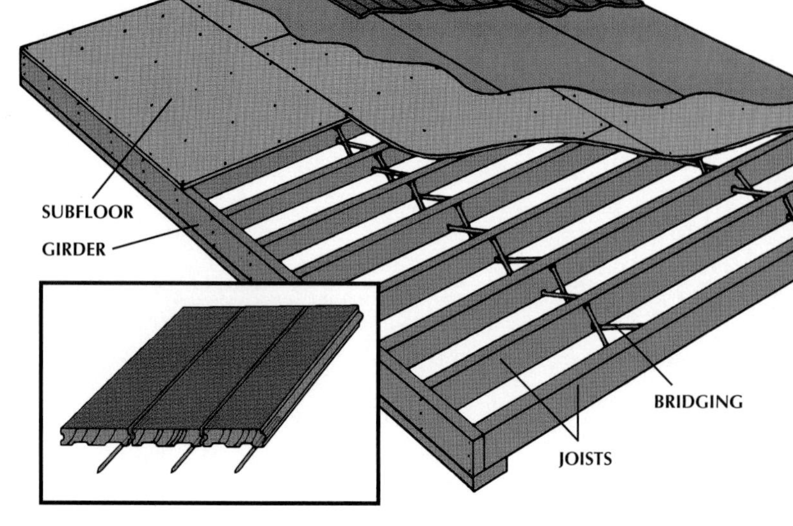

Anatomy of a floor.
A typical floor is constructed in layers. Parallel 2- by 9-inch joists, laid on girders and braced by diagonal bridging, provide structural support. In older homes, the subfloor is often wide planks or tongue-and-groove boards laid diagonally. In later homes, $\frac{3}{4}$-inch plywood was used. A layer of heavy felt or building paper over the subfloor was often omitted in older floors. Wood finish flooring commonly has interlocking tongues and grooves on the sides and ends. Strips are attached by driving and setting 3-inch flooring nails at an angle above the tongue, where the heads will be concealed by the upper lips of the adjoining grooves *(inset)*. Properly installed vinyl and ceramic finish flooring is laid over an additional underlayment of hardboard, cement board, or other material. This is essential when these materials are laid over an old wood finish floor.

CORRECTING FLOOR PROBLEMS

Squeaks in the first-floor level are usually easy to correct if there is no basement ceiling so you can work from below. For upper floors or those not accessible from below, use one of the methods for working from above shown below and on the next page. A floor over a crawlspace may (and should) have insulation between the joists below. You can temporarily remove it—wearing long sleeves, gloves, goggles, and a mask—but working from above will be much easier.

Some structural faults in a floor are obvious; others show up only after a heavy object such as a loaded bookcase has burdened the floor for a few weeks. Flexing and sagging in the middle of a floor are caused by inadequate support. You can eliminate flexing by putting in a beam and shims to support joists in midspan *(page 63)*. To take out a sag, you must raise the joists with a jack *(page 64)* before putting a beam and posts in place. To avoid cracking a joist, turn the jack screw only a bit each day—no more than a half-turn in a very old house—until the sag is gone. You will need a helper for that kind of work.

ELIMINATING SQUEAKS

Shimming the subfloor.
If the subfloor is accessible from below, have someone walk on the floor while you look for movement in the subfloor over a joist. To eliminate movement, apply a bead of construction adhesive to both sides of the tapered edge of a wood shingle and wedge it between the joist and the loose subfloor. Do not force the subfloor upward or you may cause boards in the finish floor to separate.

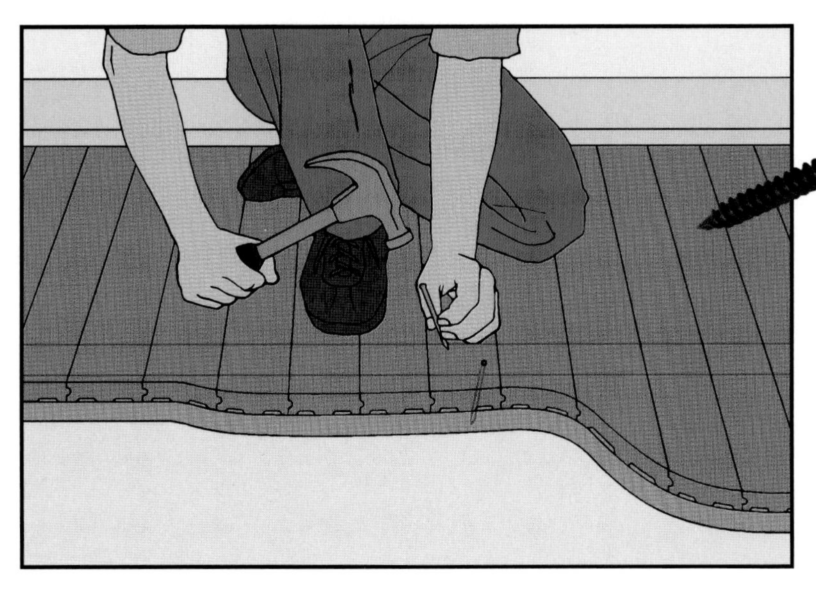

TRIM HEAD SCREW

Securing inaccessible subfloors.
If the ceiling beneath the floor is finished, refasten the loose section of subfloor to the nearest joist through the finish floor above.

◆ Use a stud finder to locate the joist. Then drill pairs of pilot holes angled toward each other and drive 3-inch finishing nails or trim head screws *(photo)* into the subfloor and joist below.

◆ Set the nailheads or countersink the screws and cover them with wood putty that has been tinted to match the color of the boards.

Anchoring floorboards from below.

◆ Select screws that will reach to no more than $\frac{1}{4}$ inch below the surface of the finish floor.
◆ Drill pilot holes through the subfloor, using a bit with a diameter at least as large as that of the screw shanks, so that the screws will turn freely. Avoid penetrating the finish floor by marking the subfloor's thickness on the drill bit with tape.
◆ Drill pilot holes into the finish floor with a bit slightly narrower than the screws.
◆ Fit the screws with large washers, apply a bit of candle wax to the threads to ease installation, and insert them into the pilot holes. As you turn the screws, their threads will bite into the finish floorboards, pulling them tight to the subfloor.

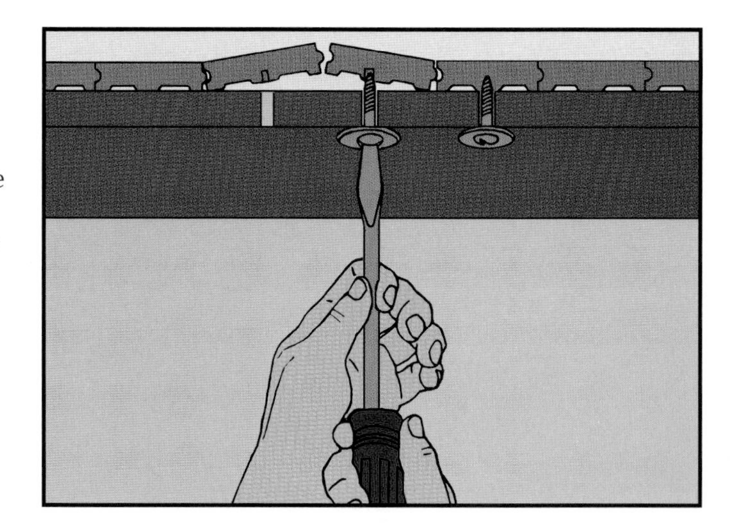

Silencing finish flooring from above.

◆ First, try remedies that do not mar the finished surface. Force powdered graphite or talcum powder into the joints between boards.
◆ If the squeak persists, insert glazier's points—the triangular metal pieces that secure glass into frames—every 6 inches and set them below the surface with a putty knife *(above)*. If the pressure of the knife is insufficient to push the points down, use a hammer and small piece of scrap metal to tap them into place.
◆ Should these solutions fail, drive finishing nails or trim head screws through the floorboards and into the subfloor, angling and concealing them as explained on page 61.

BRACING A WEAK SPOT

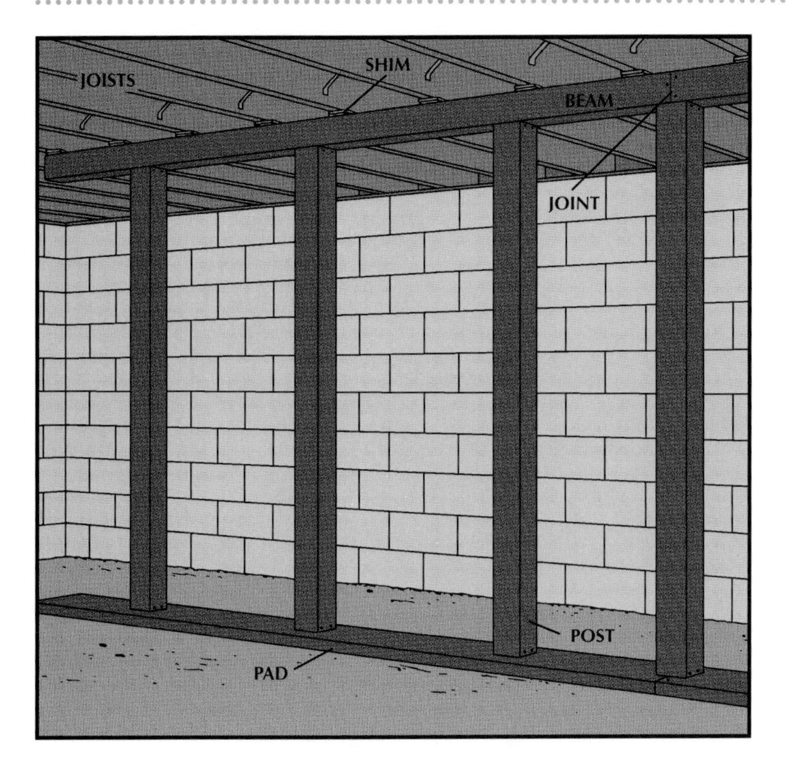

Shoring weak joists.

◆ To brace a sagging floor, make a beam of 10-foot pressure-treated 4-by-4s, laid end to end on the basement floor perpendicular to the joists.

◆ Cut three pressure-treated 4-by-4 posts for each beam section, plus an additional post for each beam joint. Make the posts $5\frac{1}{4}$ inches shorter than the measurement between the floor and the joists at the point of lowest sag.

◆ Toenail three posts to each beam section, one in the center and one 2 feet from each end.

◆ Lay a wood pad for the posts. On a dirt floor, use 10-foot pressure-treated 2-by-12s end to end; on a concrete floor, 12-inch lengths of 2-by-8 will do.

◆ With a helper, set each post-and-beam section on the corresponding pad. Tap pairs of wood shims between the beam and the joists.

◆ Plumb each post with a carpenter's level, then toenail it to the pad.

◆ Drive in the shims.

◆ Insert a post at every beam joint and then toenail the beam sections together.

LEVELING A FLOOR FROM BELOW

1. Preparing the wall.

If the side of the house is perpendicular to the floor joists, proceed as follows. Otherwise, follow the steps that begin on the next page.

◆ Unscrew nuts and remove washers from any anchor bolts that fasten the sill plate to the foundation; if the sill and joists are connected by metal straps, remove them as well.

◆ Outside the house, use a pry bar to remove a horizontal strip of siding and sheathing wide enough to expose the sill plate, the header joist, and the lower ends of the studs.

If the house has balloon framing, with no header joist and with studs that stand on the sill plate beside the joists, check that the joists and studs are fastened together with at least four $3\frac{1}{2}$-inch nails *(inset);* add extra nails if necessary.

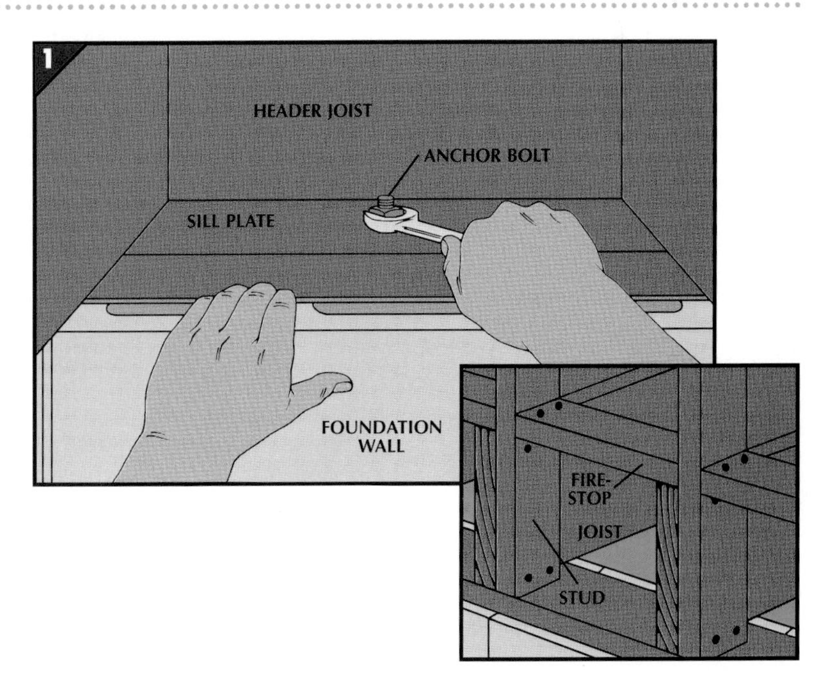

2. Setting up the jack.

◆ At one end of the wall in the basement, toenail a 10-foot 4-by-4 beam to the bottoms of joists. Run the beam parallel with the foundation wall and about 18 inches from it *(left)*. As you work, add shims to fill any gaps between joists and beam.

◆ Lay a 10-foot 2-by-12 pad on the floor under the beam.

◆ Plumb a telescoping house jack at the center of the pad and beam, and raise the jack just enough to hold it upright.

3. Jacking the beam.

◆ Raise the jack until the floor above is level, as indicated by a carpenter's level set at a right angle to the wall and directly above the jack *(right)*.

◆ When the floor is level, measure the space between the joist bottoms and the top of the foundation wall at points near the jack to gauge the thickness of lumber you need to replace the defective section of sill.

4. Supporting the beam.

◆ Cut a 4-by-4 post to fit between the pad and the beam, alongside the jack.

◆ Plumb the post, tapping it into place with a maul. Shim as needed for a tight fit *(right)*. Remove the jack.

◆ Sight along the beam to determine whether the ends are bowing down from the weight of the house. If so, set up the jack 2 feet from one end of the beam, jack that end level with the center of the beam, and insert another 4-by-4 post there. Jack and support the other end in the same way.

◆ Repeat this procedure the full length of the wall.

◆ Starting at one end of the line of beams, raise the beam another $\frac{1}{4}$ inch at each post and shim the top accordingly.

RESTORING WOOD FLOORS

Old wood floors add character to a house and are often worth preserving. Restoring such floors to their former beauty requires sanding with special equipment and then refinishing *(pages 70–73)*.

Surface Repairs: Take care of squeaks and structural repairs *(pages 61–64)* first, before working on the finish flooring as explained on the next few pages. Be sure to check the floor as shown below to make sure it can safely be sanded for refinishing.

Swapping Floorboards: Replacing missing, badly warped, or rotted boards presents no particular challenges if they do not interlock *(page 67)*. But tongue-and-groove boards—and especially those fastened directly to the floor joists without a subfloor—require special attention *(pages 68–69)* to get replacement pieces to fit correctly.

The size and look of old boards lend a floor character but make it difficult to find suitable replacements. One solution is to pull boards from inconspicuous places—closet floors, for example, or under rugs or furniture—and to replace them with new wood. Another is to forage among local wreckers and salvagers for old flooring. A third—and expensive—option is to custom-order duplicate flooring at a mill. Stain the new boards to match the old.

TOOLS

Chisel
Mallet
Putty knife (3")
Post jacks
Pry bar
Hammer
Nail set
Vise
Tack cloth

MATERIALS

Cork stopper
Wood filler
Penetrating sealer
Felt weather stripping
2 x 4 lumber
Common nails ($3\frac{1}{2}$")
Resin-coated nails ($1\frac{1}{2}$")
Flooring nails (3")
Finishing nails or trim head screws (3")
Sandpaper

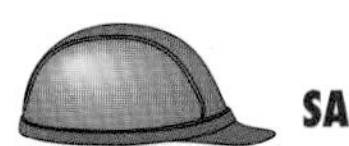

SAFETY TIPS

Safety goggles shield your eyes while you are hammering or pulling nails, chiseling, or sanding a floor. A hard hat protects against injury from joists, girders, and exposed flooring nails.

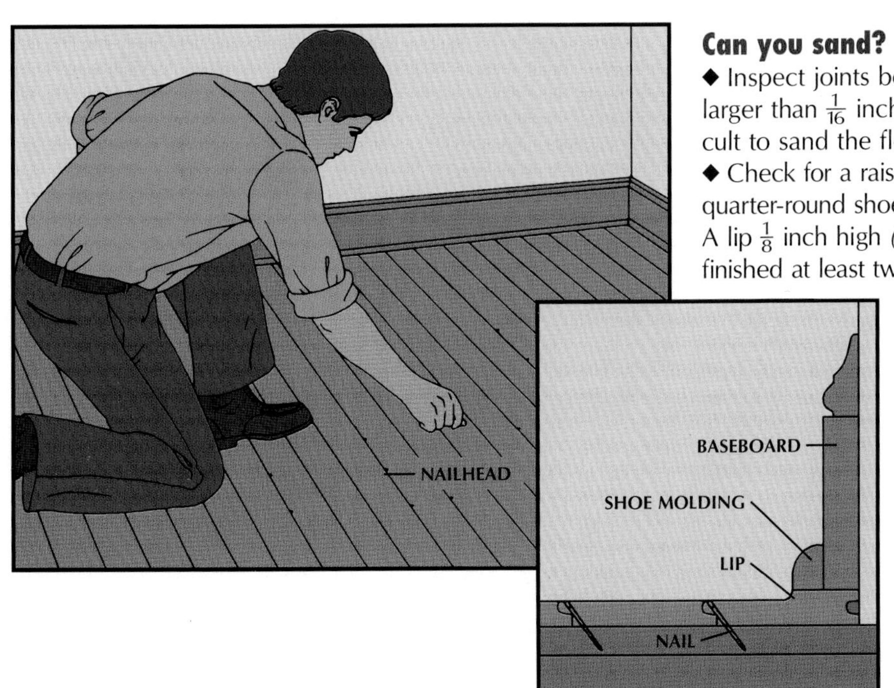

Can you sand?

◆ Inspect joints between tongue-and-groove boards: Gaps larger than $\frac{1}{16}$ inch or protruding nailheads will make it difficult to sand the floor for refinishing.

◆ Check for a raised lip at hard-to-sand areas—next to the quarter-round shoe molding or under radiators, for example. A lip $\frac{1}{8}$ inch high *(inset)* indicates that the floor has been refinished at least twice and probably cannot be sanded deeply enough to remove bad stains or lighten its color. Such a floor can only be replaced, covered over, or given a new finish.

QUICK FIXES FOR GAPS AND HOLES

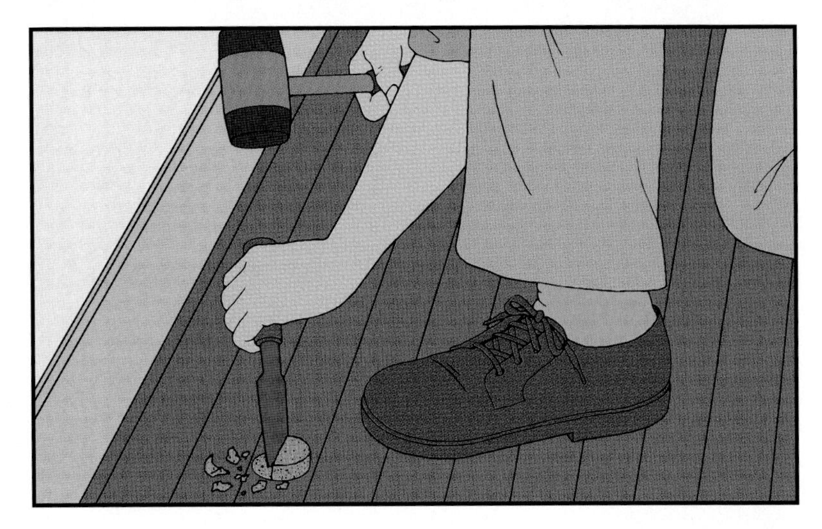

Plugging radiator pipe holes.
Wood plugs are the strongest fillers for holes, but corks are quicker and work satisfactorily in low-traffic areas.

◆ Pound into the hole a greased cork of slightly larger diameter.

◆ Chisel off the protruding end *(left)* and sandpaper the surface flush with the floor.

◆ Stain the cork to match its surroundings.

Dealing with cracks between boards.
Fill narrow cracks with either a wood filler chosen to match the floor color as closely as possible or a paste made with 4 parts sanding dust (taken from an inconspicuous part of the floor) to 1 part penetrating sealer.

For wide cracks, use a broad-blade putty knife to stuff felt weather stripping into the opening *(right)*, filling each space to a level $\frac{1}{8}$ inch below the floor surface. If the weather stripping shows, pack the last $\frac{1}{8}$ inch with wood filler.

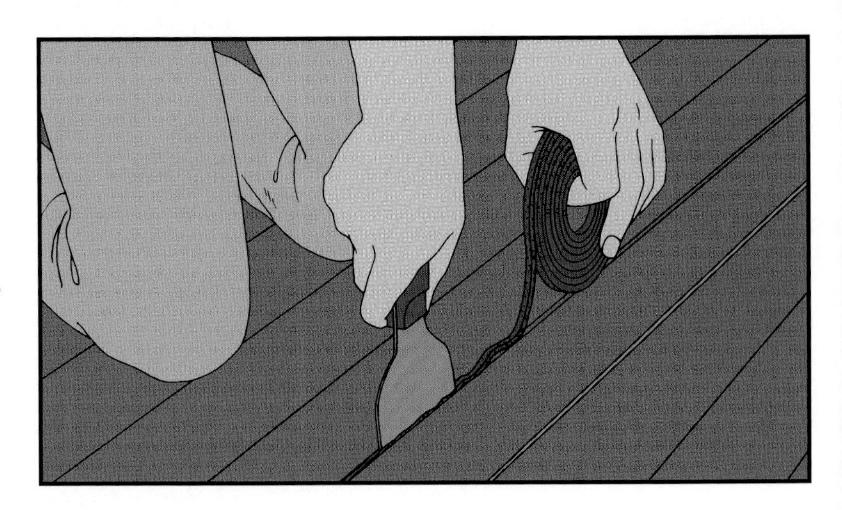

A SIMPLE BRACE FOR A SMALL SAG

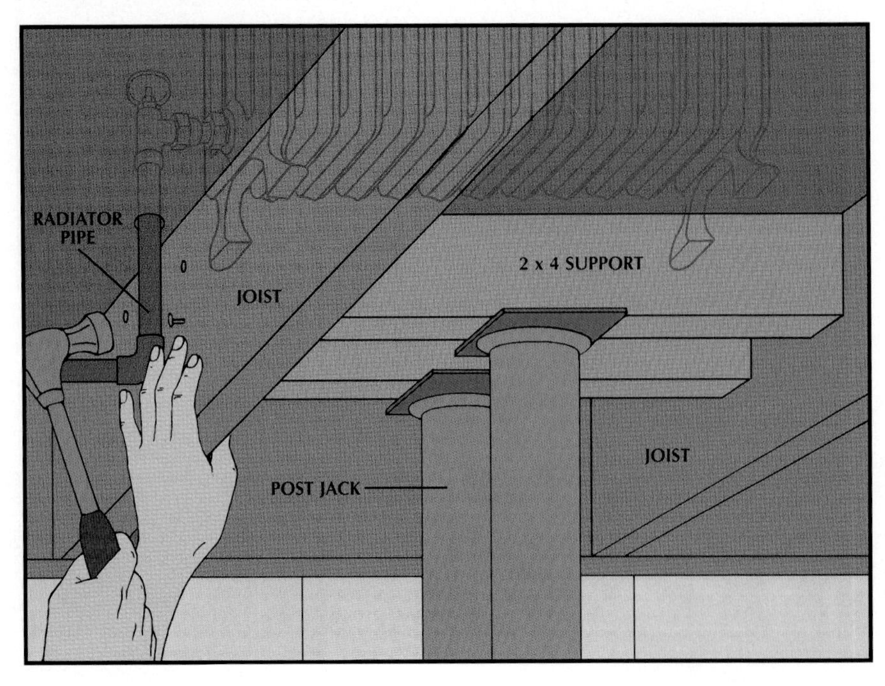

Installing supports.
Fix dips up to 30 inches long and $\frac{3}{4}$ inch deep by driving hardwood wedges between a joist and the subfloor. Level sags that fall between joists, such as those caused by a narrow radiator, as follows:

◆ Find the radiator pipes descending from the floor above. Use the pipes to determine the location of the radiator legs.

◆ Cut two 2-by-4 supports to fit between joists, and position them against the floor, directly beneath the radiator legs.

◆ Place a post jack under each support, then raise the jacks. As you do so, have a helper upstairs monitor the sag with a straight, 8-foot 2-by-4 or the factory edge trimmed from a sheet of plywood.

◆ When the floor is flat, nail through the joists into the ends of the supports to secure them *(left)*. Remove the jacks.

PATCHING PARQUET AND PLAIN STRIP FLOORING

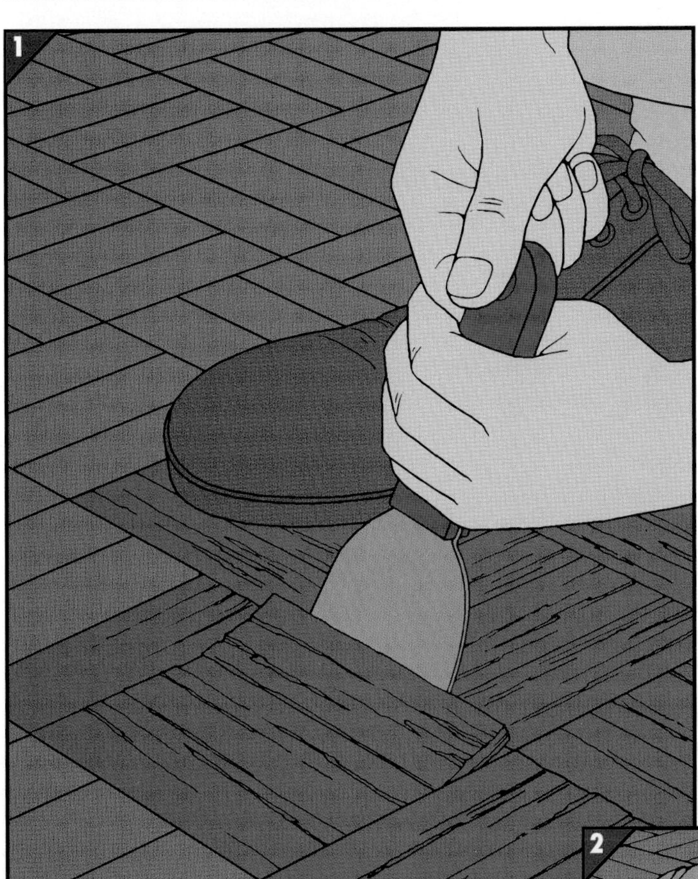

1. Removing damaged wood.

◆ For plain-edge parquet or strip flooring (without tongues or grooves), insert a 3-inch putty knife into a joint next to a damaged piece and gently pry it out, then use the opening to dislodge other deteriorated wood. If you have trouble loosening the first piece, move the knife along the joint, prying at different spots.

◆ After removing the old flooring, pull any nails that have worked through the wood and remain embedded in the subfloor.

On a parquet floor with tongue-and-groove joints, use a mallet and chisel to split damaged pieces down the middle, then pry out each half.

2. Inserting new pieces.

◆ Fit the new strips of parquet into place and tap them against the subflooring with a mallet.

◆ If the other pieces of the floor are face-nailed, drill pilot holes, matching the nailing pattern of the rest of the floor. Nail down the new pieces with $1\frac{1}{2}$-inch resin-coated flooring nails.

For tongue-and-groove parquet, blind-nail through the tongue as you would for tongue-and-groove flooring *(page 69, Step 5)*.

REPLACING TONGUE-AND-GROOVE BOARDS

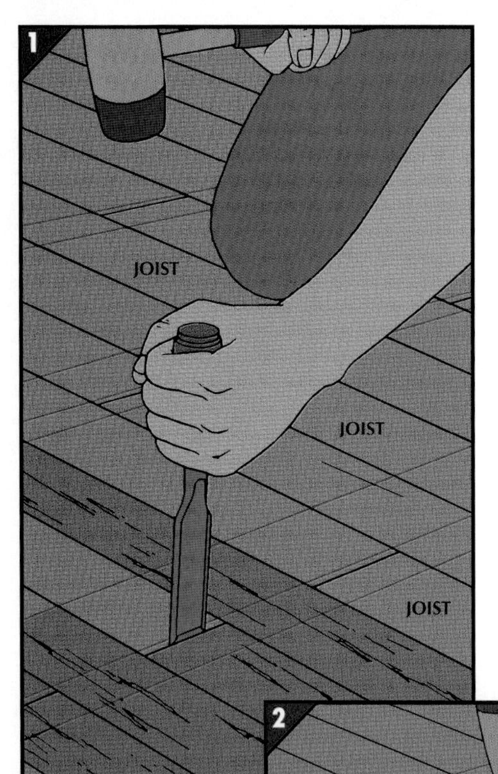

1. Freeing the floorboards.

◆ If there is no subfloor under the finish floor, use an electronic stud finder *(page 89)* to locate the joists that pass beneath the damaged section. (Joists run perpendicular to floorboards.)

◆ Plan to remove sections of board so that the end joints of adjacent replacement boards will be staggered.

◆ In order to provide a nailing surface at both ends of new boards, chisel through old ones at the centers of joists flanking the damage. To do so, first turn the bevel of the chisel toward the damaged area and cut about $\frac{1}{4}$ inch vertically into the board *(left)*. (Where a floorboard ends at a joist, omit this cut.)

◆ About 1 inch closer to the damaged area, drive the chisel toward the vertical cut—or the joint between boards—at a 30-degree angle, bevel up. Continue this process until you have cut through the board.

◆ Repeat the procedure to free both ends of all sections to be removed.

Where a subfloor is present, you need not locate joists. Make the cuts as near the damage as possible; later you can nail floorboards to the subflooring.

2. Removing the boards.

◆ To extract a damaged floorboard without harming the tongues and grooves of sound neighbors, chisel two parallel incisions along each damaged board as shown at left. Rock the blade in the incisions to split the board.

◆ Insert a small pry bar into a split at the center of the damaged area and pry out first the middle strip, then the groove side, and finally the tongue side of the board.

◆ Working from the center outward, pry up the remaining boards in the same fashion.

◆ Pull any exposed nails or hammer the heads below subflooring or joist surfaces using a nail set.

3. Cutting the tongue from a board.

To prepare a replacement board for fitting, chisel off the tongue where the new board will fit between two old ones. To do so, proceed as follows:

◆ Secure the board, tongue side up, in a vise.

◆ Make a vertical cut across the tongue to mark the section to be removed.

◆ Tap the chisel, bevel up, against the end of the tongue to split it off up to this cut.

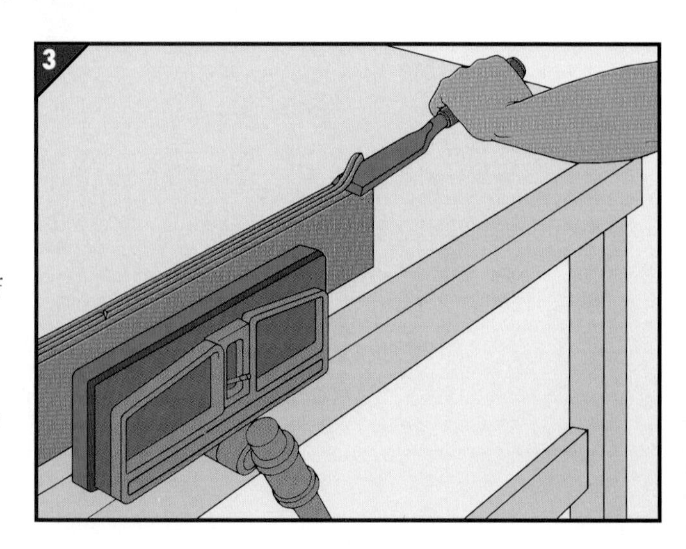

4. Inserting boards.

◆ To insert a new board *(left),* tilt it so that the groove engages the tongue of the adjacent board.

◆ Fit a scrap of floorboard onto the untrimmed section of the new board's tongue and tap the scrap gently with a mallet to snug the board into place.

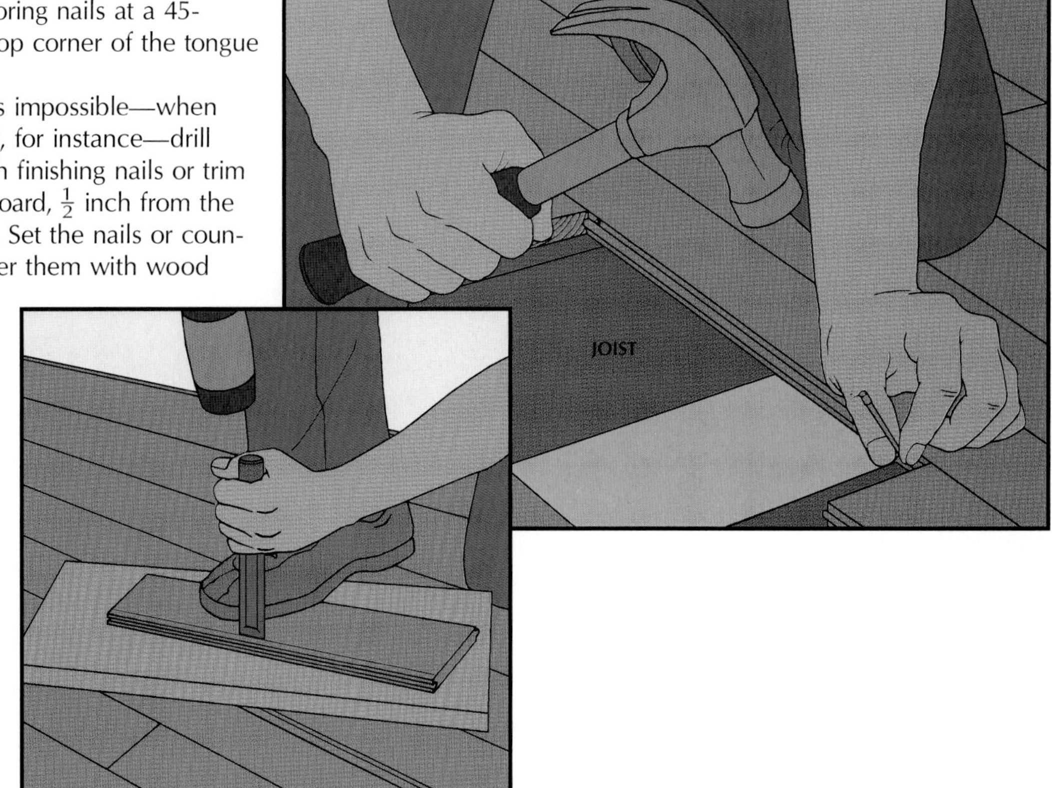

5. Blind-nailing a board in place.

◆ Drive and set 3-inch flooring nails at a 45-degree angle through the top corner of the tongue of the new board.

◆ Wherever blind-nailing is impossible—when you're fitting the last board, for instance—drill pilot holes and drive 3-inch finishing nails or trim head screws through the board, $\frac{1}{2}$ inch from the edges and 12 inches apart. Set the nails or countersink the screws and cover them with wood filler tinted to match the floorboard.

◆ To prepare the last board for fitting, lay it upside down on a piece of scrap wood and chisel off the lower lip of the groove as indicated by the blue line in the inset. Then tap the board into place tongue first, drill pilot holes, and nail it to every joist or the subfloor.

A NEW FACE FOR A WOOD FLOOR

Restoring the natural beauty of a wood floor, whether it is varnished or painted, necessitates removal of the old finish before the new one can be applied. The first step is to take all furniture out of the room and to seal drapes in plastic bags. Lift off floor registers and cover the vents with plastic.

Fasten loose boards and replace badly damaged ones *(pages 67–69)*. Drive protruding nailheads $\frac{1}{8}$ inch below the floor surface with a nail set. Beginning at a door, remove shoe moldings from baseboards by driving the nails through the molding with a pin punch no larger than the nailhead.

Getting to Bare Wood: Some laminated floorboards are too thin to sand; remove the old finish with a chemical stripper. On thicker boards, use a drum sander *(below)*.

Multiple sandings are required. For rough or painted floorboards, begin with 20-grit sandpaper, then proceed to 36-grit, 50-grit, and finally 80-grit. Varnished or shellacked floors need only three sandings beginning with 36-grit. Sand parquet floors first with 50-grit followed by 80- and 100-grit.

Removing Stains: First try to remove a stain by hand-sanding. If it remains, apply a small amount of wood bleach to its center. Let the spot lighten, then apply enough bleach to blend the treated area with the rest of the floor. Rinse away the bleach with a vinegar-soaked rag. If the stains remain even after bleaching, replace the boards *(pages 67–69)*.

A Two-Step Glaze: To protect the wood and emphasize the grain, apply a sealer, which is available in both natural wood hues and a clear, colorless form *(page 72, bottom)*. For a final protective glaze over the sealer, select a urethane floor finish, which becomes exceptionally tough as it hardens.

Both oil- and water-based sealers and finishes are available. If you plan to stain the floor, oil-based products provide richer, more even color than water-based products, which dry faster and are easier and safer to handle.

If you choose water-based products, apply and smooth them with tools made of synthetic material, avoiding natural-bristle brushes and steel wool. Use a synthetic abrasive pad instead. Clean the floor with a lint-free rag rather than a tack cloth.

CAUTION *Sanding produces highly flammable dust. Seal the doorways into the work area with plastic, and ventilate the room with a fan (opposite).*

TOOLS

- Nail set
- Pin punch
- Drum sander
- Edging machine
- Floor polisher
- Paint scraper
- Paintbrushes
- Lambs wool applicator
- Putty knife

MATERIALS

- Sandpaper
- Wood bleach
- Vinegar
- Tack cloth
- Lint-free rags
- Sealer
- Urethane floor finish
- Abrasive pads (steel-wool or synthetic)
- Tinted wood putty

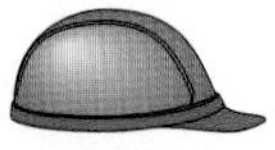

SAFETY TIPS

Sand floors wearing goggles, ear protection, and dust mask. When applying wood bleach, sealer, or finish, put on goggles and rubber gloves, as well as long pants and a long-sleeve shirt.

TOOLS TO RENT

A refinishing job calls for professional equipment. One such tool is a drum sander *(right)*. Make sure the machine has a tilt-up lever for lifting the spinning drum from the floor (not all have this feature). The second is an edging machine, a sander with a rotating disk for working along baseboards and other places that the drum sander cannot reach. Finally, to smooth each coat of sealer or new finish, rent a commercial floor polisher. Fit it with a round pad of steel wool—or a synthetic abrasive pad if using a water-based finish.

Before leaving the shop, check that the machines are working and that their dust bags are clean. Take with you any special wrenches for loading the drum sander and plenty of sandpaper—at least 10 drum-sander sheets and 10 edger disks of each grit for an average room. Because sanders need grounding, they must have three-pronged plugs; if your house has two-slot receptacles, you will need grounding adapters.

1. Loading the drum sander.

◆ With the sander unplugged, thread a sheet of sandpaper into the loading slot, turn the drum one full revolution, and slip the other end of the sheet into the slot.

◆ To secure the paper, tighten the drum's internal clamp by turning the boltheads at both ends of the drum with the wrenches provided by the dealer. With fine-grit sandpaper, fold a strip of the material in half, grit exposed, and slip it into the slot between the two ends to keep them from slipping out *(inset).*

Filtered Ventilation

A window fan with a furnace filter helps clear the air in a room while you are sanding. Buy a filter large enough to cover the entire fan, and tape it to the intake side; duct tape works well for the purpose. Place the fan in a window with the intake side inward, and turn it on. The filter will catch a large portion of the dust so it does not collect in your fan or blow into the neighborhood.

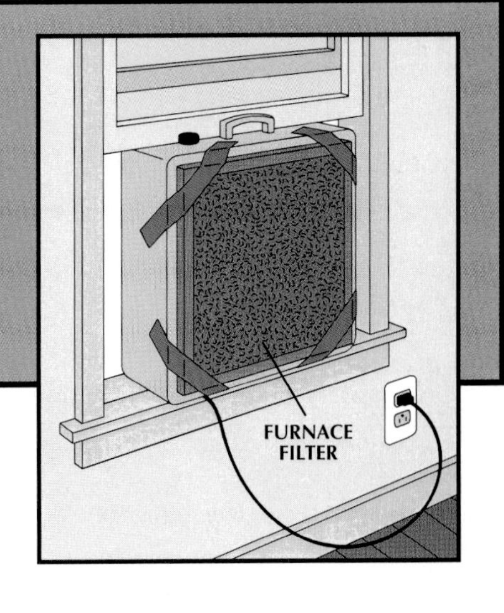

2. The first sanding.

◆ Standing with a wall about 3 feet behind you, lift the drum from the floor with the tilt-up lever, start the sander, and when the motor reaches full speed, lower the drum to the floor. Let the sander pull you forward at a slow, steady pace. Sand boards along the wood's grain unless they undulate slightly. In that case, or if the floor is patterned with varying grain directions, do the first sanding diagonally.

◆ At the far wall, raise the drum from the floor, move the cord behind you to one side, then lower the drum and pull the sander backward over the area you just sanded.

◆ Lift the drum and move the machine to the left or right, overlapping the first pass by 2 or 3 inches.

◆ Continue forward and backward passes across the room, turning off the sander occasionally in order to empty the dust bag, then turn the machine around and sand the area next to the wall.

CAUTION *Keep the sander in motion to prevent it from denting or rippling the wood.*

3. Completing the sanding.

◆ Sand areas missed by the drum sander with the edger, loaded with coarse-grit paper.

◆ Repeat both the drum and edge sandings, with successively finer sandpaper. On floorboards, these sandings, like the first, should be made with the grain *(inset, top)*. On parquet floors, do the second sanding on the opposite diagonal to the first, and the final sanding along the length of the room *(inset, bottom)*.

◆ Smooth the floor with a floor polisher *(opposite)* and a fine abrasive pad, suited to sealer and finish. This will lessen the boundary between drum- and edge-sanded areas.

4. Scraping the tight spots.

In areas that neither the drum sander nor the edging machine can reach, remove the finish with a paint scraper. At a radiator, remove collars from around the pipes for a thorough job. Always pull the scraper toward you, applying firm downward pressure on the tool with both hands. Scrape with the grain wherever possible, and replace the blade when it gets dull. Sand the scraped areas by hand.

APPLYING PROTECTIVE COATS

1. Spreading sealer.

◆ Ventilate the room. Vacuum the floor and pick up dust with a tack cloth, or a dry rag if using water-based sealer.

◆ Starting next to a wall and away from the door, apply sealer liberally over a 3-foot-wide strip of floor with a rag. Use long, sweeping strokes along the grain of the wood or along the length of the room if the grain directions vary.

◆ Between 8 and 20 minutes after it is applied, the sealer will have penetrated the wood, leaving shallow puddles of the liquid on the surface. Have a helper, using rags in both hands, mop up the excess sealer.

◆ As your helper works on the first strip, start applying sealer to the second strip. Try to work at a pace that keeps both of you moving together with your knees on dry floor until the job is almost finished. On the last strip, the helper will have to back across wet sealer to the door.

◆ Finally, let the sealer dry according to the manufacturer's specifications.

2. Smoothing the sealed wood.

◆ Fit a floor polisher with a heavy-duty scrub brush and press a fine abrasive pad into the bristles of the brush *(inset)*. Run the polisher over the floor to smooth irregularities in the surface caused by tiny bubbles in the sealer coating.

◆ Scour the edges and corners of the floor by hand with a small abrasive pad, then vacuum the entire floor and go over it thoroughly with a tack cloth or damp rag, according to the finish, to pick up any remaining dust.

3. Finishing the floor.

◆ Apply the finish slowly and evenly with a wide brush. With an oil-based finish you may use a lambs wool applicator *(inset)*. Work along the grain. If grain directions vary, work along the room's length. Stroke in one direction and do not go back over finish that has begun to set. If working alone, do edges and corners first with a small brush, then work on the rest.

◆ When the first coat is dry, smooth the surface *(Step 2, above)*.

◆ Clean the floor with a vacuum and tack cloth or damp rag. Force wood putty, tinted to match, into cracks and nail holes with a putty knife.

◆ Apply a second coat of finish in the same way. Water-based urethane, thinner than oil-based, needs a third coat.

◆ Wait 24 hours. Replace shoe moldings, registers, radiator-pipe collars.

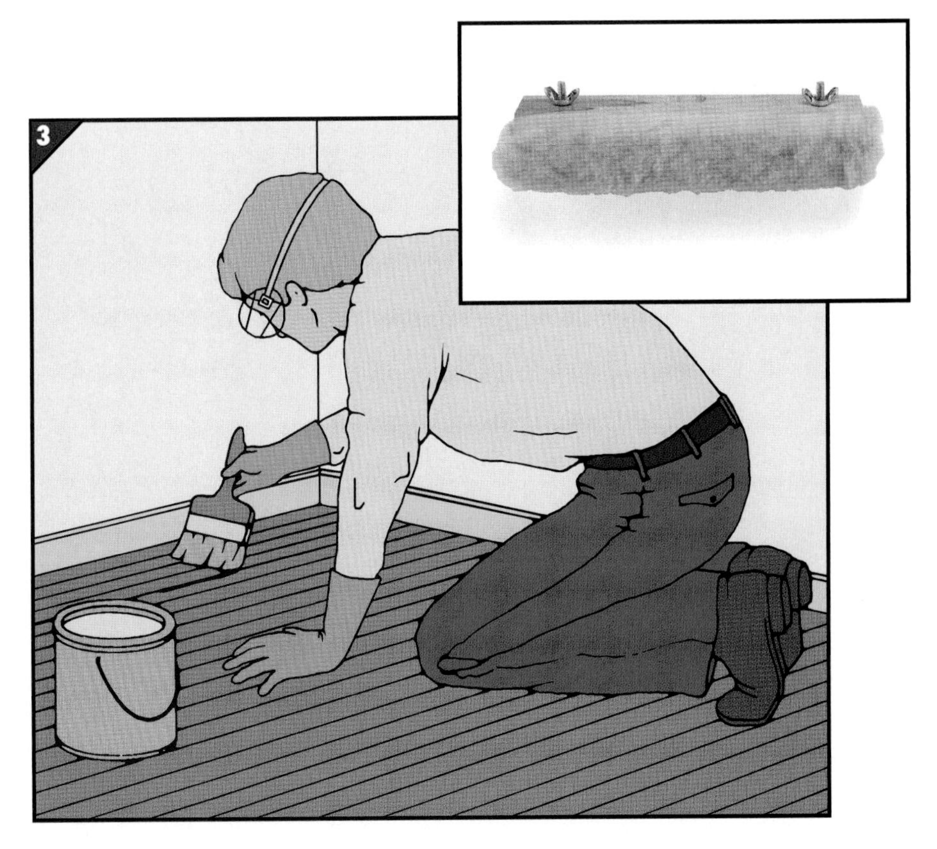

REPAIRING RESILIENT FLOORS

The tough surface of resilient flooring—typically vinyl tiles or sheet flooring—will resist wear and stains for many years. If damage does occur, you can usually repair it yourself, or at least reduce the visibility of the scars.

Common-Sense Precautions: A resilient floor should be kept as dry as possible, even when being cleaned, so that water does not get underneath and destroy the bond of the adhesive that holds it in place.

Resting furniture feet on plastic or rubber coasters will help protect the floor from punctures and gouges. When heavy furniture or appliances must be moved across the floor, slide them over pieces of plywood.

Curing Minor Ailments: To conceal a shallow scratch in a vinyl floor, gently rub it lengthwise with the rim of an old coin. This will press the edges of the scratch together so only a thin line remains. Deeper cuts can be closed by carefully heating the vinyl with an iron and aluminum foil, as explained on page 77.

If a tile has come loose, first determine whether water from leaking plumbing is the cause; if it is, repair the leak before fixing the floor. Use water-based latex adhesive to glue the tile down.

Mending Major Flaws: The best remedy for a ruined tile is a replacement; similarly, a badly damaged section of sheet flooring will need a patch. But before removing any resilient flooring or adhesive, read the asbestos warning on the opposite page.

If you cannot find any spare matching tiles or sheet flooring, look for replacements in inconspicuous areas of your floor—under a refrigerator or at the back of a closet, for instance. Cut and remove the section from the hidden area and substitute a nonmatching material of equal thickness.

If your resilient floor is glued to an asphalt-felt underlayment, the felt may tear as you remove damaged flooring. Usually you can glue the felt back together with latex adhesive; allow the adhesive to dry before continuing the job. If the felt is too badly torn, cut out the damaged section and glue down enough replacement layers of 15-pound asphalt felt to maintain the same floor level.

TOOLS

Putty knife
Utility knife
Iron
Notched trowel
Metal straightedge

MATERIALS

Latex adhesive
Replacement vinyl tiles or sheet flooring

SAFETY TIP

Protect your hands with rubber gloves when working with adhesive.

SIMPLE FIXES

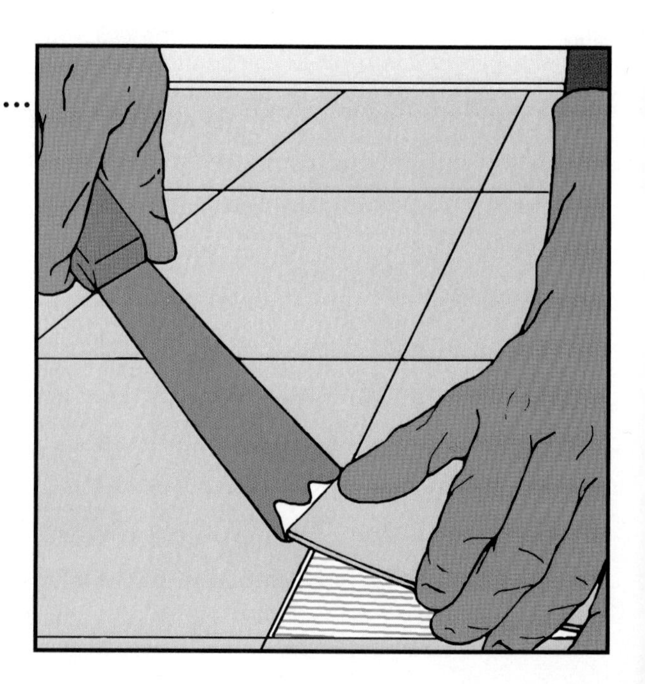

Securing a loose tile.

◆ Lift the loose portion of the tile and spread a thin coat of latex adhesive on the underside of it with a putty knife. If only a corner of the tile has come unstuck, loosen more of it until you can turn the tile back far enough to spread the adhesive.

◆ Press the tile into place so that it is level with those tiles that surround it. Hold it down with a 20-pound weight for at least an hour.

Deflating a blister, method 1.

◆ Following a line in the flooring pattern if possible, score then slice along the length of a blister with a utility knife *(right)*. Extend the cut $\frac{1}{2}$ inch beyond the blister at both ends.

◆ With a putty knife, spread a thin layer of latex adhesive through the slit onto the underside of the flooring.

◆ Press the vinyl down; if one edge overlaps because the flooring has stretched, use it as a guide to trim the edge beneath. Remove trimmed-off scrap, then press the edges together and put a 20-pound weight on the repaired area for at least 1 hour.

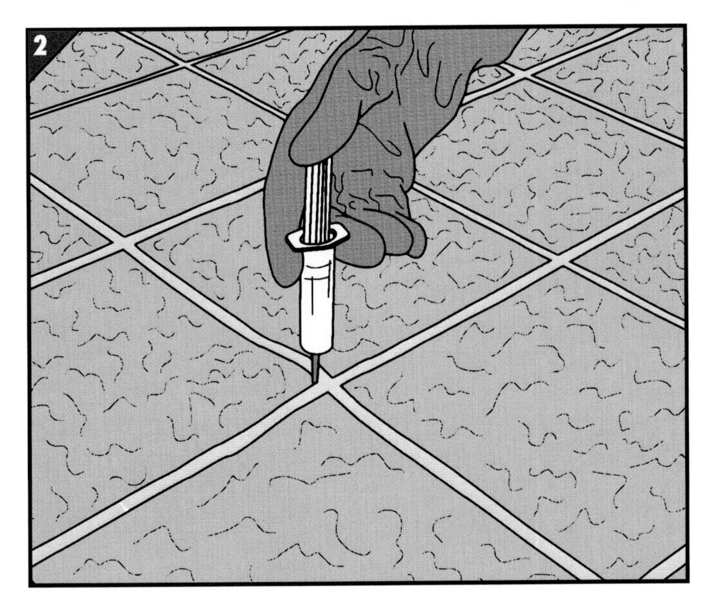

Deflating a blister, method 2.

◆ Use a syringe-style glue injector with a metal needle, available from a flooring supplier.

◆ Insert the needle into the center of the blister, preferably at a point on a pattern line.

◆ Press gently on the plunger, injecting $\frac{1}{4}$ ounce of glue for every square inch of blister.

◆ Roll a hand roller back and forth over the blister to spread out the glue underneath.

◆ With a damp cloth, wipe up any excess glue around the needle hole, then cover the blister with a cloth and place several books on it until the glue dries.

CAUTION

Asbestos Warning

If your resilient floor was installed before 1986, the flooring or the adhesive underneath may contain asbestos. When damaged, these materials can release microscopic asbestos fibers into the air, creating severe, long-term health risks. Unless you know for certain that your floor does not contain asbestos, assume that it does, and follow these precautions when making any repairs:

- *Always wear a dual-cartridge respirator. Asbestos fibers will pass right through an ordinary dust mask.*
- *Never sand resilient flooring or the underlying adhesive.*
- *Try to remove the damaged flooring in one piece. If it looks likely to break or crumble, wet it before removal to reduce the chance of raising dust.*
- *When scraping off old adhesive, always use a heat gun to keep it tacky or a spray bottle to keep it wet.*
- *If vacuuming is necessary, rent or buy a wet/dry shop vac with a HEPA (high-efficiency particulate air) filtration system.*
- *Place the damaged flooring, adhesive, and HEPA filter in a polyethylene trash bag at least 6 mils thick, and seal it immediately.*
- *Contact your local environmental protection office for guidance as to proper disposal.*

REPLACING DAMAGED RESILIENT TILES

1. Removing tiles.
To remove a damaged tile that is still securely bonded to the underlayment, lay a straightedge across the tile about 1 inch from its edge to protect the adjacent tile from the heat gun. Cut through the tile along the straightedge with a linoleum knife.
◆ Sweep the nozzle of the heat gun back and forth along the slit until the adhesive is soft enough to allow the insertion of a putty knife under the edge of the tile, then work the tile loose and remove it. Remove adjacent damaged tiles the same way.
◆ If any damaged tiles were cut when installed to fit against a wall or around an obstruction, use them as templates to make matching replacement tiles.

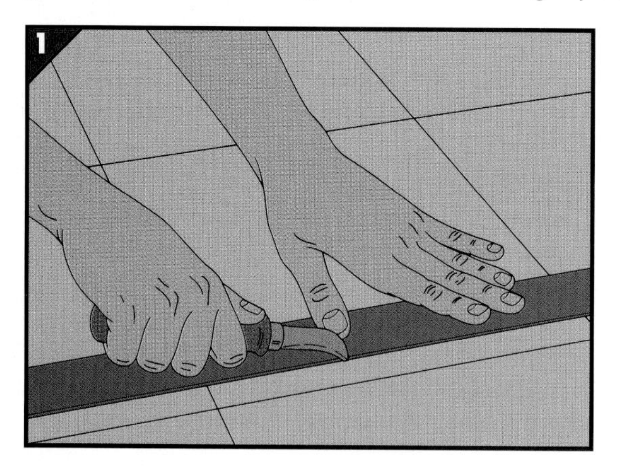

2. Spreading the adhesive.
◆ Remove the old adhesive from the underlayment with a heat gun and putty knife.
◆ With a notched spreader, coat the underlayment with vinyl-tile adhesive, leaving ridges, and let it set according to the manufacturer's instructions.

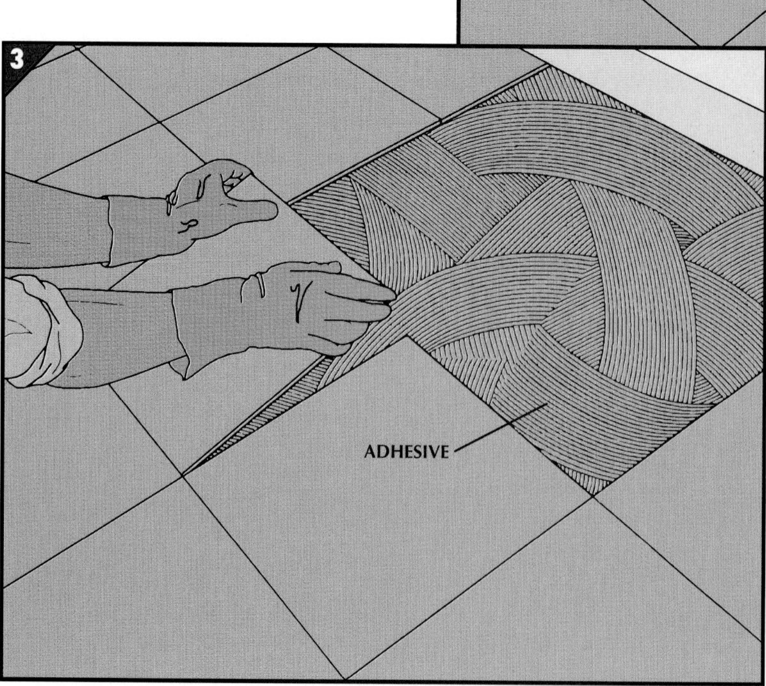

3. Installing the new tiles.
◆ Fit a replacement tile in a corner of the opening where it abuts two existing tiles.
◆ Lay whole tiles first, and finish with those that have been cut to fit.
◆ With a hand roller, firmly press down all the new tiles flush with each other and the surrounding tiles.
◆ With a damp cloth, immediately wipe up any excess adhesive. Don't walk on the replacement tiles until the adhesive has dried completely. This usually takes 24 hours.

PATCHING SHEET FLOORING

1. Cutting the patch.

◆ Place over the damaged spot a spare piece of matching flooring larger than the area to be patched, aligning the design of the replacement piece with that of the floor. Secure it in position with tape *(left).*

◆ With a metal straightedge and a utility knife, score the top piece, following lines in the pattern where possible. Using the scored line as a guide, cut through the replacement piece and the flooring underneath. Keep slicing along the same lines until you have cut through both sheets.

◆ Set the replacement piece aside and loosen the adhesive under the section you are replacing as shown in Step 1 *(opposite).* Remove the damaged section and the old adhesive.

2. Installing the patch.

◆ Spread adhesive over the exposed subfloor with a notched trowel and set the replacement patch in position as you would a tile *(opposite, Step 2).*

◆ Hide the outline of the patch by a careful application of heat: Cover the edges of the patch with heavy aluminum foil, dull side down, and press the foil several times with a very hot iron *(inset).* This will partly melt the cut edges of the flooring so they form a solid and almost undetectable bond.

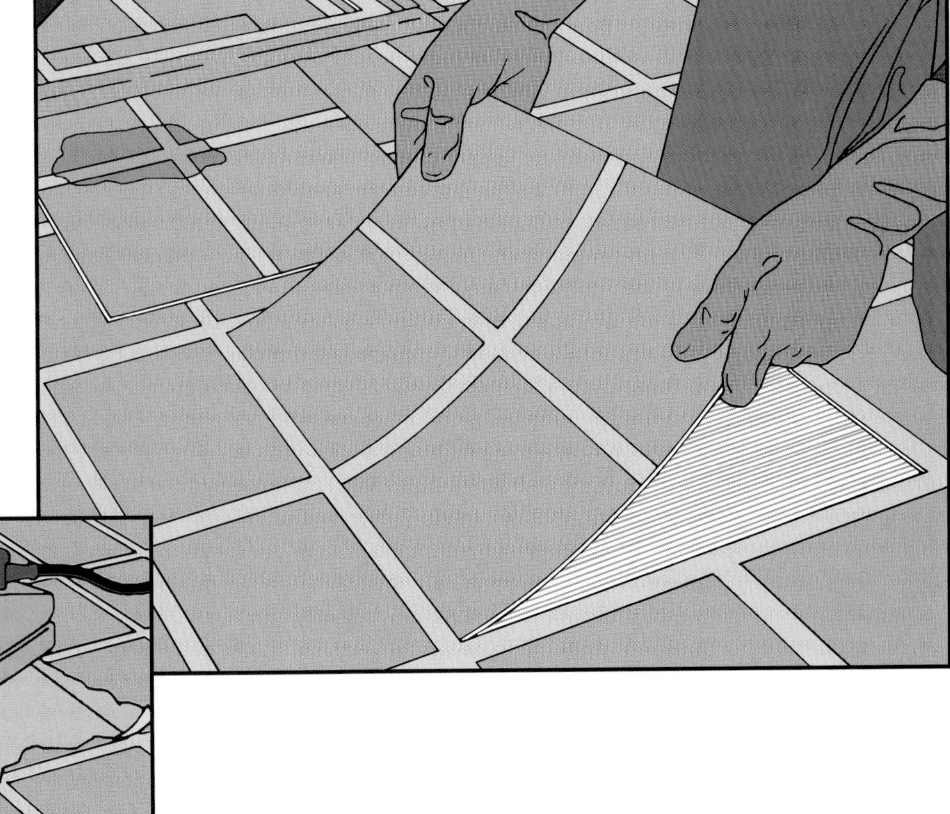

STAIRS: SILENCING A SQUEAKY TREAD

Squeaks, a common problem in older, carriage-supported stairways, are caused by treads that have separated slightly from the carriage or by the riser's rubbing against other stair parts when stepped on. You can stop the squeak by making the separated portion stay down or by inserting a thin wedge as a shim underneath it.

The repairs described on these pages will also work on modern prefabricated stairways with housed stringers, though they develop squeaks far less frequently. A special technique for replacing a glue wedge that has worked loose from the tread and housed stringer is shown at the bottom of page 80.

Locating the Squeak: Use a carpenter's level to find warps, twists, or bows in the treads. While a helper climbs the stairs, listen, watch for rise and fall, and—resting your hand on the tread—feel for vibration.

If the tread spring is minimal, you can eliminate it with angled nails *(below)* or trim head screws. If the tread movement is substantial, use wedges *(opposite, top)*.

Such repairs from the top are usually sufficient. But if you can get to the stairway from underneath you can make a sound and simple fix, preferable because it is invisible, by adding glue blocks to the joint between the tread and the riser, the most common source of squeaks. If the tread is badly warped or humped in the center, rejoin it with a screw through the carriage *(page 80, top)*.

TOOLS

- Carpenter's level
- Electric drill with bits ($\frac{1}{8}$", $\frac{1}{4}$", $\frac{3}{32}$")
- Hammer
- Nail set
- Utility knife
- Screwdriver
- Putty knife
- Chisel

MATERIALS

- Finishing nails ($2\frac{1}{2}$")
- Wood putty
- Trim head screws ($2\frac{1}{2}$")
- Hardwood wedges
- Glue
- Common nails (2")
- Construction adhesive
- Wood screws (3" No. 12)

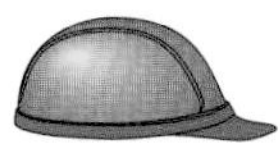

SAFETY TIP

Goggles protect your eyes from dust and flying debris while you are hammering, chiseling, or drilling.

WORKING FROM ABOVE

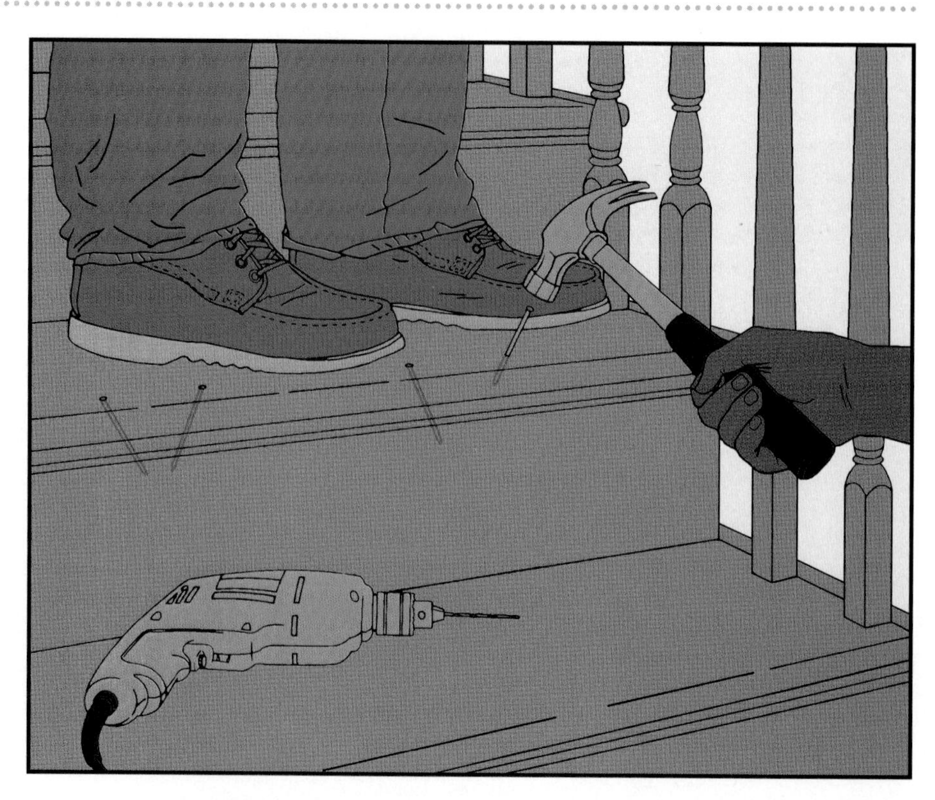

Nailing the tread down.

◆ With a helper standing on the tread, drill $\frac{3}{32}$-inch pilot holes angled through the tread and into the riser at the point of movement. If the squeak comes from the ends of the tread, angle the holes into the carriage.

◆ Drive $2\frac{1}{2}$-inch finishing nails into the holes, sink the heads with a nail set, and fill with wood putty.

If the tread spring is too great for nails to close, drill pilot holes as above and secure the tread with $2\frac{1}{2}$-inch trim head screws. Apply paraffin wax to the threads to make the screws turn easily in oak. Countersink the heads and fill the holes with wood putty.

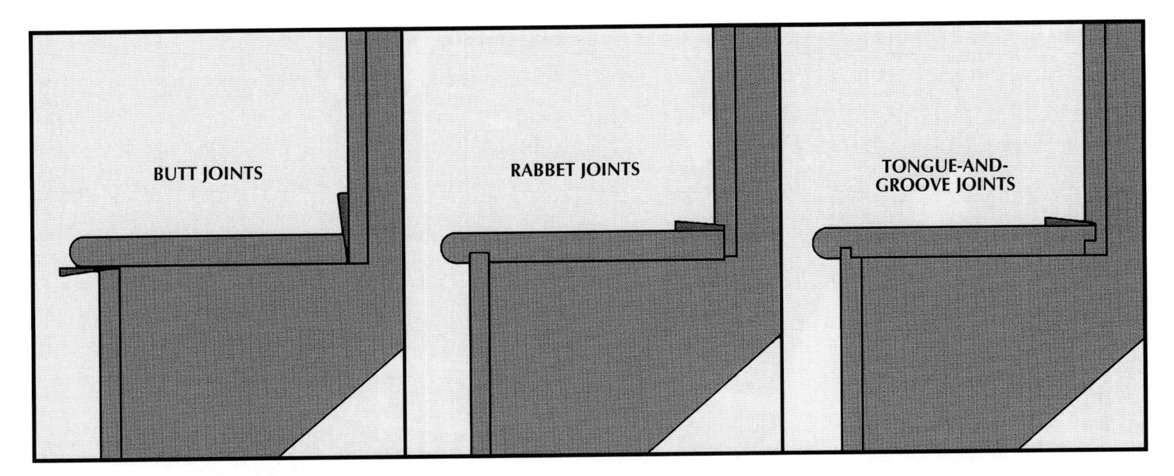

Wedging treads tight.

◆ Remove the scotia molding under the tread nose and insert a knife into the tread joints in order to discover the kind of joints that were used. With butt joints, the knife will slip vertically into the joint behind the tread and horizontally under the tread; with rabbet or tongue-and-groove joints, the knife-entry directions are reversed.

◆ Drive sharply tapered hardwood wedges coated with glue into the cracks as far as possible in the indicated directions.

◆ Cut off the wedges' protruding ends with a utility knife; replace the scotia molding. Use shoe molding to cover joints at the back of the treads.

WORKING FROM BELOW

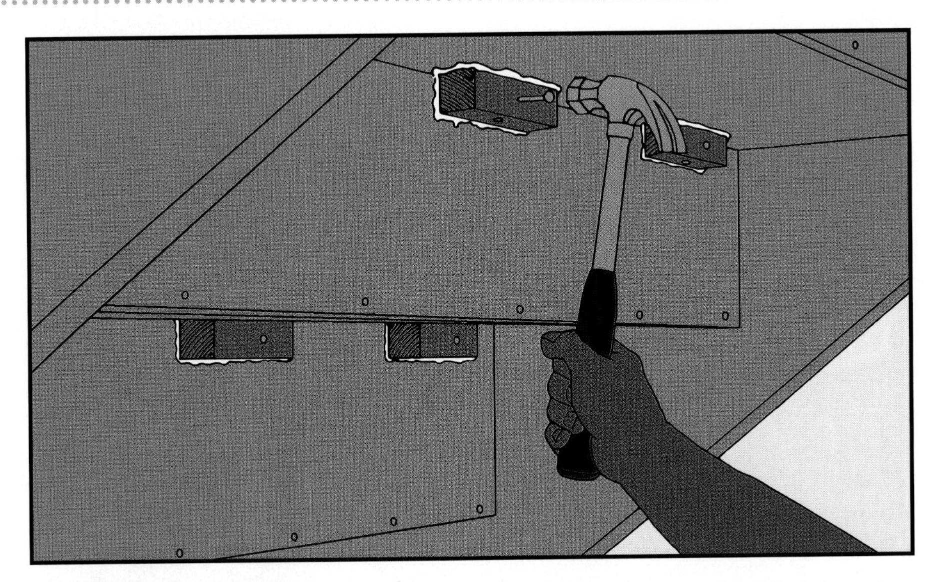

Installing glue blocks.

◆ If the joint has old blocks that have come partly unstuck, pry them off with a screwdriver or putty knife and scrape the dried glue off the tread and riser.

◆ Spread glue on two sides of a block of wood $1\frac{1}{2}$ inches square and about 3 inches long. Press the block into the joint between the tread and the riser and slide it back and forth a little to strengthen the glue bond.

◆ Then fasten the block with a 2-inch common nail in each direction. Add two or three more blocks to each joint.

Drilling through the carriage.

◆ About 2 inches below the tread, chisel a shallow notch into the carriage. With a helper standing on the tread, drill a $\frac{1}{8}$-inch pilot hole angled at about 30 degrees through the notch and $\frac{3}{4}$ inch into the tread *(left)*. Then enlarge the hole through the carriage with a $\frac{1}{4}$-inch bit.

◆ With the helper off the tread, spread a bead of construction adhesive along both sides of the joint between the tread and the carriage, and work it into the joint with a putty knife.

◆ Have the helper stand on the tread again and install a No. 12 wood screw 3 inches long.

RE-SHIMMING A PREFAB STAIRWAY

Replacing loose wedges.

◆ Split out the old wedge with a chisel *(below)*, and pare dried glue and splinters from the notch.

◆ Plane a new wedge from a piece of hardwood to fit within an inch of the riser. Coat the notch, the bottom of the tread, and the top and bottom of the wedge with glue.

◆ Hammer the wedge snugly into the notch, tap it along the side to force it against the notch face, then hit the end a few more times to jam the wedge tightly under the tread.

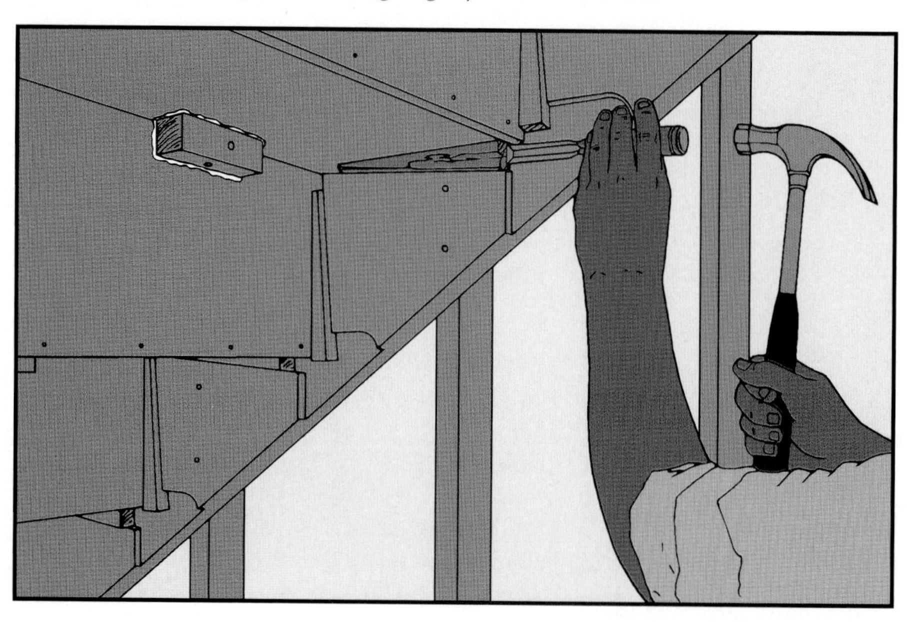

STAIRS: REPAIRING A BALUSTRADE

A balustrade consists of a railing that runs between newel posts and is supported by balusters. It is both decorative and functional. For safety as well as the best appearance, any broken or loose elements should be fixed without delay.

Three Types of Baluster: Tighten a loose baluster with glue, nails, or small wedges; but if it is cracked, dented, or badly scraped, replace it. First, determine how your balusters are fastened. Square-topped balusters usually fit into a shallow groove in the railing. Blocks of wood called fillets are nailed into the grooves between balusters. Sometimes balusters also end at the bottom in the groove of a lower rail, called a buttress cap, that lies on top of a stringer nailed to the ends of the treads and risers *(page 83)*.

Balusters with cylindrical tops fit into holes in the railing. If they do not overlap the return nosing, balusters are also doweled at the bottom, even though a square section may abut the treads. Balusters that overlap the return nosing are probably joined to the tread by a dovetail joint, and you will have to remove the return nosing to make the replacement.

Obtaining a New Baluster: Save the broken baluster as a pattern for a new one. If you cannot match it, have a cabinetmaker turn one. Instead of cutting a dovetail, pin a doweled baluster into the dovetailed tread with a nail *(page 82)*.

Cures for a Shaky Railing: The cause of a wobbly railing is usually a loose starting newel post. For a post in a bullnose tread, run a lag screw up through the floor into the foot of the post. Where there is no bullnose, the solution is to drive a lag screw through the newel and into the boards behind it *(page 83)*.

TOOLS

- Compass saw or keyhole saw
- Pipe wrench
- Electric drill with bits ($\frac{7}{32}$", $\frac{5}{16}$")
- Spade bit
- Folding rule
- Chisel
- Pry bar
- Forstner bit ($\frac{3}{4}$")
- Hammer
- Miter box
- Socket wrench

MATERIALS

- Glue
- Finishing nails ($1\frac{1}{2}$")
- Lag screws ($\frac{5}{16}$" x 3" and 4") and washers
- Scrap wood for pry block
- Putty
- Scrap 2 x 4 lumber for gauge block

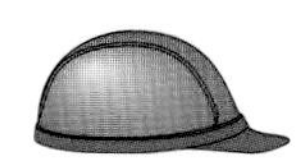

SAFETY TIP

Protect your eyes with safety goggles when you are hammering nails, using a hammer and chisel, drilling at or above waist level, or levering wood with a pry bar.

REPLACING A DOWELED BALUSTER

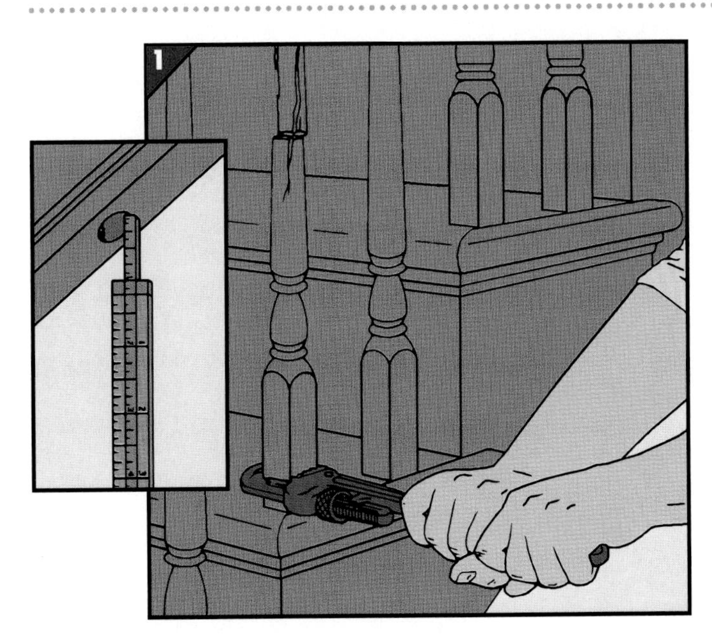

1. Removing the damaged baluster.

◆ Saw the baluster in two and sharply twist the bottom piece with a pipe wrench to break the glue joint at the base *(left)*. Then remove the top piece; if it is stuck, use the wrench.

◆ If the joints do not break, saw the baluster flush, using cardboard on the tread to guard it from the saw. Then drill out the dowel ends with spade bits the size of the dowels on the new baluster.

◆ Trim the bottom dowel to a $\frac{3}{16}$-inch stub.

◆ With a folding rule, measure from the high edge of the dowel hole in the railing to the tread *(inset)* and add $\frac{7}{16}$ inch. Cut off the top dowel to shorten the new baluster to this length.

2. Installing the new baluster.

◆ Smear glue in the tread hole, angle the top dowel into the railing hole, and pull the bottom of the baluster across the tread, lifting the railing about $\frac{1}{4}$ inch.

◆ Seat the bottom dowel in the tread hole. If the railing will not lift, bevel the top dowel where it binds against the side of the hole.

DEALING WITH A DOVETAILED BALUSTER

1. Removing the return nosing.

◆ Use a chisel to crack the joints.

◆ While protecting the stringer with a pry block, insert a pry bar and remove the return molding and return nosing *(below)*.

◆ Saw through the old baluster and hammer it out of the dovetail.

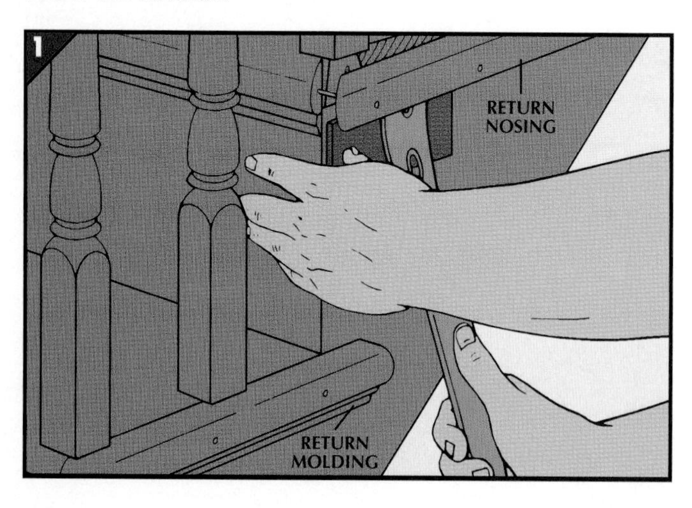

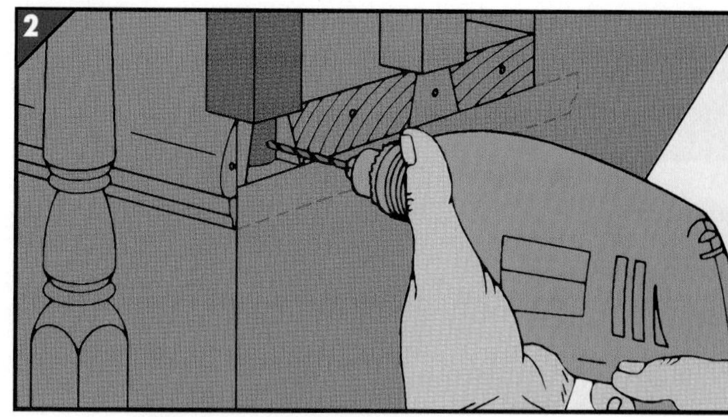

2. Securing the new baluster.

◆ Insert the top of a cut-to-length doweled baluster into the railing hole and set its base in the tread dovetail. Shim behind the dowel, if necessary, to align it with its neighbors.

◆ Drill a $\frac{1}{16}$-inch pilot hole through the dowel into the tread, and drive a $1\frac{1}{2}$-inch finishing nail through the hole into the tread.

◆ Renail the return nosing and return molding through the old holes; putty over the nailheads.

A NEW FILLETED BALUSTER

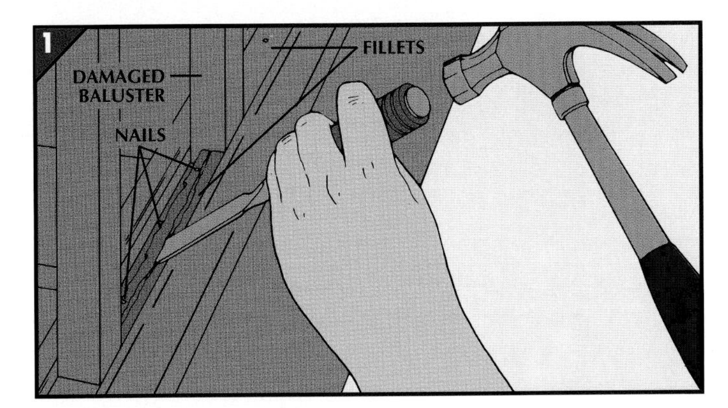

1. Taking out the old baluster.

◆ With a chisel, remove the fillet in the buttress cap on the downstairs side of the damaged baluster *(above)*. Then chisel out the railing fillet on the upstairs side of the baluster.

◆ Hammer each end of the baluster toward the chiseled-out fillet grooves to remove the baluster. Pull any nails left behind and scrape old glue from the grooves.

◆ Obtain the angle for the new baluster ends and fillets by placing the old baluster on top of the new one. Mark the angle on the new baluster and saw it to length.

2. Fastening the new baluster.

◆ Set the baluster against the existing fillets and toenail it to the railing and buttress cap with two $1\frac{1}{2}$-inch finishing nails through each end. Start the nails where the new fillets will hide them, and set the heads.

◆ Measure the length of each new fillet, mark the angle cuts using the old baluster, and cut with a miter box.

◆ Coat the backs with glue and fasten them in the railing and buttress-cap grooves with $1\frac{1}{2}$-inch finishing nails.

TIGHTENING A SHAKY NEWEL

Installing a lag screw.

◆ Hold a gauge block *(box, right)* against the newel, 4 inches from the floor, the hole centered on the post. Guide a $\frac{3}{4}$-inch Forstner bit through the block, and drill a hole $\frac{3}{4}$ inch deep in the newel *(below, right)*. Extend the hole through the newel with a $\frac{5}{16}$-inch bit and into the carriage with a $\frac{7}{32}$-inch bit.

◆ With a socket wrench, drive a $\frac{5}{16}$-inch lag screw 4 inches long fitted with a washer *(overhead view, inset)*. Plug the hole with a dowel, then cut it flush.

To steady a newel set in a bullnose tread, drive two nails through the flooring near the newel. From beneath, measure from the nails to locate the center of the newel dowel. Drill shank and pilot holes and install a $\frac{5}{16}$-inch lag screw 3 inches long. Pull the nails and putty the holes.

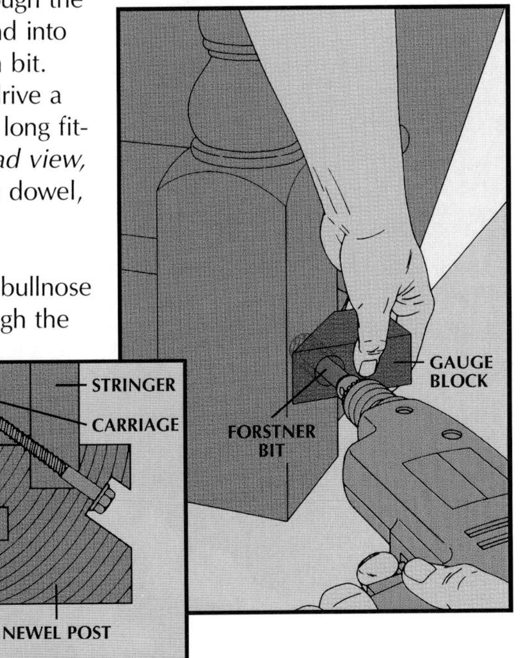

A GAUGE BLOCK FOR ANGLED DRILLING

A gauge block like the one shown in the photograph above simplifies the drilling of an angled hole into a newel post. To make a gauge block, use a Forstner bit to bore a $\frac{3}{4}$-inch hole through the edge of a block of 2-by-4. Then cut the block through the hole at the angle you wish to drill.

3

C H A P T E R

WALLS, CEILINGS, WINDOWS, AND DOORS

To give the interior of your house a major lift, spruce up the condition of the walls and ceilings and make sure the windows and doors fit tightly and operate smoothly.

Vintage old houses have substantial walls covered with plaster; those of less age have walls of prefabricated gypsum panels. In either kind of construction, minor cracks and gouges are simple to repair. More extensive damage can also be repaired but may indicate an underlying condition that needs to be corrected first. This chapter explains wall structure and shows you how to repair or replace the surface materials as necessary. It also shows you how to repair decorative details such as plaster molding.

Doors and windows that bind, rattle, or don't close tightly are a common complaint in an aging house. Structural settling and repeated painting over many years often interfere with their operation. You'll discover in this chapter how to deal with the most common door and window problems, and how to keep sliding pocket doors operating smoothly.

Peachtree Road

▷ *Right:* A door may need to be refitted or rehung because the framing in an old house has settled over the years. Many problems require only a bit of sanding or some shims to adjust the hinges.

▽ *Below:* Surface-mounted locks and porcelain knobs are period features well worth preserving when restoring an old house. Cleaning and simple repairs are often all that is required.

▷ *Right:* Pocket doors, ranging from a simple style like this to the ornate doors in Victorian parlors, are great space-savers and highly practical as well—if you keep the rollers working freely and correct any binding or sticking problems.

◁ *Left:* Double-hung sash windows are a classic feature in many older homes. Keep them operating smoothly by replacing sash cords and cleaning away built-up dirt and paint.

△ *Above:* Decorative moldings and details enrich many old houses. Repairs are often simple, using the same techniques for wood as for plaster.

▷ *Right:* Plaster or wallboard walls and ceilings are the background for your interior furnishings. You can repair cracks and patch or replace damaged sections to keep your rooms in excellent condition.

EXAMINING YOUR LIVING SPACES

Defects in walls and ceilings often go unnoticed because they frequently develop slowly, and living with them every day, we don't pay close attention to the first signs.

That's why it is important to make periodic, critical inspections of the finished interior surfaces in your home—to spot and correct problems before they become serious, and expensive to deal with.

Sometimes visible damage correlates with flaws you have noted elsewhere: a drip under a bathroom sink or in the attic may result in stains and then cracks in the ceiling or wall below. Peeling wallcovering may be the result of adhesive failure, or of deterioration of the wall surface itself. A door that sticks or one that repeatedly swings open may indicate a structural sag shift that will eventually cause cracks in the wall as well.

The check points listed below tell you what to look for when you inspect your living spaces. The information on the following pages tells you how walls and ceilings are constructed and how to repair them, as well as how to correct common problems with windows and doors.

SAFETY TIPS

When inspecting or working on plaster, wear a dust mask and safety goggles for protection from falling debris. For ceiling work, be sure not to set up a stepladder where a door could be opened and hit it. Block the door securely or lock it.

Check points for inspection.

◆ Check plaster walls and ceilings for areas of previous patching and any cracks wider than $\frac{1}{4}$ inch. Wide vertical cracks in a corner, horizontal cracks widening toward the center along the intersection of the ceiling and a partition wall, or large cracks that radiate from doorframes and window frames generally indicate weak or twisted wall framing. In that case, surface repairs will not be sufficient.

◆ Check, too, for actual gaps between walls and the floor or ceiling; they are signs of structural problems that also require more than surface work.

◆ If a crack wider than $\frac{3}{8}$ inch crosses the center of a plaster ceiling, look for a visible sag, indicating that the plaster is pulling away from its lath—a condition that requires immediate replastering or patching with gypsum wallboard. However, if a bulge in a wall or ceiling does not have associated large cracks and if you can press it back into place with your hands, you may be able to refasten it securely with plaster washers *(page 98)* rather than having to replace the entire section.

◆ Check wallboard for loosened joint tape or popped-up nails; both are easy-to-fix cosmetic problems.

◆ In a bathroom, kitchen, or laundry room, check for stains—often along what appear to be thin surface cracks —and powdering or flaking of the wall surface. These indicate water damage, probably from inside the wall rather than from surface condensation.

◆ Check doors to see that they operate smoothly and fit precisely in their jambs. Door tops planed at angles indicate previous adjustments for structural sags that probably were not corrected. A wedge-shaped gap between a door top and the jamb head may indicate a developing problem.

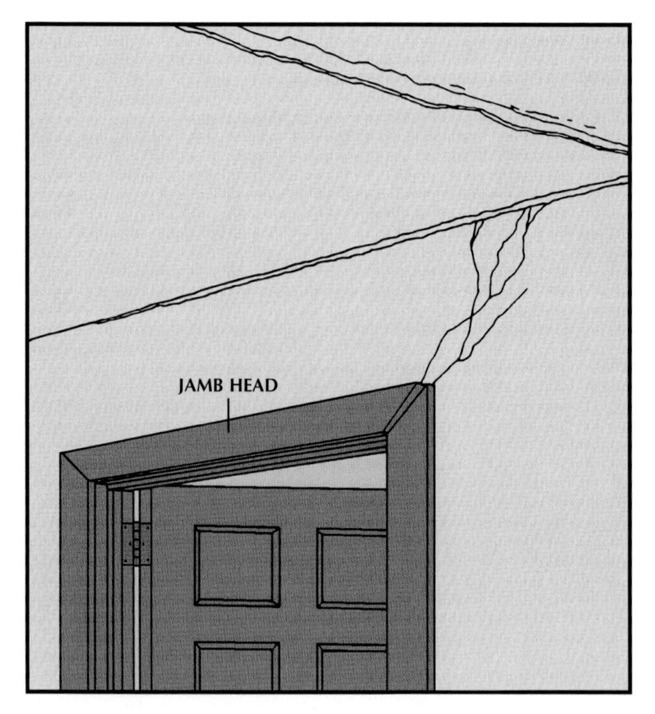

Check that latches work properly and hold a door closed without rattling. Make sure that hinges move smoothly and are tightly fastened to the door and the jamb.

◆ Check that windows open and close smoothly and do not rattle. Racked frames are common in old windows, as is binding caused by accumulated layers of paint. Check the condition of sash cords in double-hung windows. If frayed or rotted, replace them with nylon cord or sash chain. Check the hardware on casement and sliding windows, where dirt and lack of lubrication often affect operation.

INSIDE WALLS AND CEILINGS

There's more to walls and ceilings than meets the eye. As the illustrations on the following pages show, the wallboard or plaster surface is nothing more than an attractive skin for the skeleton of a house.

Wood-Framed Construction: Of the various surface-and-structure combinations shown in this chapter, wood-framed walls and ceilings covered by wallboard are the most common. The walls consist of vertical members, called studs, and horizontal members, the top plates and sole plates—all usually cut from 2-by-4 stock.

Larger boards called joists define every ceiling and support the floor of any living space overhead; hence the terms "ceiling joist" and "floor joist" are often used interchangeably. The box below describes several techniques for finding studs and joists in a finished wall or ceiling.

Masonry Walls: Older houses with exterior walls built of solid masonry are often finished inside with plaster laid on brick, but most such dwellings have ceilings and partition walls framed with wood joists and studs. Studs also lie behind the brick facades of many houses that are actually brick veneer, in which a single layer of brick is added to the outside of wood-framed walls.

Walls That Bear Weight: A wall that supports the roof or other upper structural parts of a house is known as a load-bearing wall, or bearing wall. In masonry houses, interior bearing walls are usually built of masonry. In a few frame houses, the studs of bearing walls are closer together than the standard 16-inch spacing for greater strength. Ceiling joists run perpendicular to bearing walls.

Finish Surfaces: Walls in most old houses were finished with three layers of plaster: a coarse, thick first or base coat applied over a surface of closely spaced wood strips (lath) or, later, wire mesh (metal lath); a rough "brown coat"; and a surface layer about $\frac{1}{8}$ inch thick of smooth white finish plaster.

In the late 1940s, this "wet plaster" wall construction was replaced by the use of prefabricated panels of gypsum sandwiched between layers of heavy paper, commonly called wallboard or drywall *(page 102)*. Because it does not require drying time, wallboard is easily and quickly installed.

LOCATING CONCEALED STUDS AND JOISTS

For most wall and ceiling work, you need to know where studs and joists are. Typically they are 16 inches apart; finding one helps locate others. One way of detecting studs and joists is to tap the wall or ceiling, listening for the solid sound of wood behind wallboard or plaster.

Alternatively, check for visual clues to stud and joist locations. Examine wallboard close up for traces of seams or nailing patterns; this is best done at night with a light shining obliquely across the surface. If the work you plan requires removing the baseboard, look behind it for seams or nails that hold wallboard panels to studs.

The easiest approach is to use an electronic stud finder *(left)*, which indicates changes in structure density with a column of lights. As the tool is guided across wallboard or plaster, the lights turn on sequentially as it approaches a stud or joist. The top light glows when the stud finder reaches the edge of a framing member. You can approximate its center by finding the midpoint between the two edges.

No method is perfect. In each case small test holes drilled in an inconspicuous spot may be needed to pinpoint a stud or joist and to confirm the spacing between them.

WOOD FRAMING BEHIND THE SURFACE

Wallboard over studs and joists. On this wood-framed wall, 4-by-8 panels of wallboard are secured horizontally with adhesive and nails or screws to vertical 2-by-4 studs. The studs are nailed between the sole plate (a 2-by-4 at floor level) and a top plate of doubled 2-by-4s at ceiling level. Studs are normally spaced at 16-inch intervals, center to center. Short pieces of 2-by-4 called firestops are sometimes nailed horizontally between studs at staggered levels to retard the spread of flames in case of fire.

Alongside door and window openings, studs are doubled, and a beamlike header forms the top of each opening. Short "cripple studs" extend above each header and below each window opening's rough sill, a 2-by-4 that runs across the bottom of the opening.

On the ceiling, wallboard covers 2-by-10 joists, 16 inches apart. Joist ends are toenailed to the upper surfaces of the top plates of two bearing walls.

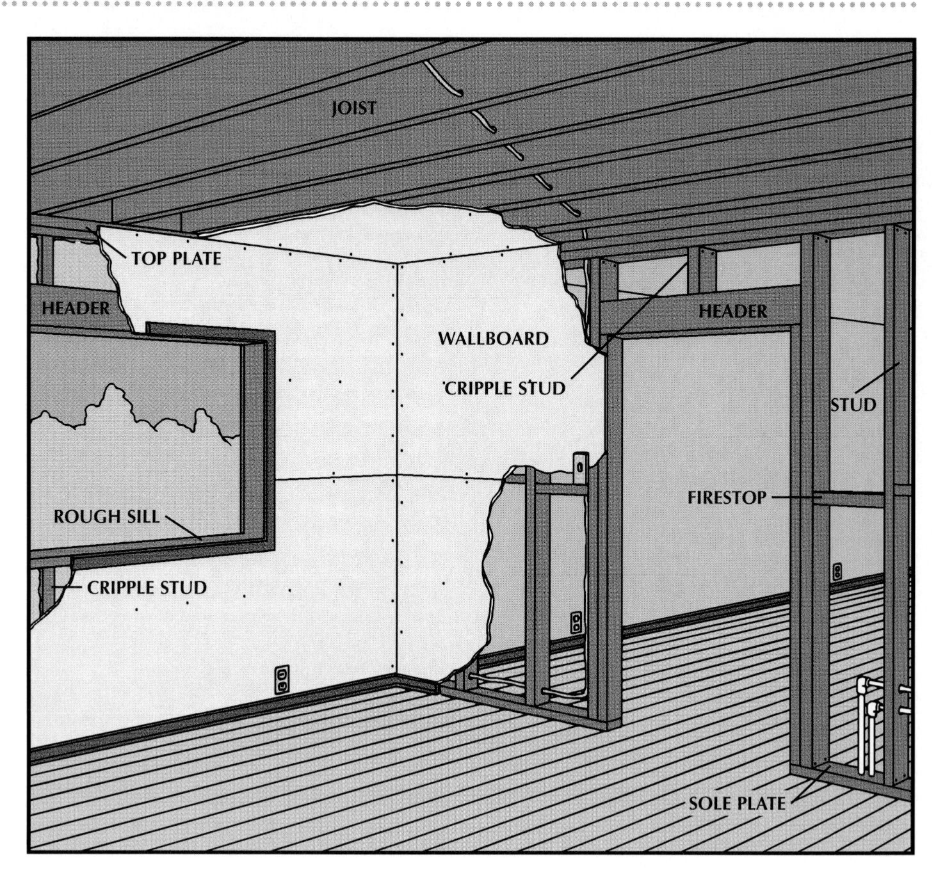

Plaster over wood lath. The plaster finish that covers this wood-framed wall and ceiling is typical of house construction before 1930. The layout of wall studs and ceiling joists here is identical to modern frame construction *(above)*, except that spacing between the framing members varies from 12 to 24 inches.

A pattern of wood strips, called lath, anchors the plaster. Generally $\frac{5}{16}$ inch thick and $1\frac{1}{2}$ inches wide, the strips span up to four studs or joists, in staggered groups of four to six. The strips are spaced $\frac{1}{4}$ inch apart so that the plaster can ooze between them for a good grip. At corners, the wood lath is strengthened with a 4- to 6-inch-wide strip of metal lath.

MASONRY WALLS WITH WOOD-FRAMED CEILINGS

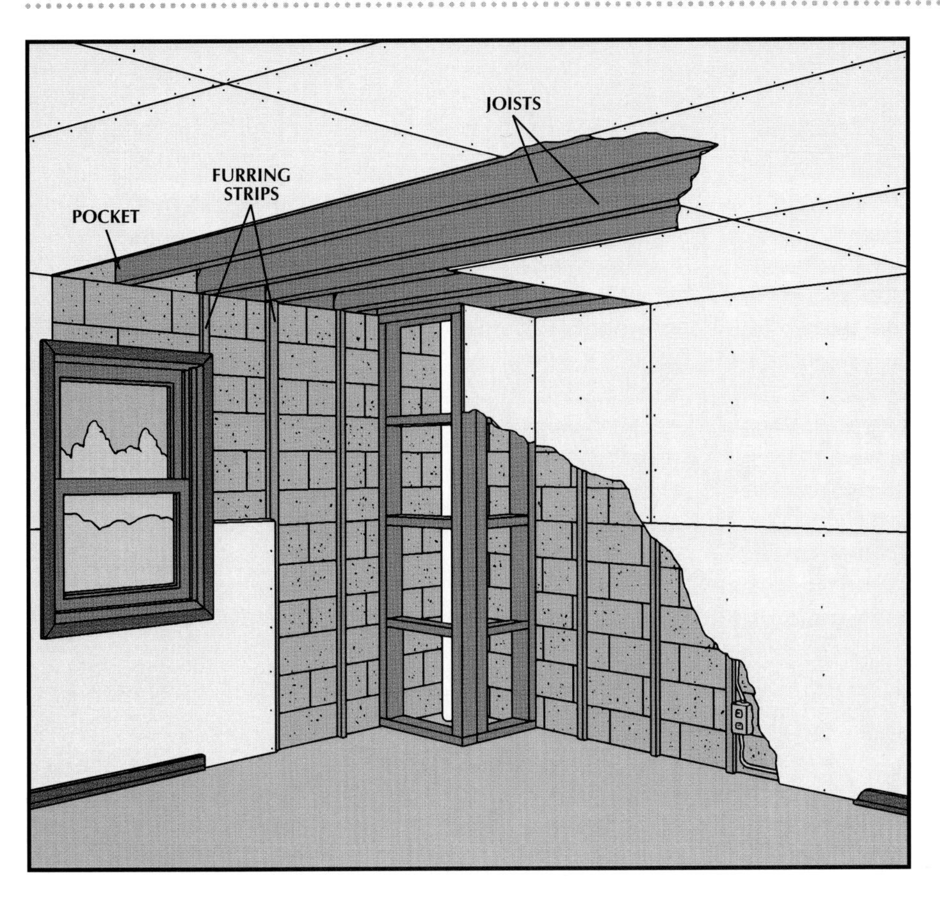

Furring strips under wallboard. On a concrete-block wall, wallboard is nailed to vertical 1-by-3 wood strips, called furring strips. They are spaced at 16-inch intervals and secured to the blocks with masonry nails, adhesive, or a combination of the two. Enclosures built of 2-by-3s or 2-by-4s hide any exposed pipes.

On the ceiling, wallboard is attached to 2-by-10 ceiling joists whose ends rest in pockets made in the masonry walls at the time of construction.

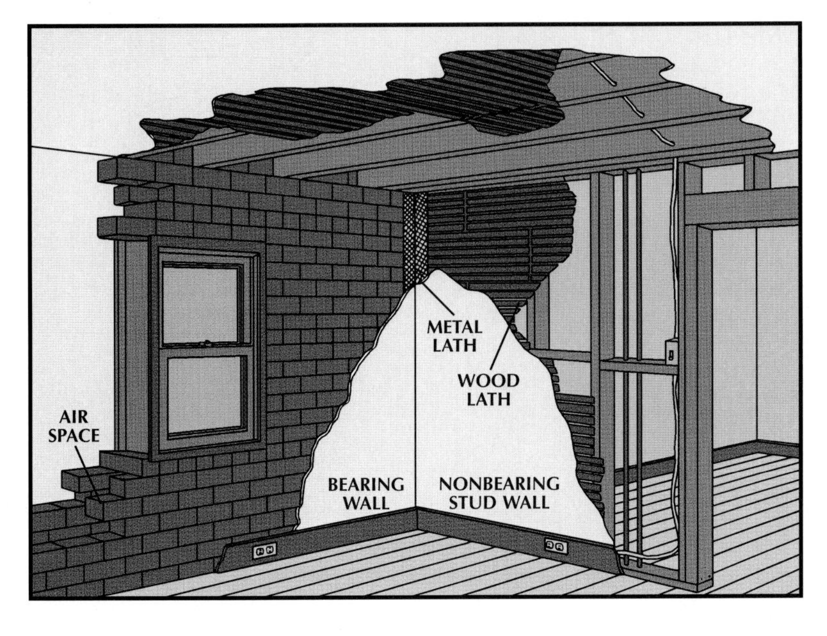

Plaster over masonry walls. In this masonry house, typical of the early 1900s, all exterior walls as well as interior bearing walls consist of two layers of brick separated by a narrow air space. Nonbearing interior walls are framed with wood studs. The ends of the ceiling joists rest in pockets that were made in the brick walls at the time of construction.

The plaster finish on interior masonry walls may be applied directly to the bricks, or to metal or wood lath fastened to furring strips secured to the bricks. On wood-framed walls and on ceilings the base underlying the plaster is metal lath or wood lath reinforced at corners with metal lath.

REPAIRS IN WALLBOARD AND PLASTER

A wall or ceiling finished in plaster requires different repair techniques from one covered in wallboard (drywall), but the materials used are the same for both surfaces. For example, small defects in either kind of wall are filled with ready-mix vinyl spackling compound or joint compound, and large holes patched with wallboard.

Repairing Wallboard: It is not uncommon for drywall nails to pull away from the studs and joists and protrude. They are easily reseated and hidden with joint compound *(below)*. Corner beads may also need to be refastened to the wall and the corner reshaped *(opposite)*.

When patching anything much larger than a nail hole, you must first provide a foundation for the repair material. Stuff holes up to an inch across with newspaper. Insert a wire screen for holes 1 to 6 inches wide *(page 94)*. And when large wallboard patches are needed, add braces for holes 6 to 12 inches across *(pages 94–95)* and cleats for those more than a foot wide *(pages 95–97)*.

Fixing Plaster Walls: To repair cracks and small holes in plaster, you must clear away the damaged material, fill the opening with joint compound, and sand the area flush with the wall. Undercutting the holes will allow the compound to bond better *(page 97)*. Large holes can be repaired with wallboard, but particular care must be taken not to damage the surrounding plaster *(pages 99–100)*.

TOOLS

- Nail set
- Hammer
- Putty knives
- Sanding block
- Metal file
- Utility knife
- Carpenter's square
- Wallboard saw
- Keyhole saw
- Electric drill
- Drywall knives
- Electronic stud finder
- Chalk line
- Cold chisel

MATERIALS

- Wallboard
- Drywall screws (1", $1\frac{1}{4}$", $1\frac{5}{8}$")
- Joint compound
- Sandpaper (coarse and fine)
- Wire screening
- Patching plaster
- 1 x 3s, 2 x 4s
- Joint tape (paper or fiberglass)
- Wood screws (3")
- Plaster washers
- Plywood ($\frac{1}{4}$")
- Construction adhesive

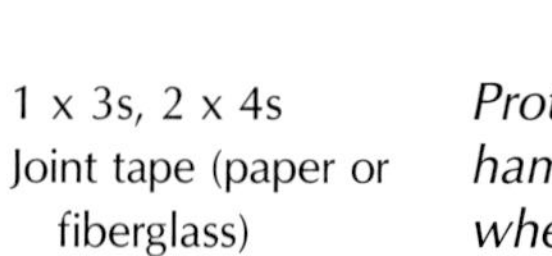

SAFETY TIPS

Protect your eyes with goggles when hammering, drilling, and sawing and when chipping away plaster. A hard hat guards your head from falling material when you are working overhead, and a dust mask protects your lungs when you are sanding and demolishing plaster.

RESEATING POPPED NAILS

1. Securing and dimpling the nail. Hammer the nail flush with the wallboard. Then carefully drive the nail a fraction of an inch below the surface, so the hammer's face creates a small depression, or dimple, in the surrounding wallboard without breaking the surface. (A driven and dimpled nail is shown to the right of the joint here.)

If the nail refuses to stay put, insert a new nail 2 inches directly above or below it. Dimple the new nail, then reseat the original one.

2. Patching the dimples.

◆ Apply a thin, smooth layer of joint compound over each dimple with a putty knife *(left)*. Let the compound dry; as it does, its color will change from dark to light beige.

◆ Apply a second layer of joint compound over a slightly larger area than the first layer.

◆ Smooth out any rough spots, especially at the edges, and let the patch dry.

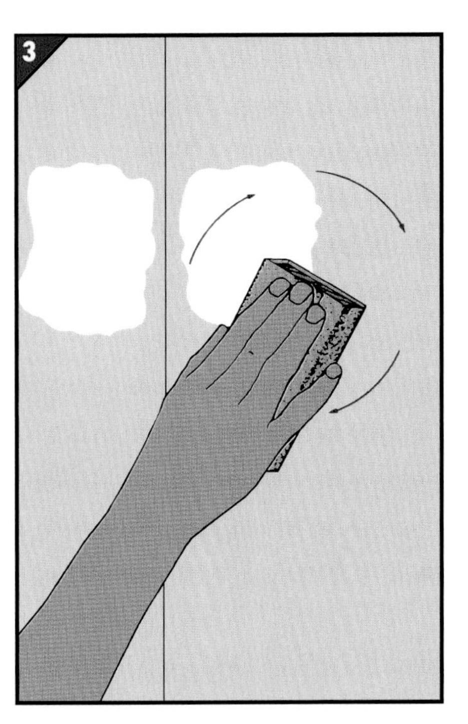

3. Leveling the surface.

◆ Gently sand the patches with fine-grit sandpaper wrapped around a sanding block. For smoothest results, rub the block across the patch in a circular motion.

◆ Feather the edges of the patches to blend smoothly with the surrounding surface, and clear away the dust before repainting.

REPAIRING DAMAGED CORNERS

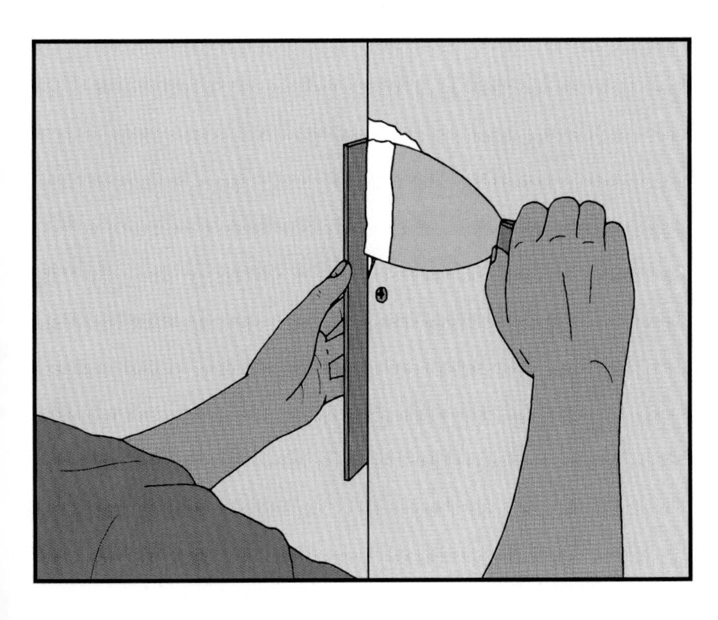

Rebuilding a corner.

◆ If the corner bead has been damaged, reseat it with $1\frac{5}{8}$-inch drywall screws and flatten any protruding bends with a metal file.

◆ Roughen the damaged surface on each side of the corner with coarse sandpaper, then brush clean and dampen.

◆ Holding a flat piece of wood against one side of the corner, apply joint compound to the other *(left)*. Reverse sides and repeat, taking care not to dent the fresh joint compound.

◆ Scrape off excess compound and let the area dry for 24 hours.

◆ Repeat this step as required, using fine-grit sandpaper on a sanding block to smooth the patch after each coat.

FIXING SMALL HOLES IN WALLBOARD

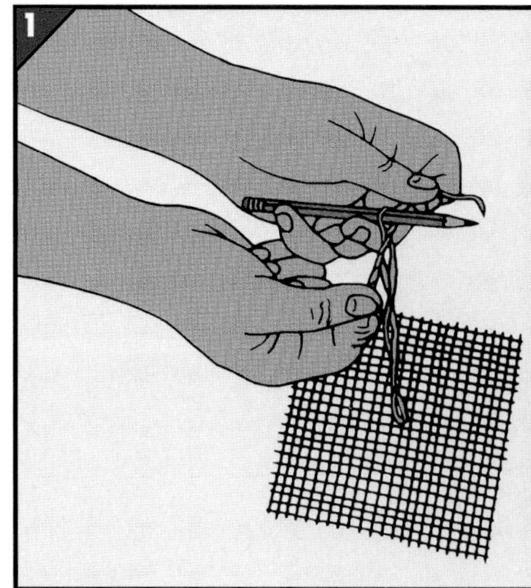

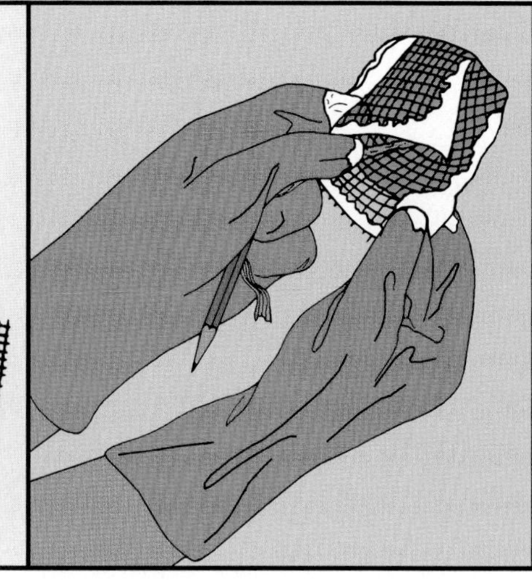

1. Installing a backing.

◆ Pull out loose pieces of wallboard and cut away torn surface paper with a utility knife.

◆ Roughen the edges of the hole with coarse sandpaper and brush away the dust.

◆ Cut a piece of wire screening slightly larger than the hole and loop a string through the center.

◆ Tie a pencil to it, with 4 to 6 inches of slack *(near right).*

◆ Wearing rubber gloves, coat the edges of the screen backing with patching plaster, roll the backing, and work it into the hole, maintaining a grip on the pencil *(far right).*

◆ Reach into the hole, in order to dampen the edges of the wallboard, and then coat them with plaster.

◆ Carefully pull the backing flat against the hole.

◆ Wrap the string around the pencil, then twist it against the wall to hold the backing in place.

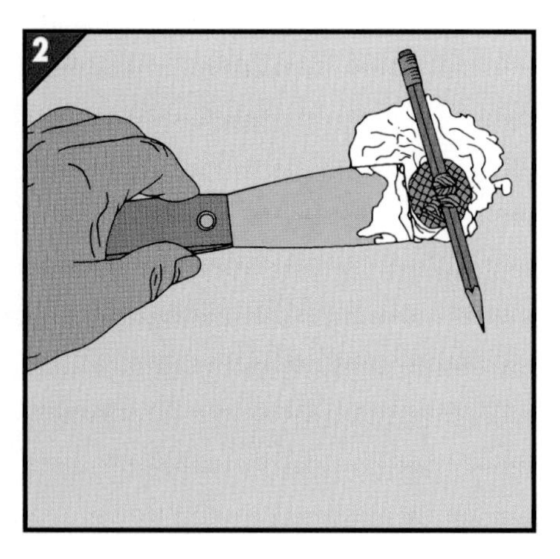

2. Applying the first coat.

◆ Using a 2-inch putty knife, gently fill the hole nearly flush with the wallboard surface, leaving a gap around the string *(left).*

◆ Let the plaster set for 30 minutes.

◆ Cut the string as close to the screen as possible, freeing the pencil.

◆ Dampen the edges of the center gap, then fill it with fresh plaster.

◆ Fill the hole flush with the wallboard surface, then allow the patch to dry.

◆ Spread joint compound or spackling compound over the patch with a wide-blade putty knife. Make this top layer wider than the underlying patch.

◆ After the compound has dried for 24 hours, sand it with a fine-grit paper on a sanding block, feathering the patch's edges.

PATCHING EXTENSIVE DAMAGE

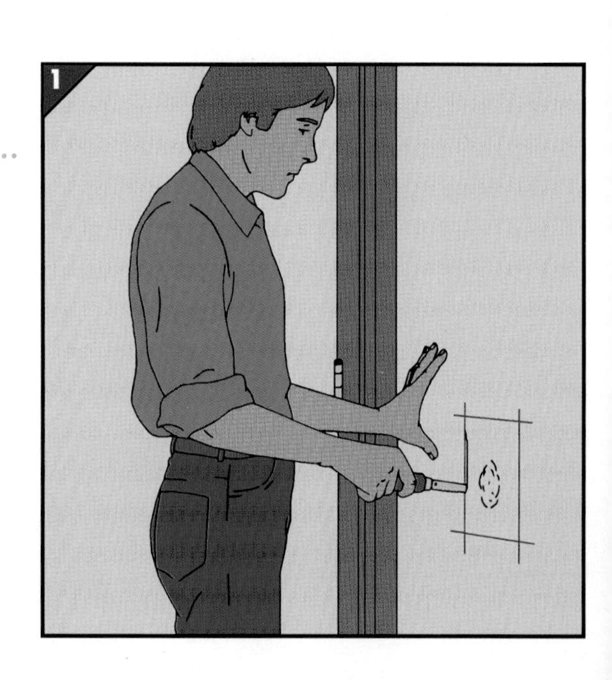

1. Cutting out the damage.

◆ With a carpenter's square, pencil a rectangle around the damaged area.

◆ Cut along the edges of the rectangle using a wallboard saw or a keyhole saw. With a wallboard saw *(right),* start the cut by forcing the pointed tip of the saw blade through the wallboard. Drill holes at the corners for a keyhole saw. As you saw around the damage, do not let the cutout drop behind the wall.

◆ Use the cutout as a pattern for a patch that is made from wallboard of the same thickness.

◆ From a 1-by-3, make two braces for the patch, each about 5 inches longer than the height of the opening in the wall.

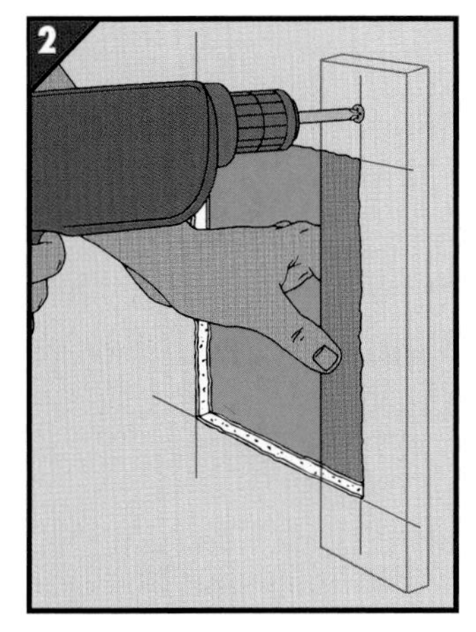

2. Installing the braces.

◆ Hold a 1-by-3 brace behind the wall so that it extends equally above and below the opening and is half hidden by the side of the opening.

◆ Drive a $1\frac{1}{4}$-inch drywall screw through the wall and into the brace, positioning the screw in line with the side of the hole and about 1 inch above it *(left)*. Drive a second screw below the opening.

◆ For holes taller than 8 inches, drive an additional screw along the side.

◆ Install the second brace on the opposite side of the opening the same way.

◆ Slip the wallboard patch into the opening, and screw it to the braces in the four corners and opposite any screws along the sides.

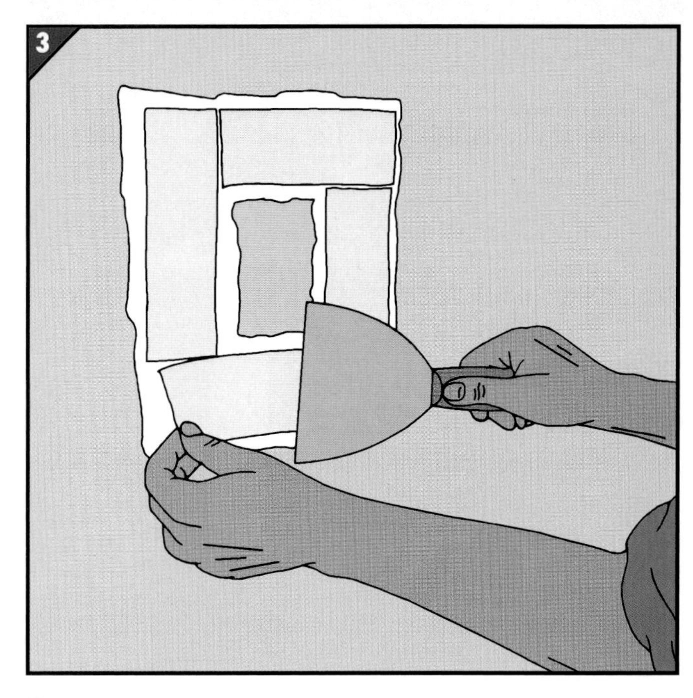

3. Taping the edges of the hole.

◆ Cover the screws and edges of the patch with joint compound, then embed strips of paper tape around the edges of the hole *(above)*.

◆ Using an 8-inch drywall knife, stroke the surface of the joint compound from the center of the patch outward, tapering the edges of the patch to the level of the surrounding wall.

◆ Allow the patch to dry for 24 hours, then apply a second coat, feathering the edges.

◆ Once the patch has dried, smooth it with fine-grit sandpaper on a sanding block, feathering the edges.

SURGERY FOR LARGE HOLES IN WALLBOARD

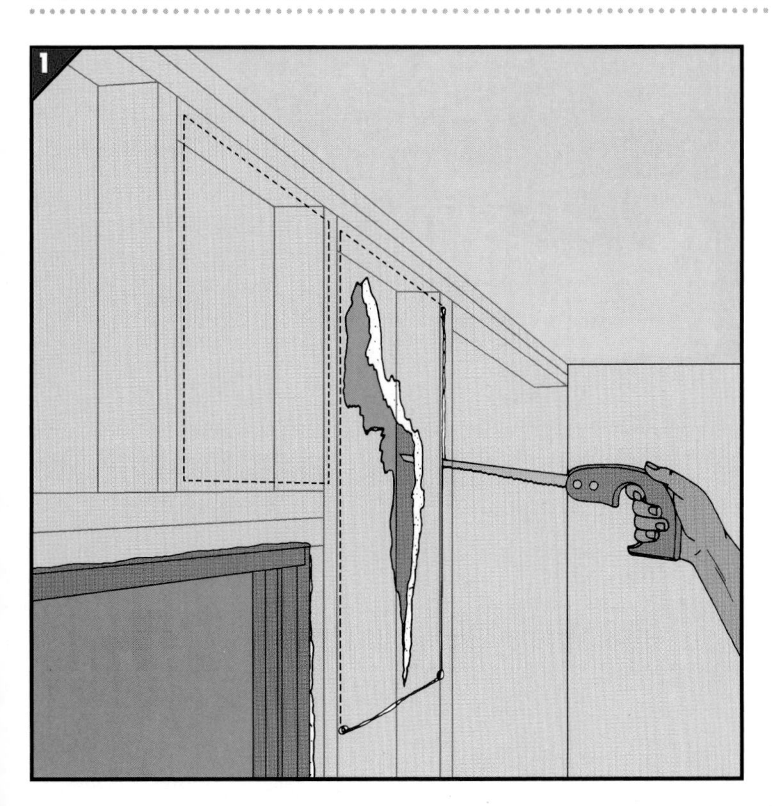

1. Cutting between studs and joists.

◆ Locate the position of the nearest stud or joist on each side of the hole *(page 89)*.

◆ Using a carpenter's square, mark an opening with 90-degree corners to be cut around the hole. Draw along the inside edges of the two studs or joists that flank the hole, and along any framing members between them. If a stud frames a window or door as shown here, continue the marks to the next stud: Doing so avoids a joint in line with the opening, which would otherwise be subject to cracking from repeated opening and closing. Where a hole lies within 16 inches of an inside corner, draw to the end of the panel to avoid forming a new joint too close to the corner.

◆ Remove any wood trim within the marked-off area. If there are electrical fixtures or outlets, turn off power and unscrew cover plates.

◆ Cut out sections of wallboard between framing members with a wallboard saw or a keyhole saw *(left)*.

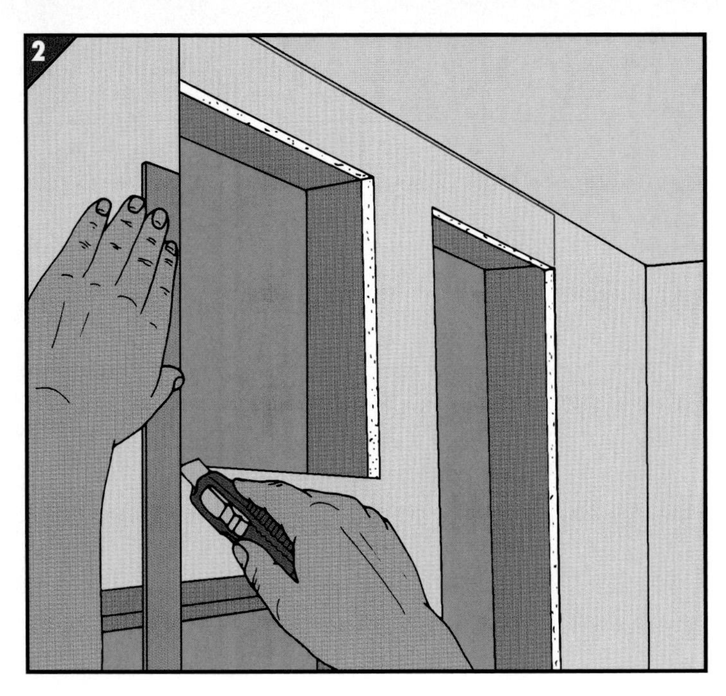

2. Removing attached or blocked pieces.

Switch to a utility knife to remove wallboard attached to studs or joists or if you encounter obstructions in the wall (such as insulation or firestops).

◆ Cut through the sections, using a straightedge as a guide *(left).*

◆ Take out any screws or nails and chip off any wallboard mounted with adhesive.

◆ Cut away joint tape and torn surface paper with the utility knife.

◆ At an inside corner, pull out pieces of wallboard wedged in the butted joint.

◆ Sand uneven edges around the opening with coarse sandpaper on a sanding block and brush debris from the exposed framing, cleaning it for the patch.

3. Making the patch.

◆ Measure each side of the opening as well as the sizes and positions of any electrical boxes, or doorframes or window frames, within it *(page 103).*

◆ Transfer the measurements to a panel of the same type and thickness as the damaged wallboard, using a carpenter's square to ensure 90-degree corners *(above).* Exclude the panel's tapered edges from the patch unless an edge of the opening falls at an inside corner.

◆ Cut out the patch, positioning the saw blade on the outline's inner edge; for an opening within the patch, cut just outside the line.

4. Adding cleats.

◆ For fastening the patch, cut 2-by-4 cleats to fit alongside the joists or studs at the edges of the opening. Where possible, cut the cleats 2 to 3 inches longer than the opening.

◆ Secure the cleats flush with the studs or joists using 3-inch wood screws driven every 4 to 6 inches along the cleat *(above).*

5. Installing the patch.

◆ Before positioning the patch, mark the location of any exposed stud or joist on the wall or ceiling near the opening.

◆ Fit the patch in the opening and drive $1\frac{5}{8}$-inch drywall screws through the patch about every 6 inches into each cleat, stud, or joist, starting at the middle and working to the edges *(left)*. Do not screw the patch to a top plate or a sole plate.

◆ Finish the repair as described in Step 3 on page 95 *(top)*.

FILLING CRACKS IN PLASTER

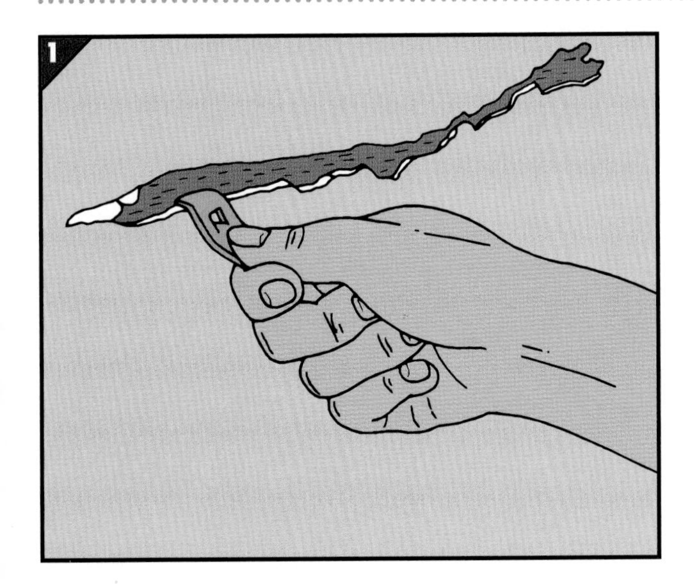

1. Preparing the crack.

This procedure applies to cracks comparable to the one shown here. Narrower cracks in sound walls do not require taping *(Step 3, next page)*.

◆ To help lock the patching material in place, scrape some of the plaster from behind the edges; a can opener works well *(above)*. Doing so makes the crack wider at the base than at the surface.

◆ Brush out dust and loose plaster, then dampen the interior surfaces of the crack.

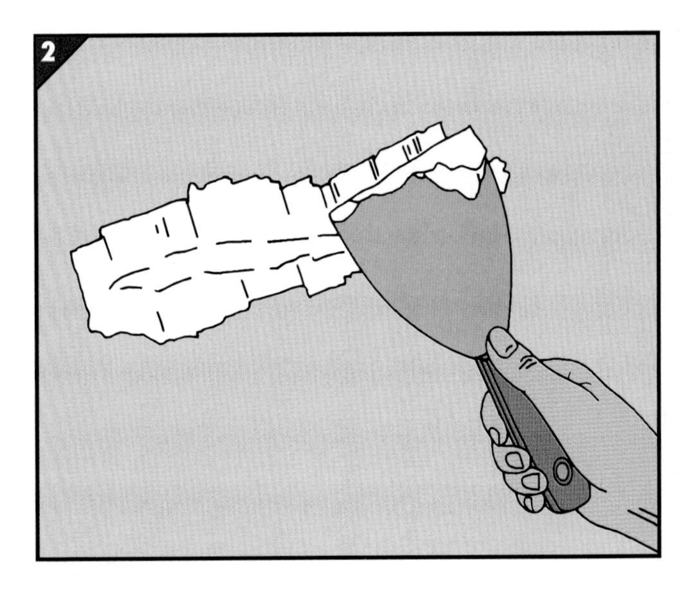

2. Filling the crack.

◆ Using a 5-inch drywall knife, pack joint compound into the crack, working it behind the undercut edges.

◆ Stroke the knife back and forth across the crack *(above)* until it is completely filled, then draw the knife along the crack to bring the patch surface flush with the wall.

◆ Allow the patch to dry for 24 hours.

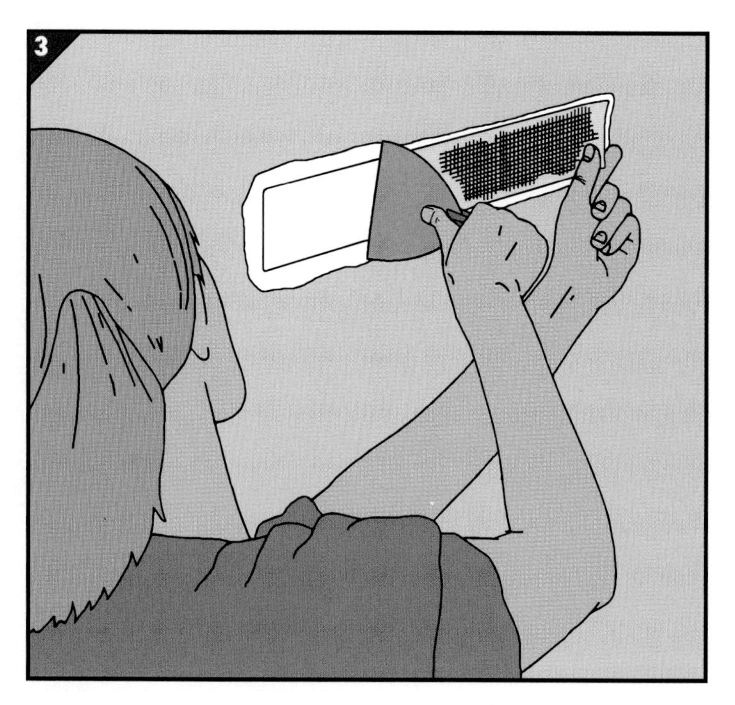

3. Reinforcing the patch with tape.
◆ Cut a piece of fiberglass tape 2 inches longer than the crack.
◆ Spread a wide layer of joint compound over the crack.
◆ Press the tape into the compound, then run the knife blade along the tape to set it in place *(left)*.
◆ Allow the area to dry, then apply a second coat, feathering the edges.
◆ After the patch dries, sand it smooth.

FIRST AID FOR BOWED PLASTER

Plaster on wood lath is the most common wall finish in old houses. After many years, it may loosen in spots and bow outward from a wall or sag down from a ceiling. This is because the keys—gobs of the base (rough) coat that protrude through the spaces between the strips of lath, locking the plaster in place—have broken off. Rather than replacing the plaster entirely, it is often possible to fasten such spots securely in place with plaster washers *(photo, right)*. Each washer is held by a single screw and is concealed by spackle, patching plaster, or joint compound. It may be necessary to first chisel or scrape away the surface layer of finish plaster under each washer in order to fasten it below the level of the surface.

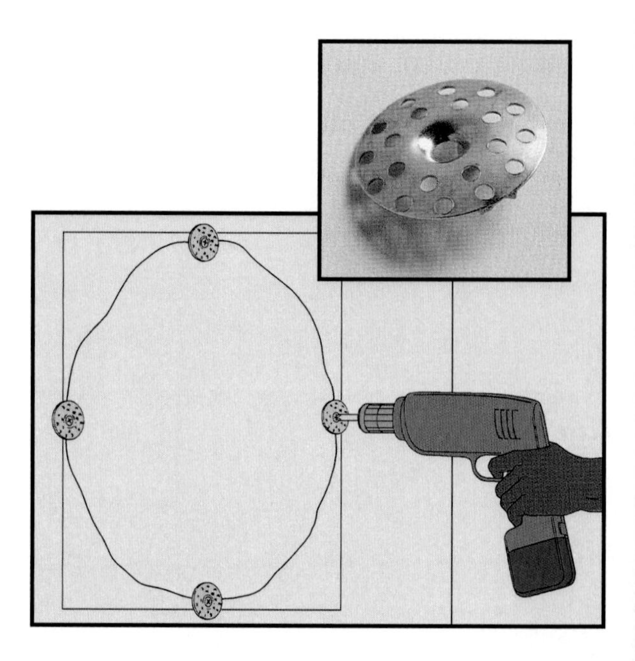

Installing plaster washers.
◆ Mark the perimeter of the loose plaster *(blue lines)*.
◆ Drill pilot holes for $1\frac{1}{4}$-inch No. 6 flat-head wood screws around the perimeter and in the center of the sag, spacing the holes 8 to 10 inches apart.
◆ Fasten a plaster washer at each hole, tightening the screw until the washer is pulled below the surface of the plaster.
◆ Cover the washer and screw with wallboard joint compound, then sand, prime, and paint.

WALLBOARD REPAIRS IN PLASTER

1. Removing the plaster.

◆ Snap a chalk line to form a rectangle that encompasses the damage.

◆ To protect sound plaster from damage while clearing deteriorated plaster from the rectangle, screw plaster washers just outside the chalked lines.

◆ Score the plaster along the chalked lines with a utility knife; then, with a hammer and cold chisel, remove the damaged plaster within the rectangle *(left).*

CAUTION *When chiseling plaster, work in small sections and tap the chisel gently. Excessive force can loosen plaster beyond the plaster washers.*

2. Attaching plywood strips.

◆ Cut strips of $\frac{1}{4}$-inch plywood, 1 inch wide.

◆ Edge each opening with the strips, loosely fastened with $1\frac{5}{8}$-inch drywall screws driven partway into the lath.

◆ Shim the strips to position a scrap of wallboard flush with the plaster *(right).* Tighten the screws.

◆ Trim the protruding shims with a keyhole saw.

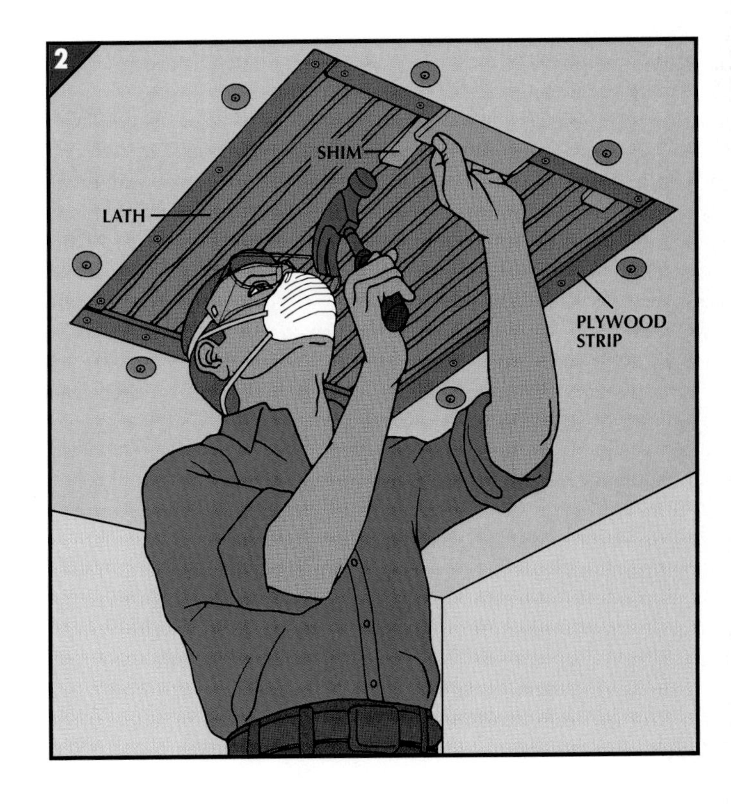

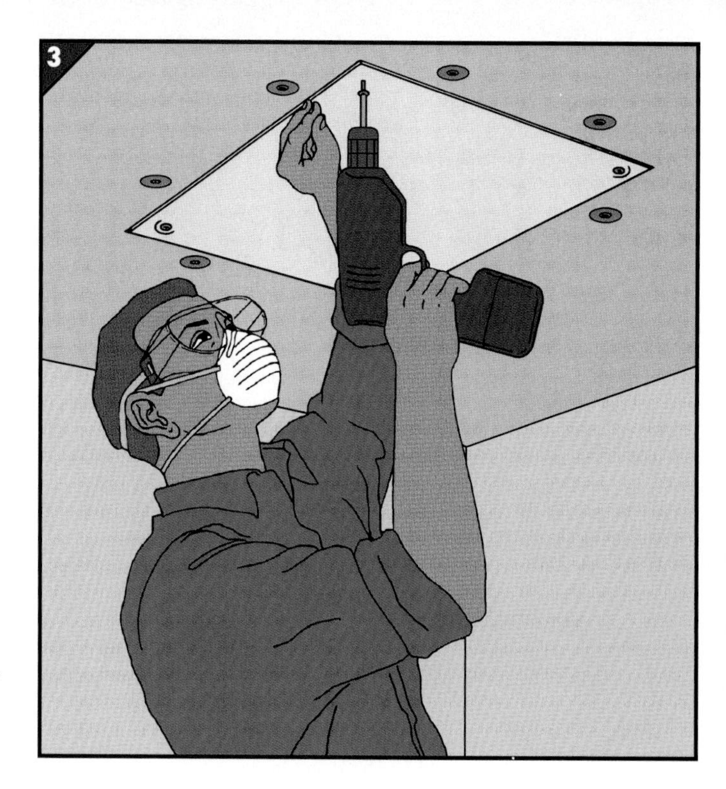

3. Installing the patch.

◆ Cut a piece of wallboard to fit the rectangle.

◆ Apply a bead of construction adhesive to each plywood strip, then press the wallboard against the adhesive.

◆ Fasten the wallboard to the plywood strips with 1-inch drywall screws 6 inches apart, starting at the corners *(right)*.

4. Taping the joints.

◆ With a 6-inch-wide drywall knife, spread a $\frac{1}{8}$-inch-thick layer of joint compound over all the joints *(left)*.

◆ Embed perforated-paper joint tape in the wet compound and run the knife over it, squeezing out excess material. Let the compound dry for 24 hours.

◆ Scrape off any ridges with the knife and apply a second layer of joint compound, called a block coat, with a 12-inch drywall knife centered on the joint. Allow the joint compound 24 hours to dry.

◆ Apply a final skim coat of compound with the 12-inch knife, feathering the material to a distance of 12 inches on both sides of the joint.

◆ When the compound is dry, smooth all the joints with fine-grit sandpaper.

REPAIRING PLASTER MOLDING

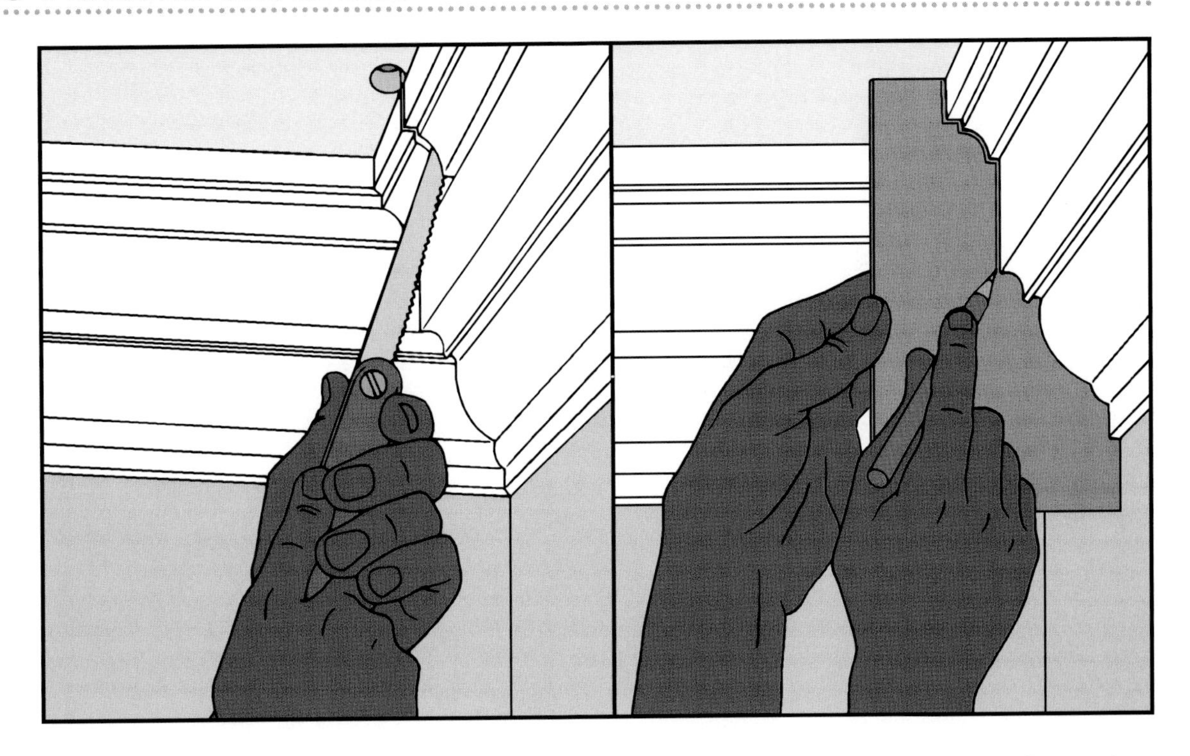

Profile molding.

◆ At one end of a damaged section of molding, drill a hole in the ceiling large enough to accommodate the blade of a keyhole saw.

◆ Insert the saw into the hole and cut a kerf (slot) straight through the molding from top to bottom *(above, left).*

◆ Slide a piece of cardboard $1\frac{1}{2}$ inches longer and wider than the molding into the kerf and trace the molding profile on the cardboard with a sharp pencil *(above, right).*

◆ Cut out the profile precisely, trace it onto a piece of stiff sheet metal, and cut the sheet metal to match. File the edges smooth and shape them as necessary by test-fitting the metal template over an undamaged section of molding.

◆ Fill damaged spots with joint compound or patching plaster, using a spatula, ornamental tool *(below),* or other tool as necessary. Use your metal template to scrape and smooth the wet patching material to match the molding profile.

Ornamental molding.

◆ Dampen the molding; then, with the pointed end of a special pointing, or ornamental, tool *(below),* press stiff plaster onto the damaged area a teaspoonful or so at a time *(right).*

◆ For sculpting, use the opposite, flat end of the tool.

◆ Finish with a moist, soft-bristled watercolor brush to smooth the plaster, redefine the design, and remove any tool marks.

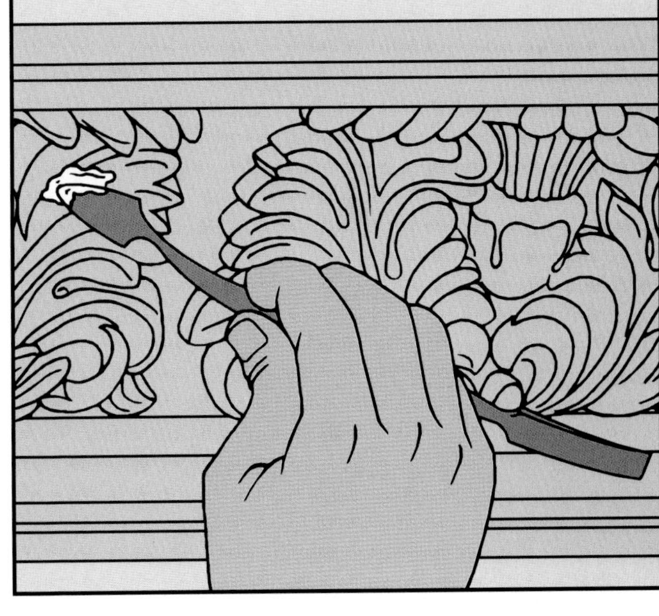

COVERING WALLS AND CEILINGS

Wallboard, the material most commonly used to finish walls and ceilings, is simply a sheet of chalklike gypsum wrapped in heavy paper *(below)*. Easy to cut and somewhat flexible, wallboard can be fastened to a variety of supporting structures: joists, furring strips, or studs of wood or metal. The joints where panels meet are concealed with either adhesive-backed fiberglass mesh or paper tape and covered with pastelike joint compound *(pages 107–110)*.

Dimensions: Wallboard is made in 4- and $4\frac{1}{2}$-foot widths 8, 10, and 12 feet long and in thicknesses of $\frac{3}{8}$, $\frac{1}{2}$, and $\frac{5}{8}$ inch; $\frac{1}{2}$-inch wallboard is considered standard, but check your local building code. Using 12-foot sheets will reduce the number of joints to be finished. But if the long sheets are too heavy and unwieldy to handle, use shorter ones.

Before You Begin: To determine how many sheets of wallboard you need, calculate the square footage of each wall, ignoring all openings except the largest, such as archways or picture windows. Do the same for the ceiling. To convert this figure into sheets, divide it by the area of the panels you intend to buy. A 4- by 8-foot sheet is 32 square feet; a 4- by 12-foot sheet is 48 square feet.

Plan to hang panels horizontally rather than vertically on walls, unless the wall is very narrow. In rooms with ceilings higher than 8 feet, use sheets of wallboard $4\frac{1}{2}$ feet wide, trimmed to fit. If the ceiling is taller than 9 feet, you'll need a filler strip. Place it at the bottom of the wall, cut edge down.

You will also need fasteners—either nails or screws *(below)*—and adhesive, which reduces the number of screws or nails required while greatly increasing the strength of the attachment.

Prior to hanging the panels, make sure the walls have sufficient insulation *(page 239)*. If necessary, add insulating batts. Fasten them to the sides of the wall studs, with the vapor barrier facing into the room.

Hanging the Wallboard: Install the ceiling first, then the walls, always beginning in a corner. Measure and cut wallboard so that end-to-end joints fall at joists or studs and are staggered by at least 16 inches in adjacent rows.

Installing wallboard horizontally on walls results in fewer joints and fewer dips and bows. To further reduce the number of joints, wherever possible arrange wallboard sections so that joints fall along the frames of doors and windows.

TOOLS

Drywall T square
Utility knife
Wallboard saw or keyhole saw
Tape measure
Chalk line
Caulking gun
Drywall hammer
Electronic stud finder
Screw gun or electric drill with screwdriver bit
Pry bar
Tin snips

MATERIALS

Wallboard
Wallboard adhesive
Drywall nails or screws
Corner bead

SAFETY TIP

Protect your eyes with goggles when driving nails or screws.

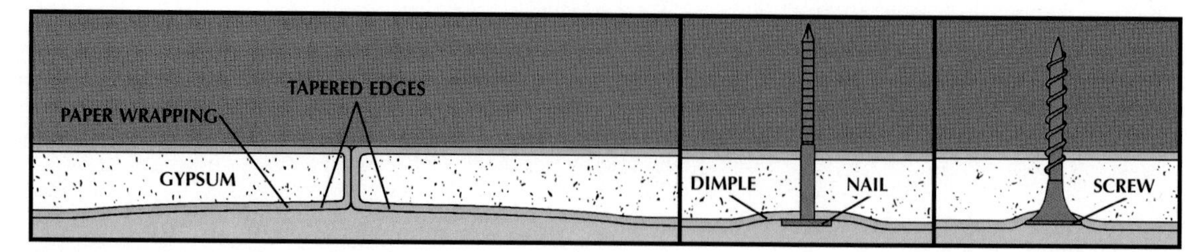

Wallboard and its fasteners.
The long edges of the wallboard panel are slightly tapered *(above, left)* starting 2 inches from the edge. When two sheets are butted side by side, they form a shallow trough for joint tape, making the seam easier to conceal.

Drywall nails *(above, center)* have broad heads and unusually sharp points. Buy nails with ringed shanks for extra grip in wood framing or furring strips. Drive the nails to a depth slightly below the wallboard surface, and fill the resulting hammerhead dimple with joint compound. Neither the nailhead nor the dimple should break the paper wrapping.

Drywall screws *(above, right)* can be used in metal or wood framing. Sink screwheads to just below the wallboard surface, leaving the paper intact.

FITTING WALLBOARD LIKE A PRO

Shortening a panel.

◆ Position a drywall T square on a wallboard panel as shown at right and cut through the paper wrapping with a utility knife.
◆ Grasp the edge of the panel on both sides of the cut and snap the short section of wallboard away from you, breaking the panel along the cut.
◆ Cock the short section back slightly, then reach behind the panel with a utility knife to make a foot-long slit in the paper along the bend.
◆ Snap the short section forward to break it off.

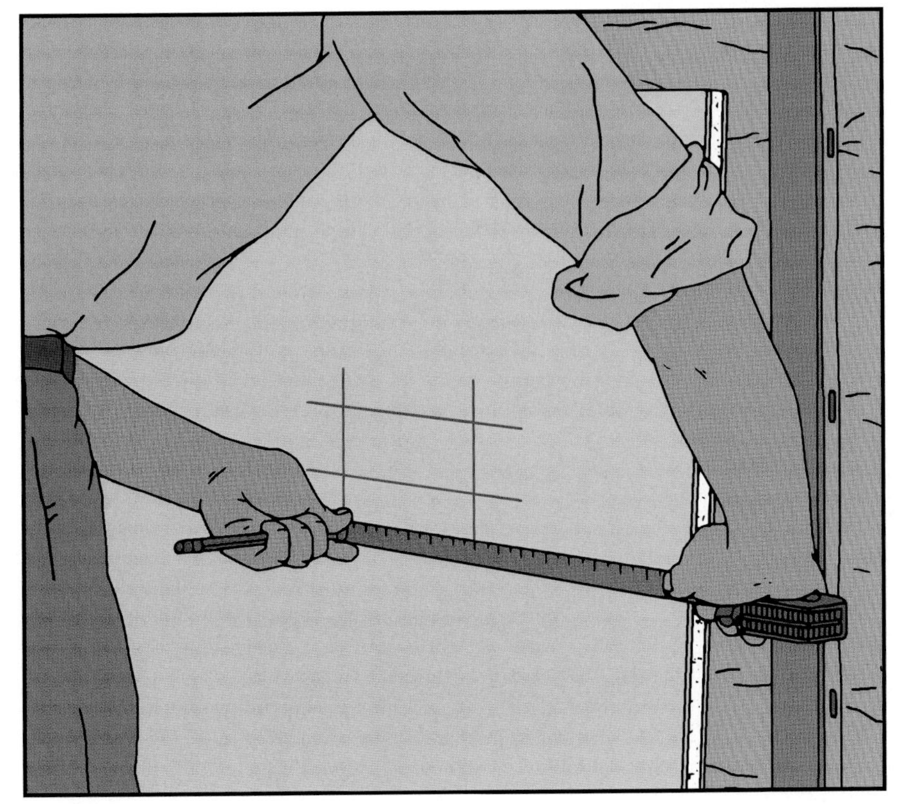

Making openings.

◆ To mark a panel for a small opening such as the hole for an electrical box, measure from the point on the wall where the edge of the sheet will rest to the near and far sides of the box.
◆ Similarly, measure from the point where the top or the bottom edge of the panel will fall to the top and bottom of the box.
◆ Transfer these measurements to the sheet: Hold the tape measure between your thumb and forefinger at the first measurement as shown at left. Rest the side of your forefinger against the edge of the panel and hold a pencil against the end of the tape with the other hand, then move both hands down the panel simultaneously to mark the first of the four edges of the opening.
◆ Repeat this procedure for each of the other three measurements.
◆ Cut the opening with a wallboard saw or a keyhole saw *(page 95)*.

For a larger opening, such as a window, mark the wallboard the same way. Cut all four sides with a saw, or saw three sides, then score and break the fourth.

HANGING A CEILING

1. Applying the adhesive.

◆ Measure and trim the first panel so the end not butted against the wall will coincide with the center of a joist edge.

◆ Mark joist locations on the panel with a chalk line.

◆ Apply a $\frac{3}{8}$-inch-thick bead of wallboard adhesive to the underside of each ceiling joist to be covered by the first panel. So adhesive will not ooze out between sheets, start and stop each bead about 6 inches from the point where the sides of the panel will fall.

◆ Also apply adhesive to the edges of the joists to which you will attach the ends of the panel.

2. Attaching the wallboard.

◆ With a helper or two, lift the panel into position against the adhesive-coated joists and drive a nail or screw into each joist at the center of the sheet. If using drywall nails, double-nail at each joist, except at the ends, driving a second nail 2 inches apart from the first.

◆ Fasten the tapered sides of the panel to each joist, 1 inch from the panel edges.

◆ Secure the ends with nails or screws spaced 16 inches apart and $\frac{1}{2}$ inch from the edge.

◆ Continue in this fashion until the entire ceiling is covered. If you find there will be a gap along the wall running parallel to the joists, trim panels to ensure that the filler strip *(opposite, Step 3)* will span at least two joists.

GIVING DRYWALL A LIFT

You can install wallboard without enlisting friends or neighbors as helpers by renting a drywall lift. This handy tool raises a wallboard panel to the desired height and holds it in position while you secure it to the wall or ceiling. Casters make the lift easy to position, and a brake keeps it from moving once it is in place.

To use the lift, rest one edge of a wallboard panel on a pair of metal hooks attached to a frame with adjustable arms that together form a cradle for the sheet. Angle the cradle for a ceiling or wall, then turn the wheel to raise the sheet of wallboard to the correct height.

TRICKS OF THE TRADE

Devising a Tapered Joint

The ends of wallboard panels, unlike the sides, are untapered. As a result, no shallow, joint-tape trough *(page 102)* is formed between sheets butted end to end, making the seam difficult to conceal. One remedy is to staple cardboard shims, $\frac{1}{16}$ inch thick, along the edges of the joists or studs on either side of the joint. The shims cause the wallboard to slope toward the joist or stud behind the joint, creating a slight depression for the joint tape.

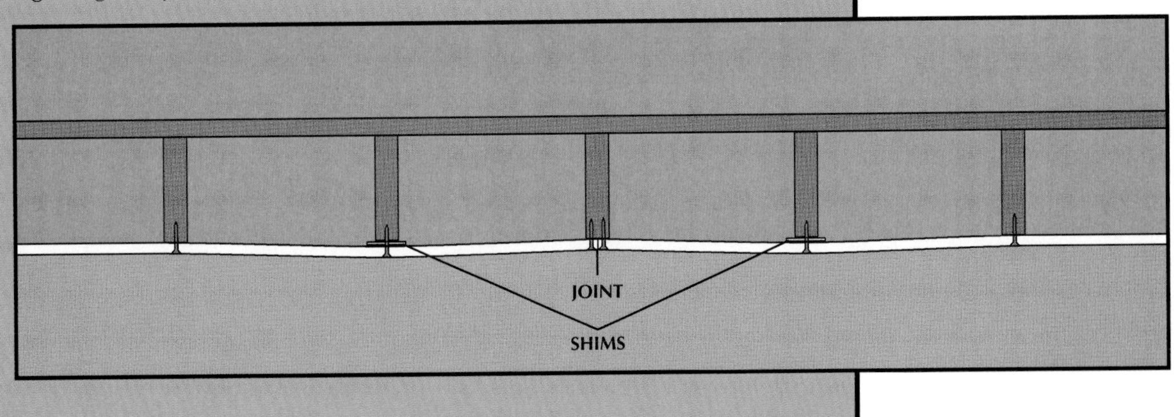

3. Adding a filler strip.
Fill gaps in the ceiling with wallboard strips cut to fit.
◆ Cut a strip from the side of a sheet and butt it against the adjoining panel so the tapered edges meet, ensuring a smooth joint.
◆ Secure the filler strip with adhesive and fasteners driven into the joists.
◆ Use a utility knife or the blade end of a drywall hammer head to trim away small amounts of excess gypsum.

SECURING WALL PANELS

1. Installing wallboard horizontally.
◆ On the ceiling and the floor, mark the centers of wall studs as a guide to fastening the sheets of wallboard.
◆ Trim the first panel to end at the center of a stud. If necessary, shim the adjacent studs to provide an even surface.
◆ As with ceiling joists *(page 104, Step 1)*, apply adhesive to the studs that will be covered by the first sheet.
◆ With a helper, lift the panel into place, tight against the ceiling. Secure it with three rows of fasteners driven into each stud an inch from the bottom edge of the panel, then across the middle, then an inch from the top edge. If using drywall nails, double-nail the midsection of the sheet *(page 104, Step 2)*.
◆ Finish attaching the sheet with fasteners spaced every 8 inches across the ends, $\frac{1}{2}$ inch from the edge—except where an end falls at an inside corner. In that case, leave the end unfastened, butt the next panel against it, and fasten the end of the second sheet to a stud. At an outside corner, lap the end of the second sheet over the end of the first, and nail the ends of both panels to their common stud.
◆ After the upper course, install a lower course, trimming the panels lengthwise to leave a $\frac{1}{2}$-inch gap at the floor. Arrange the panels so that joints in the lower course do not align with those in the upper one. With a helper, use foot levers *(Step 2, below)* to raise the panel off the floor while securing it.

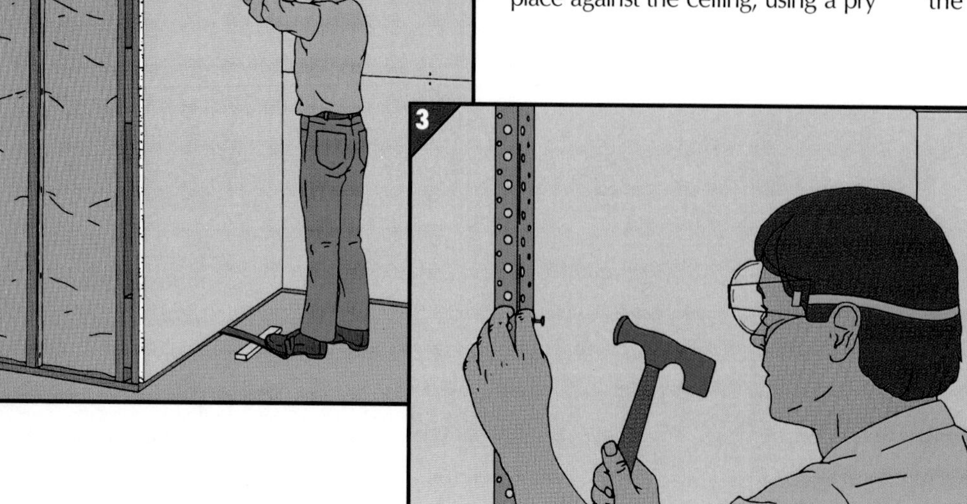

2. Installing vertical panels.
For narrow sections of wall, install panels vertically, joining them at the midpoint of studs.
◆ Apply adhesive in the pattern for horizontal panels. Lift the panel into place against the ceiling, using a pry bar on a scrap of wood as a foot lever.
◆ Secure the panel to each stud with fasteners spaced about 2 feet apart, starting 1 inch from the top and ending 1 inch from the bottom. If using drywall nails, double-nail the midsection *(Step 1, above)*.

3. Attaching a corner bead.
◆ To protect an outside corner, trim a metal corner-bead strip to the correct length by cutting through the flanges with tin snips, one flange at a time.
◆ Position the corner bead over the wallboard joint and fasten it to the stud beneath with nails or screws driven through holes in the bead.

APPLYING JOINT COMPOUND

All that remains after installing wallboard *(pages 102–106)* is to conceal fastener heads, corner bead, and the seams between drywall sheets. Joint compound is an essential element in all three tasks. Buy a 5-gallon drum of joint compound for every ten 4- by 8-foot sheets of wallboard you have installed.

Taping and Feathering: Covering fastener heads and corner bead requires only the application of joint compound. To hide and strengthen a seam between wallboard sheets, however, precede the joint compound with joint tape made of paper or fiberglass mesh *(below)*.

Paper joint tape is stuck to the wall with an underlying layer of joint compound *(opposite)*, whereas fiberglass tape has an adhesive backing to make the work go more quickly. Either tape is then covered with two layers of compound in a process known as feathering *(page 110)*.

A Final Smoothing: After joint compound dries, you must sand or sponge away grooves and ridges. Sand with 120-grit, open-coat paper wrapped around a sanding block; a sanding plate on a pole lets you reach high areas. A light back-and-forth motion works best except for rubbing down a high spot, where a circular motion is preferable.

Sponging avoids both the dust made by sanding and the risk of scratching the wallboard's paper surface. Saturate a wallboard sponge with water, wring it dry, then gently rub it across the joint compound with a smooth, sweeping motion.

Fiberglass tape.
To save time in taping wallboard joints, use fiberglass-mesh tape instead of the traditional perforated paper tape. Because the fiberglass tape is sticky on one side, you do not have to first apply a bed coat of compound to the seam. Simply stretch the mesh tape along the joint, pressing it down so that it adheres, then cover it with successive layers of joint compound *(pages 108–110)*. This tape is also excellent for making patches across surface cracks in walls and ceilings.

Joint compound
Wire coat hanger
Paper or fiberglass joint tape

Wallboard knives (5", 8", 12")
Joint compound pan
Sanding plate and pole
Sandpaper (120-grit, open-coat)
Wallboard sponge
Corner trowel
Crown trowel

HIDING FASTENERS AND CORNER BEAD

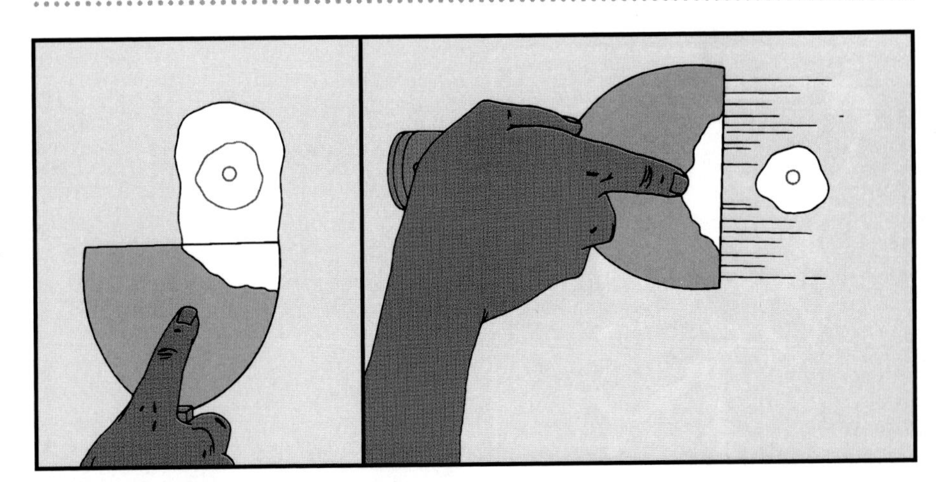

Covering a nail- or screwhead.
◆ Load half the width of a 5-inch knife blade with joint compound.
◆ Holding the blade nearly parallel to the wallboard, draw the compound across the nail- or screwhead so that it fills the dimple completely *(above, left)*.
◆ Raise the knife blade to a more upright position and scrape off excess compound with a stroke at right angles to the first *(above, right)*.
◆ Apply two additional coats in the same fashion, allowing the compound to dry between coats.
◆ After the third coat dries, lightly sand or sponge the patch smooth.

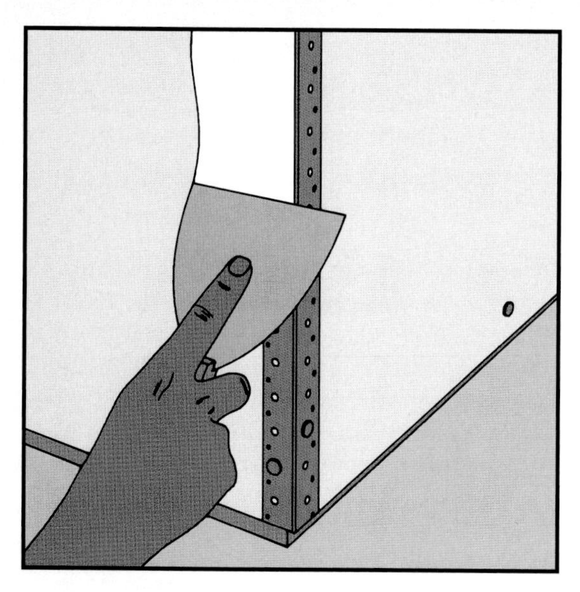

Covering a corner bead.

◆ Load the left two-thirds of a 5-inch knife with joint compound.
◆ With the right 2 inches of the knife overhanging the corner, run the knife down the left side of the bead *(left).*
◆ Load the right side of the knife and run it down the right side of the bead.
◆ Scrape the knife across the edge of a scrap of wood to clean it, then remove excess compound and smooth the joint by running the knife alternately down the left and right faces of the bead.
◆ Apply and smooth a second coat without letting the knife overhang the corner, feathering this layer about $1\frac{1}{2}$ inches beyond the first.
◆ Apply a third coat using an 8-inch knife to feather the compound an additional 2 inches on each side.
◆ Once the compound dries, sand or sponge it smooth.

APPLYING TAPE TO A FLAT JOINT

1. Applying joint compound.

When using fiberglass tape *(page 107),* skip this step and adapt the knife technique shown in Step 2 to stick the tape along the bare joint. A coat-hanger spindle, hooked to your belt, holds a roll of joint tape at the ready.
◆ Thin a batch of joint compound with a pint of water for every 5 gallons of compound, then load half the width of a 5-inch knife with the mix.
◆ Center the blade over the joint, cocking it slightly so the blade's loaded side is the leading edge, and smoothly run the knife along the joint *(right).* Hold the knife almost perpendicular to the wallboard at the start, but gradually angle it closer to the board as you draw it along the seam to fill the depression at the wallboard's tapered edges.

For an end-to-end joint, where the sheets do not have tapered edges, apply a $\frac{1}{8}$-inch-thick layer of compound.

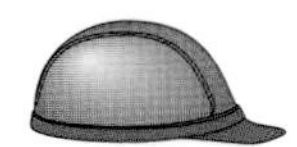

SAFETY TIPS

Goggles shield your eyes from dripping joint compound when you are working overhead. Always wear a dust mask when sanding joint compound.

2. Embedding paper tape.

◆ Press the end of the tape into the wet compound at one end of the joint.
◆ As you hold the tape over the joint with one hand, run the blade of a 5-inch knife along the joint with the other to force the tape into the compound *(left).* At the far end of the joint, use the knife as a straightedge in order to tear the tape.
◆ Run the knife along the joint a second time, pressing firmly to push the tape into the compound and to scrape off most of the excess compound.
◆ Then go over the tape a third time, pushing down on the knife to eliminate any air bubbles, and return the excess compound to the pan.

At an end-to-end joint, where the paper tape rides on the surface, do not scrape off excess compound completely. Leave a combined tape-and-compound thickness of about $\frac{1}{8}$ inch.

TAPING AN INSIDE CORNER

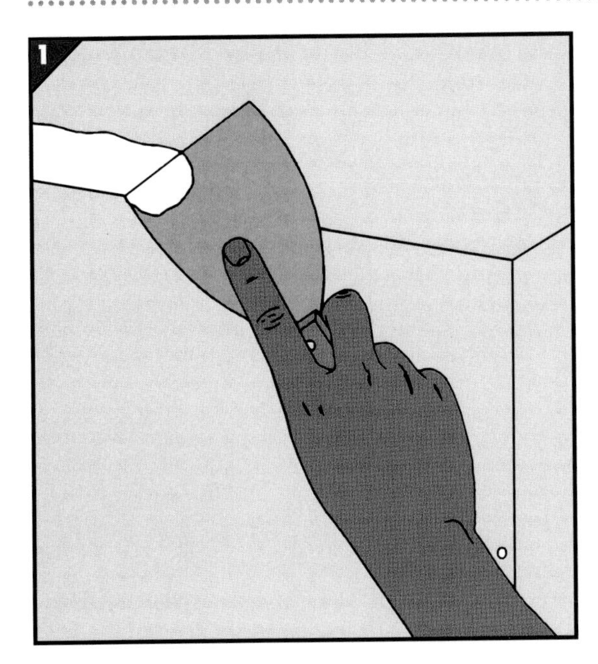

1. Applying the compound.
Fiberglass tape *(page 107)* requires no initial application of compound; simply crease the tape down the center and press it into the corner. To apply paper tape:
◆ Load half the width of a 5-inch knife with joint compound.
◆ Run the knife along one side of the corner joint, then the other, lifting the inside of the blade slightly to create a thicker layer of compound at the joint. Do not be concerned if you scrape off some of the compound on the first side while coating the second.

A corner trowel *(right)* has angled faces for applying joint compound to both sides of a corner at once.

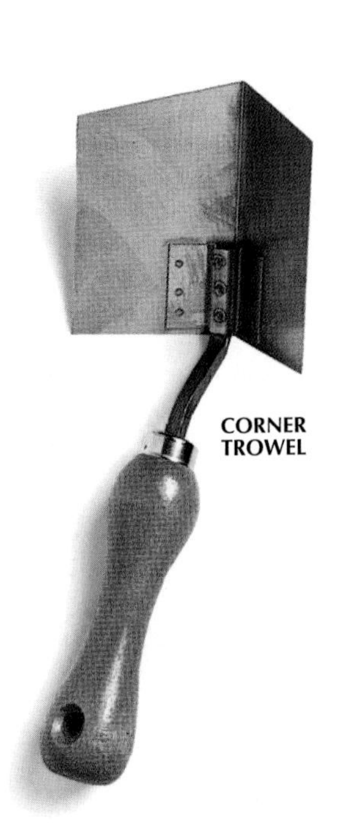

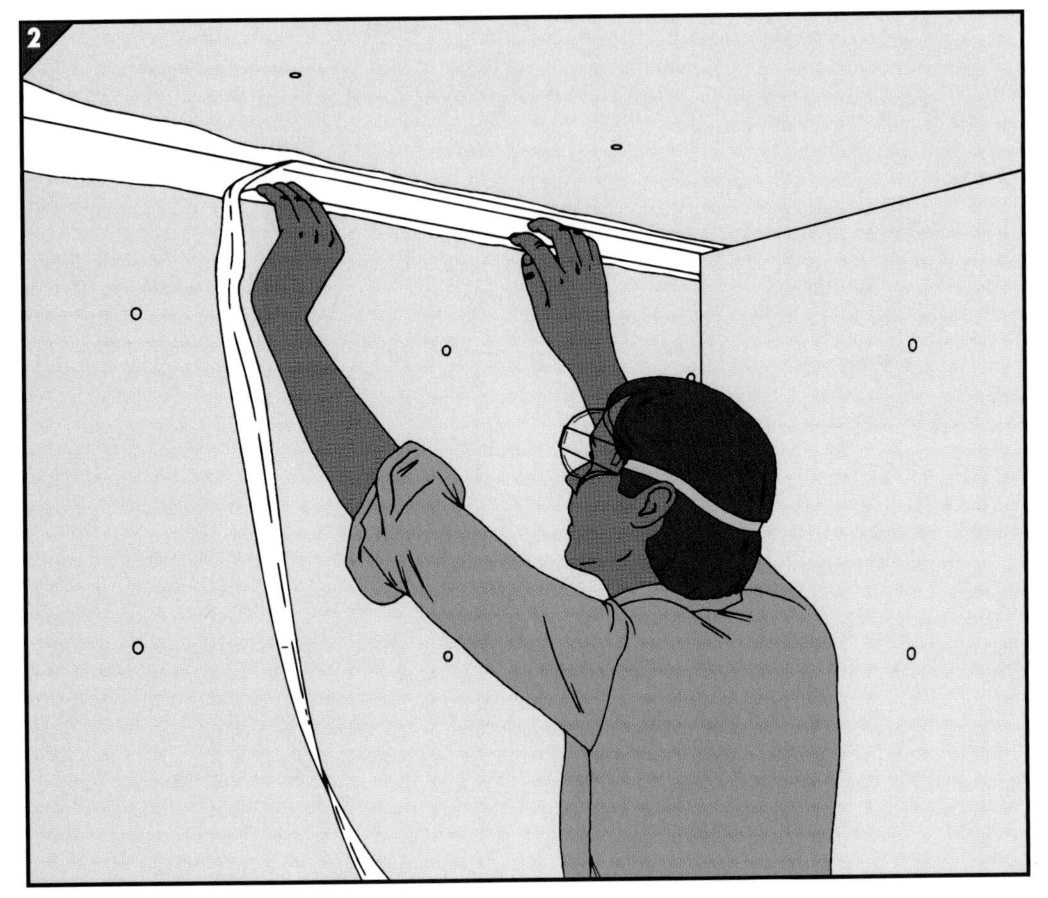

2. Embedding the tape.
◆ Fold the tape along its lengthwise crease line and press it lightly into the joint compound with your fingers.
◆ Run a 5-inch knife or corner trowel lightly along both sides of the crease, applying just enough pressure to make the tape stick to the compound. Then repeat, using more force to squeeze out excess compound.
◆ Finally, coat the tape lightly with some of the excess, and run the knife or trowel over it one last time, leaving a film of compound on the tape.

FEATHERING JOINT COMPOUND AT SEAMS

Completing a flat seam.
◆ For paper tape, thin the compound as described in Step 1 on page 108. With fiberglass tape, use the compound as it comes from the can.
◆ Load the full width of an 8-inch knife with joint compound and cover the tape with an even layer of the material.
◆ Clean the knife and draw it over this layer, holding the blade slightly off center and lifting the edge nearer the joint about $\frac{1}{8}$ inch. Do likewise on the other side of the joint to create a slight ridge that feathers out evenly on both sides.
◆ Let the compound dry and lightly sand or sponge it smooth.
◆ For paper tape, thin the compound with a quart of water for every 5 gallons and apply a final layer with two passes of a 12-inch knife: On the first pass, rest one edge of the knife blade on the center ridge and bear down on the other edge; on the second pass, repeat this procedure on the other side of the ridge.
◆ Let the compound dry and give it a final sanding or sponging.

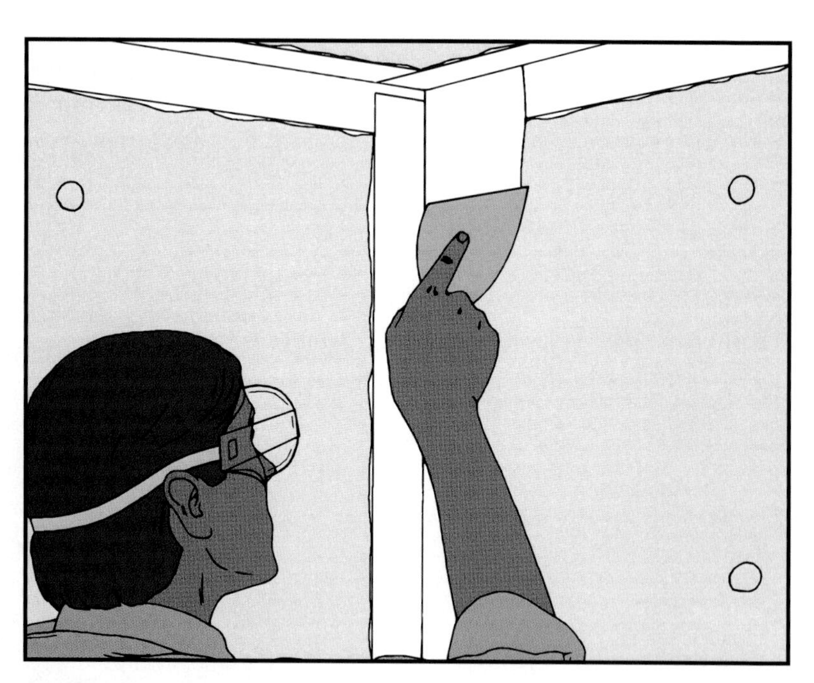

Feathering an inside corner.
For this procedure, thin the joint compound as you would for a flat seam *(above)*.
◆ Load the full width of a 5-inch knife with joint compound and spread an even layer of compound over one side of the corner.
◆ Scrape off any compound that laps onto the corner's second side, then draw the knife down the first side again, bearing down on the outside edge of the knife in order to feather the compound.
◆ Smooth this layer one more time, removing any excess and scraping off any compound that was left on the wall beyond the feathered edge.
◆ After the first side of the corner has finished drying, apply joint compound to the second side in the same fashion.
◆ Then repeat this procedure on both sides with an 8-inch wallboard knife.

An Arched Trowel to Speed the Work

A tool called a crown trowel, or wallboard trowel, makes it easy to create a ridge in the joint compound over a flat seam. With a $\frac{1}{8}$-inch curve to the blade, it creates a ridge along the wallboard seam with a single swipe, instead of the two passes required with a flat 8-inch knife. After this ready-made ridge dries, sand or sponge it, then apply the last layer of joint compound with a 12-inch wallboard knife as described above.

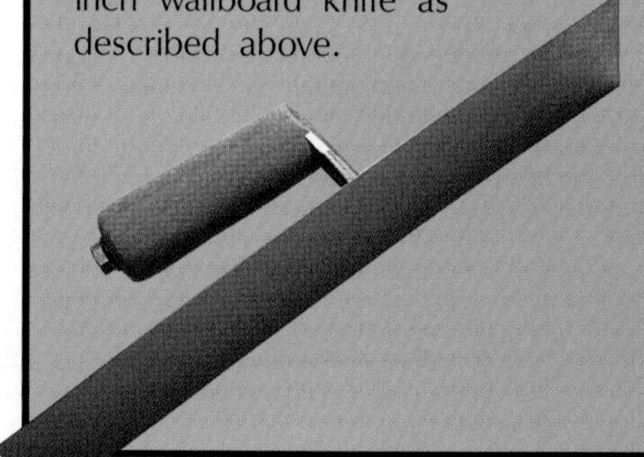

REPAIRING BALKY WINDOWS AND DOORS

Doors and windows are among the most vulnerable parts of a house: They are often exposed to the ravages of the weather; constant use wears out their hardware; and moisture and age cause them to warp, sag, and swell.

Balky Windows: Most older houses have double-hung windows. All too often the sashes bind or they are frozen shut by layers of paint. Or sash cords—especially the lower ones—break, resulting in windows that won't stay open. When replacing a broken cord on one side of a window, renew the other cord as well. If your windows have metal pulleys with wide grooves, you can replace the cords with indestructible metal sash chains.

Doors that Bind: When a door sticks or drags, first check for loose hinges. If the screw holes are stripped, glue in wood dowels and redrill the screw holes. Shimming the hinges or planing the door edge may be in order if the house has settled and the doorframe is no longer square. Where the frame is square but the door is not, you can realign the door.

Pocket doors, which disappear into walls and roll either on the floor or on overhead tracks, have special difficulties. Diagnosis of a problem is complicated by a bewildering variety of construction methods. If the repairs shown on pages 116 and 117 fail, the only solution is to remove a section of the wall to get at the trouble.

Working with Wood and Plaster: Moisture swells unsealed wood, so a sash or door planed in humid weather is likely to become loose during the winter. The best time to repair windows and doors is during a dry season; seal planed or sanded edges with paint or varnish as soon as possible after you fix the door.

When working with window or door casings or repairing a pocket door, remember that old materials are brittle. Remove wood moldings with care—they often can't be matched—and avoid jarring the walls, which could shake plaster loose from its lath.

TOOLS

- Window opener
- Hammer
- Pry bar
- 1" paint scraper
- Long-nose pliers
- Carpenter's nippers
- Wire brush
- Bar clamp
- Electric drill
- Drill bits ($\frac{5}{16}$" and $\frac{1}{2}$")
- Drum-rasp drill attachment
- Drill guide
- Mallet
- Wood chisel
- Screwdriver
- Block plane
- Jack plane
- Putty knife

MATERIALS

- Scrap lumber
- 2 x 4
- Sandpaper
- Paraffin
- Sash cord or chain
- Finishing nails ($1\frac{1}{4}$")
- Fluted dowels ($\frac{5}{16}$" and $\frac{1}{2}$")
- Wood glue
- Cardboard
- Metal washers
- Lipstick
- Plywood sheet
- Wood putty
- Metal screw eyes
- Heavy-gauge wire
- Wood screws ($1\frac{1}{2}$" No. 6)

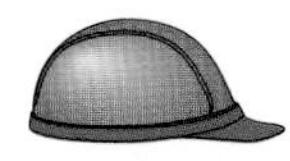

SAFETY TIPS

To protect against dust and splinters when repairing doors and windows, wear gloves and a dust mask. Add goggles when working at eye level or higher, or using a drum rasp.

LOOSENING A STUCK WINDOW

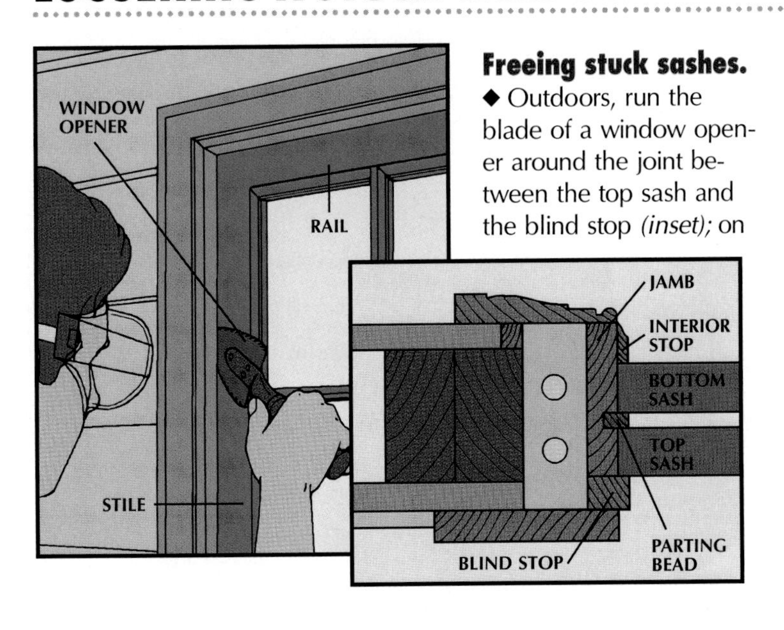

Freeing stuck sashes.

◆ Outdoors, run the blade of a window opener around the joint between the top sash and the blind stop *(inset);* on the bottom sash, insert the blade between the sash and the parting bead.

◆ Inside, run the window opener between the top sash and the parting bead, and between the bottom sash and the interior stop.

◆ If the bottom sash remains frozen, place a wood block at one end of the outside sill. Wedge a pry bar between the block and the rail, directly under the stile. Carefully pry the sash up, alternating from one side of the window to the other.

◆ On the top sash, carefully pry out the top blind stop. Wedge the pry bar between the top rail and a block of wood placed in the corner of the jamb, and pry the sash down.

CAUTION *Pry only at the ends of rails; pressure elsewhere could cause a windowpane to break.*

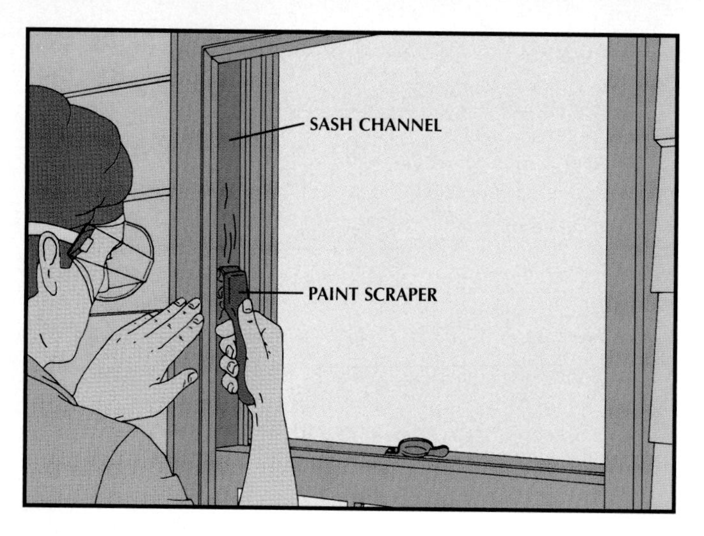

Easing a tight sash channel.
◆ Use a 1-inch paint scraper to pare paint and dirt from the sash channels, including the stops and parting bead.
◆ Sand the channels smooth, using a wood sanding block slightly narrower than the channel, then lubricate the channels with a block of household paraffin.

REPLACING SASH CORDS

1. Removing a bottom sash.
◆ Remove the interior stop on one side of the window.
◆ Raise the sash slightly and angle its side free of the jamb, then rest the sash on the window sill.
◆ Grip the knot in the end of the broken cord with long-nose pliers and pull it out of the sash.
◆ Untie the knot on the other side of the sash and set the sash aside.
◆ On a window with access plates *(inset),* remove the screws or nails that secure the plates and pry them out; if necessary, remove the parting bead to get at a plate. On a window without access plates, remove the casings that conceal the sash weights.
◆ Retrieve the weights from the bottom of the window frame and untie the cords.

If the window has interlocking weather stripping—the metal type that fits into a groove in the sash—remove it when you pull out the sash. To do so, raise the sash to the top of the frame and use carpenter's nippers to remove the nails that fasten the weather stripping track. Lower the sash and remove it—along with the weather stripping.

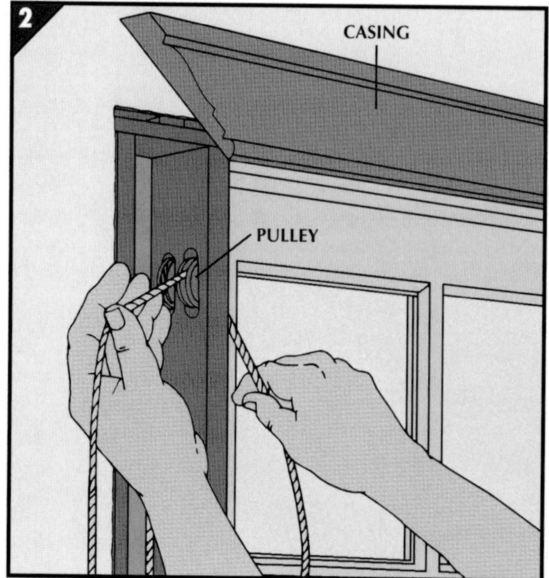

2. Threading new cords.
For a window with no access plate, knot a new cord to a counterweight at a point about 3 inches from one end of the cord. Feed the other end over the pulley *(left).* Repeat with the second cord.

For a window with access plates, tie a piece of string to a bent nail and feed the nail and string over the pulley until the nail appears at the access hole; then tie the other end of the string to the sash cord. Use the string to pull the cord down, and tie the cord to the weight. Repeat with the second cord.

3. Adjusting the cords.

◆ Set the sash on the sill.
◆ Thread the cord through its slot in the edge of the sash.
◆ Pull the cord to raise the weight to the pulley, then lower the weight about 2 inches. Knot the cord and trim it close to the knot.
◆ Repeat with the second cord.
◆ Set the sash in its channel, raise it to the top of the frame, and check that the weights are suspended about 2 inches from the bottom of the compartment. Adjust the cords as needed.
◆ Replace the casing or access plate, then fasten the stop with $1\frac{1}{4}$-inch finishing nails.

MAKING A DOOR FIT ITS JAMB

A door that scrapes the floor.

◆ For a two-knuckle hinge *(right),* lift the door off the hinge pins and slide washers onto the pins of both hinges.
◆ Experiment with washers of different thicknesses until the door no longer scrapes; the thickness of each set of washers should not exceed $\frac{1}{8}$ inch.
◆ For a hinge with interlocking knuckles and removable pins *(inset),* remove the screws fastening the lower hinge to the jamb, and wedge the bottom of the door up slightly.
◆ Cut a cardboard shim and slide it behind the hinge leaf.
◆ Experiment to find the correct shim thickness, then replace the screws.

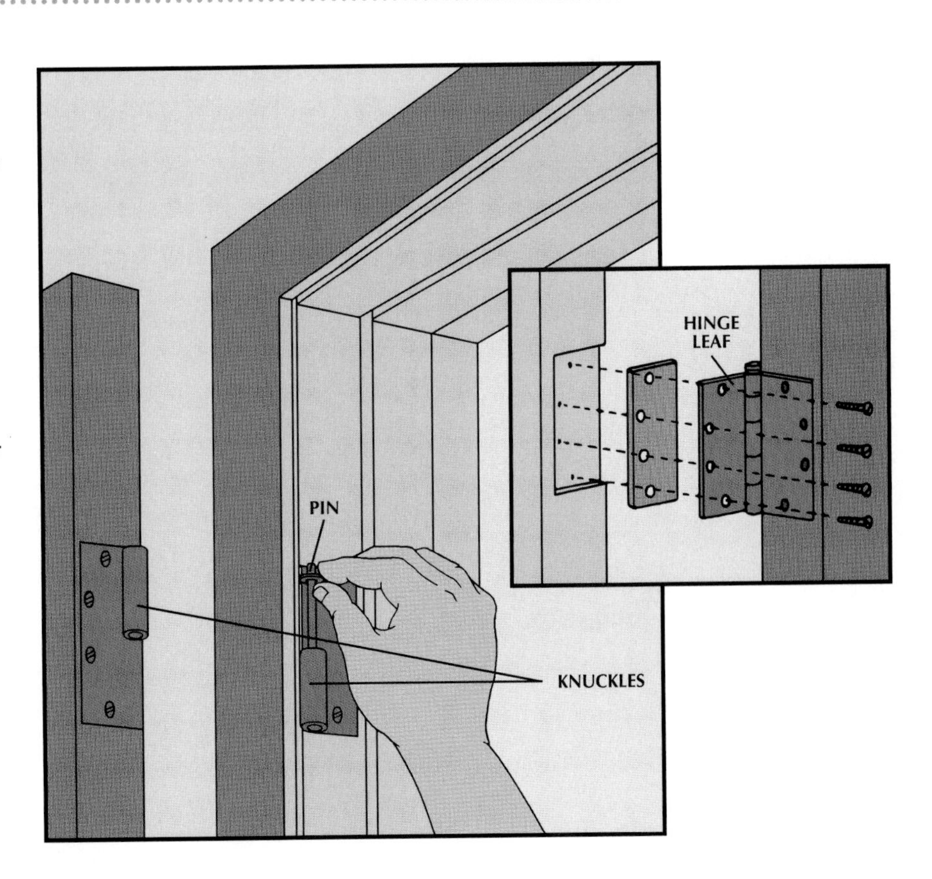

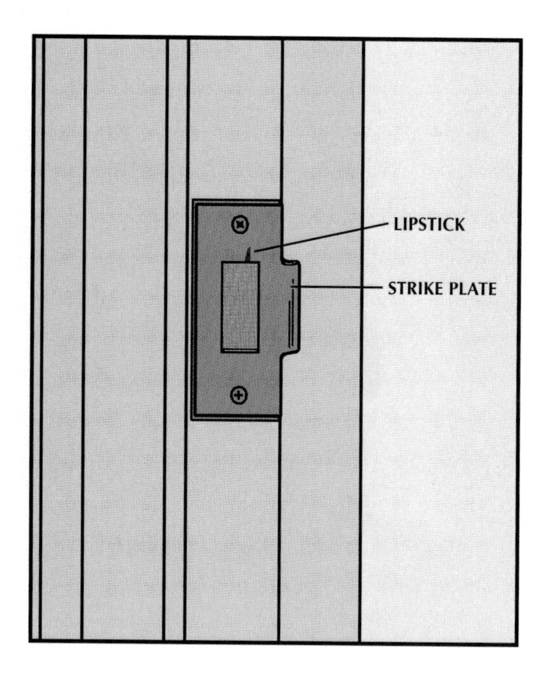

A door that will not latch.

◆ Cover the tip of the latch bolt with dark lipstick.
◆ With the doorknob turned to hold the latch bolt open, close the door, then release the knob. Turn the knob again to retract the bolt and open the door.
◆ If the imprint of the lipstick is more than $\frac{1}{4}$ inch out of line with the hole in the strike plate, remove the strike plate.
◆ Tape a piece of paper over the mortise, then repeat the steps above to mark the latch bolt's position on the paper.
◆ Align the strike plate with the imprint and mark around it for a new mortise and bolt hole, then enlarge the mortise and bolt hole with a wood chisel.
◆ Replace the strike plate and fill the exposed portions of the old mortise with wood filler.

If the imprint is less than $\frac{1}{4}$ inch off, clamp the strike plate in a vise and enlarge the strike opening with a file; do not enlarge the mortise.

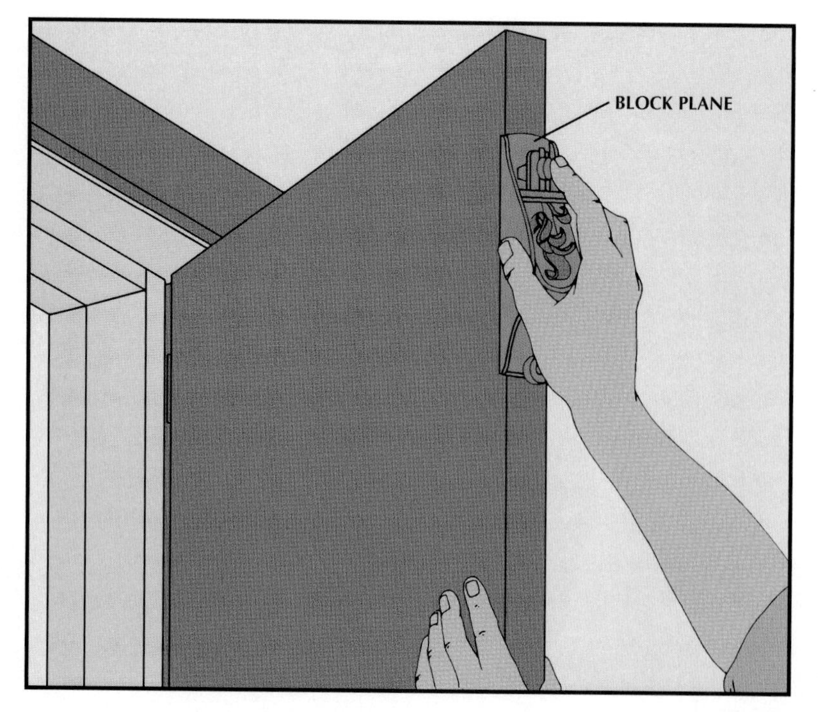

Freeing a door that binds.

For a minor problem, tap a wedge beneath the door to hold it open, then use a block plane to gradually pare the edge that binds, until the gap between the door and jamb is even.

◆ If an entire edge binds on the strike or hinge side, remove the door and unscrew the hinges.
◆ Mark a line $\frac{1}{8}$ inch from the hinge edge on both sides of the door and have a helper hold the door while you plane down to the lines with a jack plane.
◆ Test the fit of the door and mark any points that require additional planing.
◆ Widen the hinge mortises before reattaching the hinges, then rehang the door.

CAUTION *To avoid splintering when planing the top or bottom of a door, always work from a corner toward the center.*

QUICK FIXES FOR PORCELAIN KNOBS

A variety of knob repairs.

To tighten a porcelain knob that is loose on its metal stem, force a small amount of epoxy glue into the joint between the porcelain and the stem with a toothpick *(right)*.

If the screws that hold the knob to the cam are missing or worn, replace them with new screws of the same size.

Take dried paint off by covering the surrounding metal with masking tape, then wiping the knob with a paint remover. Work outdoors if good ventilation is called for.

Apply porcelain touch-up paint, found in hardware stores, to obvious chips. Sand the chipped area with fine emery cloth, brush on a thin coat of paint, let it dry, and sand again. Build up the paint in layers until the cavity is filled.

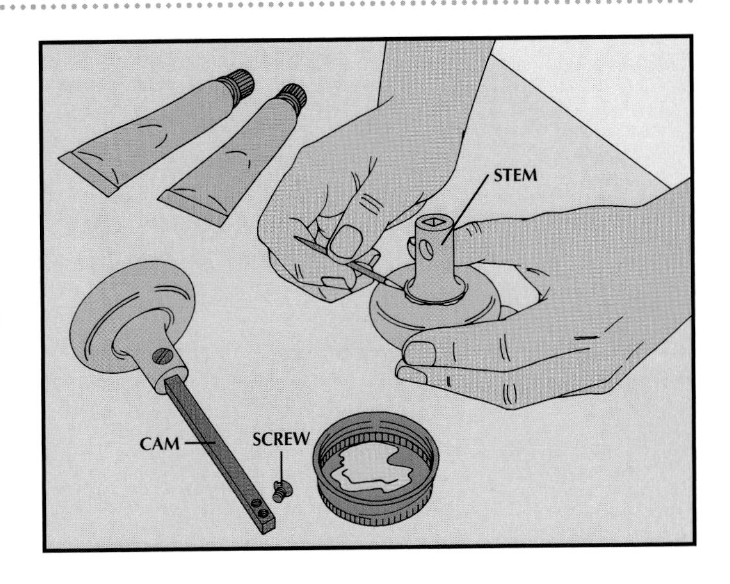

REFURBISHING INTERIOR DOOR LOCKS

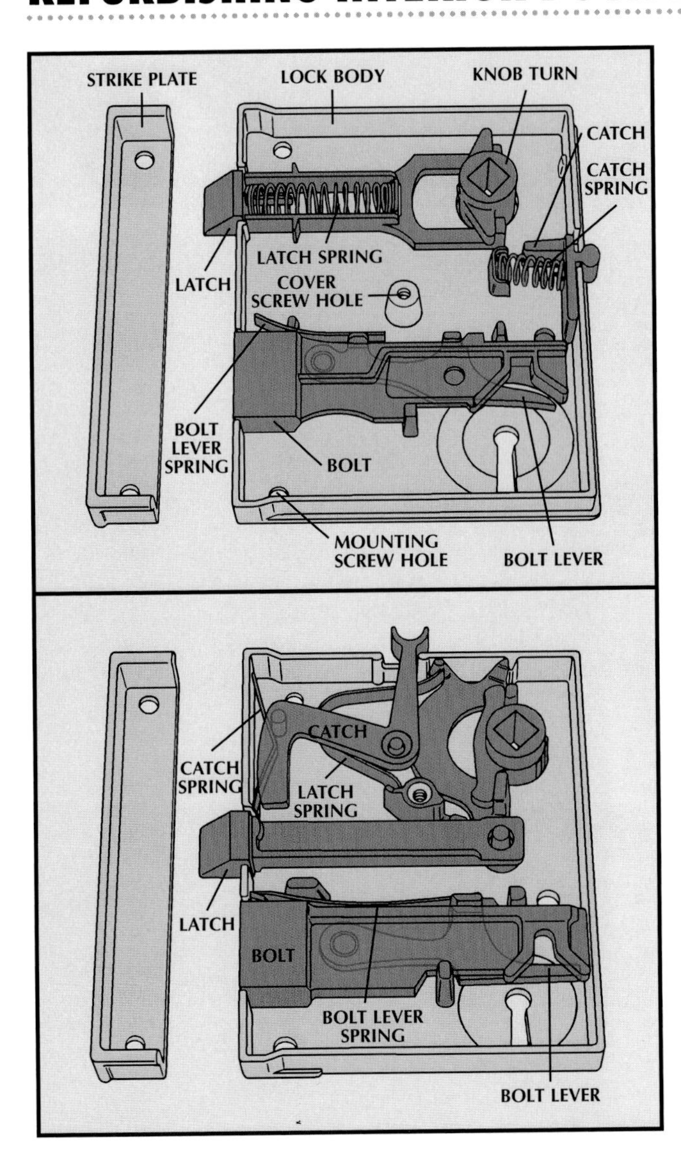

Two interior rim locks.

Surface-mounted door locks were common in old houses and often are an antique feature worth preserving. The locks illustrated at left are mounted so that their strike plates are on the rim of the jamb and their bodies on the door face. Clean or repair them as follows:

◆ Remove the knob, then detach the lock body from the door by taking out the mounting screws.

◆ Set the lock on a flat surface. With a cloth covering your hand and the lock to catch springs that may pop out, unscrew the central screw that holds the cover in place.

◆ Sketch or photograph the lock. If you have two locks, leave one assembled as you clean the other.

◆ Without disturbing the parts, look for any that are broken, misaligned, or missing. In particular, locate and check the condition of three springs, which may be flat or coiled. One presses against the bolt lever and is operated by the door key. Another holds the latch extended. The third, a catch spring, provides tension for a small catch that can lock the latch in place.

◆ Remove all the parts of the lock. Have a locksmith replace any broken or missing springs. Other metal parts may be more difficult to replace or repair. A bent bolt can sometimes be straightened in a vise, but the force may break the bolt.

◆ Bathe the strike plate, body, latch, and bolt in paint remover, lightly lubricate all moving parts, and reassemble the lock.

A PRIMER ON POCKET DOORS

Diagnosing problems.
Typical pocket doors ride on grooved metal wheels along a track on the floor or overhead. Inside the wall, the doors fit into pockets framed by narrow studs. The top of the door fits between stop moldings *(inset, top);* in some, wood pegs fit in a grooved track to hold the door in line. Double pocket doors have a center stop screwed to the edges of the jamb *(inset, bottom)* to keep doors from sliding past the middle of the opening.

Over time, bits of plaster may pile up in the pockets and can be swept or vacuumed out. A floor track within the opening may be dented or crushed and can be bent back into shape with pliers. Fixing other problems requires removing the doors. For instance, the studs in the pockets sometimes warp and bind the door, or the rollers at the bottom of the door may break. Matching rollers are no longer manufactured; look for replacements in secondhand shops, or improvise new sets from large window pulleys.

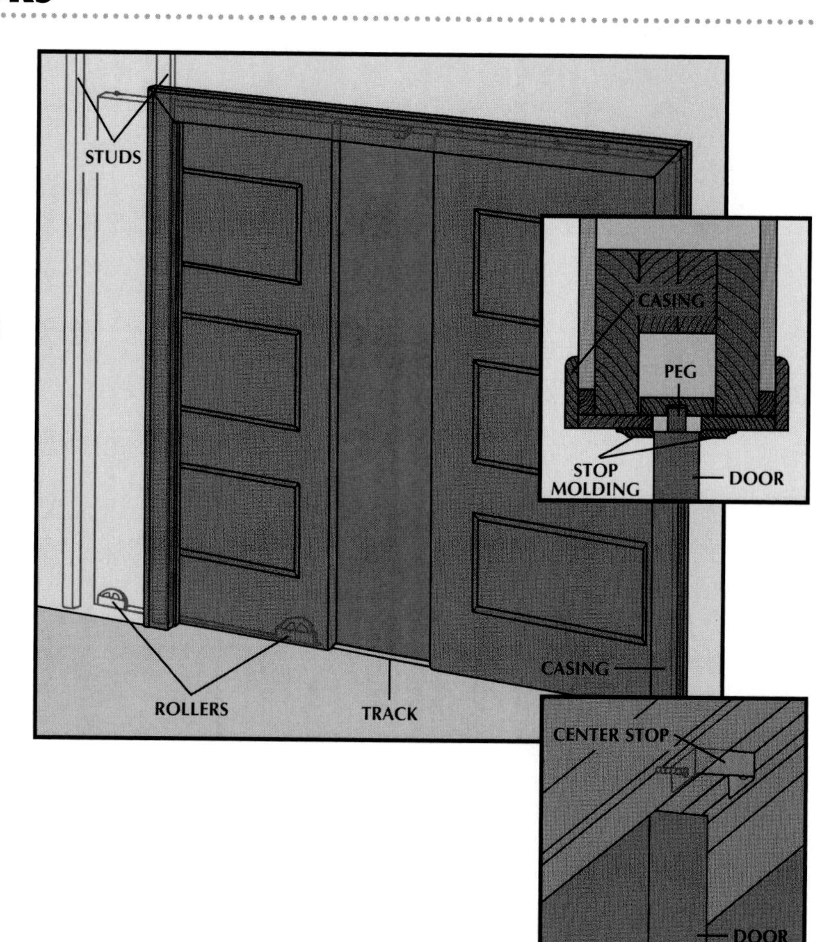

Fixing doors suspended from above.
Some pocket doors hang from overhead rollers that you can adjust if the door begins to scrape the floor. To do so, first move the door to the center of the opening. Then tap shims beneath it to lift it $\frac{1}{4}$ inch from the floor, and use a screwdriver or a nutdriver to tighten the adjustment screws on the rollers at each end of the door. If the adjustment screws are not visible at the ends—or if the door has a third roller between the outer ones—remove one of the top casings to expose the screws.

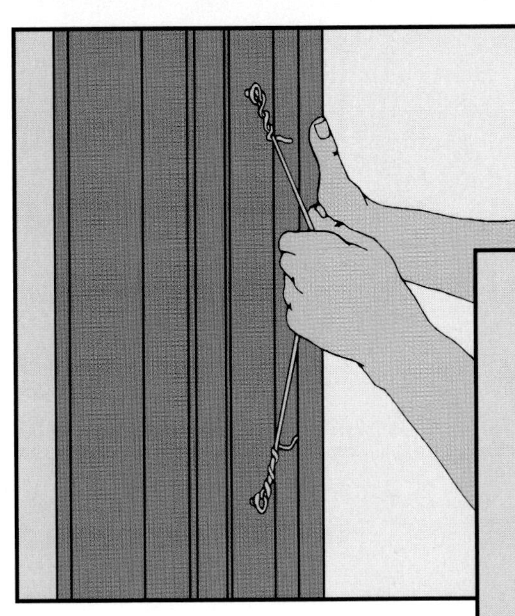

Retrieving a jammed door.

◆ Fasten metal screw eyes into the edge of the door, about 4 feet above the floor and a foot apart.

◆ Run a loop of heavy wire between them, and use the wire as a handle to drag the door out of its pocket.

Removing a door from its frame.

◆ For a double door, unscrew the center stop and slide the door to the middle of the opening, then pry off the stop molding on one side of the top jamb. For a single door, pry off the stop molding on one side of the top jamb, and remove the casing, jamb, and stop on that side as well *(opposite, top).*

◆ With a helper, lift the door off its bottom track and gradually slide the bottom of the door sideways until the top of the door is free.

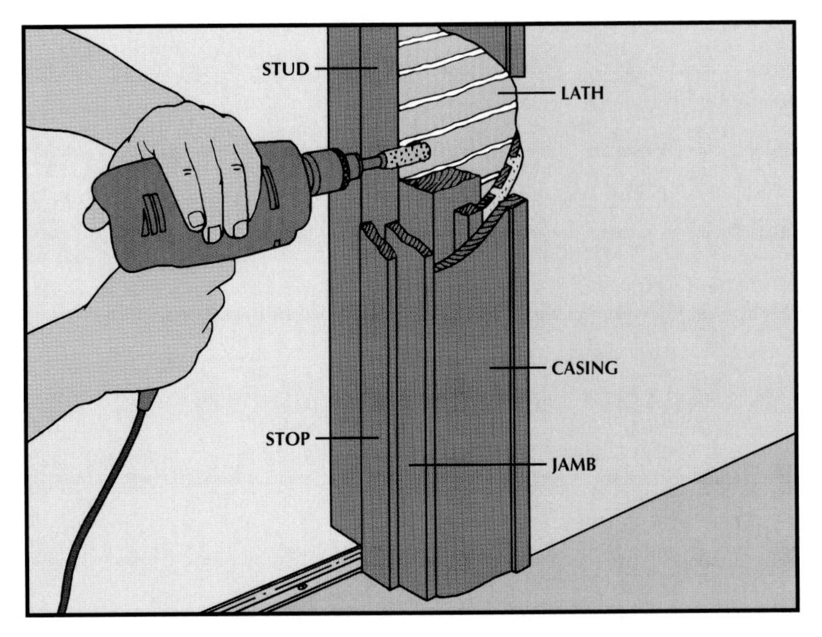

Curing doors that bind.

◆ If you have not already done so to dismount the door, pry off the casing, jamb, and stop on one side of the door.

◆ Probe inside the pocket with a piece of scrap wood as wide as the door, and note where the scrap binds.

◆ Wearing goggles and working from the middle of the stud toward the top and bottom, shave away about $\frac{1}{8}$ inch of wood with an electric drill fitted with a drum-rasp attachment; move the drill slowly and apply a light, steady pressure.

If studs at the back of the pocket are warped, break through the plaster and lath between studs to get at them, then adapt the procedure shown on pages 99 and 100 to patch the hole.

4 CHAPTER

INTERIOR PAINTING

Like putting on a new suit or dress, painting a room can make a dramatic change in its overall look. Whether your aim is to restore a room to its original elegance in an old house or to completely transform and update it, a new coat of paint on properly prepared walls, ceilings, and woodwork is by far the most important—and often the only necessary—step.

Modern nonlead paints are far superior to those of earlier years. The colors are virtually fadeproof, their surfaces do not powder, chalk, or flake, and they are almost universally washable. Water-base paints make painting especially easy. There is little or no odor and they can be rolled on in less than half the time required for brush application. Best of all, no volatile thinners or cleaners are required—everything cleans up with water.

In this chapter you'll find out how to paint the interior of your home with the greatest ease and efficiency, including how to choose exactly the right tools for your job, how to prepare all kinds of surfaces, and how to paint a room in the proper sequence, with special techniques for windows, doors, and louvers.

GULF

△ *Above:* Think about color relationships from room to room when you paint the interior. You can choose a palette of different but harmonizing colors to give individual rooms character and tie several rooms together visually.

▷ *Right:* An old house presents a clean slate for redecorating, but features such as trim, chair rail moldings, and fireplaces present painting challenges. Proper preparation and following the correct painting sequence are the keys to excellent results.

◁ *Left:* Louvered shutters and doors are not hard to paint when you use the proper technique. You may want to take them down to make painting the adjoining trim easier.

▽ *Below:* Paint trim—woodwork and moldings—with a brush after doing the ceiling and walls. A contrasting color creates a rich effect.

▷ *Right:* Bold color can be a striking background for the display of colorful objects. Use white for effective contrast without color conflict. Cut in the edges with a brush before painting the large areas.

A TOOL KIT FOR INTERIOR PAINTING

Like most jobs, painting requires a variety of tools and materials. General-purpose items—such as a hammer, a screwdriver, a sturdy knife, a can opener, and masking tape—you probably already have on hand. For cleaning up, you'll need rags and metal containers such as coffee cans or loaf pans.

You may, however, need to purchase many of the tools that are shown here, as well as other items. Buy drop cloths to protect both furniture and floors from paint drips and spatters. You'll also need a sanding block and several grades of sandpaper to smooth repairs to walls and woodwork, and a sponge to clean up dust and dirt and to wash down previously painted walls. As an auxiliary container for paint, a medium-size rustproof pail is ideal.

Appropriate protective gear includes rubber gloves, goggles, and a dust mask. A respirator may be necessary with some toxic paint removers.

Tools for repairing surfaces.
For patching wallboard, plaster, and trim before painting, you will need both stiff- and flexible-blade putty knives, and a wide-blade putty knife for taping wallboard. Extensive filling of joints around trim and baseboards requires a caulking gun.

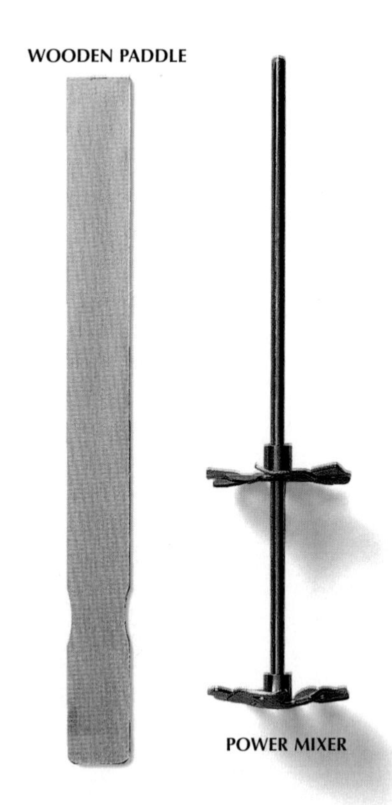

Mixing tools.
Paint must be stirred thoroughly to cover surfaces evenly. For small quantities, wooden paddles are satisfactory, but a power mixer driven by an electric drill works faster, especially when blending large quantities.

ROLLER TRAY AND GRATING

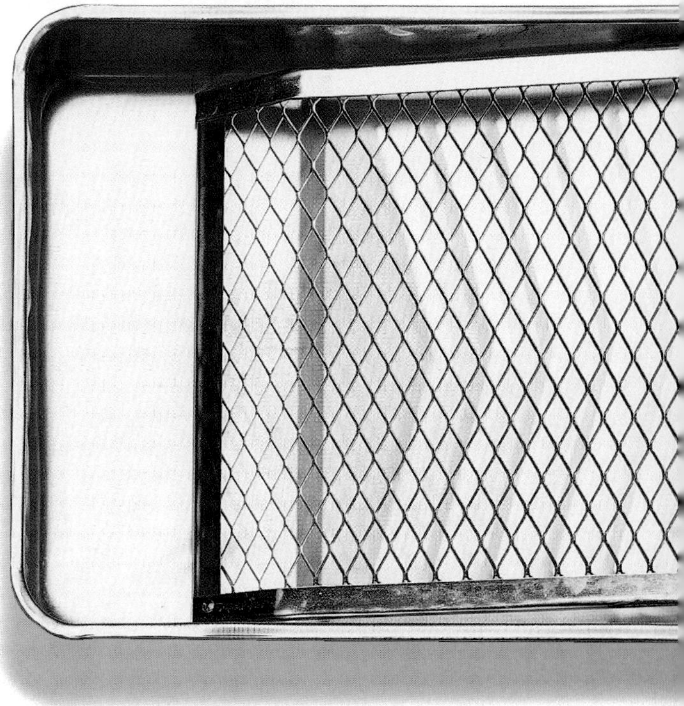

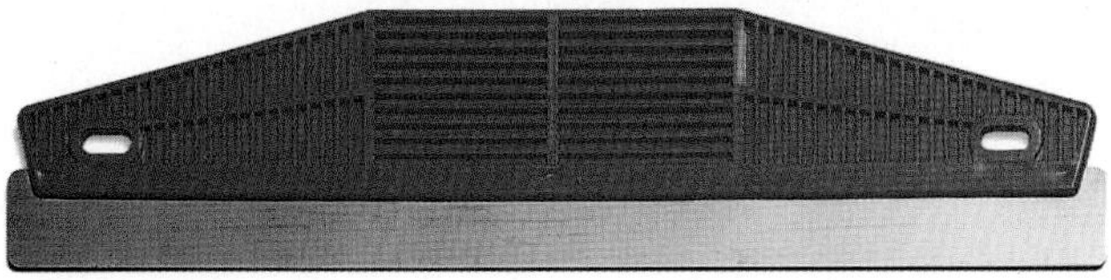

PAINT SHIELD

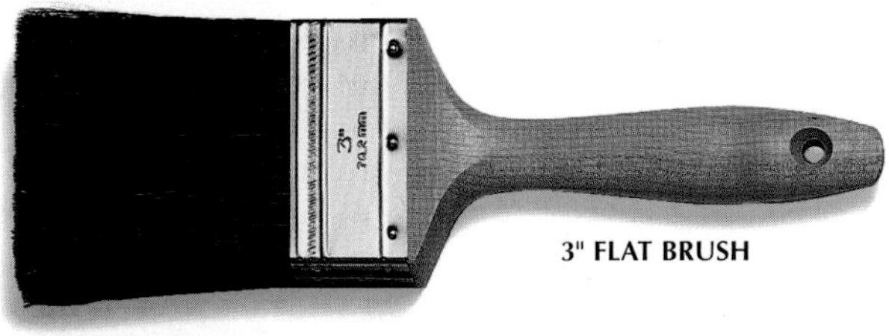

3" FLAT BRUSH

2" CHISEL-EDGE BRUSH

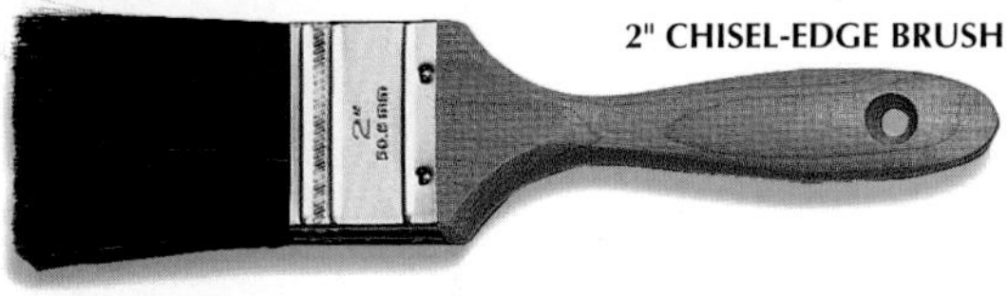

ANGULAR SASH BRUSH

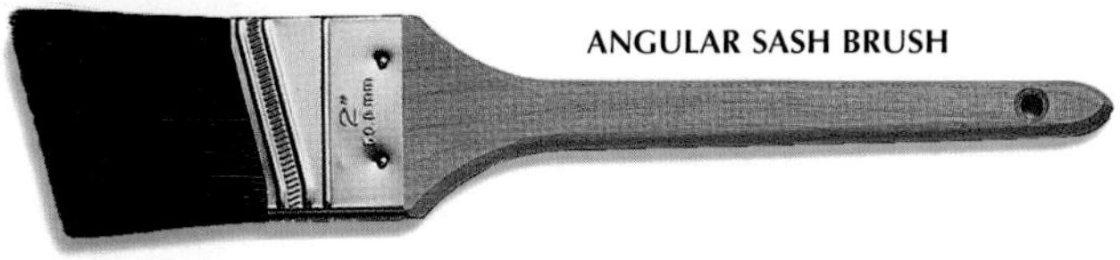

OVAL SASH BRUSH

9" SPRING ROLLER FRAME AND HANDLE

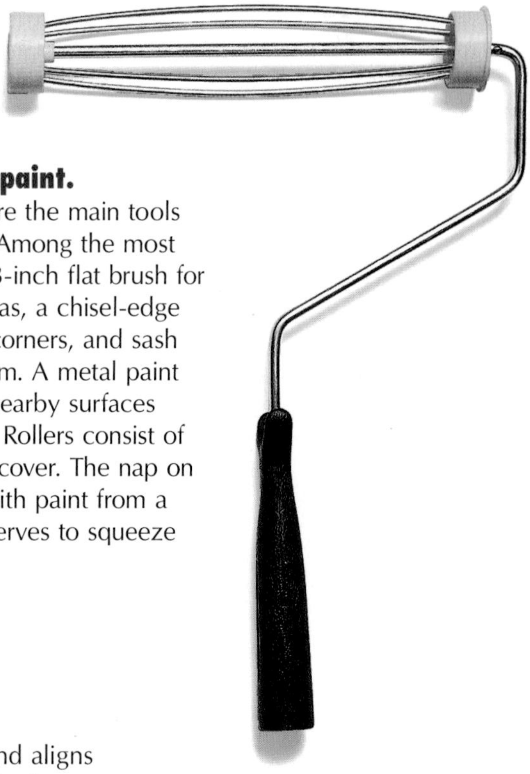

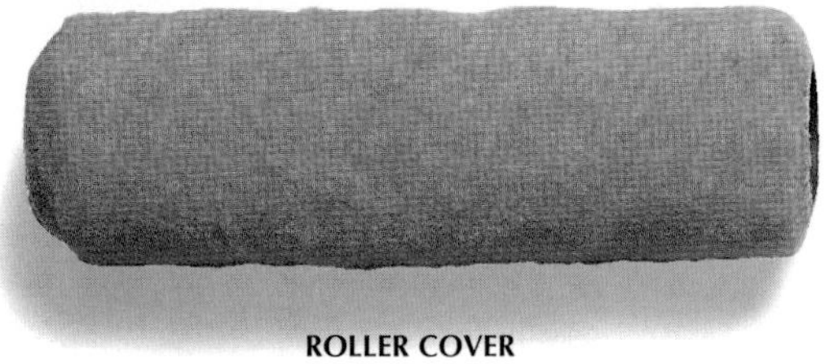

ROLLER COVER

Tools for applying paint.
Rollers and brushes are the main tools for painting interiors. Among the most useful brushes are a 3-inch flat brush for wide trim and flat areas, a chisel-edge brush for edges and corners, and sash brushes for narrow trim. A metal paint shield helps protect nearby surfaces from an errant brush. Rollers consist of a spring frame and a cover. The nap on the cover is loaded with paint from a roller tray; a grating serves to squeeze out excess paint.

WINDOW SCRAPER

PAINTBRUSH COMB

Cleanup tools.
This paintbrush comb cleans and aligns brush bristles and has a curved edge to scrape paint from rollers. The spin-drier slings solvent from rollers and brushes to help dry them. To peel dried paint from glass, use a window scraper.

SPIN-DRIER

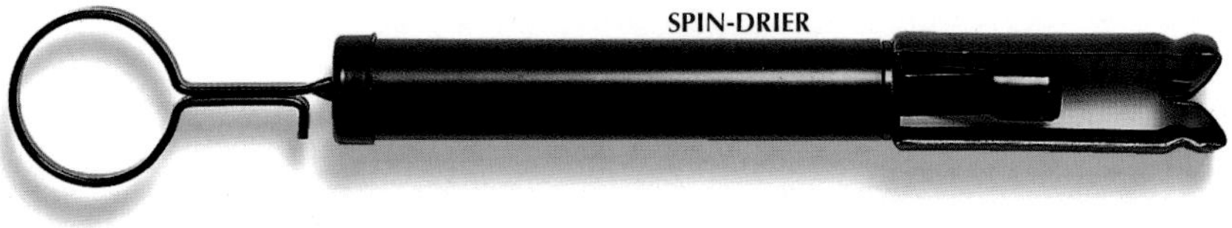

REACHING WALLS AND CEILINGS

For most interior painting and other work a stepladder *(below, left)* is highly useful. A folding sectional ladder *(page 24)* is even more versatile. To work on a large area without having to move your ladder every few feet, you can bend a sectional ladder into a low scaffold and lay planks on it. Or you can improvise a scaffold by putting doubled 2-by-12 planks or, preferably, scaffolding planks between the steps of two stepladders set no more than 6 feet apart.

A single straight ladder—perhaps one section of an extension ladder *(page 25)*—is useful reaching for extra-high walls or ceilings. Put rubber ladder shoes over the feet to protect finish flooring and prevent slipping, but never set the feet on a drop cloth. You can also use a straight ladder and a stepladder to make a work platform over a stairwell *(below, right)*. Whatever ladders you use, never set one up in front of a closed, unlocked door; either lock the door or open it.

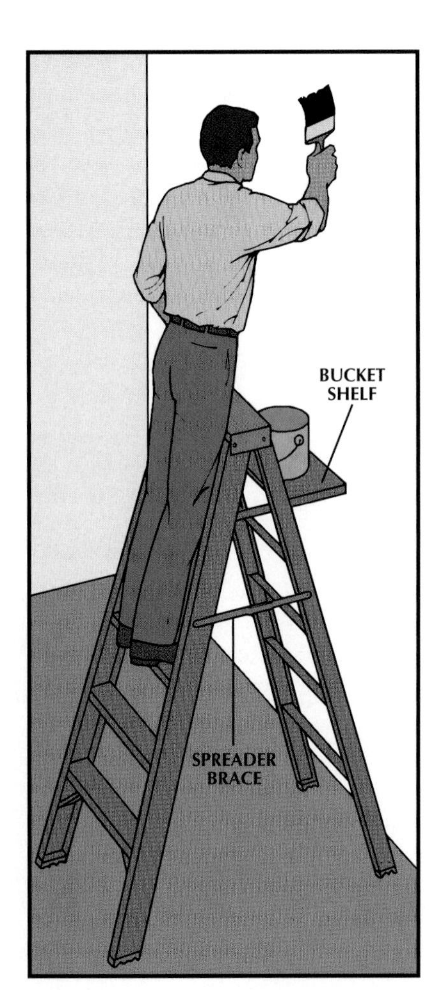

The versatile stepladder.

◆ Open the ladder to its fullest extent, lock its spreader braces into place, and push the bucket shelf down as far as it will go.

◆ Place the four legs on level ground or a level floor.

◆ Mount the ladder one step at a time, always facing the ladder and holding onto upper steps—not the side rails—with both hands as you climb.

◆ Don't stand above the second-highest step of a stepladder, and never try to support yourself by leaning or stepping on the bucket shelf.

A platform for a stairwell.

To paint the ceiling and walls above a staircase, fashion a platform from a straight ladder, a stepladder, and scaffold planks. Protect the wall above the stairwell by fitting the ladder rails with foam-rubber protectors.

◆ Place the straight ladder on the staircase and lean it against the wall.

◆ Set the stepladder at the top of the stairs.

◆ Lay the planking on a lower rung of the stepladder and on whichever rung of the straight ladder makes the planks level, or nearly so.

PREPARING INTERIOR SURFACES

The durability of any paint job depends largely on the care with which you have prepared the surfaces before you apply the paint.

For virgin wallboard, plaster, or wood, first dust the surface thoroughly, then brush a coat of primer on surfaces that you plan to paint. Check the finish paint instructions for primer information.

If you are working with finished surfaces, try to ascertain whether the material beneath the finish is wallboard or plaster, and the type of surface covering that was used. Such information will determine how you proceed with preparation treatments and will help you to select the proper undercoatings, primers, and paints. Next, inspect the room thoroughly for damage that may call for repairs.

Dealing with Old Paint: Check for blistering, cracking, or peeling paint and scrape it off *(page 130, top)* or remove it with a nylon paint stripper disk fitted to an electric drill. If it is necessary for you to remove many layers of paint, consider using a heat gun *(page 128)*. When the damaged paint is near window glass, strip it with a chemical paint remover *(page 126)* rather than risk breaking the glass with a power tool.

Concealing Flaws: Repair damaged wallboard or plaster *(pages 92–100)*, and fill in gouges, holes, and cracks in walls and trim. When choosing a filler, read the label to be sure the product is compatible with the finish you plan to use. Build up depressions and conceal nails with spackling compound. Use the same material to repair short open joints; longer gaps—along a baseboard, for example—are better caulked than patched with spackling compound.

On surfaces that are bare and those that have been painted, follow repair work with a thorough sanding. Electric sanders speed the work, but for small areas, a sanding block works well *(page 129)*.

Special Surfaces: New paint will not adhere properly to glossy surfaces; dull such finishes by raising a nap with sandpaper or a liquid deglosser. Strip off wallpaper or prepare it for painting. If floor wax has adhered to baseboards, take it off with wax remover. Brush rust from radiators, pipes, and heat ducts, and clean mildew from damp places. Interior brick and garage and basement surfaces require special preparations.

Cleaning: Dirt, grease, and even fingerprints can prevent new paint from adhering firmly. A good washing down with a heavy-duty household detergent just before painting will usually suffice for finished walls and woodwork. Finally, be sure that surfaces are completely dry before painting.

CAUTION *Paint strippers, solvents, and cleaning agents can give off harmful fumes. Follow the advice in the box on page 133.*

TOOLS

- Putty knives (flexible- and stiff-blade)
- Inexpensive paintbrush
- Sharp knife
- Long-nose pliers
- Nail set
- Hammer

MATERIALS

- Sandpaper (fine- and medium-grit)
- Spackling compound
- Wood putty
- Wood filler
- Primer
- Paint remover
- Paint solvent
- Shellac
- Caulk
- Wallpaper primer-sealer

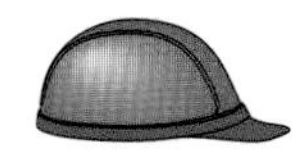

SAFETY TIPS

Protect your hands from cleaning agents and paint solvents. Wear rubber gloves and goggles to apply paint remover, and add a respirator if the product contains methylene chloride. When sanding, wear a dust mask.

CHOOSING THE RIGHT STRIPPER

Use this chart after determining the quality and condition of the wood in your interior trim. If you wish to strip fine hardwood bare, use a paint remover, chosen from the first three agents in the first column. To remove some but not all of the paint on softwood trim, consider a heat gun *(page 128)*. To clean old trim, choose from the last two entries.

A STRIPPER OR CLEANSER FOR EVERY JOB

Stripping Agent	Use	Remarks
Paint Removers		
Water-base (various formulations)	Effective on lacquers, varnishes, polyurethane, and oil-base and latex paints. Better than other removers at extracting paint from deep wood pores.	Nonflammable, nontoxic, relatively little odor. Products based on dibasic esters (DBE) may require up to 12 hours to work.
Methylene chloride	Removes lacquers, varnishes, polyurethane, oil-base paints, and thin layers of latex paint.	Nonflammable, powerful, works in minutes, still preferred by many professionals. Noxious fumes; requires extremely good ventilation. Suspected carcinogen.
Methanol, toluol, acetone mix	Works on heavy layers of latex-base and oil-base paints, lacquer, varnishes, and water-base stains.	Flammable; use with special caution.
Partial Strippers and Cleansers		
Heat gun	Removes built-up paint layers.	Useful when wood is to be repainted; will not fully clean wood surface; requires some chemical cleanup; some risk of scorching wood.
Denatured alcohol	Dissolves shellac.	Can be diluted with lacquer thinner to cut back rather than remove the finish.
Ammoniated cleansers, trisodium phosphate (TSP), sodium metasilicate	Partially removes shellac, varnish, and water-base stains.	Can be diluted with hot water to vary strength; sodium metasilicate is a nonphosphate alternative to TSP.

WORKING WITH PAINT REMOVERS

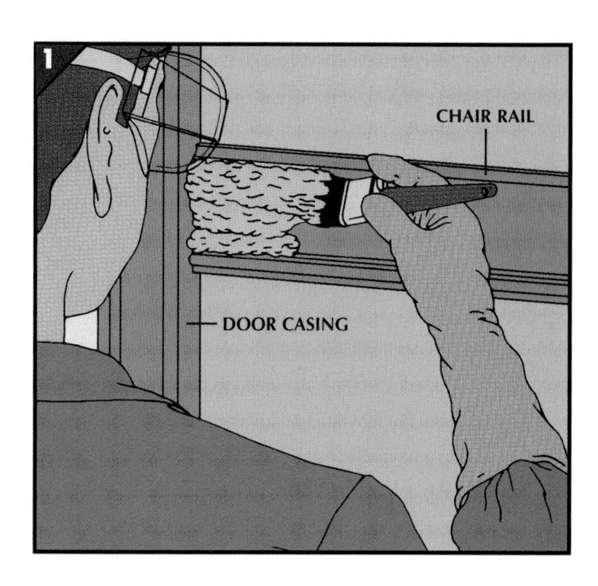

1. Applying the remover.
◆ Open the windows; protect the floor and other surfaces with cardboard. (Plastic sheets may melt.) Have scraping tools assembled and ready for use.
◆ Brush paint remover onto the wood with short strokes in one direction *(right)*. Back-and-forth brushwork would damage the chemical's bond with the finish.
◆ Let the remover stand for the length of time specified by the manufacturer, liquefying the paint into a sludge.
◆ Scrape the wood clean with a wide-blade putty knife whose sharp corners have been filed round. The sludge should come off the wood in a continuous ribbon; if it does not, brush on another coat of the paint remover and wait for a few more minutes before scraping.

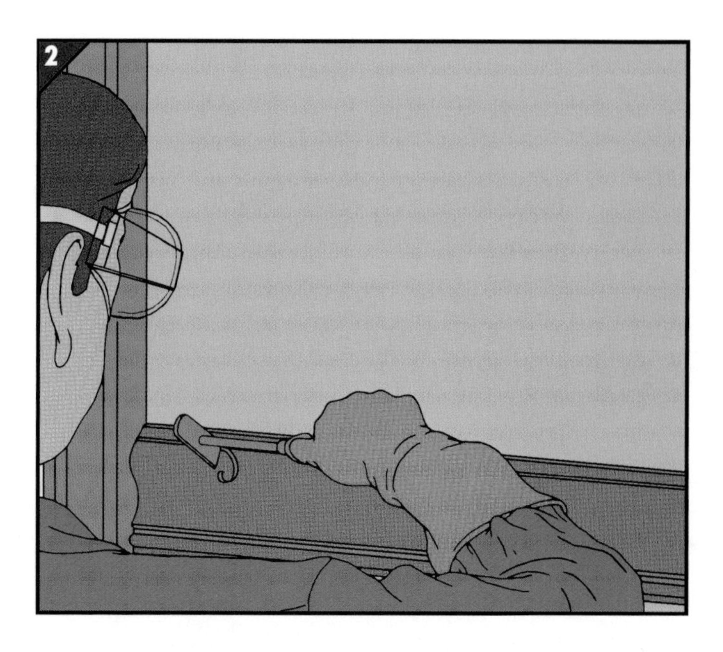

2. Cleaning contours.
◆ For grooves and corners that cannot be reached with a wide-blade putty knife, use a scraping tool with a contour as close as possible to the trim you must clean. A molding scraper, which has interchangeable blades that fit most common molding shapes, is one choice; see the box below for others.
◆ For multiple layers of paint, you may need to apply the paint remover again, waiting and then scraping as before.
◆ After the woodwork has been stripped, rinse it with the solution recommended by the manufacturer. Most paint removers can be rinsed with plain water or detergents, but some require a special neutralizer. Rub the rinse along the grain with a plastic stripping pad.

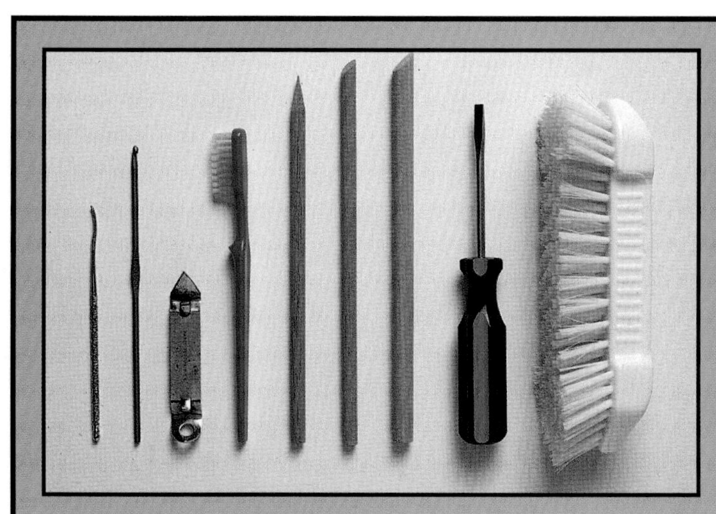

Improvised Scraping Tools

TRICKS OF THE TRADE

Instead of buying special scraping tools to strip paint, you can adapt household items to the job. Some tried and true implements include nutpicks, crochet hooks, church key can openers, old toothbrushes, screwdrivers, hand brushes, and dowels sawed off or sharpened like a pencil.

SPECIAL TOOLS FOR TAKING OFF PAINT

Using a heat gun.

◆ Cover the floor and other surfaces to avoid scarring by hot paint flakes.

◆ Set the heat output at High, or at 700°F if there are temperature settings.

◆ Move the heat gun slowly back and forth, holding it 2 to 4 inches away from the surface of the molding, until the paint begins to bubble up from the wood.

◆ If the paint does not bubble within a few seconds, raise the temperature, but always work evenly to avoid scorching the wood.

◆ Scrape the paint away with the same tools you would use with a chemical paint remover *(page 127)*.

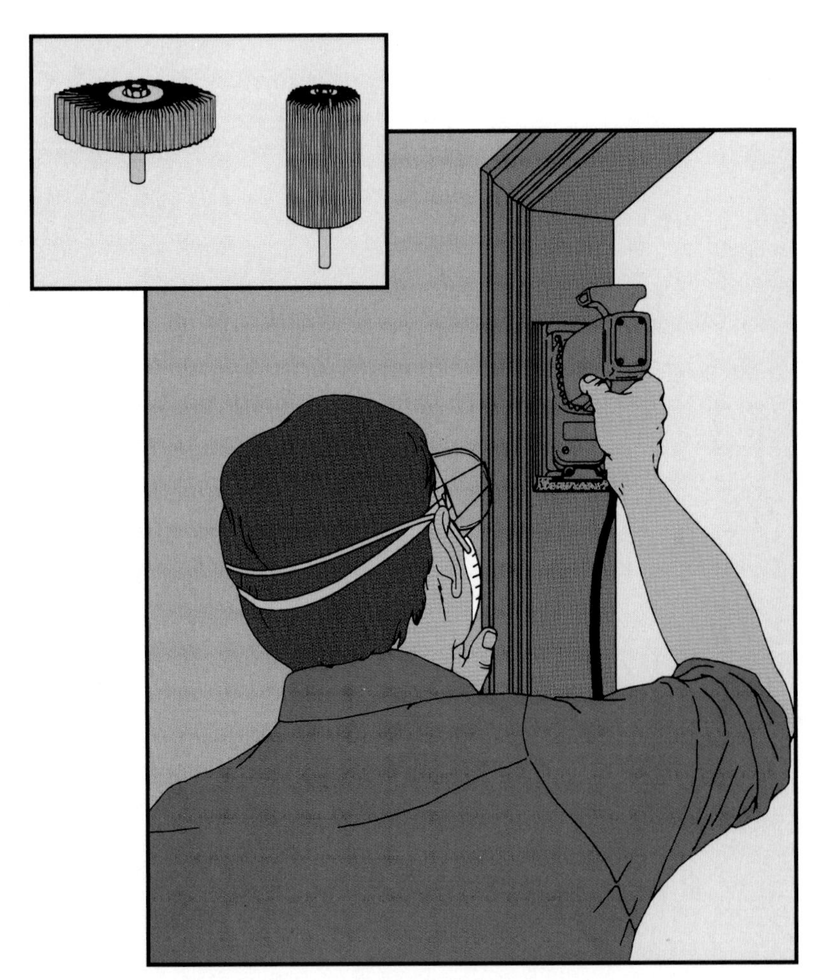

Finishing the job with a sander.

Sand away any remaining paint, adapting your method to each type of surface as follows:

Flat molding: Use an orbital sander and medium-grit sandpaper to sand traces of finish off flat molding *(left)*. Then sand by hand back and forth with fine sandpaper. Follow along the wood grain to remove any swirl marks.

Rounded surfaces: Sand these with an electric drill fitted with a large flexible-flap sanding wheel or a smaller flapped sanding drum *(inset)*; both are widely available at hardware stores. Do not use a wheel with wire flaps.

Small, concave areas: Glue a layer of felt around a small dowel, then hold sandpaper around it to form a sanding block.

SANDING TECHNIQUES

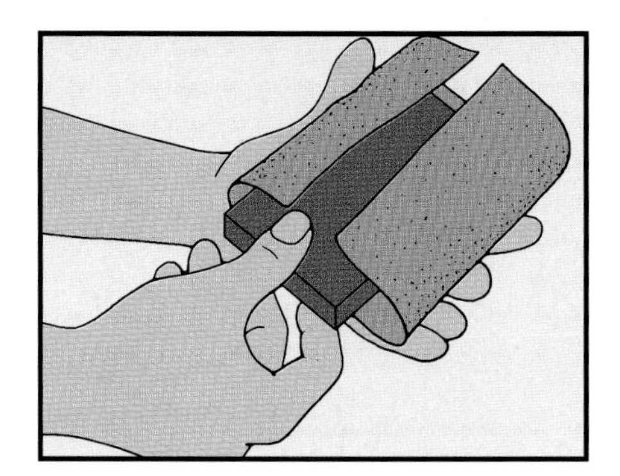

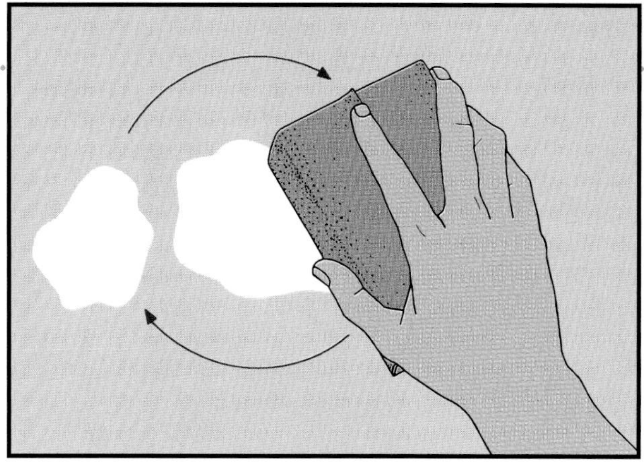

1. Making a sanding block.
You can buy a ready-made sanding block, but a homemade one works just as well.
◆ From a scrap of 1-by-3 or 1-by-4 board, cut a block 4 or 5 inches long.
◆ Cut a rectangle of sandpaper large enough to encircle the block. For previously painted surfaces, start with medium-grit sandpaper, then proceed to fine-grit paper; for virgin wood, use only fine-grit paper.
◆ Wrap the paper around the block with the grit side out.

2. Sanding flat areas.
◆ Make sure that all loose paint is removed from the area to be sanded and that any patching compounds are completely dry.
◆ Grasp the block firmly, holding the sandpaper snugly around it.
◆ On a painted surface, sand with a gentle, circular motion, and feather the edges of the area by blending the old paint or patching materials into the surrounding surface; on bare wood, work in straight strokes along the grain.
◆ Tap the sandpaper frequently on a hard surface to remove accumulated residue, and replace the paper when it becomes clogged or worn out.

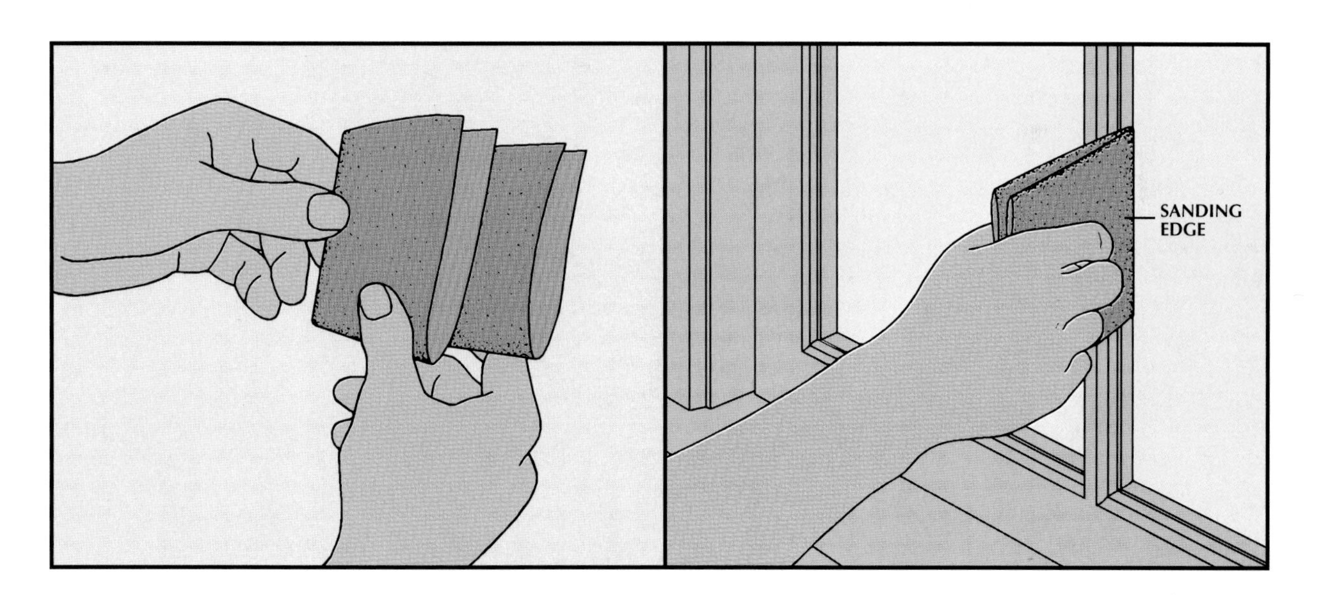

A sanding edge for intricate jobs.
◆ Fold a 6-inch square of sandpaper into quarters to make a sharp sanding edge *(above, left)*.
◆ Place the edge against the surface to be sanded *(above, right),* and gently rub the paper over the surface to blend the edges of patching material or old paint with the surrounding surface.
◆ Refold the paper as necessary to make fresh edges.

REPAIRING DAMAGED PAINT AND WOOD

Scraping paint.
Insert the edge of a $1\frac{1}{4}$-inch-wide putty knife under the loose paint and, being careful not to gouge the surface, scrape with a pushing motion. For large areas, use the scraper shown on page 45 *(middle)*.

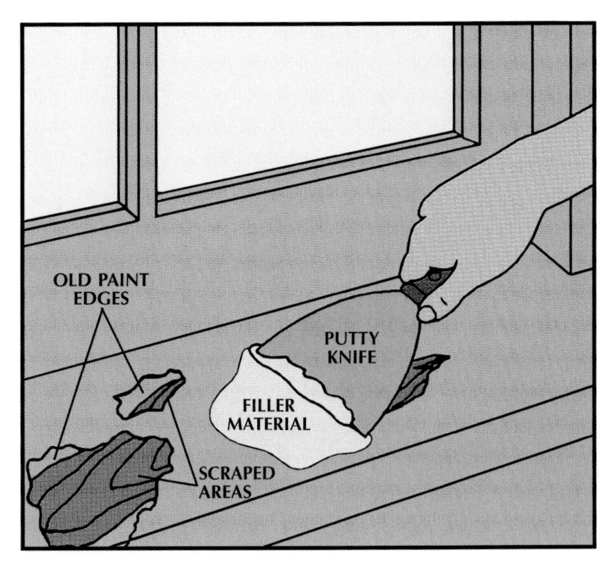

Filling in depressions.
Apply spackling compound to a small depression with a flexible-blade putty knife; use a wide-blade putty knife for extensive filling. When the filler has dried, sand it flush with the surface. Spot-prime all scraped or filled areas before repainting.

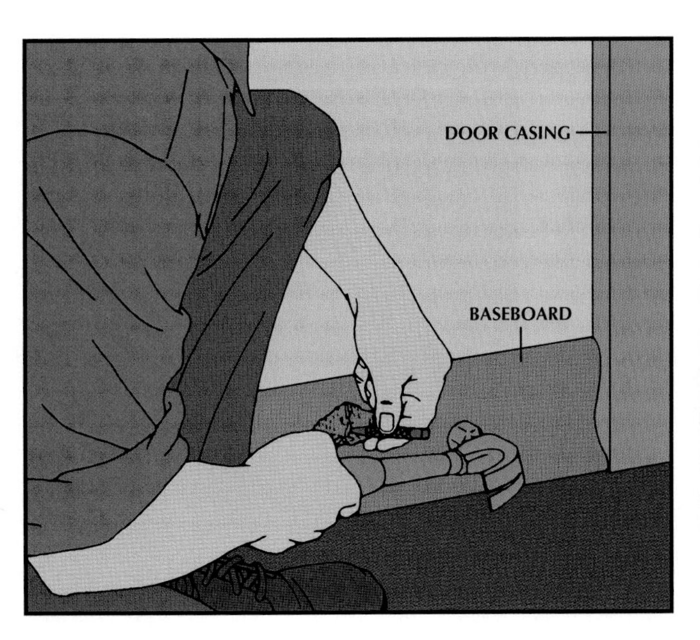

Filling wood dents and gouges.
◆ Roughen the surface of a shallow depression by gently tapping a scattering of holes into the wood with a $\frac{1}{32}$-inch nail set.
◆ Select vinyl spackling as a filler if you are going to apply paint; use water putty if you plan to stain or varnish, wood putty for areas of heavy wear—door casings, window frames, and the like. Force a thin layer of the filler into the nail set holes with a putty knife.
◆ Build upon this layer to the wood's surface.

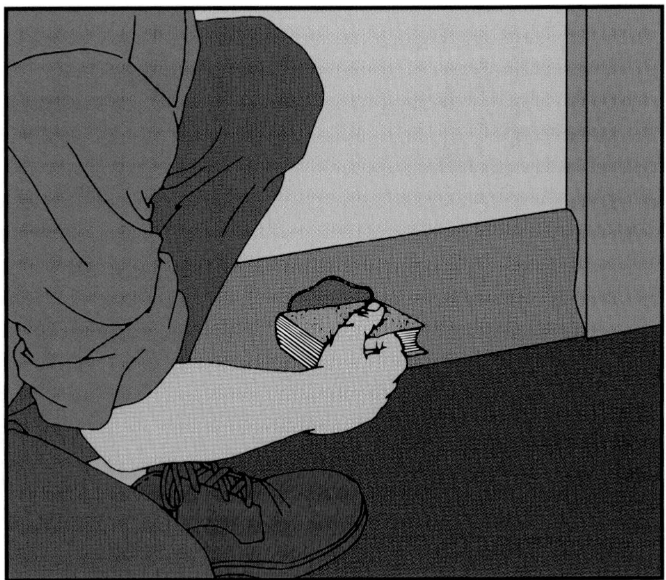

Shaping the patch.
◆ Shape the filler closely to the contours of the molding with the edge of a putty knife or with your fingers, but leave at least a slight bulge.
◆ After the patch is completely dry, sand it to shape with fine sandpaper. A sanding block formed by wrapping sandpaper around an old deck of playing cards will conform to the contours of the trim and permit you to apply even pressure to the various irregular surfaces.

COPING WITH WOOD KNOTS

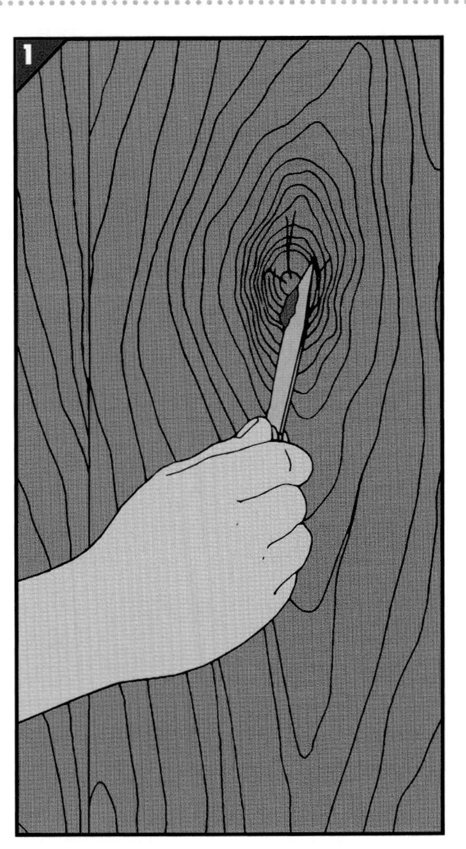

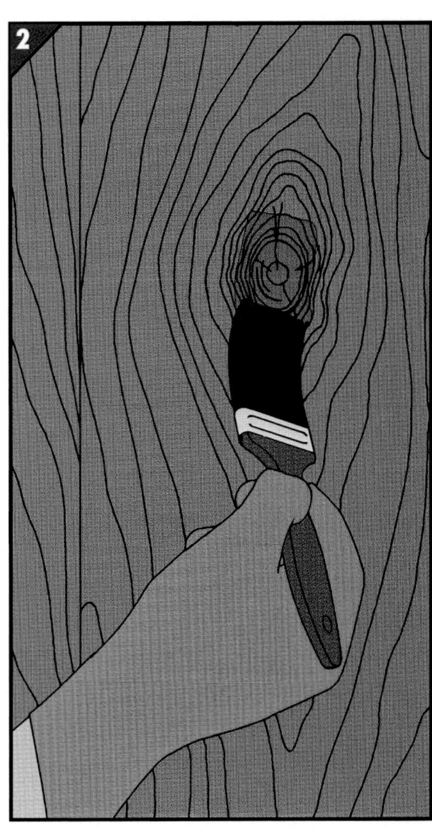

1. Preparing the surface.
◆ Scrape off any hardened resin with a sharp paring knife or similar utensil and clean the area with turpentine.
◆ If the knot is loose, remove it with long-nose pliers and fill the hole with wood putty or wood filler.

To conceal a protruding knot that you cannot remove, build up the surrounding area with putty or filler and sand to an unobtrusive slope.

2. Sealing a knot.
◆ Sand the surface lightly, then paint it with thinned shellac.
◆ When the shellac is dry, sand the surface lightly once more.

TRIM AND MOLDING

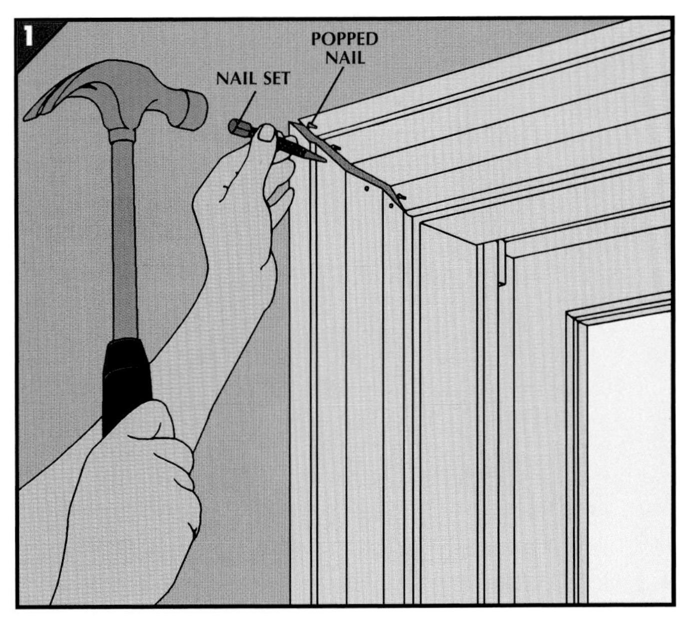

SEALED JOINT
PUTTY KNIFE

2. Filling a hole or joint.
With a flexible-blade putty knife, fill the nail holes with spackling compound or wood putty, depending on the surface you are preparing *(opposite, bottom left).*

1. Countersinking a nail.
◆ Place a nail set on the popped nailhead, with the shaft perpendicular to the surface *(above).*
◆ Strike the set with a hammer to embed the head about $\frac{1}{8}$ inch below the surface.
◆ For slightly opened joints around window frames and doorframes *(above),* apply spackling compound or wood putty, roughly shaping it to match the molding contours if the gap is wide. Caulk longer joints *(pages 46–47).*
◆ After the filler dries, check it for shrinkage and add more if needed. Sand the dried patches with fine-grit paper.

A ROOM WRAPPED UP FOR PAINTING

Thoroughly preparing a room before you paint is well worth the time and effort. Doing so not only shields room contents from the inevitable splattering of paint, but saves time when cleaning up and results in a neater job. The only tool you'll need is a screwdriver.

Begin by shifting furniture into the middle of the room and covering it with drop cloths. Cover the floor as well, taping newspaper along the baseboards. Newspaper also makes an excellent shield for radiators and other objects that can't be removed.

Electrical: Turn off the circuit breakers or unscrew the fuses for the room. Unscrew switch plates and receptacle covers, tape the screws to the plates, and set them near their original positions. If you wish, you can write the new paint brand, color, and type on a piece of masking tape and stick it to the back of one of the plates for future reference.

Loosen screws that secure light fixtures so that they stand away from the surface, allowing you to paint behind them later with a brush. Tape plastic around the fixtures, and make sure not to turn them on while the plastic is in place.

Smooth away ridges of old paint around the openings with sandpaper, taking care to observe the precautions for dealing with lead and asbestos that are outlined on page 10. Turn the electricity back on for illumination if it is necessary, but exercise caution when painting around electrical openings.

Hardware: Uninterrupted surfaces are easier to paint than those with obstructions, so remove as much hardware as possible—unless, of course, the objects themselves are to be painted. You may wish to take off items such as window-sash locks, strike plates, and cabinet handles. Masking tape will protect parts that are not easily removed, such as hinges, locks, and thermostats. Doorknobs can be removed or masked.

Window Glass: Many painters use a freehand technique to paint window sashes and dividers, but you might wish to protect the glass instead. Run masking tape around the edges of the panes, leaving a $\frac{1}{16}$-inch gap between the edge of the tape and the wood or metal so that paint can form a seal on the glass. This will prevent condensation from damaging the frame. When you are finished painting, peel the tape off.

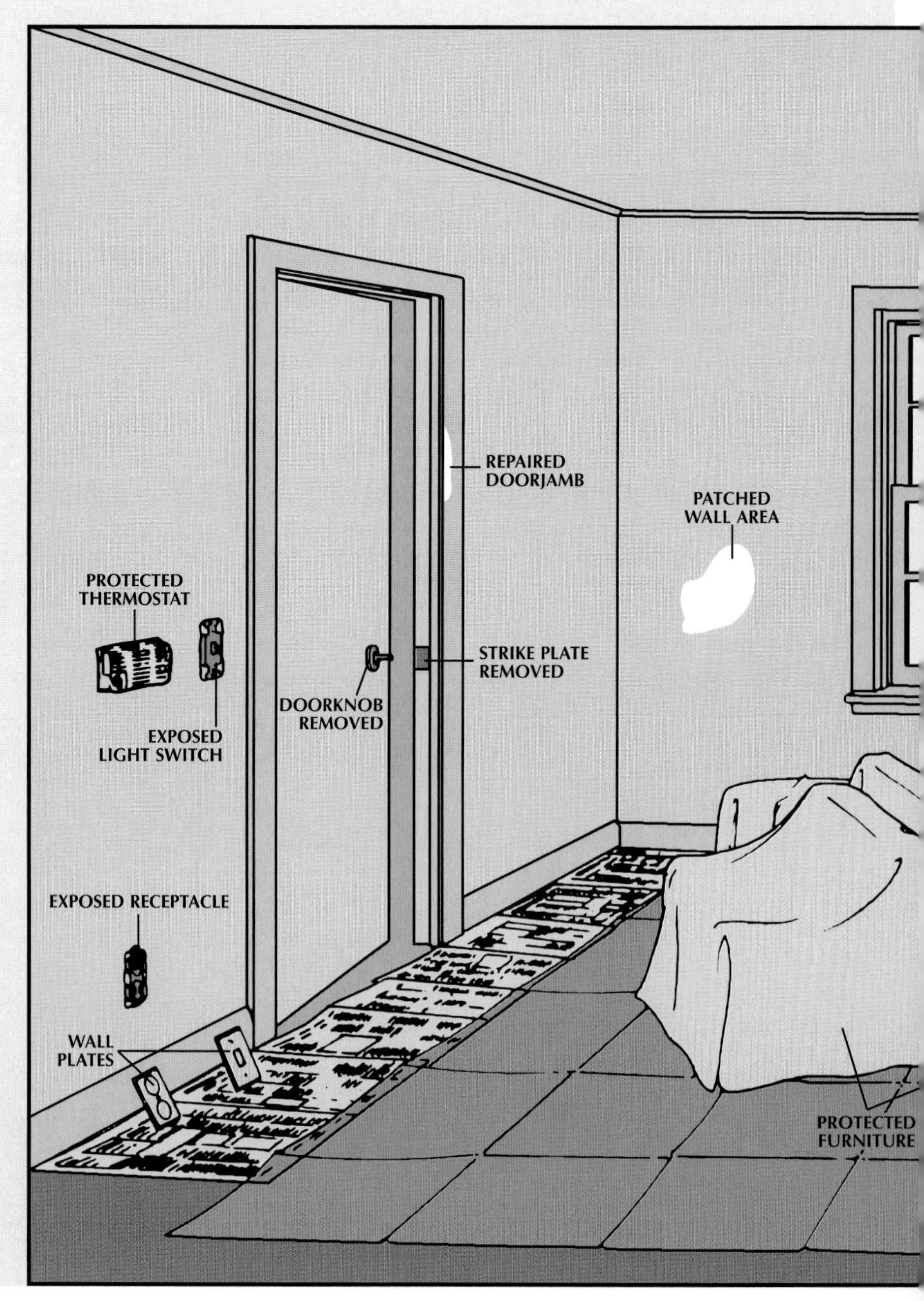

Drop cloths
Newspaper
Masking tape
Plastic sheets
Sandpaper
Rags

Preparing a room for painting.
The illustration below indicates the wide range of repairs and preparation that may be required before painting begins. Most repairs, such as patching cracks and holes or sealing wood joints *(pages 97–98, 131)*, will be necessary only from time to time.

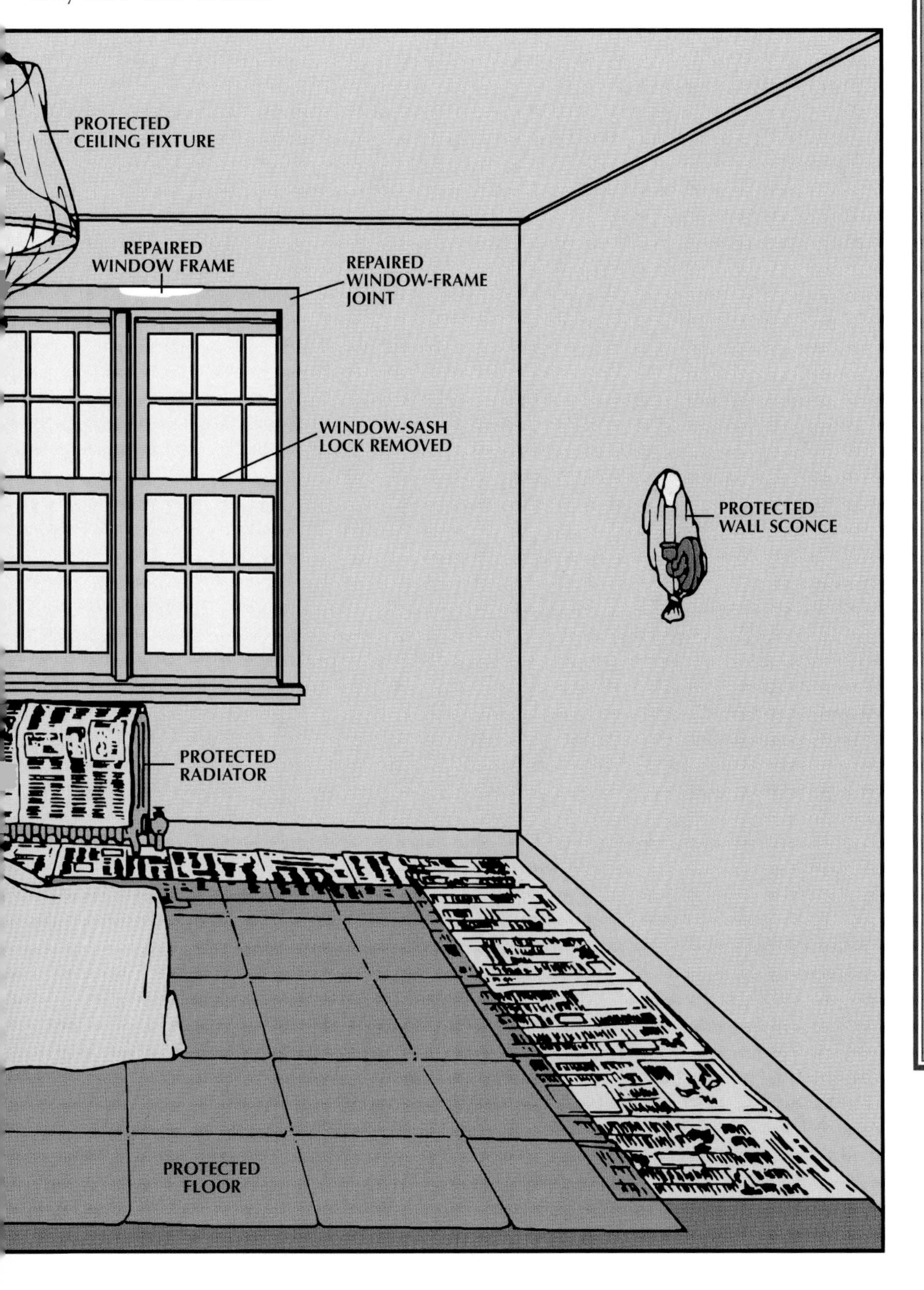

Painting the Safe Way

Many products used in painting are toxic. Water-base products, such as latex paint, are the safest, but like most chemicals they contain poisonous ingredients. Use special care in handling solvent-base coatings such as alkyd paints, as well as related products like thinners, varnishes, and strippers. The fumes of some are so toxic that you may need a respirator approved by the National Institute of Occupational Safety and Health. Many of these products are highly flammable—some even require that you extinguish gas range or water-heater pilot lights before beginning work. In addition, follow these precautions:

✔ Keep children and pets out of the work area.

✔ Read labels of products for special requirements, and keep the labels on hand should you need to call a doctor.

✔ Work only in a ventilated room. Open doors and windows, and use fans to dispel fumes.

✔ When painting a ceiling, work in a position that prevents paint from falling in your eyes.

✔ Wash any coating off your skin as soon as you can, and scrub up carefully after each session.

✔ Immediately clean paint off an animal's skin or fur—it can do serious harm, especially if the animal tries to lick it off. Wash away latex paint with plain water. Remove alkyd paint with a cloth soaked in mineral oil or cooking oil. Never use turpentine or any other powerful paint solvent: it will burn the animal's skin and will be doubly dangerous if the animal licks it off.

✔ Dispose of all paint, solvents, and other toxic chemicals in an approved manner. Call your local sanitation department or environmental protection office for advice.

WORKING WITH BRUSHES AND ROLLERS

The two major tools for any painting job are the roller and the brush. Rollers are by far the easier to use. They require none of the special handling necessary with brushes and can paint a wall or ceiling twice as fast as a brush can. On the other hand, brushes are more versatile, and most jobs need at least some brushwork to paint areas unreachable with a roller.

Choosing a Brush or Roller: While a single roller may suffice for an entire job *(opposite)*, you will need more than one brush—see the photos on page 123.

You must also match the applicator to the paint. Natural bristles and fibers lose resiliency as they absorb water from latex paint, so use synthetics with latex-base coverings. For alkyd-base paints, either a natural or a synthetic material is fine.

Preparing the Paint: Pigments sink rapidly to the bottom of a can of paint, the solvent rising to the top. So unless the paint has just been machine-agitated at the dealer's, mix it thoroughly before using. Before doing so, however, check the paint to see if a skin has formed across the top. If so, pour the paint carefully into another container. Never attempt to stir a skin back into the rest of the paint; the skin is insoluble, and stirring will only break it into tiny bits that show up on a newly painted surface.

Do not paint out of the original container. Instead, pour the paint into a pail, and keep the original can closed, so that the paint is less likely to dry out, get dirty, or spill.

Using a Brush: For the neatest results and to stave off fatigue, hold the brush correctly. The long, thin handle of a sash brush, for example, is most effectively grasped with the fingers, much as you would hold a pencil. The thick "beaver-tail" handles of wider brushes, however, are best held with the whole hand, as you would hold a tennis racket. Whatever the handle style, periodically switch hands or grips to keep your hands from getting tired.

In addition to the basic up-and-down brush stroke, there are two important techniques. The first is "cutting in," or painting a strip in corners between two surfaces of matching colors. Similarly, painting a thin, smooth line at wall and ceiling edges where two colors meet, or on the narrow dividers between windowpanes—a technique called beading—allows you to paint a sharp edge.

TOOLS

Paintbrushes
Roller cover
Roller frame
Extension handle
Roller with drop shield
Pail
Paint stirrer
Electric drill with mixer blade
Hammer
Paint shield
Corner roller
Paint pad
Roller pan with grating

MATERIALS

Paint
Cheesecloth
Wire screening
Paper plate
Finishing nail
Aluminum foil

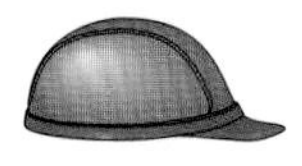

SAFETY TIPS

To minimize inhalation of paint fumes, always work in a well-ventilated area. When using alkyd-base paints and solvents, protect your hands with latex gloves.

BRUSH CONSTRUCTION

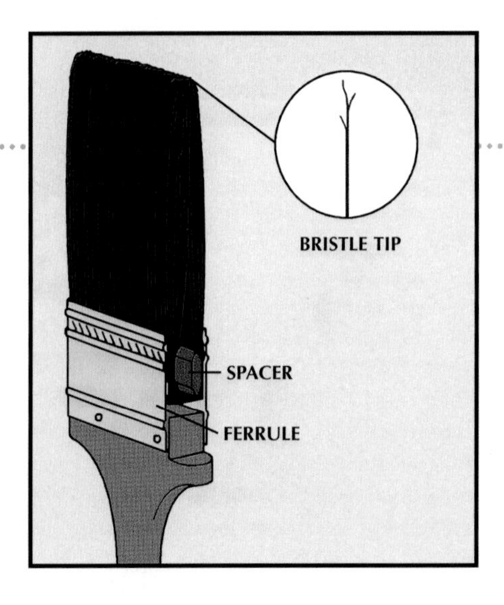

A design for efficient painting. Whether natural or synthetic, the bristles of a typical paintbrush are frayed at the working end to hold as much paint as possible *(inset)*. At the other end, they are embedded in hard plastic, which is anchored to the brush handle by a metal band called a ferrule. Inside the ferrule, a spacer spreads the bristles at the base to create a thick, springy brush edge.

What Makes a Good Brush Good?

When shopping for a paintbrush, carefully check the points listed below. These guidelines apply to synthetic- and natural-bristle brushes of any size and shape.

✔ Construction. Make sure that the ferrule is firmly attached to the handle, preferably with nails if the handle is wood. A wood handle should also have a glossy or rubberized coating, which resists moisture and is easy to clean.

✔ Balance. Grip the handle of the brush as you would for painting. The shape and the weight should feel comfortable in your grasp.

✔ Bristles. Press the brush's bristles against the palm of your hand. They should fan out evenly, and readily spring back to their original position. To check how securely the bristles are anchored, first slap the brush against the palm of your hand to shake out any loose bristles—any brand-new brush may have a few. Then tug on the bristles once or twice. No additional bristles should come out.

ALL ABOUT ROLLERS

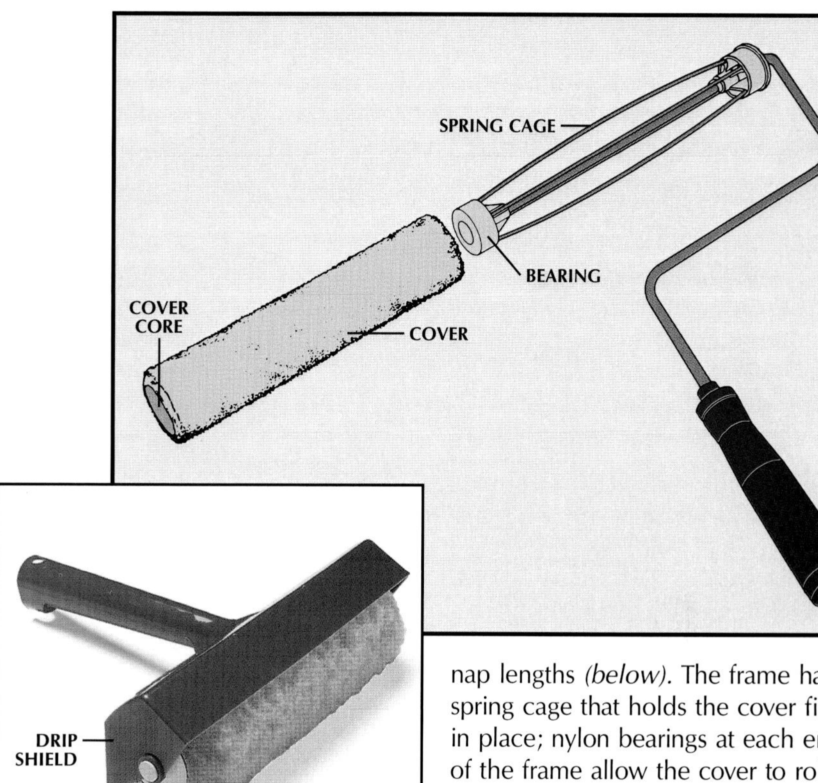

Anatomy of a roller.
Rollers consist of a cover and a frame, usually sold separately. Made of lambs wool or synthetic fibers, the cover winds around a central core of plastic or cardboard and comes in a variety of nap lengths *(below)*. The frame has a spring cage that holds the cover firmly in place; nylon bearings at each end of the frame allow the cover to roll smoothly. To reach ceilings and high walls without standing on a ladder, screw an extension pole into the handle's threaded end.

For jobs where dripping paint may be a problem—such as when painting ceilings—purchase a roller frame with a built-in drip shield *(inset)*.

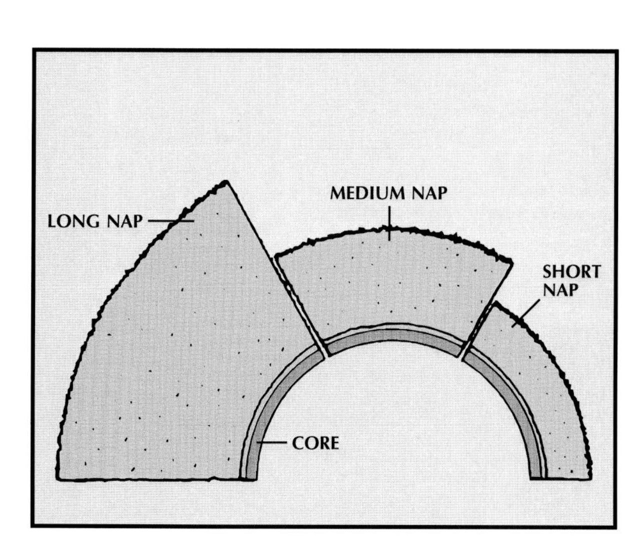

Choosing a nap.
Roller covers are available in three kinds of nap: short, medium, and long. Short nap, about $\frac{1}{4}$ inch deep, holds less paint than the others but leaves a thin, smooth coating that is ideal for glossy paint. All-purpose medium nap, between $\frac{1}{2}$ and $\frac{3}{4}$ inch deep, holds any type of paint well and produces a softly stippled effect. Long nap, from 1 to $1\frac{1}{4}$ inches deep, is good for working a thick coat of paint into textured or porous surfaces and leaves behind deep stipples in the paint.

Roller covers need no special preparation unless you are using glossy paint and a new, short-nap roller. In that case, prime the roller by sloshing it in soapy water to remove loose strands of material. Rinse the cover thoroughly and dry it completely before you begin.

PAINTING A ROOM IN SEQUENCE

To minimize drips and smears, work systematically from the top to the bottom of a room: Paint the ceiling first, then the walls, then windows, doors, and other woodwork, and finally the baseboards.

Ceilings and Walls: Plan on painting the entire ceiling and each wall without stopping. A roller attached to a 4- or 5-foot extension pole is ideal for reaching a ceiling. On a textured surface, be sure to use a roller with a long nap *(page 135)*.

On walls, some people prefer to paint in vertical portions from top to bottom. However, if you are using a roller on an extension pole to reach the top of the wall, you may find it easier to work in horizontal sections to avoid attaching the roller to—and removing it from—the pole more than once.

Windows and Doors: Painting double-hung windows in the sequence that is shown on the opposite page will solve the tricky problem of your having to move the sashes to paint surfaces that are obstructed by the lower sash. Paint the horizontal parts of the frame with back-and-forth strokes of the brush and the vertical parts with up-and-down strokes.

With doors, follow the techniques that are described on page 138 to achieve best results.

CEILINGS AND WALLS

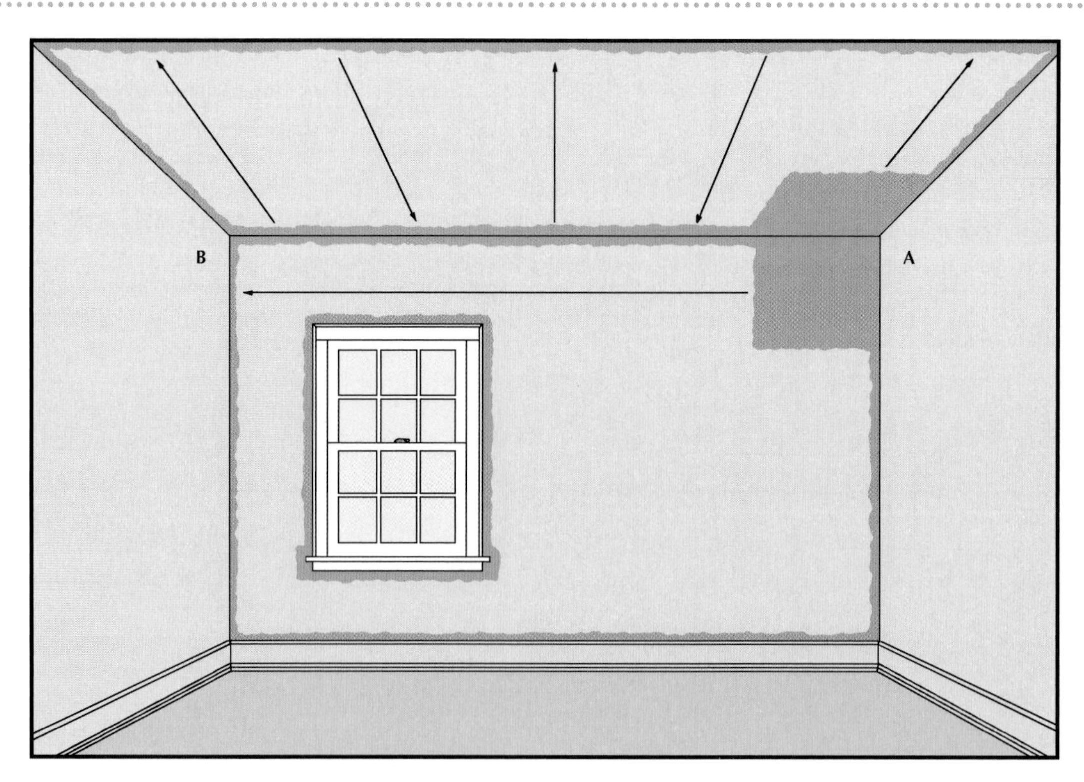

A basic pattern.

Paint a 2-inch-wide strip around the edges of the ceiling using the cutting-in technique shown above. Start painting the ceiling at a corner (A or B), then work back and forth across the short dimension of the ceiling in sections 3 feet square, as indicated by the arrows. To prevent lap marks caused when wet paint is laid over dry, blend the paint at the edges of adjacent sections before the paint on either dries. After coating the entire ceiling, check your work for missed or thin spots, and revisit them with a roller lightly loaded with paint.

Before painting a wall, cut in not only along the edges, but also around the entire frame of any door or window and along baseboards. Apply paint across the wall in tiers, beginning at corner A or B and alternating direction as with the ceiling. Check your work for missed spots.

DOUBLE-HUNG WINDOWS

1. Start on the sashes.

◆ Raise the inside sash and lower the outside sash, leaving each open about 6 inches.

◆ Paint the inner sash first, omitting the top edge. Begin with the muntins (horizontals, then verticals), followed by the sash frame (horizontals, then verticals). Bead the paint onto the wood, allowing a narrow strip—about $\frac{1}{16}$ inch wide—to flow onto the glass and form a seal between the two materials. This irregular edge of paint is straightened during final cleanup *(page 139)*.

◆ On the outside sash, paint the same parts in the same order as far as they are exposed—but do not paint the bottom edge until you paint the house exterior.

2. Complete the sashes.

◆ Push up on the bottom of the outside sash and down on the unpainted top of the inside sash, positioning them about an inch from their closed positions.

◆ In the same order as in Step 1, paint the surfaces of the outside sash that were obstructed; also paint the top edge of the inside sash.

◆ Proceed to paint the wood framing of the window, starting with the top horizontal. Coat the two side pieces next and finish with the sill.

◆ Wait until all of the paint is thoroughly dry before proceeding to the jambs in Step 3; meanwhile, work on other windows or on doors.

3. Finish with the jambs.

◆ When the paint is dry to the touch, slide both sashes up and down a few times to make sure they do not stick. Then, push both sashes all the way down to expose the upper jambs *(left)*.

◆ Paint the wooden parts of the upper jambs in the order shown by the letters A through C; metal parts are never painted. Avoid overloading the brush to prevent paint from running into the grooves of the lower jambs.

◆ Let the paint dry, then raise both sashes all the way and paint the lower halves of parts A through C.

◆ Wait for the paint to dry, then lubricate parts A and B of the jambs with paraffin or with silicone spray.

CASEMENT WINDOWS

Windows that open outward. Casement and awning windows may be made of aluminum, steel, or wood. An aluminum window does not need to be painted, but to protect the metal against dirt and pitting, consider coating it with a metal primer or with a transparent polyurethane varnish. Coat a steel casement with both a metal primer and paint, or with a paint especially suitable to metal, such as an epoxy or polyurethane paint. Treat a wood casement the way you would any other interior woodwork—unless the wood is clad in vinyl, which requires no paint.

Before painting, open the window. Working from inside outward and always doing horizontals first and then verticals, paint the parts in this order: muntins, sash frame, hinge edge, window frame and mullion, and sill. Leave the window open until all the paint dries.

DOORS AND LOUVERS

Hinged doors.

◆ Cover metal hinges, knobs, and latches with masking tape to protect them from paint spatters.

◆ Work from top to bottom when painting a door. On a panel door, shown here, paint the panels first, the horizontal rails next, and finally the vertical stiles. The top and bottom edges of a door need be painted only once in its lifetime, to seal the wood and prevent warping.

◆ Paint the latch edge only if the door opens into the room you are painting. The hinge edge of a door is painted the color of the room it faces when the door is open.

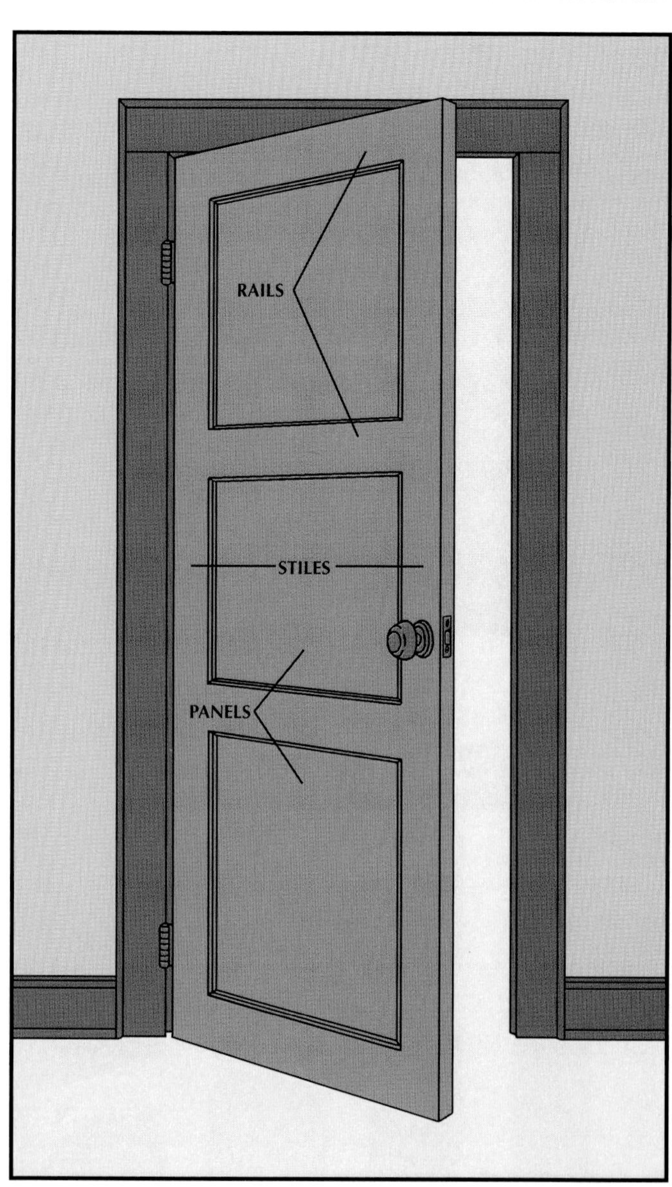

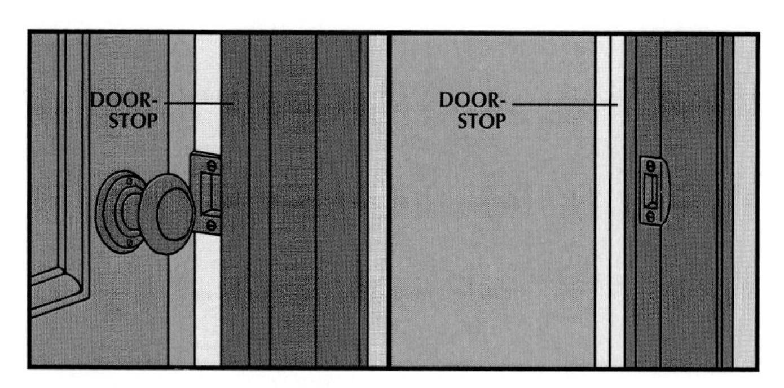

Doorframes and jambs.

◆ Paint the top of the doorframe, then the two sides, followed by the part of the jamb between the frame and the doorstop.

◆ Paint the doorstop as follows: If the door opens into the next room *(above, left)*, paint the side of the doorstop that directly faces you and the broad side that faces into the door opening.

◆ If the door opens into the room you are painting, paint only the edge of the doorstop that the door closes against *(above, right)*.

Solving the louver problem.
The narrow slats of a louvered shutter or door call for a $\frac{1}{2}$-inch brush and a slow-drying alkyd paint, so you have time to smooth drips on the slats.

◆ For an adjustable louver *(left)*, open the louver wide and set the slats to a horizontal position.

◆ Begin with the back of the panel so that you can smooth paint drips from the front.

◆ To avoid paint buildup where slats meet the frame, start painting at one end of a slat, flowing the paint toward the center in a long, smooth stroke. Repeat this technique at the opposite end of the slat.

◆ Cover as much of the slats as you can reach from the back side of the louver, opposite the adjusting rod.

◆ Turning the panel over, paint the inner edge of the adjusting rod, then wedge a matchstick or toothpick through one of its staples to keep the rod clear of the slats.

◆ Finish painting the slats one by one, smoothing out paint drips as you go.

◆ Next, paint the outer edges of the frame, horizontals first, then verticals. Paint the edges of the frame, and complete the job by painting the rest of the adjusting rod.

The slats of a stationary louver are set in a fixed, slanted position. Paint the backs first, from the ends toward the center. On the front, work the brush into the crevices between slats, then smooth out the paint with horizontal strokes.

A NEAT EDGE FOR WINDOWPANES

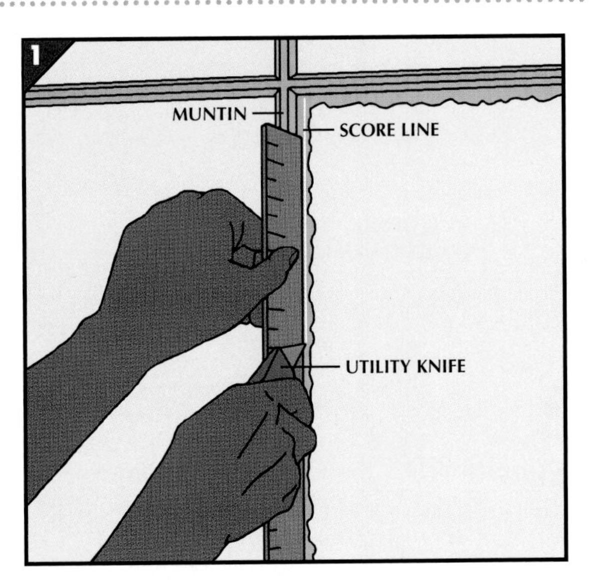

1. Scoring the paint.
With a utility knife or single-edged razor blade, score the paint on the glass, using a wide-blade putty knife or ruler as shown above to keep the score line at least $\frac{1}{16}$ inch from both sides of each muntin and from the sash or the casement frame.

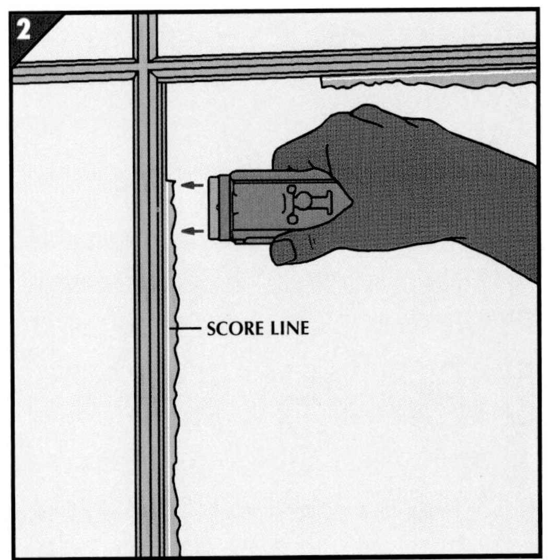

2. Removing the paint.
Position a window scraper so that the blade is parallel to the score line, and carefully push the blade under the paint, stopping at the score. The paint will come off easily, leaving a neat, straight edge.

PLUMBING

Plumbing repairs and improvements can be among the most expensive projects in an old house. Some homeowners simply grit their teeth and dig deep into their pockets to bear the expense. Others discover that there is a great deal they can do themselves, at significant savings.

Two of the most common plumbing problems in old houses are clogged drains and malfunctioning toilets. In this chapter you can learn how to solve both kinds of problems, whether they occur in a bathroom, kitchen, or laundry room. You can also learn how to avoid frozen pipes and how to give first aid if one does freeze.

When it comes to putting in new plumbing, the greatest hurdle is learning how to deal with the materials involved. Techniques for working with copper, plastic, and steel pipe and the fittings used to connect pieces of water-supply and drain pipe are explained in this chapter. There are also instructions for applying those techniques to extend plumbing to a new sink, and for installing a vanity or a pedestal-base basin, as well as a medicine cabinet on the wall. You'll be surprised at how easy many plumbing projects are.

▷ *Right:* A graceful pedestal basin is easy to install because the fittings are readily accessible.

▽ *Below:* Kitchen plumbing gets heavy use. To deal with a clogged drain or faucet problem, or to install a sink, use the same techniques as you would for bathroom plumbing.

△ *Above:* You can find basin and tub fittings to suit the period or style of any bathroom, and replacing existing fittings is not a difficult job.

△ *Above:* An antique marble washstand can be beautiful and well worth preserving. However, the faucets and drain may have to be replaced, which is not difficult. Replacement basins are also available, if the original is cracked or worn.

▷ *Right:* An easy-to-install vanity combines a washbasin with concealed storage space in any size bathroom. You can put it in place of an existing fixture, or extend water and drain lines to a new location.

INSPECTING THE PLUMBING

The original plumbing in an old house usually includes cast-iron drainpipes and either copper or galvanized-steel supply pipes. Cast-iron drains rarely present problems—and if leaks do occur, the pipe can be mended *(pages 159–160)*. Copper pipes may develop leaks at weak joints, but the piping itself has a very long life span. Steel pipes, however, begin to clog with rust after about 30 years and do not normally last more than 50 years. Plan to replace steel pipes—perhaps gradually, starting with pipes that are exposed and any that are uncovered during other repairs.

A few old houses still have lead pipes. They, too, should be replaced. As with steel pipes, this can be done over time, but before settling on a gradual approach, have the water tested for harmful levels of lead.

Assessing a Well: If your water supply comes from a private well, be sure to have it tested periodically for purity. In addition, check the well's storage capacity by turning on all the faucets and letting them run. If the water becomes muddy within 10 minutes, a larger storage tank is probably needed.

A Backyard Septic System: If your house has a septic tank, check the maintenance records. Intervals of 3 to 6 years between pumpings to empty the tank are normal; if yours requires more frequent pumping, the system needs a larger tank. You can often recognize the leaching field for your system, where effluence is discharged into the soil, by an area of lush grass in warm months or thin or melted snow in winter. The leaching field must be on a lower grade than the house, and it should never have sections of standing water or mud or produce an odor of sewage.

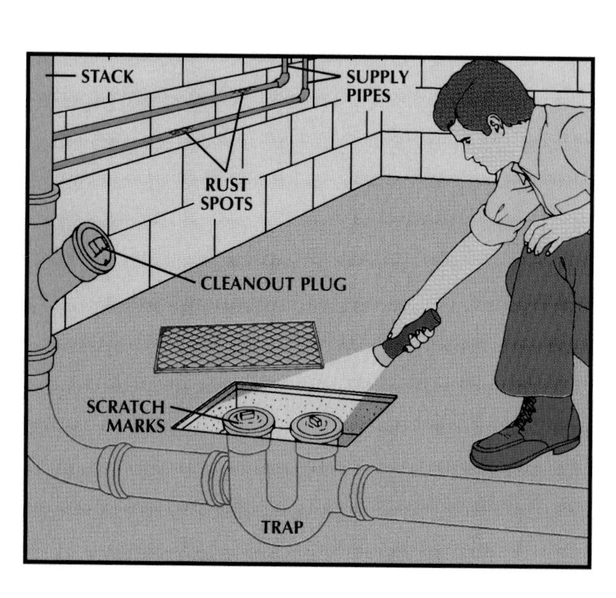

Examining exposed pipes.
◆ In the basement, locate the house trap or the cleanout plug for the stack and check for scratch marks from tools, indicating frequent removal to remedy clogging *(left)*.
◆ Inspect all visible drainpipes for signs of leaks or patching.
◆ Look for rust on galvanized-steel supply pipes. If it is confined to threaded joints, the pipes are likely to last a few more years; rust on smooth outside surfaces is a sign the pipes need to be replaced within a year.

CAUTION *Do not touch rust spots on steel pipes. You could break through an area that is weakened and cause a leak.*

Listening for leaks.
◆ Locate the main shutoff valve and make sure it works properly. A valve that is rusted open must be replaced. (Some houses have two valves, one on each side of the meter; check both.)
◆ With the shutoff valve open and all the fixtures in the house closed, listen for a gurgling or murmuring sound in a supply pipe *(right)*—a sign that a leak somewhere in the house is letting the water move.
◆ With the valve closed, listen for leaking in the supply pipe leading from the street main. If you hear gurgling, there may be a leak in that line.

Checking the water heater.

◆ Look for a temperature-pressure relief valve at the top of the tank or high on the side; normally the valve leads to a discharge pipe. If there is no relief valve, one must be installed.

◆ Check the relief valve and the drain valve for dampness or drips. Leaking valves must be replaced.

◆ Look for other signs of leakage—corrosion on the tank, water stains on the floor, or rust under the burner of a gas water heater *(left)*. Any such evidence of leaks means that the entire tank must be replaced.

◆ Finally, read the plate that lists the capacity/recovery rate—how many gallons of hot water the unit holds and how many it can heat in an hour. In the case of a four-person family, a 40/40 rating is usually adequate for a gas water heater; a 40/50 rating is necessary for an electric unit.

Testing the water pressure.

◆ In the highest bathroom in the house, turn on the cold-water faucets in the tub and washbasin full force. Then have a helper turn on a faucet in the lowest part of the house. If the flow at the bathroom faucets loses a quarter or more of its original force *(left)*, supply lines inside or outside the house may be partially clogged, requiring replacement before long, say 3 to 5 years.

◆ Turn off the cold water and repeat the test with the hot-water faucets; if the pressure drops again, the hot-water pipes—which run only inside the house—are also becoming clogged.

Inspect the caulking around the edge of tubs and examine the wall and floor tiles; deterioration can cause water damage in the rooms below. Loose tiles and cracked or missing caulking should be replaced as soon as possible.

Checking the toilets.

◆ Grip the rim of the bowl with both hands and try to wobble it *(right)*. If it moves at all, there may be a broken seal, which can permit leakage at the base of the bowl. Over time, such leaks can cause extensive damage to wood in the underlayment and subfloor.

◆ Remove the tank top and look for a date stamped on its underside; this is frequently a clue to the age of the original plumbing and therefore its probable life expectancy.

◆ Inspect the tank mechanism for corrosion, which may require the replacement of some parts. Flush the toilet to see how long recovery takes before water stops running and whether there is a strong swirling action in the bowl.

A TOOL KIT FOR PLUMBING

Many of the tools necessary for plumbing repairs and improvements are multipurpose instruments, such as screwdrivers, pliers, hammers, and adjustable wrenches. With the addition of the few specialized tools shown here, you can be ready not only to meet most plumbing emergencies but also to install and replace pipes and fixtures.

Included in this tool kit are implements for loosening and tightening plumbing hardware, cutting and soldering pipe, and clearing clogged sink and toilet drains. There is no satisfactory substitute for any of these tools, which are designed for the hardware unique to plumbing or for work in awkward spaces, such as under the sink.

Seat wrench.
The repair of faucet leaks caused by worn valve seats requires a seat wrench. With a square tip on one tapered end and an octagonal tip on the other, the wrench fits the two most common types of seats in a wide range of sizes.

Spud wrench.
The wide-spreading, toothless jaws on this wrench firmly grasp large nuts found on toilets and sinks. The jaws, which lock in place once opened to the desired width, are shaped to fit into tight spaces.

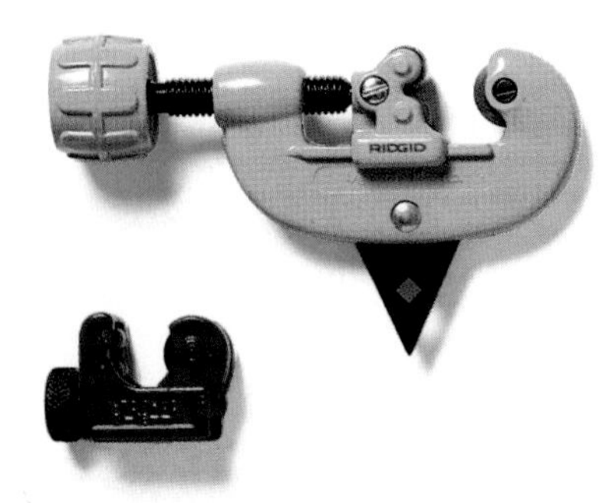

Tube and pipe cutters.
Depending on the type of cutting wheel installed, these devices cut either plastic or copper pipes. The built-in triangular reamer on the larger cutter scrapes away burrs around the cut edge, leaving it smooth. A minicutter is handy when working in tight spaces.

Pipe wrench.
The serrated teeth and spring-loaded upper jaw of this durable tool tightly grip pipes while you hold or turn them. The spring allows you to release the wrench's grip and reposition the tool without readjusting the jaws.

Basin wrench.
This self-adjusting tool's long handle is used primarily to reach otherwise inaccessible nuts that fasten faucets to washbasins and kitchen sinks.

Plunger.
A fold-out plunger has a flexible extension called a funnel. Extended as shown here, the funnel helps to unclog toilet drains. Folding it inside the cup converts the plunger for clearing tub, sink, and shower drains.

Faucet-handle puller.
To remove stubborn faucet handles, enlist the aid of this device. The jaws of the puller fit under the handle and pull it free as the threaded center shaft is tightened against the faucet stem.

Propane torch and flameproof pad.
To solder copper pipe or tubing—or to disassemble soldered joints—use a propane torch. With a flame spreader attached, the torch also thaws frozen pipes *(page 169)*. For any of these applications, protect nearby house framing with a flameproof pad.

Augers.
The trap-and-drain auger, shown here coiled with its handle, is used for clearing sink and tub drains; the handle slides along the snake as it progresses into the drain. For toilets, use a closet auger, which is shaped to direct the flexible shaft into the toilet trap and has a handle at the top.

WORKING WITH PIPES AND FITTINGS

Pipes and fittings, the prime constituents of a household plumbing system, not only can be assembled in any number of configurations but also exhibit considerable variety in their own right. For example, several different materials may be used for the supply pipes in residential systems, and still other materials are acceptable for the drain-waste-vent (DWV) portion of the network. (To determine what kind you have, simply examine the pipes in your basement, garage, or behind an access panel, and match them to the photographs on these pages.) As for fittings, they are designed for many roles—splicing straight lengths of pipe (called a run), allowing direction changes and branching, linking pipes of differing diameters, and so on. Some common sorts of fittings for the supply lines are shown opposite; DWV counterparts appear on page 150.

Keys to Buying Materials: Cost, durability, and ease of installation are among the important factors in choosing the materials for a repair job or an addition to your plumbing system. But before you make a purchase, check the code of your local jurisdiction. Some codes prohibit a particular material in one part of a plumbing system but not in another, and the local code may dictate the method used to join components. Among allowed materials, you can mix and match: Special transition fittings will create secure connections between dissimilar pipes; and if the pipes are made of different metals, an appropriate fitting will prevent an electrochemical reaction that could corrode a joint.

All piping is sized by inside diameter. When replacing pipe, determine its inner diameter *(page 150)* and buy new pipe of the same size.

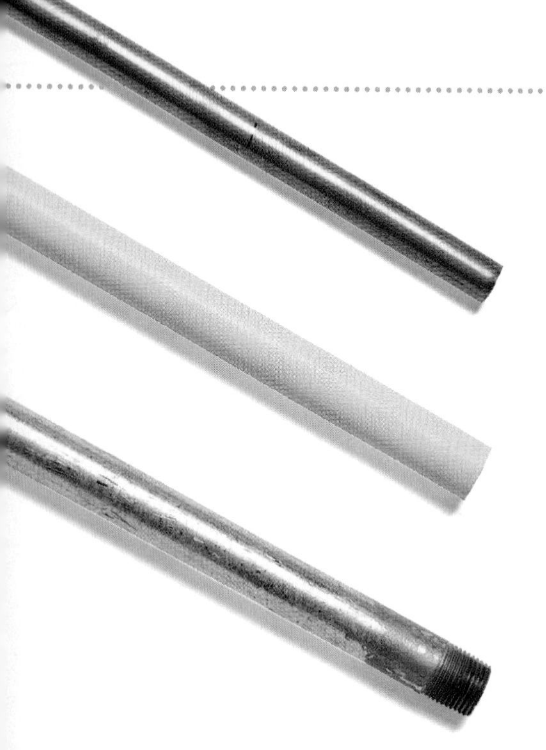

SUPPLY PIPES AND FITTINGS

Rigid copper.
This metal, joined with durable solder, resists corrosion and has smooth surfaces for good water flow. A thin-walled version called Type M is the least expensive and will serve well for most repairs.

Chlorinated polyvinyl chloride (CPVC).
A rigid plastic formulated with chlorine so that it can withstand high temperatures, CPVC is a popular supply-pipe material for its low cost, resistance to corrosion, and ease of assembly: Fittings are secured by solvent cement. For residential use, most codes specify a so-called Schedule 40 pressure rating, stamped on the pipe.

Galvanized steel.
Used for supply as well as drain-waste-vent lines, this material is found only in older homes. Although it is the strongest of supply-pipe materials, galvanized steel is prone to corrosion over time. Runs of threaded pipe are joined by threaded fittings; the entire length between fittings must be removed and replaced to complete a repair.

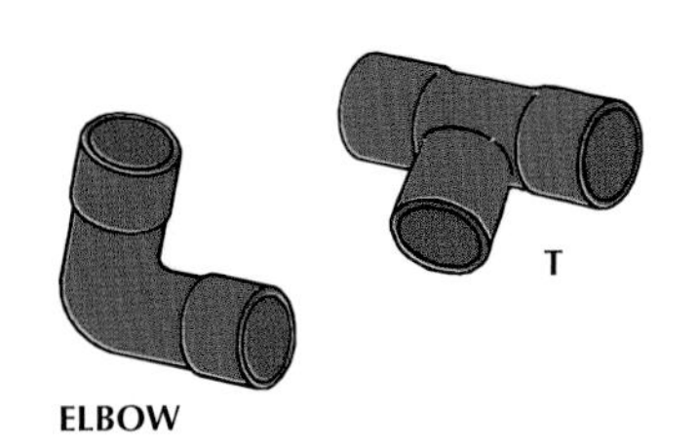

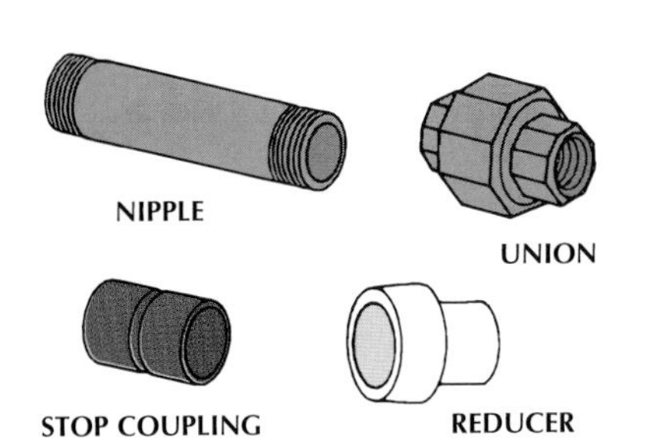

Bends and branches.
The direction of a supply pipe is changed by a fitting called an elbow or ell, available in 45- and 90-degree turns. A T fitting joins a 90-degree branch run to a straight run of pipe.

Straight-line fittings.
Many sorts of fittings are used to join pipes in a straight run. A straight piece of pipe called a nipple extends a run or fitting a short distance—from 1 to 12 inches. A union holds two pipes within an assembly joined by a threaded nut, allowing disassembly without cutting. Couplings, unlike unions, are unthreaded and permanent. A stop coupling like the one shown here has interior shoulders for a secure fit in new installations; a slip coupling, which has no shoulders, slides over existing pipe and is used for repairs. A reducer, also known as a bushing, attaches pipes of different diameters by reducing the opening at one end.

Transition fittings.
As the name implies, these fittings allow a run of pipe to change from one material to another. Copper-to-CPVC adapters join the two most common kinds of supply pipe, both unthreaded. Threaded adapters join threaded pipe to unthreaded—and also are used to connect pipes to a variety of other plumbing components, such as a spigot or tub spout. Connecting steel pipe to copper requires another special-purpose fitting: a dielectric union, which prevents an electrolytic reaction between the two metals.

DRAINPIPES AND FITTINGS

Cast iron.
This is the strongest material available for DWV piping, and its heavy weight helps contain noise generated by active drains. Cast-iron pipe comes in two types, identified by the methods used to join them: hubless *(left)*, which uses easily installed fittings; and hub and spigot, joined by a cumbersome procedure utilizing molten lead and oakum.

Copper.
Although mostly chosen for supply lines, copper pipe also comes in larger drain-waste-vent forms. Because copper DWV pipe is comparatively costly, however, it is seldom chosen for new installations.

ABS.
This plastic pipe, acronymically named for acrylonitrile butadiene styrene, is less expensive and more durable than PVC, but many codes prohibit its use because of its low resistance to chemicals and low ignition point. Where ABS is allowed in homes, a Schedule 40 pressure rating is recommended.

Polyvinyl chloride (PVC).
A rigid plastic pipe material like CPVC but less able to withstand heat, PVC is lightweight, easy to install, corrosion resistant, and inexpensive. In addition to its DWV uses, it can serve for cold-water supply lines. Codes usually specify a Schedule 40 rating for residences.

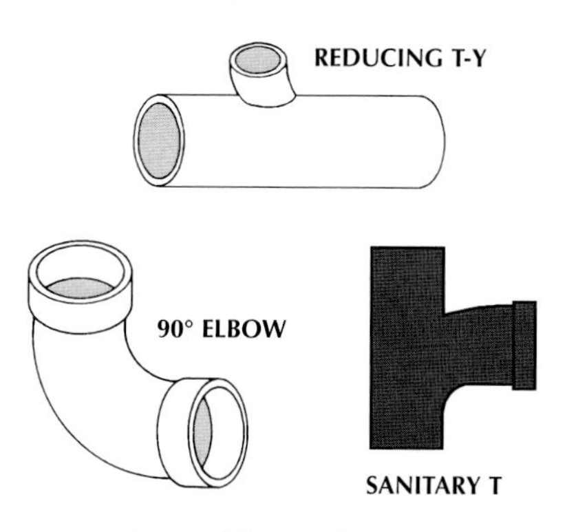

Bends and branches.
A 90-degree elbow fitting (also known as a quarter-bend) makes a right-angle turn in DWV piping. Among the fittings that join two runs of drainpipe are a reducing T-Y, which connects a branch pipe to a larger diameter drainpipe, and a sanitary T, a fitting that joins a fixture drain to a vertical stack.

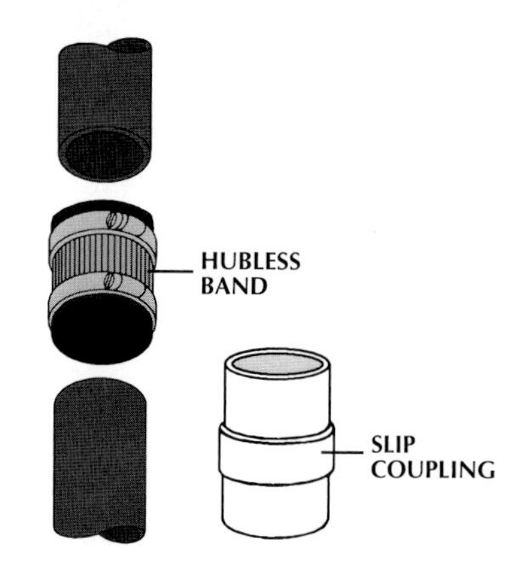

Straight-line fittings.
A hubless band—used to join hubless drainpipe—consists of a tightly fitting neoprene sleeve that is held in place over a joint by a stainless steel collar and clamps. A slip coupling, like its supply-system counterpart, slides over pipes to connect them in a repair.

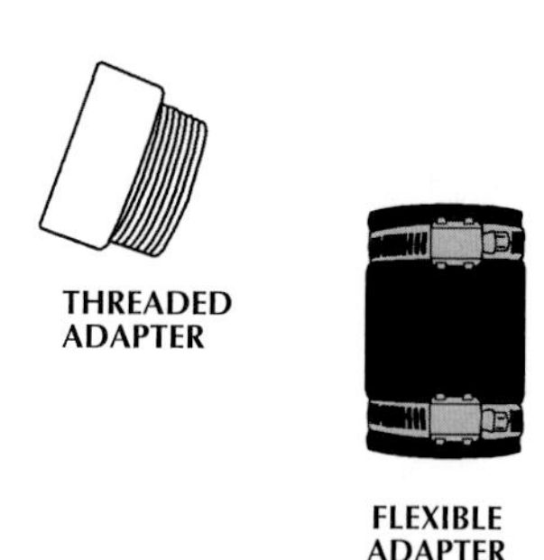

Transition fittings.
A threaded adapter, as in the supply system, joins threaded pipe to unthreaded and also connects pipe to various special drain-system components, such as cleanout plugs and traps. A flexible adapter made of a rubberlike, specially treated PVC connects unthreaded drainpipes of any material; the fitting is slipped over the pipe ends and its built-in clamps tightened.

MEASURING PIPES

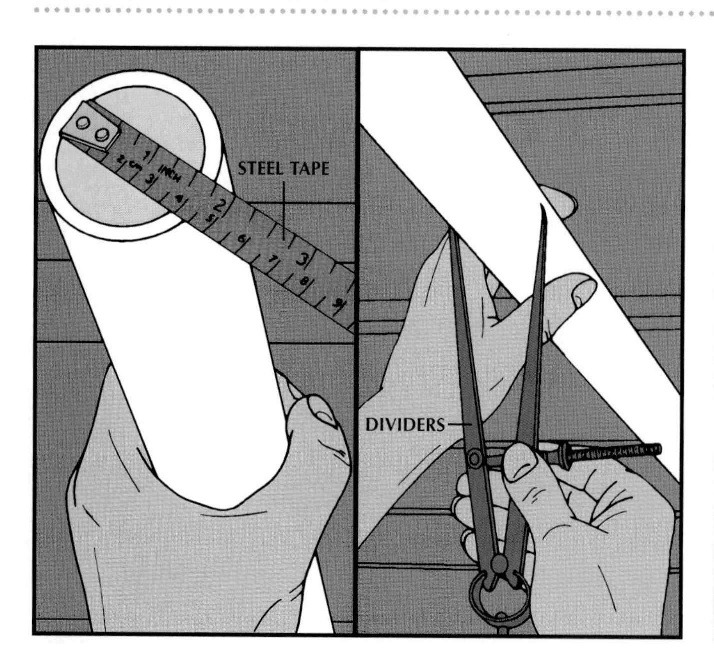

Finding the inside diameter.
Pipes and fittings are sized according to their inside diameter, called nominal size.

◆ To determine this figure for cut pipe, simply hold a ruler or steel tape across an end of the pipe and measure from one inner wall to the other *(above, left)*.

◆ If the pipe is part of an uncut run, you must proceed indirectly. First, fit dividers *(above, right)*, calipers, or a C clamp against the pipe, then measure the space between the instrument's arms to get the outside diameter; repeat several times and average the readings. Take that measurement to your pipe supplier to get an exact match.

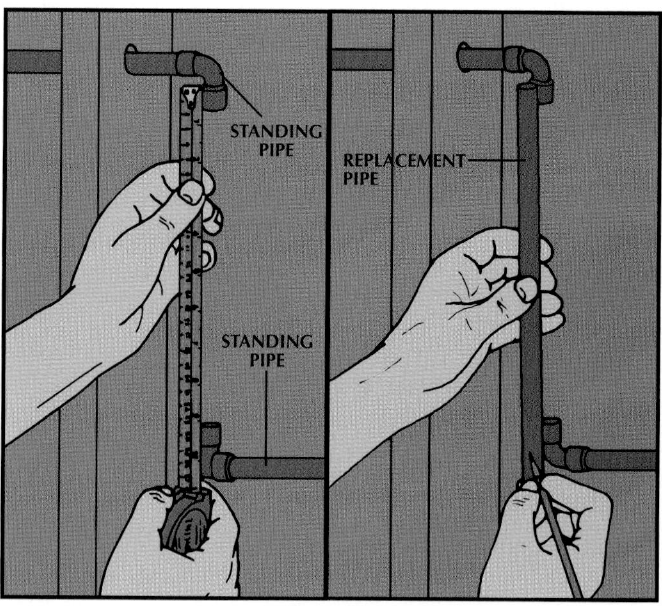

Measuring the replacement pipe.

◆ After cutting out or unthreading damaged pipe, buy the appropriate type of replacement pipe, making sure the piece is several inches longer than the gap. (See pages 152 to 160 to determine the correct pipe material and adapters for the plumbing being repaired.)

◆ Attach the new fittings on the ends of the standing pipes.

◆ Hold a steel tape to the farthest point the new pipe can extend into each of the two fittings *(above, left)*. Alternatively, hold the replacement pipe up to the gap and mark the exact length—including the depth of the fittings—with a pencil *(above, right)*.

◆ Cut the replacement pipe to fit.

REPAIRING AND REPLACING PIPE

A plumbing system's pipes, no matter what kind, are unlikely to remain problem-free forever. Sooner or later—perhaps because of corrosion, a leak at an aging joint, or the bursting of a frozen pipe—some mending will probably be necessary.

Measure for the replacement pipe as explained opposite, and begin any supply-line repair by draining the system *(box, right)*. The methods for making repairs depend on the material of the pipes involved. You can use pipe and fittings that match your current piping, or introduce a different material—replacing a run of copper with CPVC, for example. Some of the most common ways of mending broken pipe are described on the following pages.

Copper Piping: Copper is connected to copper by heating the metal with a propane torch and drawing molten solder into a pipe-and-fitting joint—a process called "sweating." The solder for supply pipes must be lead-free; other solders are acceptable for copper drains. Because the flame can be a hazard to your home's structure and its wiring, cover the area behind the piping with a flameproof pad. Keep a fire extinguisher nearby, and turn off the torch before setting it down. For complex repairs, do as much of the assembly as possible at your workbench.

Connect copper to plastic with transition fittings; several types are available.

Plastic Piping: Assemble rigid plastic pipe only when the air temperature is above 40°F. Different types of plastic require their own primers and cements: Never use PVC primer on a CPVC repair, for instance. The basic methods used to join PVC and CPVC are the same, however *(page 158)*.

A third type of plastic, ABS, requires no primer. To repair ABS pipe with PVC replacement pipe, install a rubber adapter or consecutive male and female adapters in conjunction with primer on the PVC side and a light green transition cement on both sides.

CAUTION *Solvent cements are toxic and flammable. When you apply them, you must make sure the work area is well ventilated.*

SHUTTING DOWN THE SUPPLY SYSTEM

Before making repairs to the supply system, shut off the house water supply. First, close the main shutoff valve. Then, working from the top level down, open all hot- and cold-water faucets—including all tub, shower, and outdoor faucets—and flush all toilets. Open the drain faucets on the main supply line, the water heater, and any water treatment equipment you may have. To refill the system after the repair has been completed, close all the faucets, then open the main shutoff valve. Trapped air will cause faucets to sputter momentarily when you first turn them on again.

SAFETY TIP

Goggles and gloves provide important protection when you are soldering copper pipe.

TOOLS

- Tube cutter
- Hacksaw
- Plumber's abrasive sandcloth
- Metal file
- Round file
- Wire fitting brush
- Flux brush
- Groove-joint pliers
- Striker
- Propane torch
- Flameproof pad
- Small, sharp knife
- Adjustable wrench
- Fine-tooth hacksaw or minihacksaw
- Pipe wrenches
- Ratchet pipe cutter
- Nut driver or socket wrench

MATERIALS

- Replacement pipe and fittings
- Clean cloth
- Paste flux
- Solder
- Miter box
- Adapters
- PVC or CPVC primer
- PVC, CPVC, or ABS cement
- Applicator brushes
- Plumbing-sealant tape
- Grounding clamps
- Grounding wire
- 2 x 4 lumber
- Stack clamps
- Chalk
- Newspaper or paper towels

REPLACING COPPER WITH COPPER

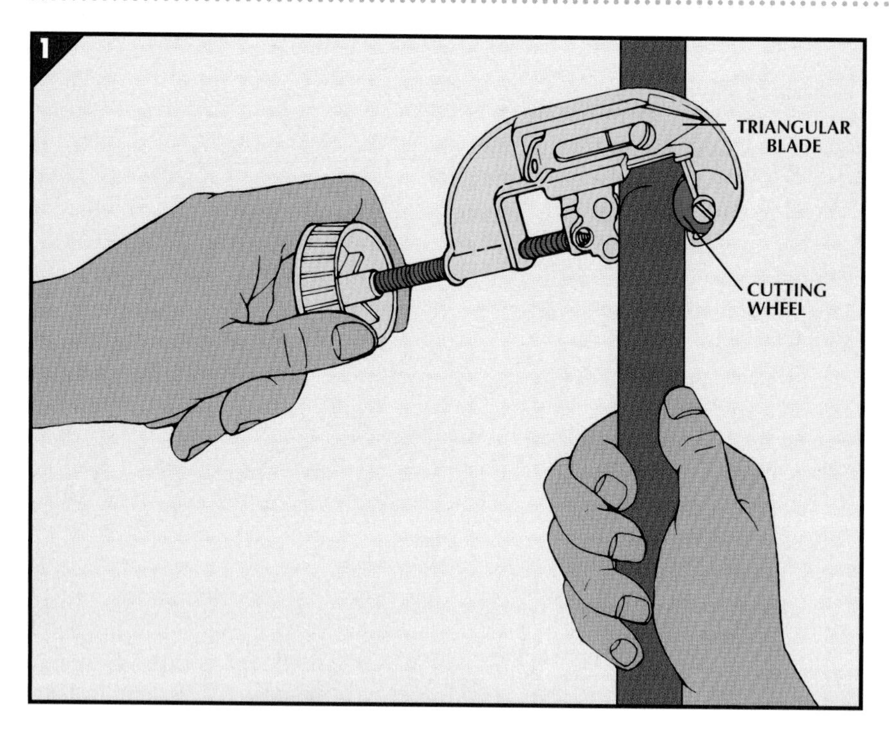

1. Using a cutter.
Although a hacksaw may be needed for a hard-to-reach section of broken copper pipe, use a tube cutter if possible.
◆ Slide the cutter onto the pipe and turn the knob until the tube cutter's cutting wheel bites into the copper. Do not tighten the knob all the way.
◆ Turn the cutter once around, retighten the knob, and continue turning and tightening. Once the piping is severed, loosen the knob, slide the cutter down the pipe, and cut through the other side of the broken section.
◆ With the cutter's triangular blade, ream out the burr inside the standing pipe. Remove the ridge on the outside with a file. (For a hacksaw cut, remove the inner burr with a round file.)
◆ Use the tube cutter to cut and ream replacement pipe.

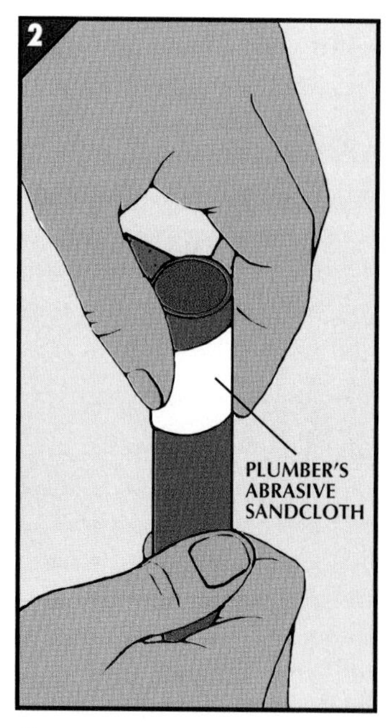

2. Preparing the cut ends.
With a piece of plumber's abrasive sandcloth—not a file or steel wool—clean the cut pipe ends to a distance slightly greater than the depth of fittings that you will use to connect them. Rub until the surface is bright.

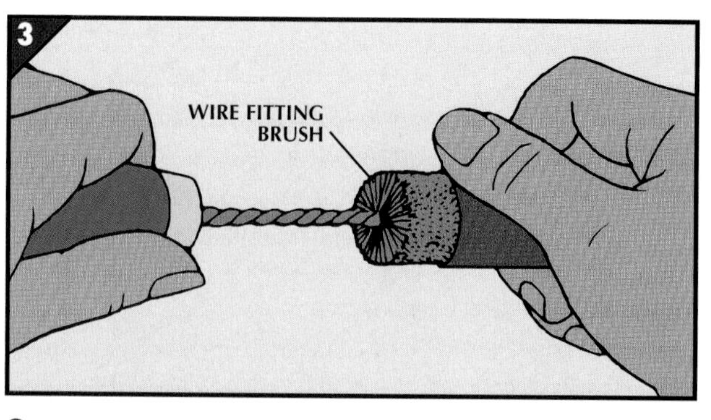

3. Cleaning the fittings.
Scour the inner surfaces of the sockets of each fitting with a wire fitting brush. Once the surfaces of the fittings and pipes have been cleaned, do not touch them: Even a fingerprint will weaken the joint.

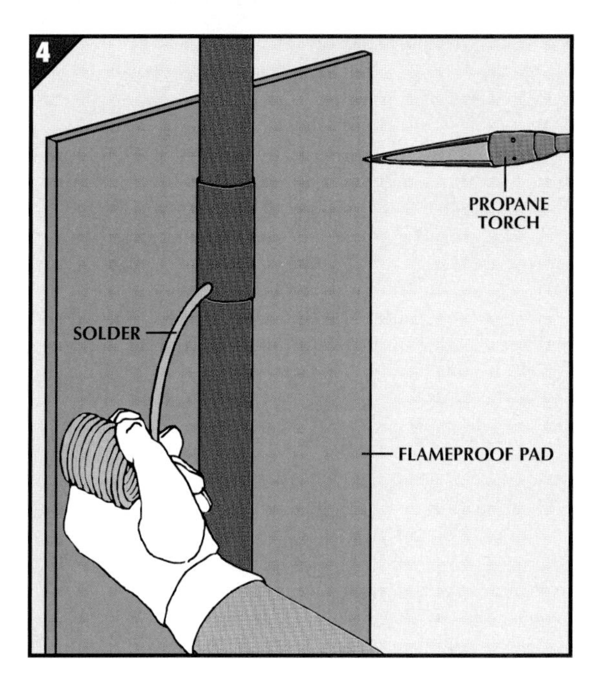

4. Assembling and heating a joint.

◆ Brush a light coat of flux over the cleaned surfaces, place the fitting between the standing pipe and the replacement section, and twist it a quarter-turn.
◆ For a slip coupling on a vertical pipe, shown here, gently crimp the coupling with groove-joint pliers just enough to hold it in place.
◆ Place a flameproof pad in back of the joint.
◆ Light the torch with a striker. Holding the tip of the flame perpendicular to the metal and about a half-inch away, play it over the fitting and nearby pipe.
◆ Touch a piece of solder to the fitting *(left)* until it melts on contact. Do not heat further or the flux will burn off and the solder will not flow properly.

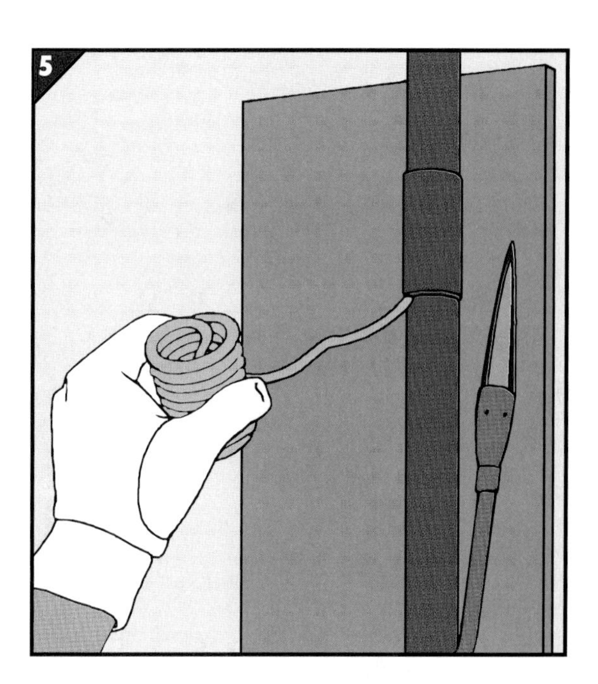

5. Soldering the joint.

◆ Touch the solder tip to the pipe where it enters one end of the fitting. Keep the solder at that point while the capillary action of the flux draws molten solder into the fitting to seal the connection.
◆ Remove the solder from the joint when a bead of metal completely seals the rim.
◆ Wipe away excess with a clean cloth, leaving a shiny surface.
◆ Apply solder to the other end of the fitting in the same way, then sweat the other joint.

TRICKS OF THE TRADE

Dos and Don'ts of Sweated Joints

Good sweated joints *(below, left)* are achieved by careful handling of flux and solder. Spread the coat of flux thinly and evenly. Excessive residue can cause corrosion; too little flux will create gaps in the bond between solder and copper. Do not overheat the fitting or direct the flame into the socket: If the flux burns—indicated by a brownish black coloring—the bond will be imperfect. Never direct the flame at the solder, and be sure to remove the solder as soon as capillary action sucks it around the full circumference of the joint. If solder drips, it has been overheated or overapplied, and the capillary action will fail. Thick, irregular globs of solder at the edges of sweated joints are a sign of a bad job *(below, right)*.

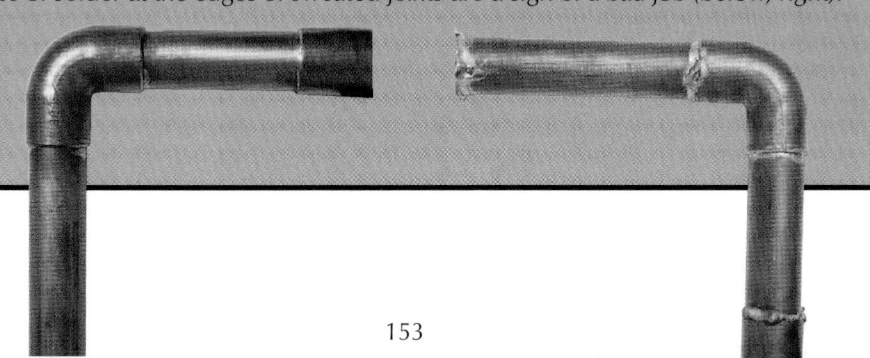

JOINING PLASTIC TO COPPER

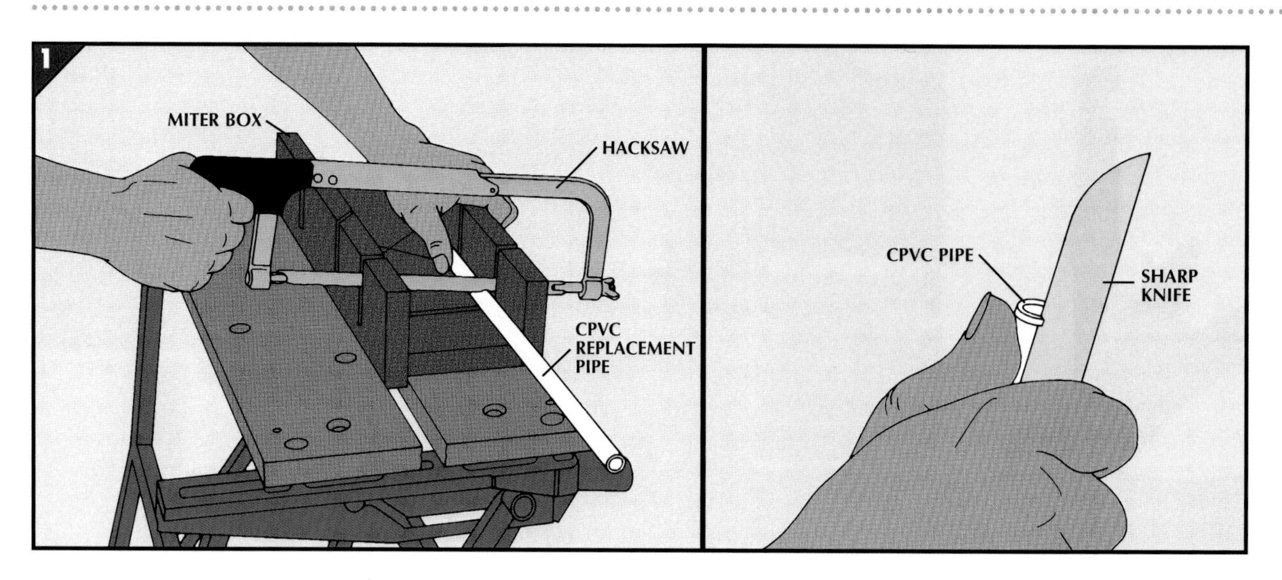

1. Cutting the pipes.

◆ Cut out the broken section of copper pipe with a tube cutter or hacksaw and ream the ends of the standing pipes *(page 152)*.

◆ Cut the CPVC replacement pipe with a tube cutter or hacksaw. If you use a hacksaw, place the pipe in a miter box and brace it with your thumb as you make the cut *(above, left)*.

◆ Ream the ends of the replacement pipe.

◆ With a small, sharp knife *(above, right),* trim the ends' inside edge to aid water flow and the outside edge to improve the welding action of the solvent.

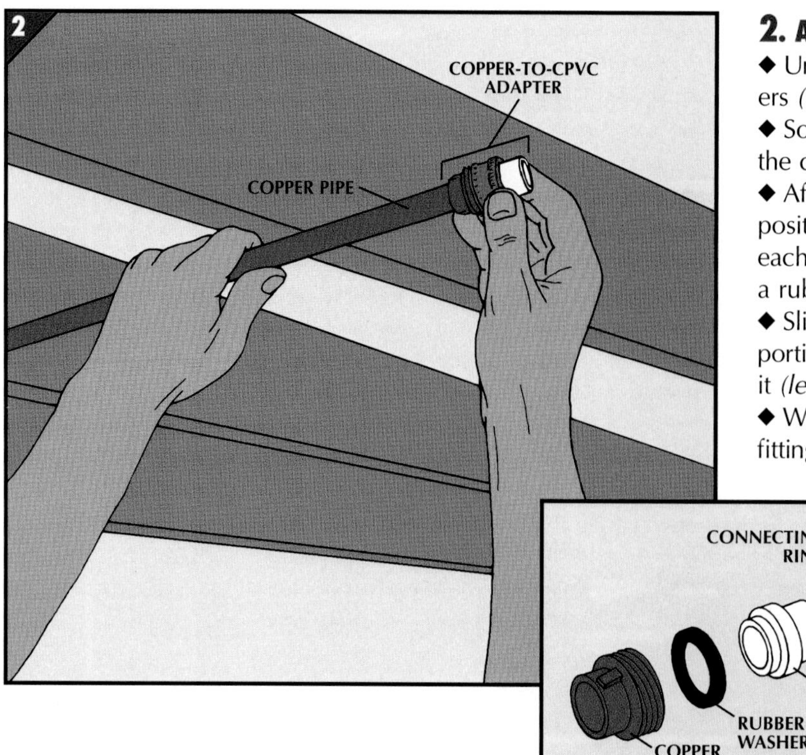

2. Adding the adapters.

◆ Unfasten two copper-to-CPVC adapters *(inset)*.

◆ Solder the copper ends of the fittings to the cut ends of the copper pipe *(page 153)*.

◆ After the soldered joints have cooled, position the threaded CPVC portion of each fitting against the copper portion with a rubber washer placed between them.

◆ Slide the connecting ring over the CPVC portion of each fitting and hand-tighten it *(left)*.

◆ With an adjustable wrench, tighten the fittings just beyond hand tight.

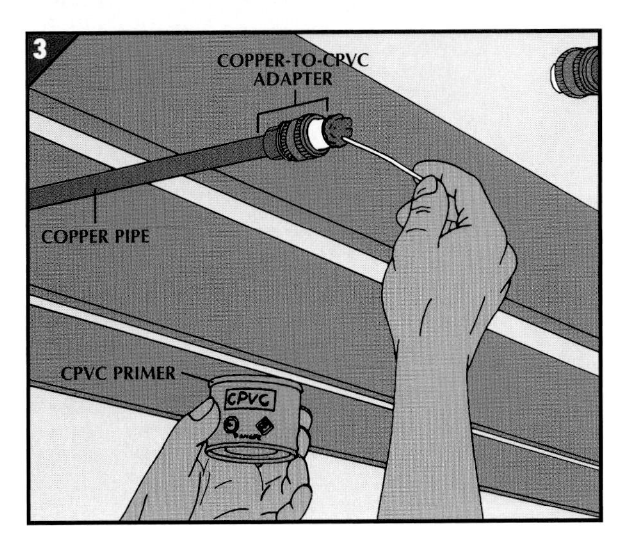

3. Priming and cementing the joints.
Work as quickly as possible with solvent cement. It sets in less than 30 seconds.
◆ With an applicator or clean cloth, apply a coat of primer to the inside of the sockets of the adapters *(left)* and to the outside pipe surfaces that will be fitted into the adapters.
◆ With a second applicator, spread a coat of CPVC cement over the primed surfaces at the ends of the CPVC pipe.
◆ Spread a light coat of cement inside the adapter sockets.

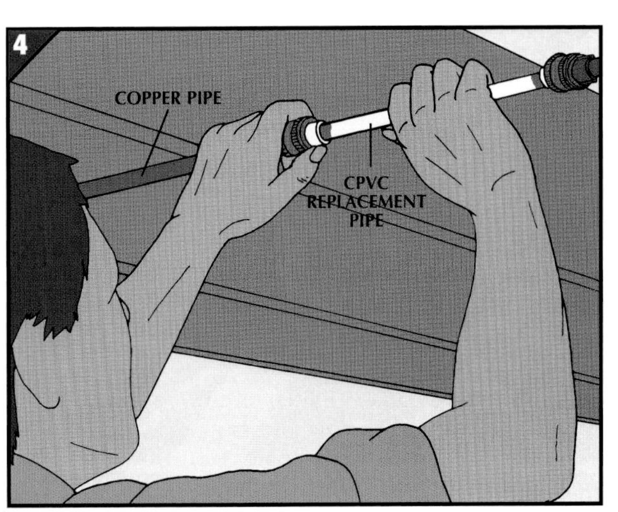

4. Fitting the replacement pipe.
◆ Working rapidly, push one end of the CPVC pipe into an adapter.
◆ Pull the free ends toward you until enough space opens for the CPVC pipe to slip into the second adapter *(right).*
◆ Give the CPVC pipe a quarter-turn to evenly distribute the cement inside the sockets.
◆ Hold it firmly for about 10 seconds.
◆ Wipe away any excess cement with a clean, dry cloth. Do not run water in the pipe until the cement has cured (about 2 hours at temperatures above 60°F).

REPAIRING STEEL PIPE WITH PLASTIC

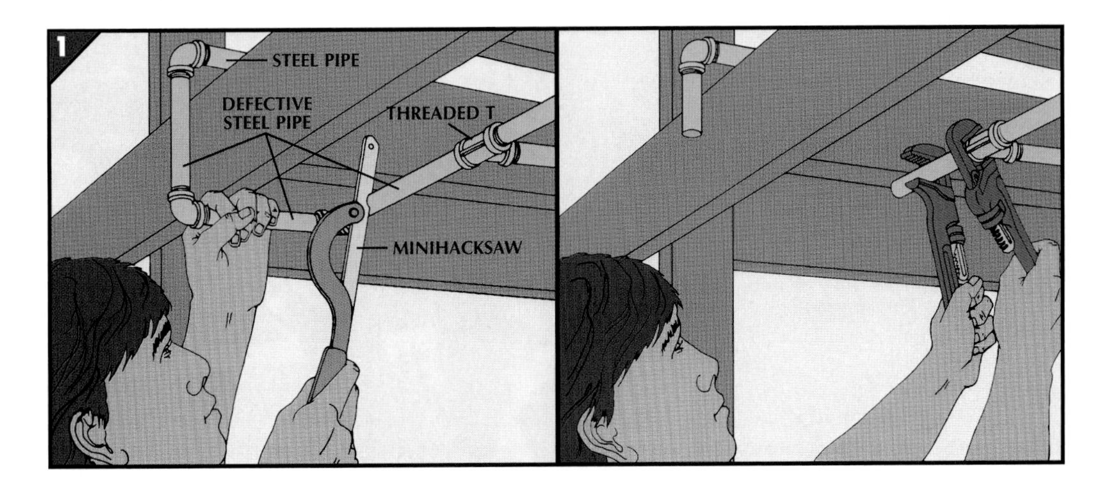

1. Removing the steel pipe.
Once in place, a threaded pipe cannot be unscrewed as one piece. In the situation here, CPVC replaces three runs of damaged pipe.
◆ Near the outer ends of the damaged section, cut the pipe with a fine-tooth hacksaw or minihacksaw *(above, left).* Remove the intervening piping.
◆ Unthread the remaining stubs of pipe from their fittings. Hold a fitting stationary with one wrench and turn the pipe with another wrench. The jaws must face the direction in which the force is applied *(above, right).*

If a union is near a damaged section, cutting is unnecessary. Hold the pipe steady with one wrench, unscrew the union with a second, then unscrew the other end of pipe from its fitting.

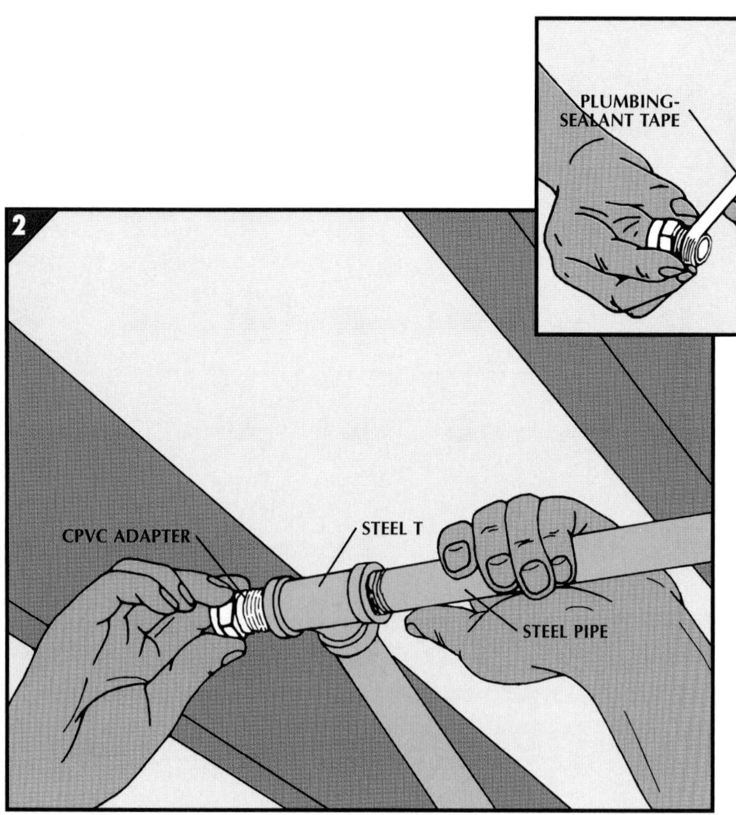

2. Adding CPVC adapters.

◆ Wrap plumbing-sealant tape around the threads of two CPVC adapters *(inset)* and screw them into the steel fittings by hand *(left)*.

◆ With an adjustable wrench, tighten the adapters just beyond hand tight.

3. Measuring and test-fitting replacement pipe.

◆ Push CPVC pipe into an adapter socket as far as it will go. Mark the desired length, allowing for the socket depth of the fitting that will go at the other end.

◆ Cut that section of pipe to length with a hacksaw in a miter box *(page 154)*.

◆ Push the fitting—in this case, an elbow—on the other end. Measure and cut the next length of CPVC pipe, push it into the next fitting, and continue dry-fitting the replacement piping in this way.

◆ At each connection, draw a line across the fitting and adjacent pipe *(right)* as a guide for reassembly and cementing.

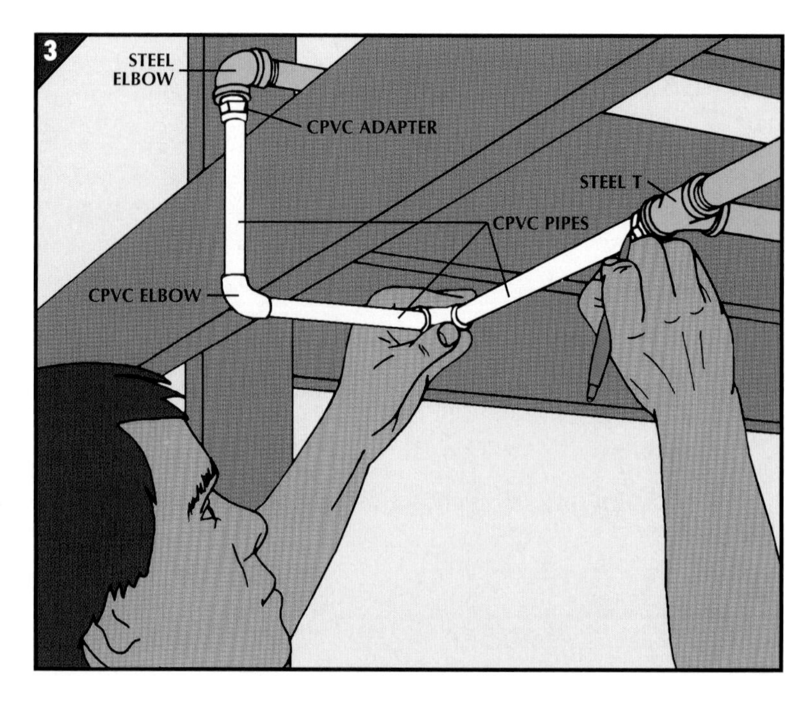

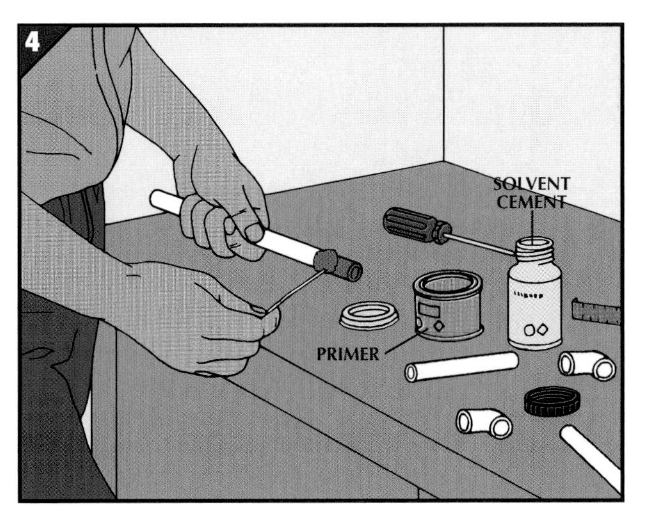

4. Cementing the CPVC pipe.

◆ Disassemble the dry-fitted pipe sections.

◆ At a well-ventilated workbench, ream and trim all pipe ends *(page 154).*

◆ Apply primer and solvent cement *(page 155)* to a pipe and fitting that will form an outer section of the assembly *(left).*

◆ Push the pipe into the fitting, give it a quarter-turn, and align the marks. Hold the pieces together for about 10 seconds.

◆ Continue cementing pipe and fittings together until all but the last pipe is in place. Leave this pipe detached.

5. Beginning the installation.

◆ Check to make sure that the CPVC adapters are dry. If they are not, dry them with a clean cloth.

◆ Apply primer to the sockets of both CPVC adapters.

◆ Spread solvent cement in the socket of the adapter that will receive the pipe at the completed end of the CPVC assembly. Apply primer and then a coat of cement to the end of that pipe.

◆ Push the pipe into the adapter socket as far as it will go. Give the pipe a quarter-turn to spread the cement.

◆ Line up the marks on the pipe and adapter and hold the pieces together for about 10 seconds *(right).*

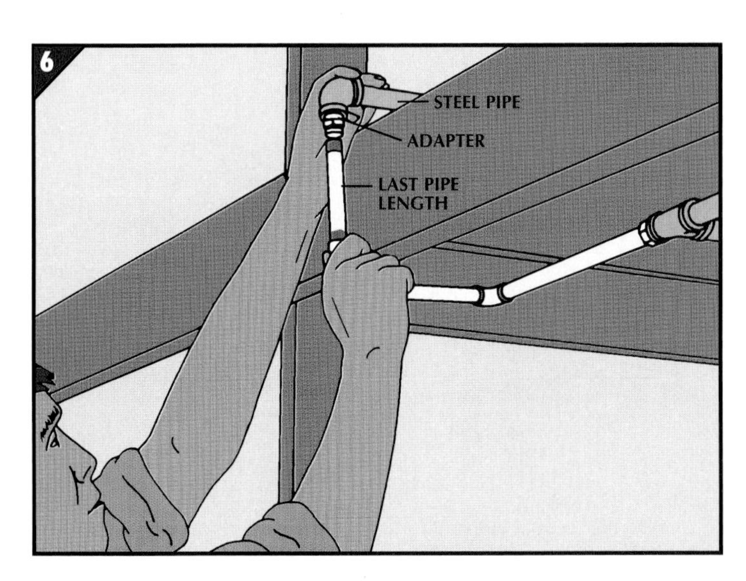

6. Adding the last pipe.

◆ Apply primer and cement to the second adapter, the last fitting on the CPVC assembly, and both ends of the unattached pipe.

◆ Push one end of the pipe into the assembly fitting. Gently maneuvering the assembly *(left),* push the other end into the adapter socket as far as it will go.

◆ Give the pipe a quarter-turn to spread the cement, and hold the pieces together for about 10 seconds. Do not run water in the pipe until the cement has cured (about 2 hours at temperatures above 60°F).

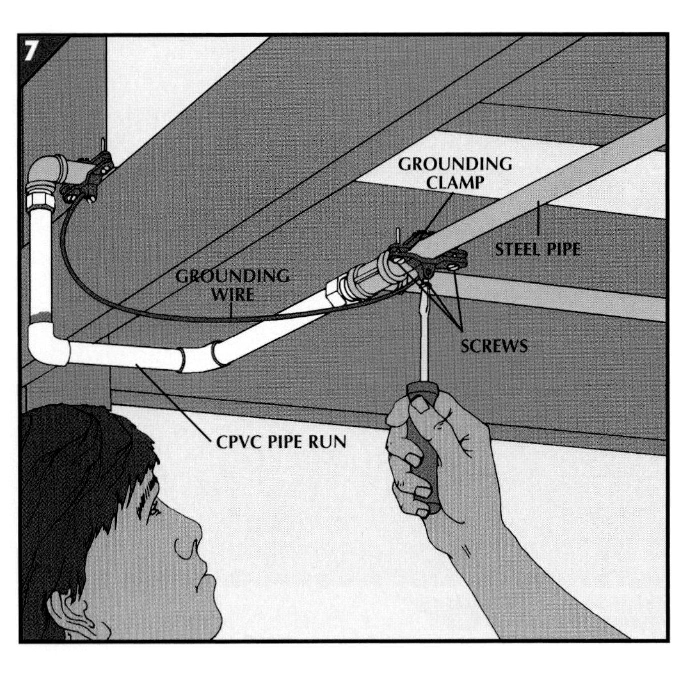

7. Installing a grounding jumper.
If the replaced section of steel pipe was part of your home's electrical grounding system, you must install a grounding jumper to maintain continuity.
◆ At one end of the cut steel pipes, fit both pieces of a grounding clamp *(above)* around the circumference of the pipe. Fasten the two pieces together with screws on either end of the clamp.
◆ Measure and cut a length of grounding wire to extend between the clamp and the other cut steel pipe.
◆ Insert the wire into the small opening on top of the clamp and secure it with the corresponding screw.
◆ Install a clamp on the other steel pipe and secure the end of the wire in its opening *(left)*.

FIXING PLASTIC PIPE

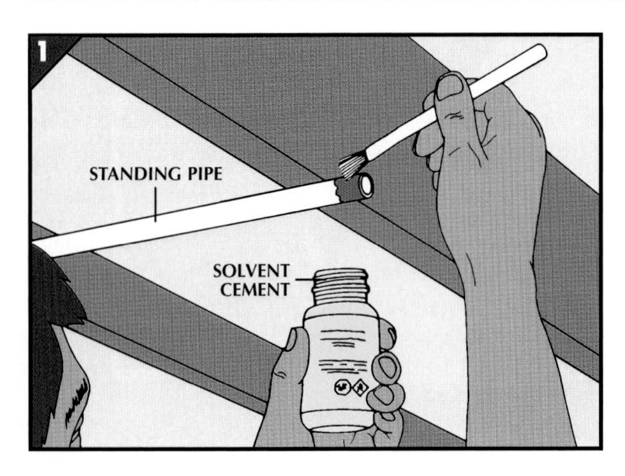

1. Preparing the joint.
◆ Cut out the damaged pipe with a hacksaw or tube cutter.
◆ Hold the replacement pipe against the gap and mark it, then cut it with a tube cutter or hacksaw and miter box.
◆ Ream and trim the pipe ends *(page 154)*.
◆ Prime the ends of the standing pipes and one socket on each of two couplings.
◆ Apply a liberal coat of solvent cement to the coupling sockets and on the ends of the standing pipes *(left)* to a distance matching the socket depth.
◆ Push the couplings onto the pipes, give them a quarter-turn to spread the cement, and hold the pieces together about 10 seconds.

2. Inserting the replacement pipe.
◆ Prime the exposed coupling sockets and ends of the replacement pipe, then apply cement.
◆ Working quickly, push one end of the replacement pipe into a coupling, then gently bend the pipes until the opposite end fits into the other coupling *(right)*.
◆ Give the pipe a quarter-turn to spread the cement, and hold the pieces together for about 10 seconds.
◆ Wipe off any excess cement around the pipe or fittings with a clean, dry cloth. Do not run water in the pipe until the cement has cured (about 2 hours at temperatures above 60°F).

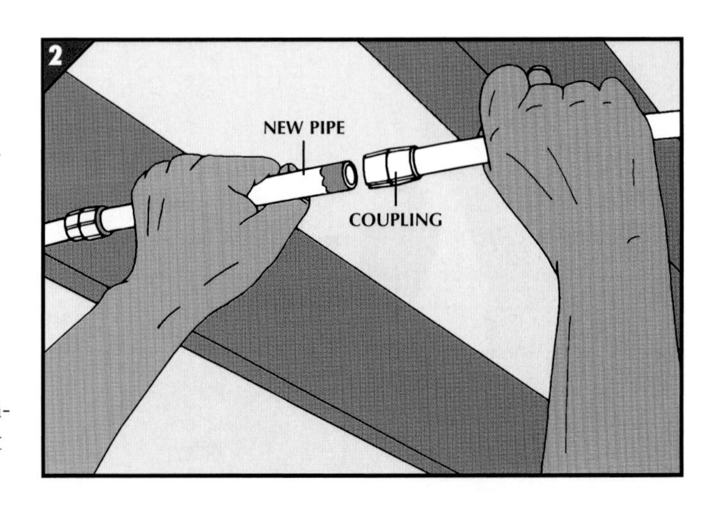

MENDING CAST-IRON DRAINPIPE

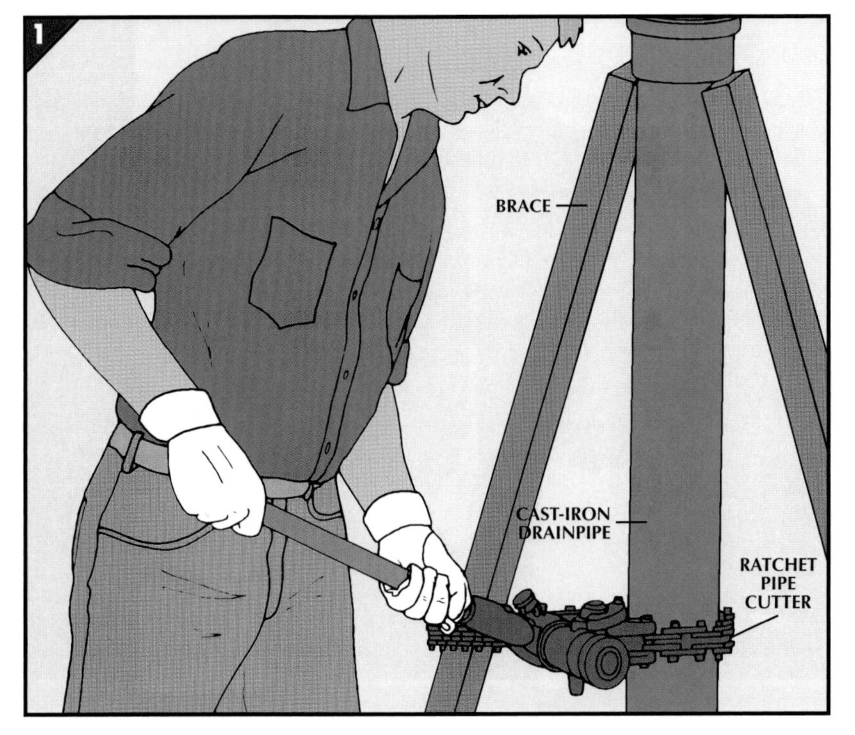

1. Removing the broken pipe.

The easiest way to cut cast-iron pipe is with a ratchet pipe cutter, available at rental stores. Before cutting vertical drainpipe, support it with stack clamps, available at plumbing stores, or brace 2-by-4s against a joint above the section to be removed *(left),* hammering the braces into position for a secure fit. Make sure that no one runs water in the house during the repair.

◆ With chalk, mark off the area to be cut out.
◆ Wrap the chain around the pipe and hook it onto the body of the tool.
◆ Tighten the knob, turn the dial to CUT, and work the handle back and forth until the cutting disks bite through the pipe.
◆ If badly corroded pipe crumbles under a pipe cutter, rent an electric saber saw and metal-cutting blade.

2. Cutting the replacement pipe.

◆ Immediately after removing the damaged section, stuff newspaper or paper towels into the standing pipes *(left)* to block dangerous sewer gas.
◆ Measure the gap in the pipe and transfer that measurement, less $\frac{1}{4}$ inch, to a cast-iron, PVC, or ABS replacement pipe.
◆ Lay cast-iron pipe across two level 2-by-4s, spaced to support the pipe ends, and cut it to size with a ratchet cutter or saber saw.
◆ Cut PVC or ABS with a hacksaw and miter box.
◆ With a sharp knife, ream and trim the ends of the plastic pipe *(page 154).*

3. Inserting the replacement section.

Hubless bands *(page 150)* join cast-iron drainpipe to replacement pipe.

◆ Slide a clamp onto each standing pipe and tighten the clamps to hold them temporarily in place.

◆ Slip the neoprene sleeves of the fittings onto each pipe until the pipe ends bottom out inside the sleeves *(near right)*.

◆ Fold the lip of each sleeve back over the pipe.

◆ Work the replacement pipe into the gap between the sleeves *(far right)* until it is properly seated.

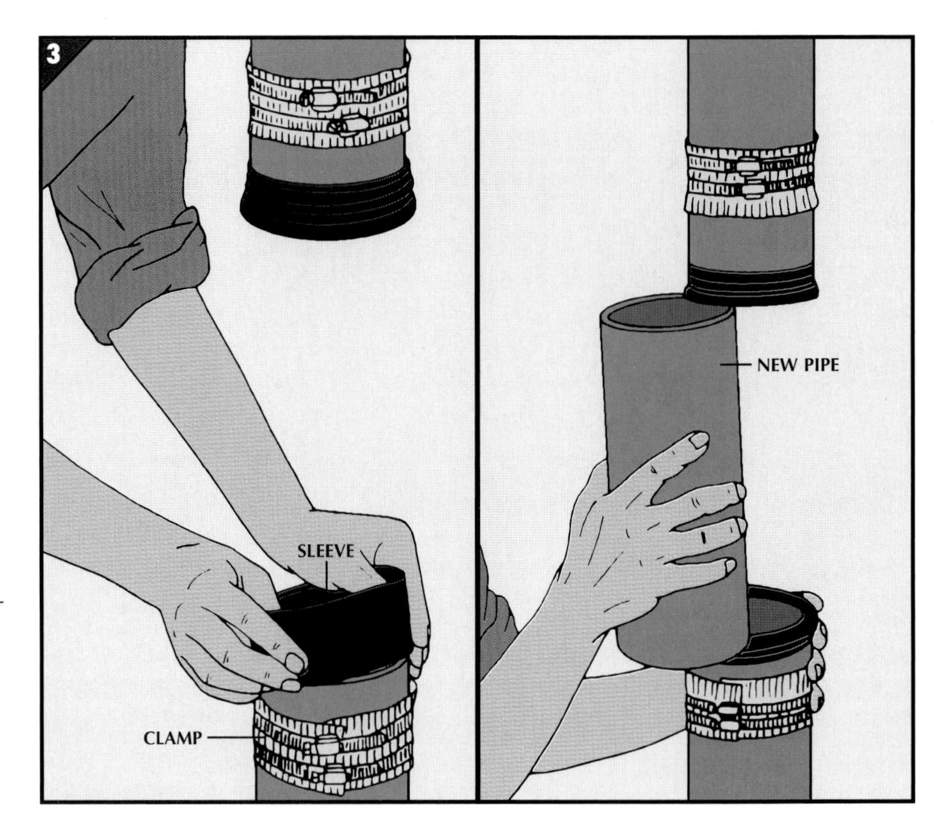

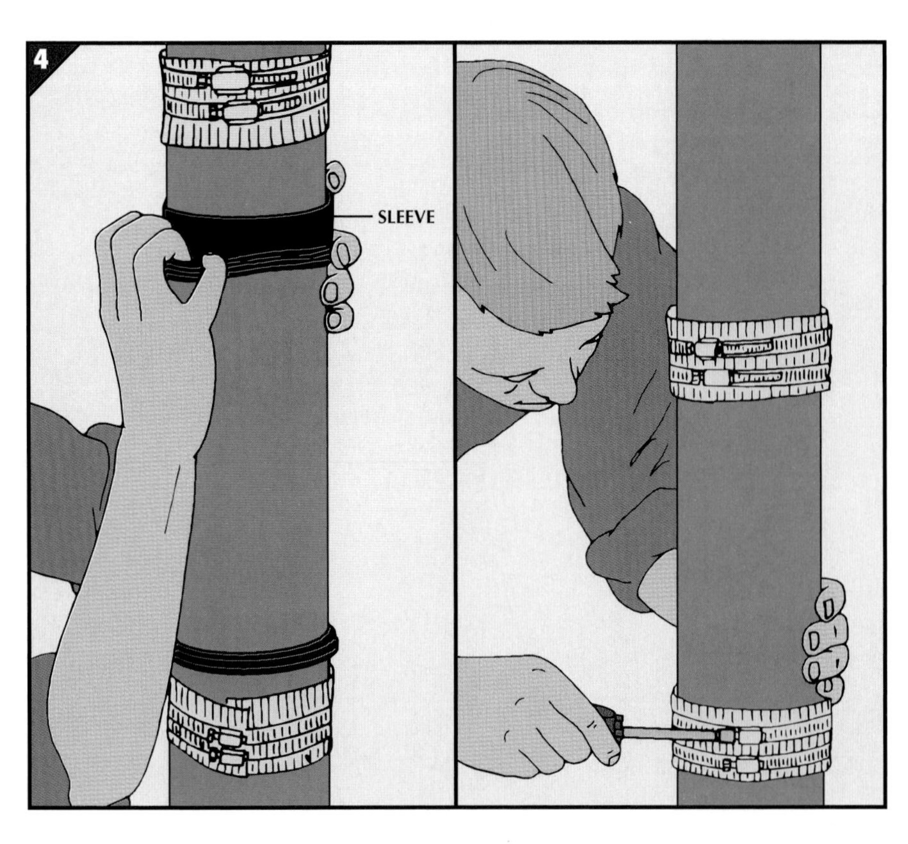

4. Completing the repair.

◆ Pull the folded lips of the sleeves over the replacement pipe *(far left)*.

◆ Loosen the clamps and slide them toward the replacement section until they are centered over the joints. Tighten them again with a nut driver *(near left)* or socket wrench.

◆ Run water through the drainpipe in order to test the repair; if a joint leaks, take it apart and reassemble the hubless band.

EXTENDING PLUMBING TO A NEW SINK

With a little ingenuity, you can apply the techniques of cutting and connecting pipes *(pages 152–160)* to move a fixture such as a vanity or add it to existing plumbing. In some situations, like the one illustrated below, you can complete the entire job outside the wall. Other projects may require cutting open and patching a small section. If the new piping runs exposed along a wall *(page 162, bottom)*, you often can conceal it behind a set of shelves or inside a floor cabinet.

For almost any extension, plastic pipes (CPVC for supply lines, PVC for drainpipes) are easiest to work with. Cut the old piping and add a branch fitting of the same material. Join the new piping to it with the appropriate adapter *(pages 149–150)*.

Locating Old Pipes: Before starting work, you must find the stack inside the wall. Determine the stack's general location by observing where it exits the roof, then pinpoint it with an electronic stud finder. Supply lines, also called risers, may run beside the stack or take a more circuitous route. You can often find the risers with the stud finder—or turn on the water, one faucet at a time, and listen for the flow with your ear against the wall.

Keeping It Simple: Once you know where the plumbing is, plan the job to avoid complications. For instance, always place the fixture within a few feet of the drain stack to avoid the need for a separate vent. Avoid adding a connection for a new sink drain to the stack below a washing machine or toilet connection; doing so would also require adding a new vent. Check your local code for other restrictions.

Make sure the drainpipe has room to slope properly and that the lower end will not be below the level of water standing in the trap. The placement of supply lines is less critical, but if the lines follow the same slope they will be easy to drain; keep the two lines about 6 inches apart.

TOOLS

- Electronic stud finder
- Drill with screwdriver and twist bits
- Utility knife
- Steel tape measure
- Soil-pipe cutter
- Tube cutter
- Hacksaw
- Propane torch
- Flameproof pad
- Drywall knife

MATERIALS

- CPVC supply pipe
- PVC drainpipe
- Supply and drain fittings
- Rubber sleeves and clamps
- Pipe anchors
- Adapters
- Plumbing-sealant tape
- Solder
- Flux
- PVC and CPVC primer and cement
- Stack clamps
- 2 x 4s
- Drywall
- $1\frac{1}{2}$-inch drywall screws
- Fiberglass-mesh tape
- Joint compound

SAFETY TIP

When soldering adapters to existing copper pipe, wear gloves and eye protection.

THREE SCHEMES FOR SUPPLY AND DRAIN LINES

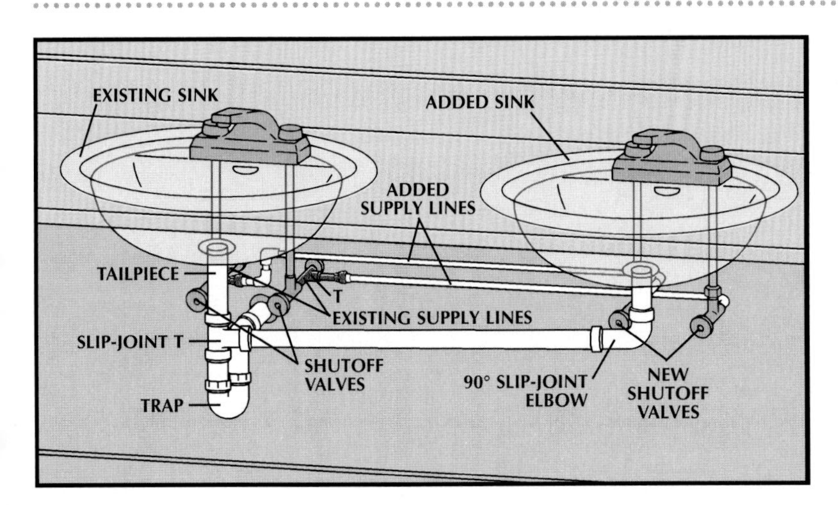

Side-by-side fixtures.
This arrangement requires no work on the stack—the new sink is tied into the trap of an existing one so that both empty into the stack together. The drainpipe between the two fixtures slopes downward from the new one $\frac{1}{4}$ inch per foot, and there can be no more than 30 inches between the drain holes of the two fixtures. Slip-joint fittings, including a slip-joint T above the trap of the old fixture, simplify the drain connections. The new supply lines run from T fittings added behind the old shutoff valves to the existing sink. At the added sink, a second pair of shutoff valves regulates water to that faucet.

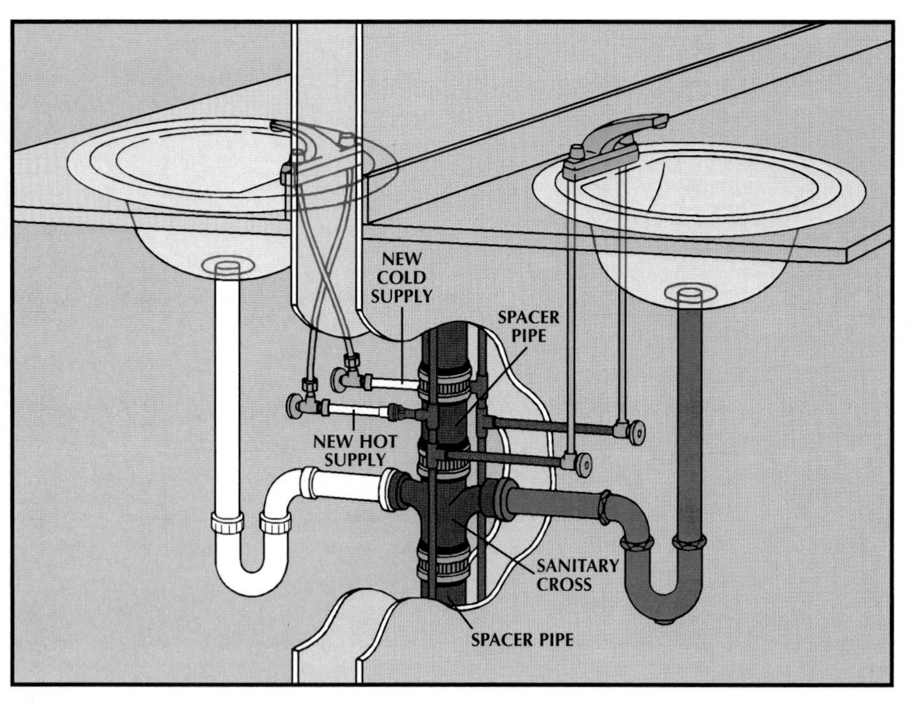

Back-to-back fixtures.
If an existing sink drains into a stack in the wall behind it, a new fixture can be installed back to back with the old one *(left)*. A two-inlet fitting called a sanitary cross, sandwiched between two spacer pipes, replaces the original drain connection, and the new supply lines run from T fittings added to the risers. Under the new sink, the supply tubes cross each other to bring hot water to the left side of the new fixture and cold water to the right.

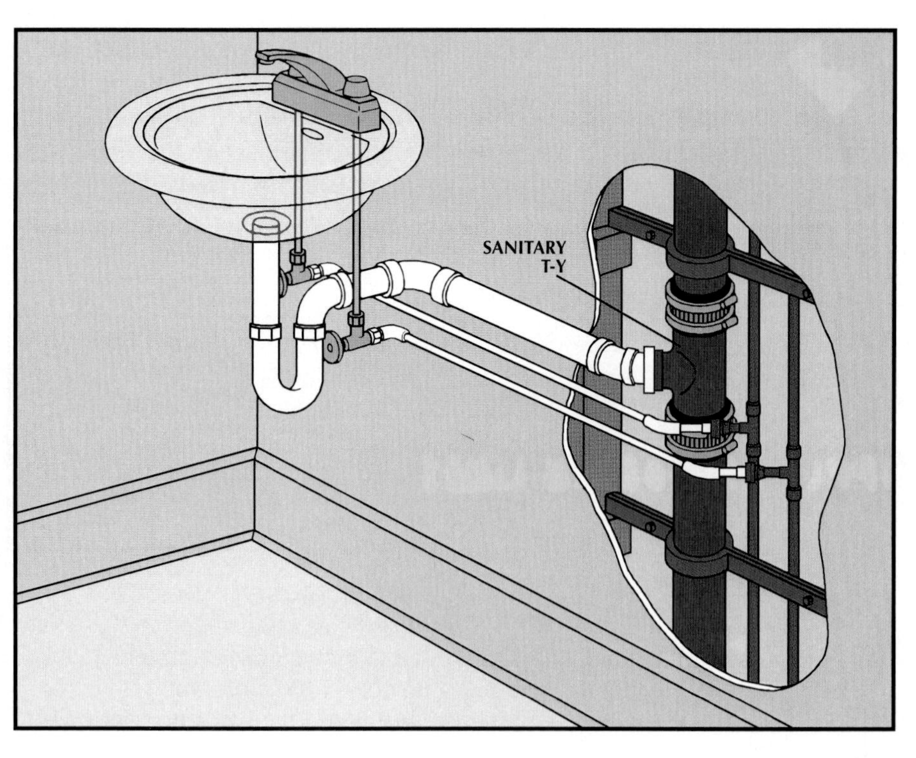

A fixture anywhere.
This method lets you install a fixture at any point close enough to a stack for a $\frac{1}{4}$-inch-per-foot drainpipe slope. A sanitary T-Y fitting or a sanitary T *(page 150)* makes the connection between the new drainpipe and the stack; supply lines are accommodated with T fittings on the risers. Both the drain and supply lines come outside the wall and run along it to the new fixture.

INSTALLING A VANITY AND WALL CABINET

Storage space is often at a premium in a bathroom. A simple way to make more room is to install a larger medicine cabinet or a supplementary one, mounted on the wall. For even more space, you can discard a stand-alone washbasin and instead install a vanity with a sink in the countertop.

Considerations for a Vanity: Ready-made cabinets are available in many widths. Choose a vanity that is at least wide enough to cover the holes left in the wall by the bracket for the old washbasin but not so large that the bathroom becomes cramped.

Installing a Medicine Cabinet: A surface-mounted cabinet *(page 167)* can be hung virtually anywhere in a bathroom. If you prefer to have a mirror flat on the wall over the basin, you can hang a medicine cabinet in any convenient spot where you can locate the wall studs.

TOOLS

- Wrenches
- Screwdriver
- Cold chisel
- Saber saw
- Electronic stud finder
- Utility knife
- Pry bar
- Level
- Electric drill with screwdriver bit
- Backsaw
- Drywall saw

MATERIALS

- Wood shims
- $2\frac{1}{4}$-inch No. 6 drywall screws
- Adhesive caulk
- $1\frac{1}{2}$- and $2\frac{1}{2}$-inch finishing nails
- $\frac{3}{4}$-inch brads
- Scribe molding
- Shoe molding
- Hollow-wall anchors
- 2-by-4s
- Wallboard

CLEARING THE WAY FOR A VANITY

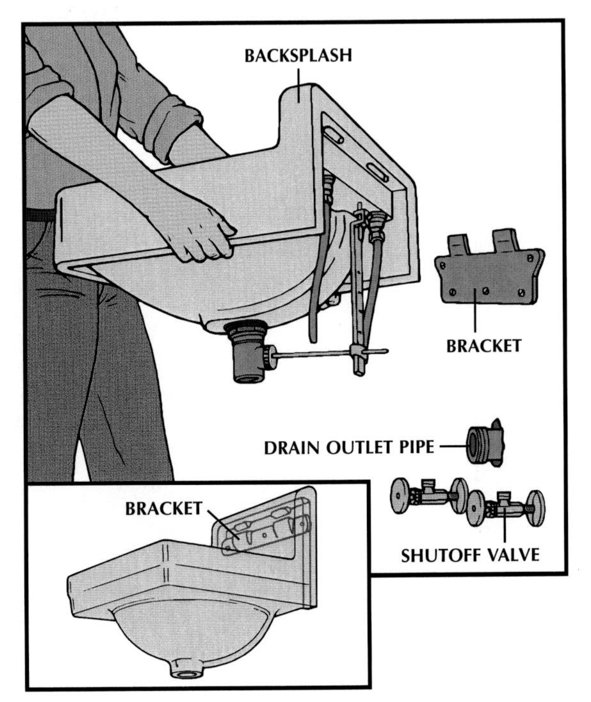

Dismounting wall-hung basins.

◆ Turn off the water at the basin shutoff valves or at the house's main valve. Disconnect the supply lines and the drainpipe assembly.

◆ To remove a basin hung on a bracket behind the backsplash as shown in the drawings at left, simply lift the basin straight up.

◆ Unscrew the bracket from the wall.

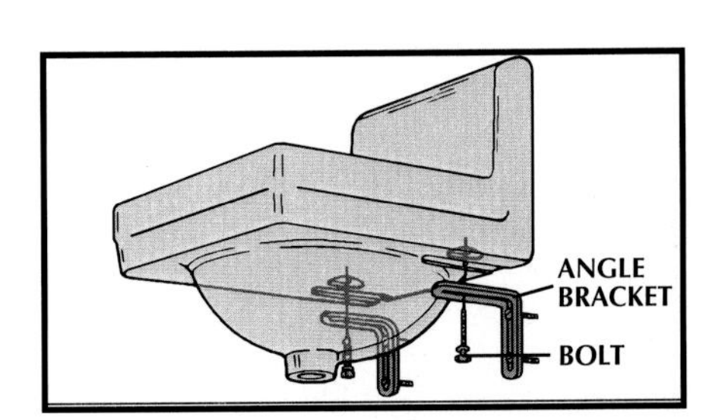

An angle bracket mounting.

To detach a basin supported from below by angle brackets, have a helper hold the basin while you loosen the mounting bolts with a wrench and remove them. Set the basin aside and unscrew the brackets from the wall.

DEALING WITH PEDESTAL BASINS

If you are installing a vanity in place of a pedestal basin in your bathroom, follow the steps below to remove the old fixture. However, if you want to install a pedestal basin, start at the last item in Step 2 and work backwards. That is: Install the wall bracket for the basin, mark the position of the pedestal on the floor, and drill holes for the floor bolt or other fasteners. Put the pedestal in place and install the fasteners. If the sink is not a single molded unit, install the threaded connecting rod according to the directions with the unit. Mount the faucets and drain assembly on the basin, and run a bead of adhesive caulk along the back edge. Place the basin in position on the pedestal, engaging it properly with the wall bracket as you do so. Secure the basin to the pedestal by screwing nuts on the threaded rod or tightening the other fasteners supplied with the unit. Finally, make the drain and water supply connections.

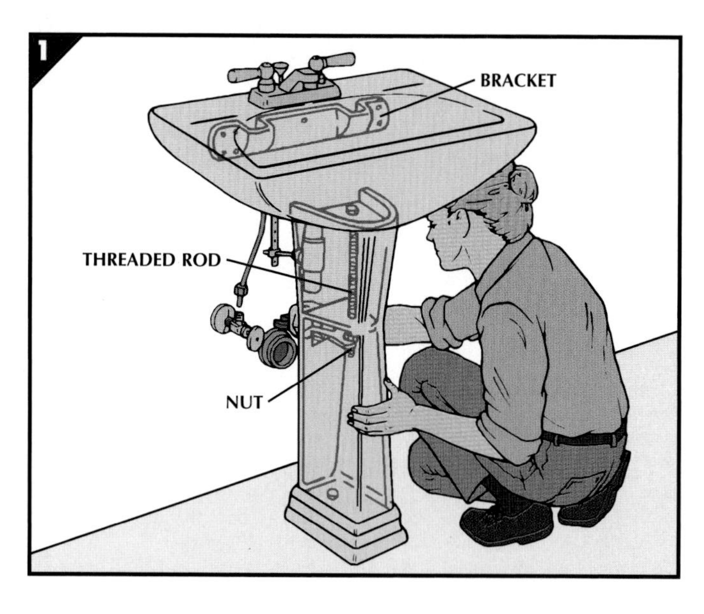

1. Removing a two-piece pedestal basin.

◆ Shut off the water and disconnect the water-supply lines and drainpipe assembly.

◆ Look inside the pedestal for a long threaded rod connecting the basin to its base. In the absence of such a rod, simply lift the basin from its wall bracket and set it aside. Otherwise, reach inside the pedestal with a wrench and remove the nut at the lower end of the rod *(left).* Lift the basin off its pedestal and wall bracket, then remove the rod from the basin.

2. Removing the pedestal.

◆ Unscrew any fasteners you find holding the pedestal base to the floor *(right),* then lift the pedestal away.

◆ If the pedestal is secured to the floor with grout, gently rock it back and forth to break the seal. Loosen old grout from the floor with a cold chisel.

◆ For a pedestal and basin molded as a single unit, unscrew the pedestal from the floor. Then lift the entire fixture free of the basin wall bracket.

◆ Detach the basin bracket from the wall.

ANCHORING A VANITY BASE AND COUNTERTOP

1. Aligning the cabinet.

◆ Position the vanity so that shutoff valves and drainpipe are roughly centered within the frame. If the vanity has a back, mark openings for the pipes, then cut the holes with a saber saw.

◆ Push the vanity against the wall. Mark the outline of the cabinet on the wall with light pencil lines, then set the cabinet aside.

◆ With a stud finder, locate wall studs that fall within the cabinet outline. Mark the center of each stud above the outline as shown here.

2. Dealing with baseboard.

◆ For wooden baseboard, run a utility knife along the joint between the wall and the top of the baseboard section extending across the planned area for the vanity, breaking any paint seal.

◆ At one end of the baseboard section, tap a small pry bar into the joint. Place a shim behind the bar *(above)*, then lever the molding away from the wall. Slip a shim into the gap.

◆ Continue prying and shimming to loosen the baseboard section, then pull it free and set it aside.

To remove vinyl molding, cut it at the cabinet outline with a utility knife guided by a straightedge. Peel away the piece below the pipes.

3. Securing the vanity.

◆ Reposition the vanity against the wall and level it from side to side by inserting shims under the cabinet *(far left)*. Level the cabinet from front to back by shimming it away from the wall *(near left)*.

◆ Mark each shim at cabinet edges. Remove one shim at a time, saw it to length, and slide it back into place.

◆ For wallboard or plaster walls drive $2\frac{1}{4}$-inch No. 6 drywall screws through the back of the cabinet about $\frac{3}{4}$ inch from the top and into the studs that were marked earlier.

4. Mounting the countertop.

◆ Attach as many of the faucet and drain fittings to the countertop as possible.

◆ Apply a bead of adhesive caulk along the top edges of the cabinet, then press the countertop into place. Wipe off excess caulk immediately.

5. Finishing up.

◆ Connect the water-supply lines and the drain.

◆ If you detached a section of wooden baseboard earlier, use a backsaw to cut the baseboard at the lines marking the sides of the vanity. Discard the center section and nail the others to the wall with $2\frac{1}{2}$-inch finishing nails.

◆ Cover gaps at the sides of the vanity with scribe molding that matches the cabinet finish; attach the molding with $\frac{3}{4}$-inch brads *(above)*. Cover a gap at the floor with shoe molding secured with $1\frac{1}{2}$-inch finishing nails.

INSTALLING A SURFACE-MOUNTED MEDICINE CABINET

1. Hanging the cabinet.

◆ Locate studs where the cabinet will go *(page 89)*. Have a helper hold it with at least one upper mounting hole on a stud. Mark through the upper holes *(right)* and lower the cabinet. With a level, align the marks.

◆ If both marks are over studs, drive screws into the studs until the heads are $\frac{1}{8}$ inch from the wall.

◆ Otherwise, mark for the lower mounting holes as well. For marks not on a stud, drill holes for hollow-wall anchors, tap the anchors into place, and tighten. Loosen both anchor screws $\frac{1}{8}$ inch from the wall.

◆ Slip the cabinet's mounting holes over the screwheads. Drive screws through the other holes and tighten them all.

2. Adding shelves and doors.

◆ Position the shelves on the interior brackets.

◆ Attach the door hinges and the doors. Mounting systems vary, but doors commonly are first attached to the upper hinge, then adjusted for fit at the bottom hinge *(left)*.

◆ Complete the installation by affixing door catches and any hardware provided by the manufacturer.

FIRST AID FOR FROZEN PIPES

A house that is properly constructed and heated is safe from plumbing freeze-ups even in the midst of a severe cold snap—unless the heating system breaks down. If that should happen, the best way to keep pipes from freezing and bursting is to drain the entire plumbing system *(box, page 151)*. Also drain the plumbing in a house that will be left empty for the winter *(page 170)*.

Although a house may be well built, if its pipes run through a basement, crawlspace, laundry room, or garage that is unprotected, they may be vulnerable to cold. To avoid resulting problems, consult the checklist at right.

Coping with Leaks: If a pipe freezes, the first symptom may be a faucet that refuses to yield water. But all too often, the freeze-up is announced by a flood from a break. Ruptures are especially likely near joints or bends in the plumbing. When a leak occurs, turn off the water supply and apply a temporary repair sleeve, available at plumbing supply stores.

Getting Ready to Thaw Pipes: As you prepare to warm a frozen section of pipe, close the main shutoff valve most of the way. The movement of water through the pipe aids thawing and helps protect against later refreezing. Keep the affected faucet open to let water vapor and melted ice run out. Since leaks may go undetected until the pipe thaws, guard against water damage by spreading plastic drop cloths, and have extra pots and pails ready. Then warm the pipe by one of the methods at right or on page 170.

Electrical heaters of one kind or another are generally safest for thawing both metal and plastic pipe. Since electricity and water together pose a shock hazard, plug the appliance into a GFCI-protected outlet *(page 213)*, which cuts power to the appliance if it detects conditions that could lead to injury.

- Electric heating tape
- Propane torch with flame spreader
- Hair dryer
- Heat gun
- Heating pad
- Heat lamp
- Work lamp

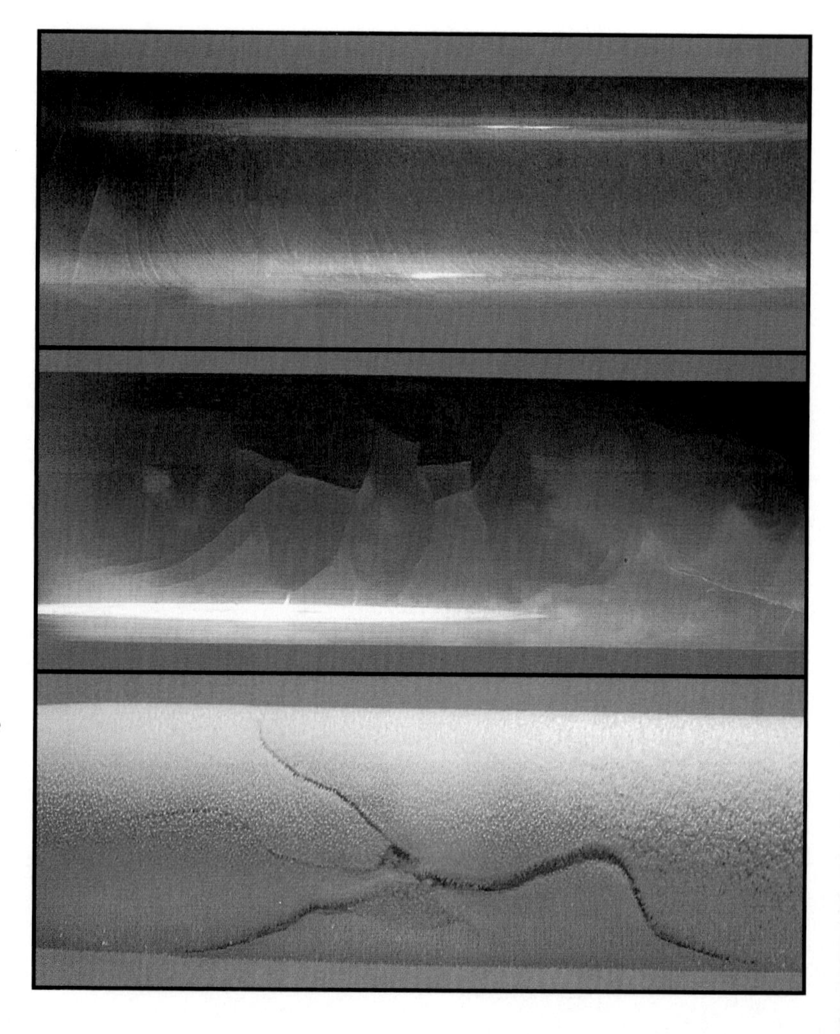

Three steps to a ruptured pipe.
Unlike most substances, water expands when it freezes—a fact that can easily burst a pipe. Three stages in the freezing and rupture of a pipe are shown in the transparent tubing at right. Frost forms first on the inner surfaces of the pipe *(top photograph)*, then ice crystals begin to take shape *(middle)*. With freezing complete, the pipe cracks *(bottom)*. By melting freeze-ups quickly, you may be able to avoid the final stage—and preserve your supply pipes from further harm.

How to Keep Pipes from Freezing

✔ Protect exposed pipes ahead of time with insulation made to retard freezing, or warm them with thermostatic heating tape *(right).*

✔ When no commercial insulation is at hand and pipes must be protected immediately, wrap several layers of newspaper loosely around the pipes and tie the paper on with string.

✔ If you have no time to install insulation, open faucets so a trickle of water moves through the pipes.

✔ Keep a door ajar between a heated room and an unheated room with pipes so that the unprotected area will receive heat.

✔ If power is available, plug in an electric heater or heat lamp, or hang a 100-watt bulb near vulnerable pipes. Keep the heat source a safe distance from walls, floors, ceilings, and nearby combustibles.

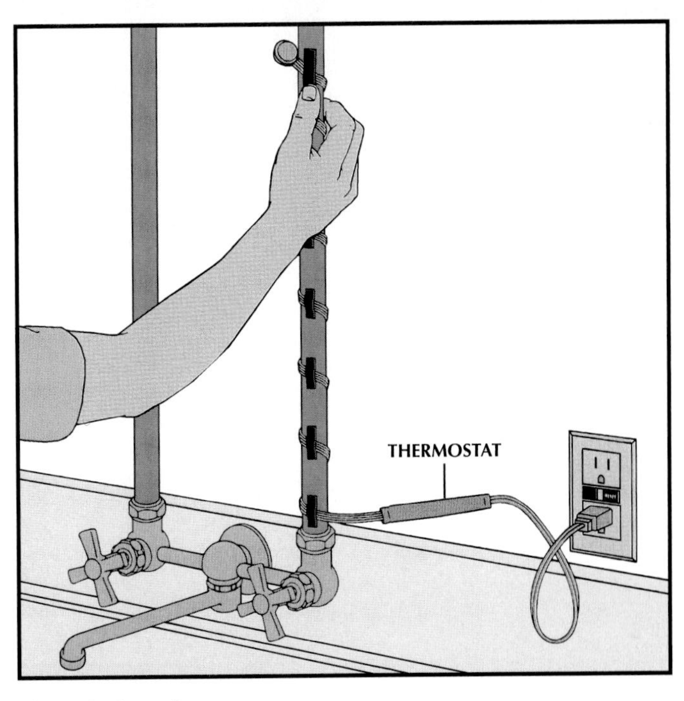

Electric heating tape.
To thaw a frozen pipe, wrap the tape in a spiral around the pipe, allowing about two turns per foot. Secure the spiral with PVC-type electrical tape *(above),* which will stay in place during temperature changes.

Most electric heating cables come with built-in thermostats and can be left plugged in permanently: When the temperature drops toward freezing, the thermostat activates the cable and warms the pipe. Cover the pipe and heating cable with nonflammable fiberglass pipe insulation as a second layer of protection against freezing.

A propane torch.
Equipped with a flame-spreader attachment, available at most hardware stores, a propane torch can thaw metal pipes rapidly and effectively during a power outage, if used with care. Place flameproof sheeting between the pipe and nearby framing. Apply heat near an open faucet first, then work gradually along the pipe *(arrow).*

A hair dryer.
If you have power, use a hair dryer instead of a propane torch; the dryer will work more slowly, but you will avoid dealing with an open flame in close quarters. An electric heat gun can also be used to thaw pipes. As with a torch, make sure pipes never become too hot to touch.

CAUTION *Use a torch only on metal pipes, not plastic ones. Never let the pipe get too hot to touch; boiling water and steam inside a pipe can cause a dangerous explosion.*

A heating pad.
Wrapped and tied around a frozen pipe near an open faucet, an ordinary heating pad can be left in place to thaw ice slowly but effectively.

A heat lamp.
If a suspected ice blockage is behind a wall or above the ceiling, set an electric heat lamp nearby. Keep it at least 6 inches from the wall to avoid scorching paint or wallpaper. For greater flexibility in handling, you can screw the bulb into the socket of a portable work lamp *(above).* Do not leave a heat lamp unattended for long. If you use a ladder as shown, make sure it can't be knocked over or moved by an opening door.

WINTERIZING AN EMPTY HOUSE

When you leave a house empty and unheated for the winter, take steps to weatherproof the plumbing. First turn off water to the house. Cut power to the water heater. For a hot-water heating system, turn off power to the boiler and drain it. Next, open the radiator valves, and remove an air vent from a radiator on the top floor.

Then empty the rest of the plumbing, including the water heater and any water-treatment devices *(see box, page 151)*. For a well system, drain the storage tank and dry off the pump, unless it is submerged in the well.

Flush and bail out each toilet. Then pour at least a gallon of plumber's antifreeze—not the toxic automotive variety—into the tank and flush the toilet again. Doing so frostproofs both the trap and the flushing channels.

For other fixtures, pour antifreeze down the drain very slowly so that it displaces water in the trap rather than mixing with it.

METHODS FOR UNCLOGGING DRAINS

When a bathroom drain stops or slows, see if other drains are affected. If so, the problem may lie elsewhere in the house's plumbing.

A Hierarchy of Solutions: If only one drain is blocked, try a plunger *(right)*. Prepare the drain by removing the strainer, pop-up plug, and overflow plate, if present; take apart a tub's drain hardware as shown in Step 1 on page 174. Stuff any overflow opening with rags.

If the plunger fails, you can sometimes clear a tub or shower drain with water *(below)*. A third method is to use an auger—a trap-and-drain auger for a tub, sink, or shower, and a closet auger for a toilet. Avoid compressed-air devices, which often compact the blockage and may cause old pipe joints to break apart.

Chemical Drain Cleaners: Do not pour chemical cleaning agents into a blocked drain. Many contain lye, and you could be exposed to the caustic as you continue work on the stoppage. Cleaners can be helpful once a tub, sink, or shower drain is open; applied regularly, they prevent buildup of debris. Never put such cleaners in a toilet, however. They do no good and can stain the porcelain.

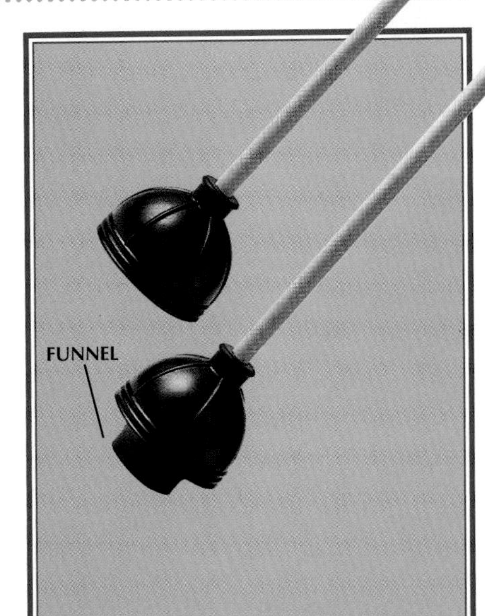

A Multi-Role Plunger

An ordinary force-cup plunger is suited to many drains, but it will not fit a toilet. For the bathroom, purchase a foldout plunger instead. As shown above, its cup can take on two different shapes.

With a tub, sink, or shower drain, keep the funnel portion tucked inside *(upper photo)*. Coat the rim of the cup with petroleum jelly and center it over the drain. Make sure that standing water covers the cup completely; if it does not, add more water. Without breaking the seal between drain and cup, pump the plunger down and up several times, then jerk it away. When the drain opens, run hot water through it to flush it clean.

For a toilet, extend the plunger's funnel lip *(lower photo)*. If a clogged toilet is too full, bail out some of the contents. If the bowl is empty, add water by hand, not by flushing. Fit the plunger over the opening near the bottom of the bowl and pump vigorously, then jerk it away. If the bowl empties, pour in water to confirm that the drain is fully opened.

CLEARING A STOPPAGE WITH WATER

Flushing a drain with a hose.
A hose-mounted drain flusher, available at most hardware stores, will work in a shower or tub drain.

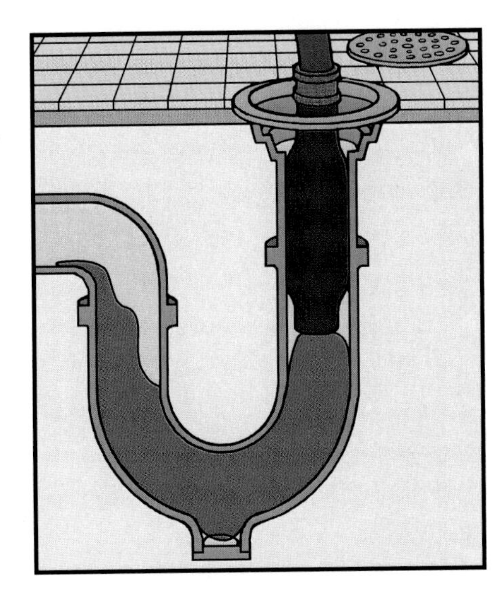

◆ Attach the drain flusher to a garden hose and push it into a shower drain; in a tub, insert it through the overflow opening past the level of the drain. Connect the other end of the hose to a faucet; for an indoor faucet, you will need a threaded adapter.

◆ Have a helper slowly turn on the hose water. The flusher will expand to fill the pipe so that the full force of the water is directed at the clog.

CAUTION *Do not flush a clogged drain that contains caustic cleaners, and never leave a hose in any drain. The cleaner could splash into your face, and the hose could draw wastewater into the supply system if the pressure should drop.*

OPENING A SINK DRAIN

Force-cup plunger
Trap-and-drain auger
Adjustable pipe wrench
Bucket
Bottle brush

Mop, rags, and sponges
Plastic bag
Petroleum jelly
Electrical tape
Plumbing-sealant tape
Penetrating oil

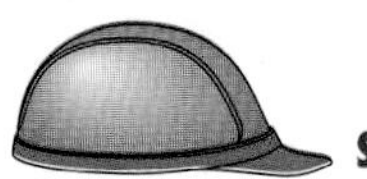

SAFETY TIP

Wear rubber gloves and safety goggles when using drain cleaners or working through a cleanout in a stack or main drain.

1. Starting with a plunger.

◆ Remove the sink strainer. In a double sink, bail out one side—the side with the garbage disposer, if there is one—and plug the drain with a rag in a plastic bag. In a washbasin, remove the pop-up drain plug; most lift out or can be turned and then lifted. Make sure there is enough water in the sink to cover the base of the plunger cup.

◆ Spread petroleum jelly on the cup's rim. Lower the plunger at an angle and compress the cup to push out air. Then seat it over the drain. Without breaking the seal, pump the plunger up and down 10 times, then quickly pull it away. If the drain stays clogged after several attempts, try an auger *(below)*.

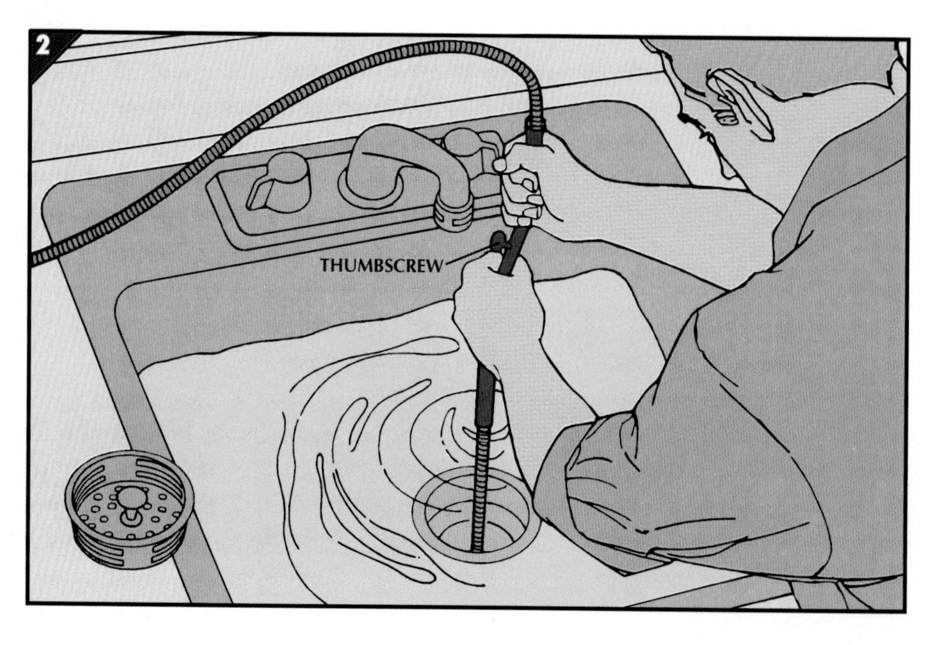

2. Using an auger.

◆ Push the tip of the auger into the drain until you feel it meet the obstruction, then slide the handle within a few inches of the drain opening and tighten the thumbscrew.

◆ Crank the handle clockwise with both hands while advancing the auger into the drain. Continue cranking and pushing the auger, repositioning the handle as necessary, until the auger breaks through the obstruction or will not go any farther.

◆ Withdraw the auger by cranking it slowly and pulling gently.

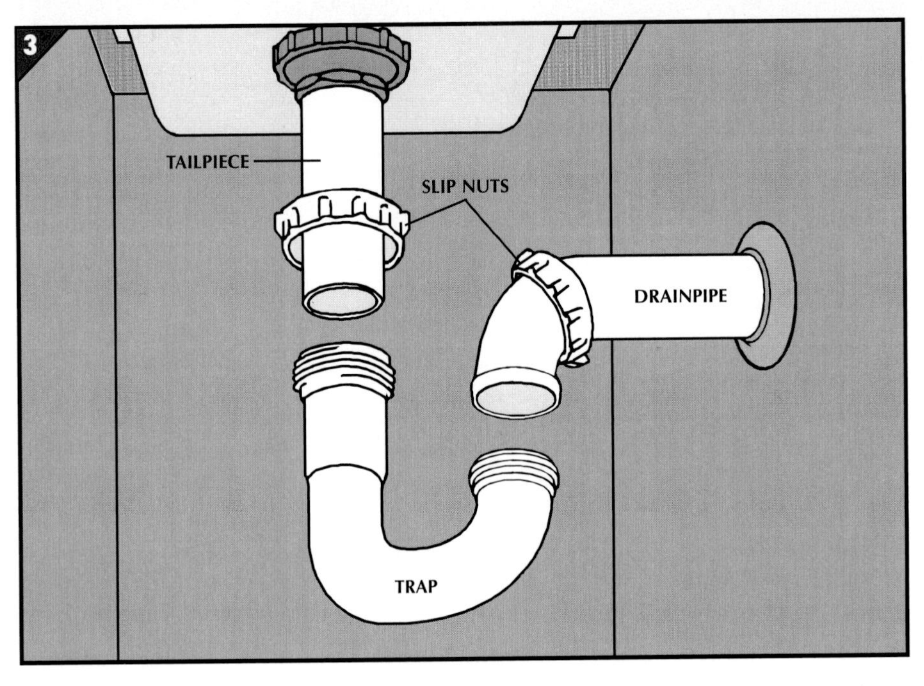

3. Removing the trap.

◆ Bail out the sink and place a bucket under the trap. Wrap the jaws of a pipe wrench with electrical tape, then loosen the slip nuts holding the trap to the tailpiece and drainpipe. Lower the trap slowly, allowing water to run into the bucket.

◆ If you find an obstruction in the trap, remove it, then clean the trap and the drainpipe with a bottle brush and detergent solution. Wrap the threads at both ends of the trap with plumbing-sealant tape, then replace the trap and tighten the slip nuts.

◆ If the trap was not blocked, clear the branch drain *(below)*.

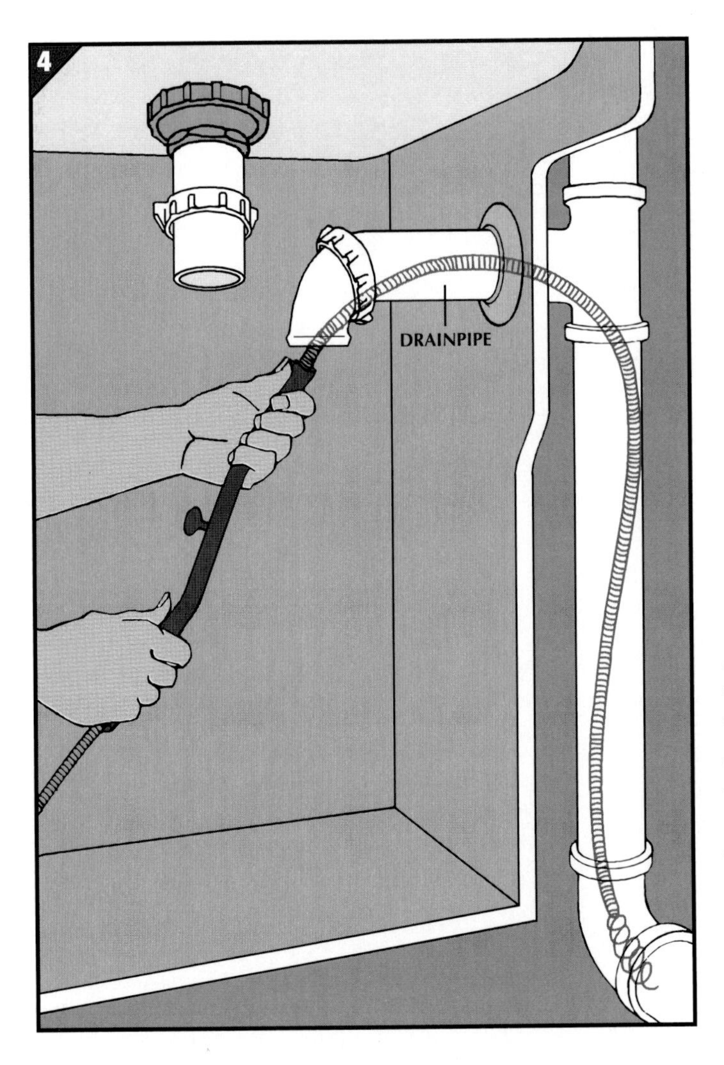

4. Cleaning beyond the trap.

With the trap removed, crank the auger into the drainpipe. The blockage may be in the vertical pipe behind the fixture or in a horizontal pipe—a branch drain—that connects with the main drain-vent stack serving the entire house. If the auger goes in freely through the branch drain until it hits the main stack, the blockage is probably in the main drainage system. In that case, identify the most likely location of the blockage, open the drain just above it, and use the auger to clear the pipe.

BREAKING UP A CLOG WITH A TRAP-AND-DRAIN AUGER

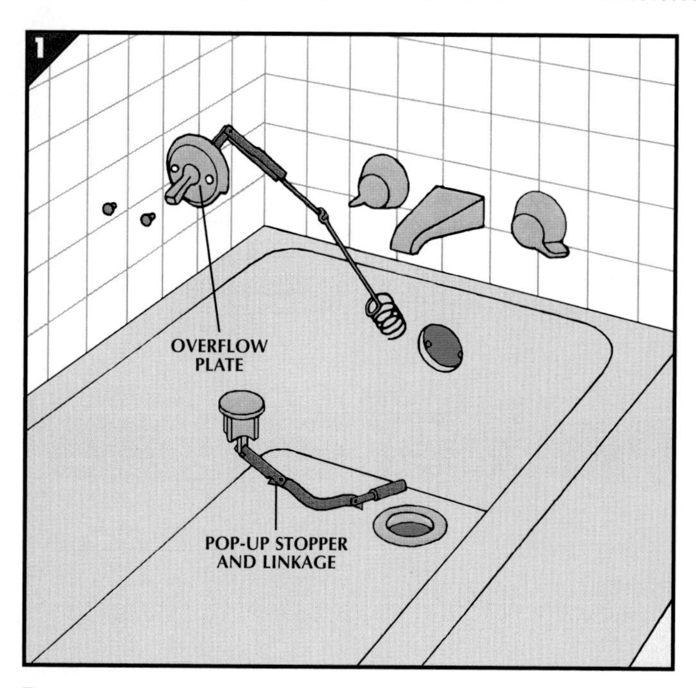

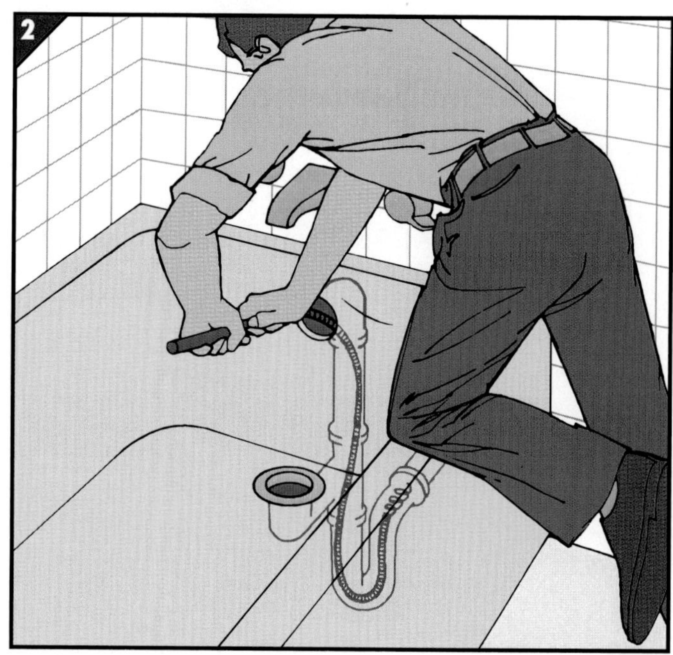

1. Gaining access to the drain.
To unclog a bathtub, unscrew the overflow plate and lift it up and out. Draw out the pop-up stopper and its linkage. Note how the parts line up so that you can put them back in the same way.

2. Inserting the auger.
◆ Cranking the auger handle clockwise, feed the auger tip through the tub overflow opening.
◆ When the auger wire reaches the blockage, move the auger slowly backward and forward while cranking. Continue to crank clockwise as you withdraw the auger wire; doing so helps to prevent you from dropping the material that caused the blockage.
◆ After clearing the drain, run hot water through it for 2 to 3 minutes.

OPENING A TOILET DRAIN WITH A CLOSET AUGER

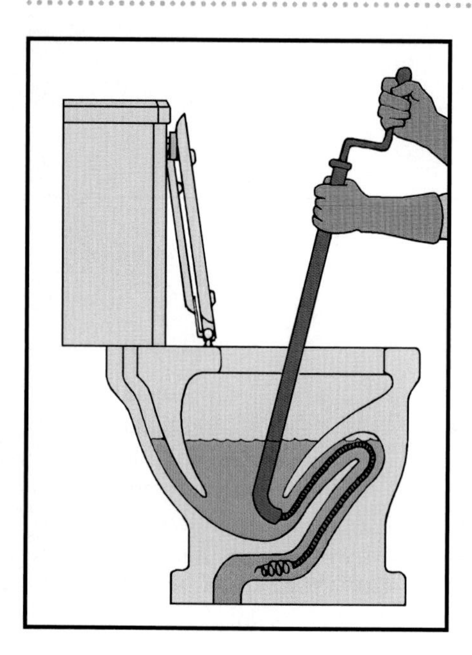

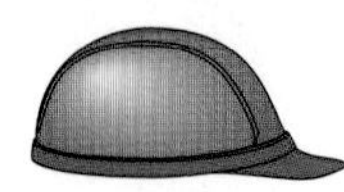

SAFETY TIP

If human waste is present when you are unclogging a toilet, wear goggles and rubber gloves.

An auger meant for toilets.
The cranking handle of a closet auger attaches to a long sleeve shaped to help guide the tip of the auger into the trap. Closet augers work equally well in toilets with a front drain opening, as shown here, or with the opening at the back.
◆ Hold the sleeve near the top and position the other end against the drain opening. Crank the auger tip slowly clockwise into the trap until you hook the obstruction or break through it.
◆ Withdraw the auger while cranking the handle clockwise. If the drain remains clogged, repeat the process.
◆ When the drain seems clear, test it with a pail of water before attempting to flush the toilet.

REPLACING DRAINS AND TRAPS

Over time, corrosion in the trap and drain under your bathroom washbasin can cause leaks, which are best remedied by the replacement of all or part of the drain assembly. You may also want to replace a worn pop-up plug and drain body when installing a new faucet.

For best results, spray the threaded connections in the drain assembly with a penetrating lubricant several hours before disconnecting the old fittings. Drain configurations vary, but most include slip-nut connections that can easily be dismantled with a wrench. If you intend to reuse a trap, be sure to put new washers under the slip nuts before putting the trap back in.

Selecting the Right Parts: If the sink is mounted in a vanity top or on a pedestal, and you are replacing all of the drain assembly, use polyvinyl chloride (PVC) fittings like those pictured here. Such pipes are durable, rustproof, and easy to work with. To replace the entire drain assembly under a wall-hung basin, chrome-plated parts are an elegant alternative. If you are replacing only some of the drain fittings, match the material of those that remain.

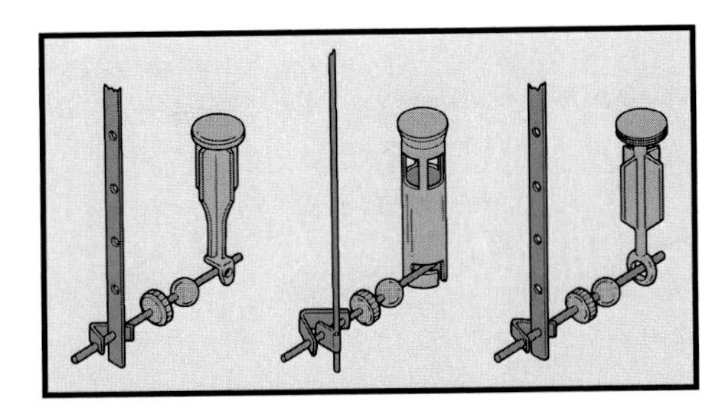

Pop-up drain plugs.
The method for removing a pop-up drain plug depends on its type. Some plugs sit atop the pivot rod and just lift out *(far left)*. Others require a quarter-turn to free them from the rod *(left, center)*. To remove the type of plug at near left, you must disengage the pivot rod from the T connector under the basin and then lift out the plug.

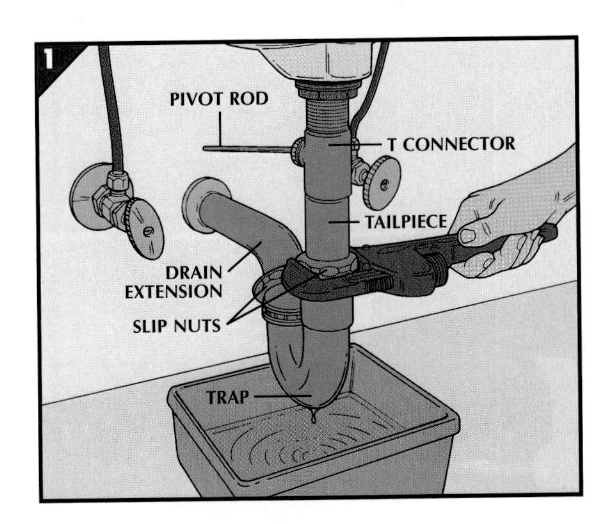

1. Removing the trap.

◆ Place a shallow container underneath the trap to catch any water remaining inside.

◆ With a pipe wrench or a monkey wrench, unscrew the slip nuts on either end of the trap, disconnecting it from the tailpiece and the drain extension *(above)*.

◆ Remove the pop-up plug as outlined above, as well as the lift rod and clevis *(page 176, Step 4)*. With pliers, unscrew the retaining nut at the back of the T connector and remove the pivot rod.

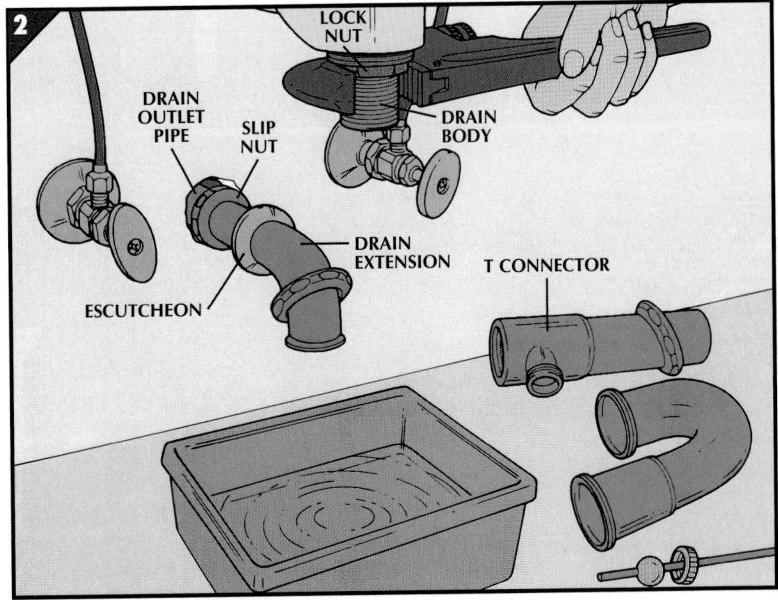

2. Removing the fittings.

◆ With a pipe wrench, unscrew the T connector from the drain body, remove the lock nut and washer holding the drain body to the basin *(above)*, and push the drain body up and out through the hole in the basin.

◆ If replacing all of the drain assembly, pry the escutcheon from the wall. Unscrew the slip nut behind it, then gently remove the drain extension, being careful not to move or break pipes inside the wall. Clean the threads of the drain outlet pipe.

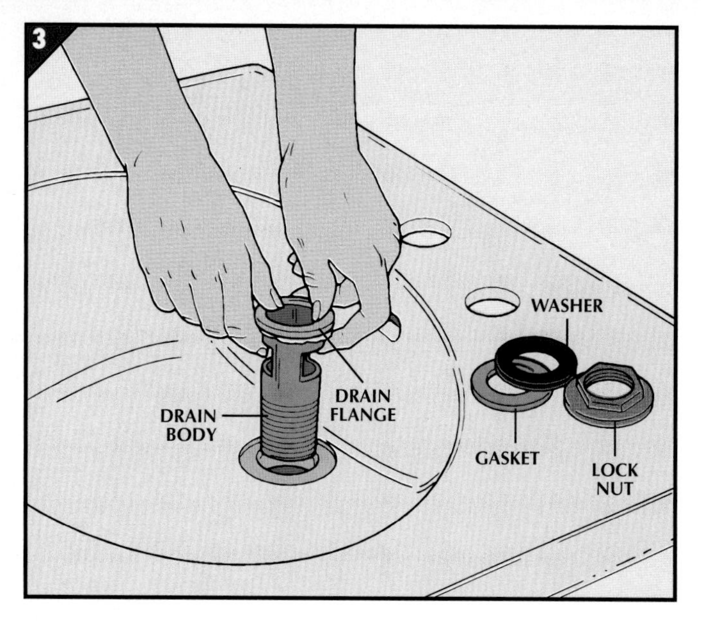

3. Sealing the new drain flange.

◆ Inside the washbasin, scrape off any old putty from around the drain opening and clean and dry the surface.
◆ Roll a short rope of plumber's putty and press it under the edge of the flange at the top of the drain body. Lower the drain body through the opening in the sink *(left)* and press down on the flange.
◆ Underneath the basin, push the gasket, washer, and lock nut onto the drain body. Hand tighten the lock nut against the bottom of the basin, then tighten one more turn with a pipe wrench. Wipe away any excess putty with a finger.
◆ If you are replacing the faucet, install the new one now, as well as the new lift rod and clevis.

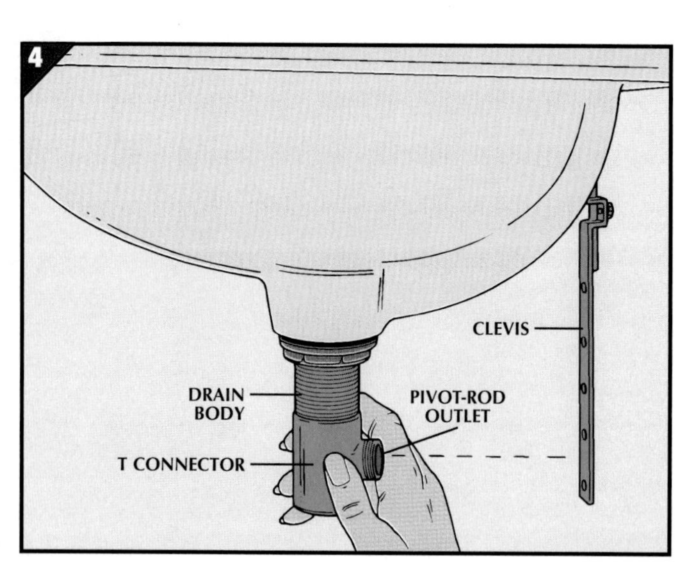

4. Aligning the T connector.

◆ Wrap plumbing-sealant tape around the threads on the lower part of the drain body.
◆ Screw the new T connector onto the drain body so that the pivot-rod outlet faces toward the clevis *(dotted line, left)*.
◆ Insert one end of the pivot rod into the T connector and attach the other end to the clevis with a spring clip or other fastener supplied with the drain.
◆ Tighten the pivot rod's retaining nut on the T connector and adjust the position of the pivot rod on the clevis as necessary.

5. Installing a new plastic trap.

◆ Wrap plumbing-sealant tape around the threads of the tailpiece and hand tighten it into the T connector. Slide a plastic slip nut and washer *(not visible)* onto the tailpiece.
◆ If replacing the entire drain assembly, loosely connect the replacement trap and the new drain extension with a plastic slip nut. Slide the escutcheon, a nut, and a washer onto the extension and insert it into the drain outlet pipe. The washer fits between the extension and the outlet pipe, but the nut slips over the pipe's outside.
◆ Align the top of the trap with the tailpiece *(right)*. Loosely connect the pipes with the nut.
◆ When the drain assembly is properly aligned, hand tighten the nuts at each connection. Turn each nut once more with a wrench. Push the escutcheon against the wall.
◆ Close the pop-up plug, fill the sink with water, then open the drain and check for leaks. Tighten any leaking joints slightly.

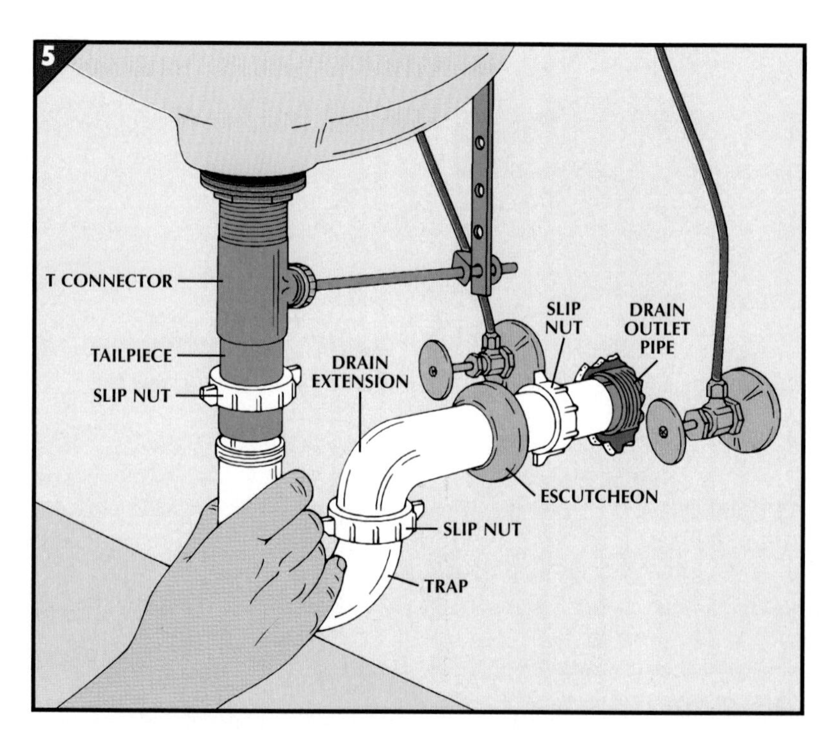

TOILET REPAIRS

Toilets, the most heavily used plumbing fixtures in the home, routinely require small repairs and adjustments—most of which can be performed in minutes.

Common Problems: When the working parts inside a toilet tank wear out or corrode, the likely result is either a continuously running toilet or an inadequate flush. A weak flush can also mean flushing holes are blocked. Diagnose and correct the specific cause as shown here and on pages 179 to 182.

To identify a costly but hidden leak from tank to bowl, pour food coloring into the water tank and wait 20 minutes. If the water in the bowl becomes tinted, replace the flapper or tank ball *(page 178, bottom)*. Visible leaks from the tank usually result from loose bolts or worn washers and gaskets *(page 179)*. Finally, clear a clogged toilet with a fold-out plunger or closet auger, as described on page 174.

Pressure-flush toilets are more likely to need the services of a professional.

Avoiding Complications: Whether you are repairing or installing a toilet, place the tank lid in a safe place to avoid chipping or breaking it. Also be careful in tightening bolts. Porcelain cracks easily, and when it does the entire toilet usually must be replaced.

Some toilets have plastic nuts. These are made to be turned by hand and could be cracked or crushed by a wrench. Use a wrench only when an old plastic nut cannot be removed by hand and you do not plan to reinstall the nut.

TOOLS

- Adjustable wrench
- Long-nose pliers
- Screwdriver
- Spud wrench
- Locking-grip pliers
- Diagonal pliers
- Putty knife
- Level

MATERIALS

- Sponge
- Flapper ball
- Lift chain
- Plumbing-sealant tape
- Washers, bolts, nuts
- Penetrating oil
- Special-purpose gaskets
- Spud washer
- Float-cup ball cock
- Float ball
- Pressure-flush fittings
- Closet bolts and nuts
- Closet-bolt caps
- Sheet metal (for shims)
- Caulk

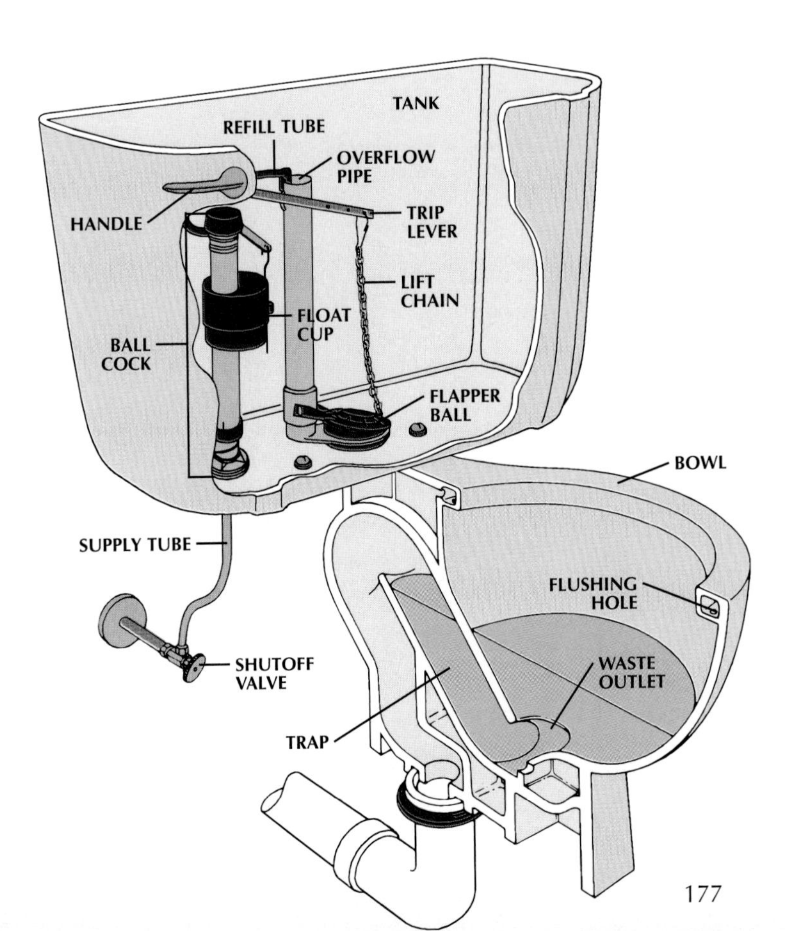

How a standard toilet works.
In a typical modern toilet *(left)*, a flapper ball seals the hole between the tank and the bowl except during a flush cycle. When the handle is pressed, it operates a trip lever and chain that raise the ball. Water rushes into the bowl through flushing holes inside the rim and then out the waste outlet. As the water level falls in the tank, a float cup buoyed by the water drops as well. The float cup is part of a mechanism called a ball cock, and the cup's descent triggers the ball cock to let in water from the toilet's supply tube. Most of the water flows into the tank, but some is directed through a refill tube to replenish the bowl and the toilet's internal trap. After the flush, the flapper ball settles back into place, resealing the tank. The float cup then rises with the incoming water, shutting off the ball cock when the water level is back to normal. If some maladjustment causes the tank water to rise too high, water spills through the overflow pipe into the bowl.

RESTORING A TOILET TO PROPER OPERATION

Adjusting the handle.
When a handle must be held down to complete a flush, the cause may be a loose connection to the trip lever. Grasp a loose handle and tighten the retaining nut inside the tank by turning it counterclockwise (the opposite direction from most nuts), with your hand for a plastic nut and with an adjustable wrench for a metal one *(left).*

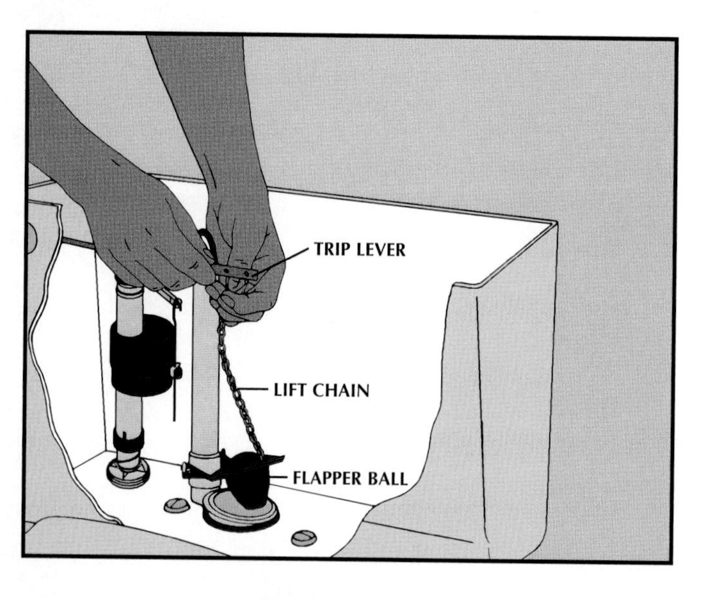

Servicing the lift chain.
Another cause for a handle that must be held down is a lift chain that is too long. To shorten it, unhook the chain from the trip lever and adjust it to allow about $\frac{1}{2}$ inch of slack: Hook the chain through another hole in the lever *(left)* or use long-nose pliers to cut and remove links.

A slow flush may indicate a short or broken chain. Replace it; pin or paper clip repairs cause corrosion. Some chains have a small float attached that regulates the amount of water in each flush to match a level marked inside the tank. If the volume of the flush is too low or too high, adjust it by sliding the float along the chain.

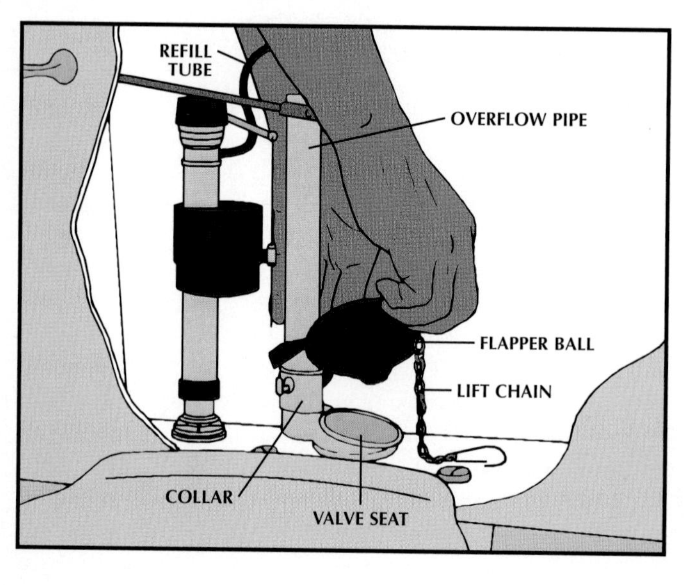

Replacing the flapper ball.
Stop tank-to-bowl leaks with a new flapper ball:
◆ Turn off the water, flush the toilet, and sponge out the tank.
◆ Unhook the ball's lift chain and take the refill tube out of the overflow pipe. Remove the flapper ball by sliding the collar up and off the pipe.
◆ To ensure a good seal, wipe a plastic valve seat with a soft cloth; gently scour a metal one with fine steel wool or a plastic cleansing pad.
◆ Slide a new flapper ball and collar down the overflow pipe. Position the ball and screw the collar in place.
◆ Attach the lift chain from the ball to the trip lever; reseat the refill tube in the overflow pipe.
◆ Turn the water back on.

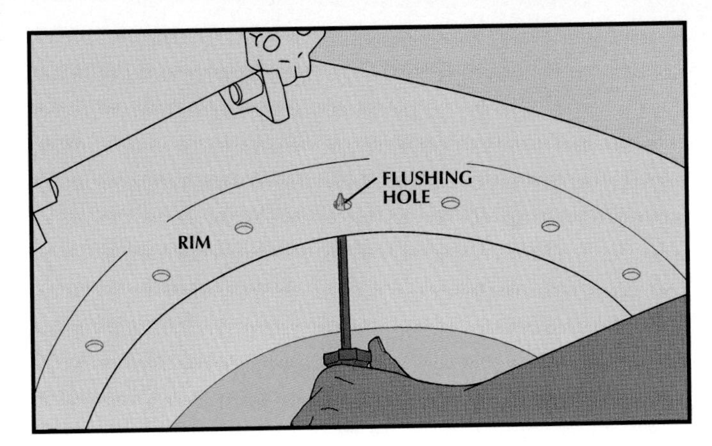

Clearing the flushing holes.

If water flows unevenly down the walls of the bowl during a flush, mineral deposits may have clogged some of the flushing holes under the rim. Insert the blade of a small screwdriver or pocket knife into the flushing holes and scrape them clean. If there is a small hole opposite the waste outlet at the base of the bowl, turn off the water, flush the toilet, and scrape inside that hole as well; then turn the water back on.

STOPPING LEAKS

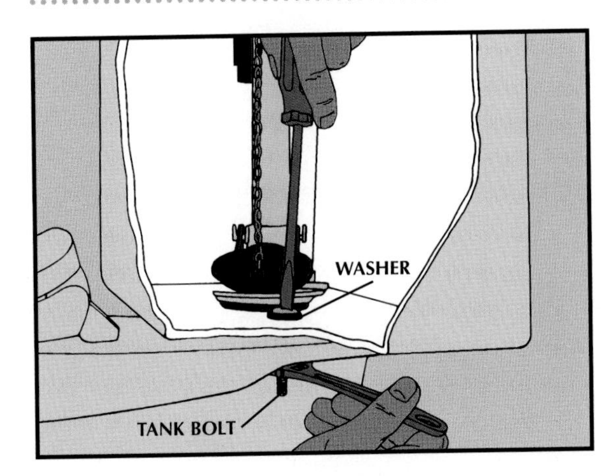

Sealing leaks under the tank.

Condensation can cause water drips on the floor under the tank. More often, the cause is a leak from the tank.

◆ To fix a leaking tank bolt, secure it inside the tank with a screwdriver and tighten the nut with an adjustable wrench *(left)*. If leaks persist, replace the bolt washers.

◆ Tighten a loose lock nut at the base of the ball cock: Turn a plastic nut with your hand, a metal nut a quarter-turn at a time with an adjustable wrench. If a finger-tight plastic nut still leaks, remove it and wrap plumbing-sealant tape on the exposed threads, then reattach the nut.

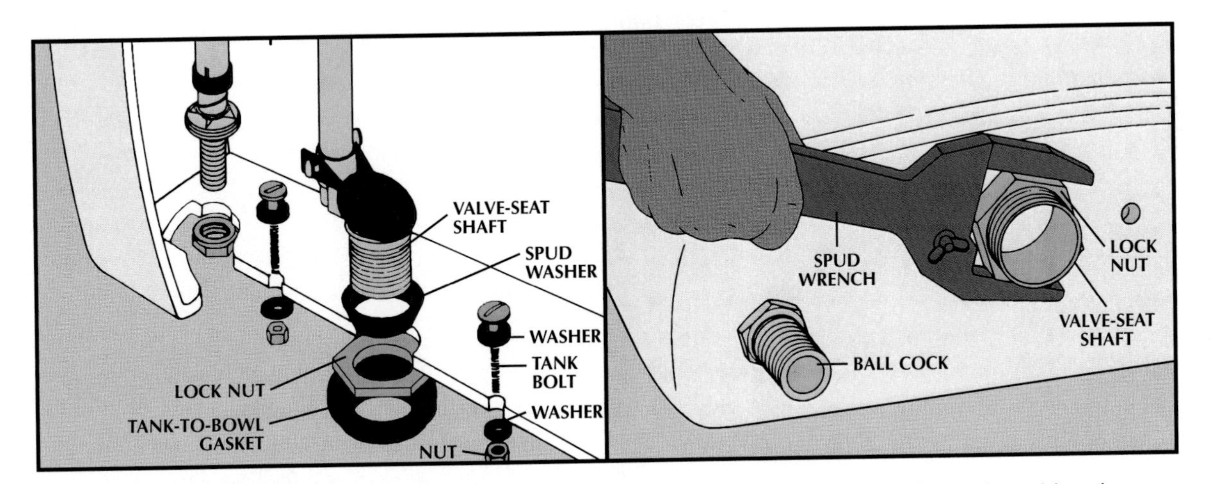

Servicing the flush-valve connection.

Pooled water near where the bowl meets the tank may be a sign of a poor tank-to-bowl connection *(above, left)*. To fix it, you must remove the tank.

◆ Shut off the water, flush the toilet, and sponge out the tank.

◆ With an adjustable wrench, loosen the coupling nut at the top of the supply tube and detach the tube from the tank.

◆ Remove the tank bolts, reversing the tightening procedure shown above.

◆ Lift the tank straight up and off; set it aside. Pry or scrape the gasket from the tank and bowl.

◆ Turn the lock nut with a spud wrench *(above, right)*. If necessary, apply penetrating oil.

◆ Pull the valve-seat shaft into the tank. Replace the old spud washer, then push the shaft back into place, securing it with the lock nut. Push a new tank-to-bowl gasket up over the nut.

◆ Ease the tank onto the bowl and attach it with new tank bolts, nuts, and washers. Reconnect the supply tube.

◆ Turn on the water slowly. Tighten any leaking nuts a quarter-turn.

REPLACING THE FILL MECHANISM

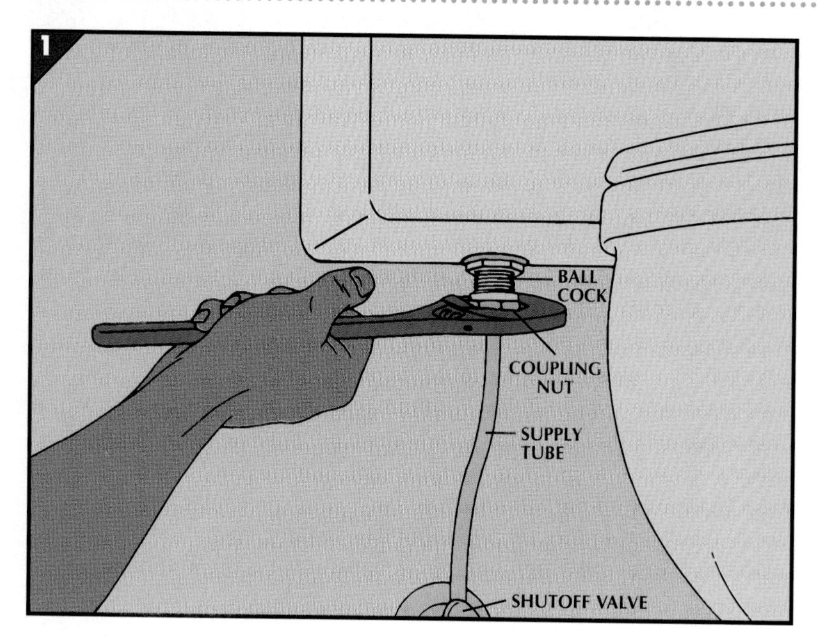

1. Detaching the supply tube.
You can often identify a worn-out ball cock by a whistling sound or tank vibration after a flush. Possible other symptoms include a low tank water level or, conversely, nonstop filling. Replace the ball cock as follows:

◆ Set a container on the floor beneath the tank to catch water runoff.

◆ Turn off the water supply. Flush the toilet and sponge out the tank.

◆ Disconnect the supply tube from the base of the ball cock by loosening the coupling nut, turning a plastic nut by hand and a metal one with an adjustable wrench *(left)*.

◆ Free the top of the ball cock by unclipping the refill tube from the overflow pipe. For an old-style ball cock *(page 182)*, also take off the float rod.

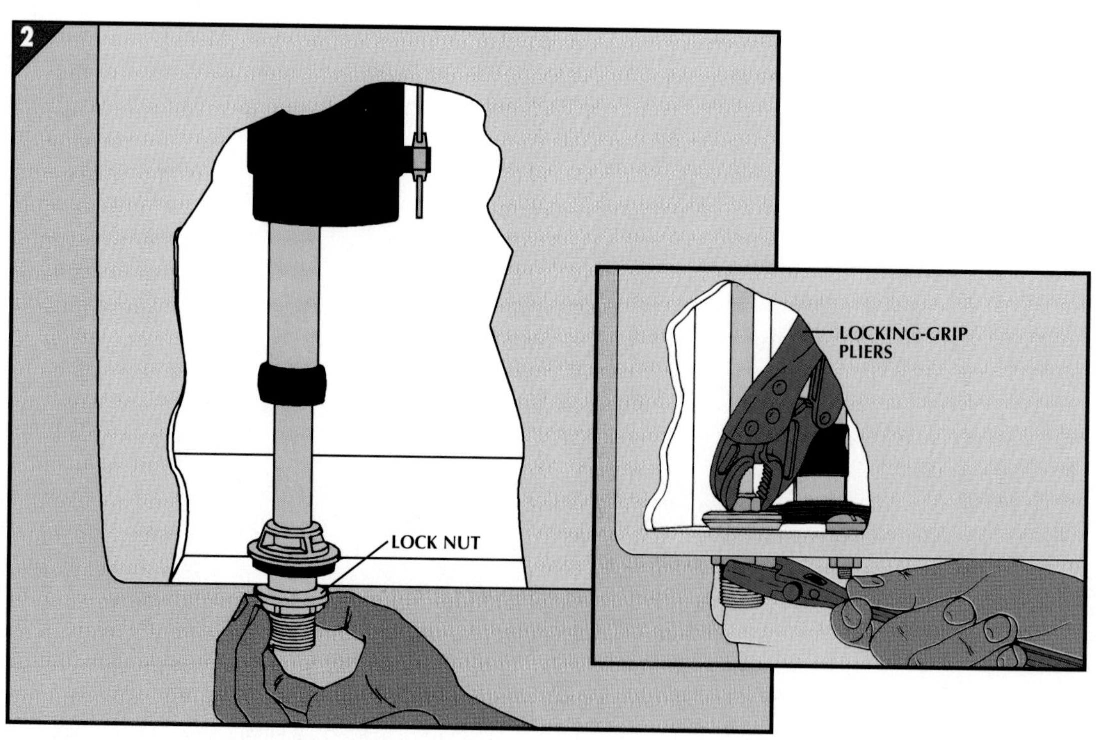

2. Removing the old ball cock.

◆ Working under the tank, unscrew a plastic lock nut at the base of the ball cock by hand *(above)*. Discard the nut.

◆ For a plastic nut that will not turn, or for a metal lock nut, attach locking-grip pliers to the lowest part of the ball cock inside the tank and wedge them against the tank wall to prevent the ball cock from turning; then remove the lock nut with an adjustable wrench *(inset)*. Apply penetrating oil to a metal nut that does not turn.

◆ Pull the ball cock up and out.

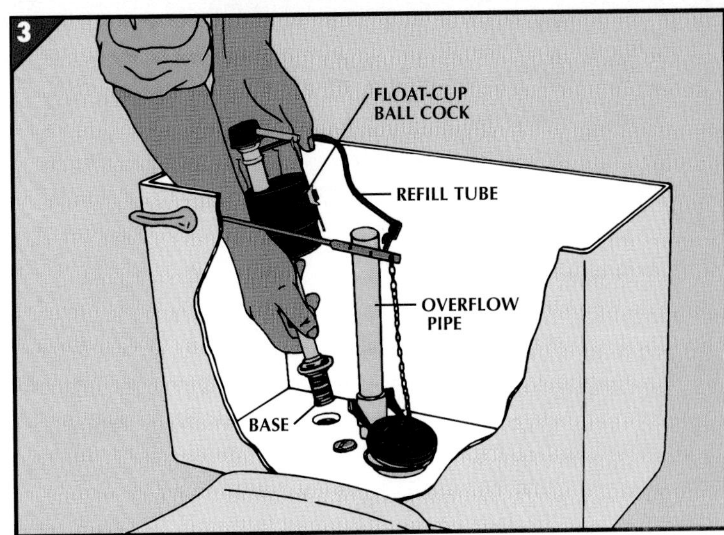

3. Installing a ball cock.

◆ Insert a new ball cock into the tank hole *(above),* making sure it stands straight without touching the sides. Clip the refill tube to the overflow pipe.

◆ Holding the ball cock with one hand, slip a washer and plastic lock nut over the base of the ball cock under the tank. Tighten the lock nut by hand.

◆ Reconnect the supply tube and slowly turn on the water.

◆ If a leak occurs, do not tighten plastic nuts with a wrench; instead, disassemble the connections and wrap plumbing-sealant tape around the exposed threads before reattaching.

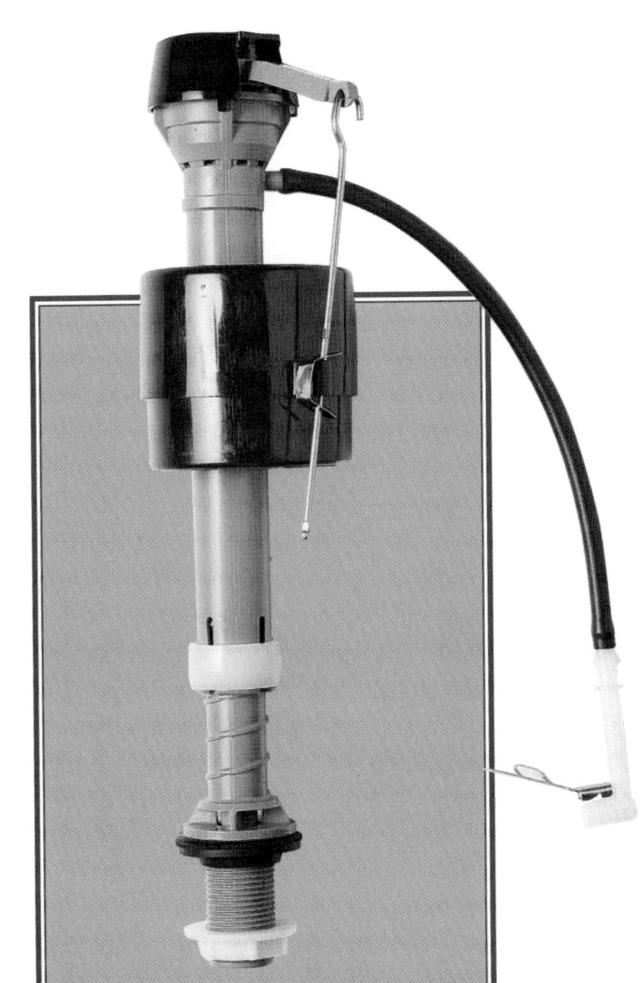

A SAFER BALL COCK

Household water pressure can drop suddenly—for example, if a local main breaks. Toilet tank water, including any chemical cleansers, may then be siphoned backward into the neighborhood water supply. To prevent that, many ball cocks are sold with an antisiphon device; in the model shown, an air intake stops siphon action. Most local codes require such features, but ball cocks without them are available. Make sure the packaging for yours specifies antisiphon protection.

4. Adjusting the float cup.

◆ Flush the toilet, let the tank refill, and check the water level; it should be $\frac{1}{2}$ to 1 inch below the top of the overflow pipe and should be just below the handle.

◆ Adjust the level by pinching the clip at the side of the float cup and sliding it $\frac{1}{2}$ inch at a time—up to raise the water level or down to lower it.

REPAIRS FOR A FLOAT-BALL ASSEMBLY

Although float-cup ball cocks like the one on page 181 are common, some older toilets have float-ball assemblies like the one shown below. In that arrangement, the flush mechanism and the water-supply connection are the same as for any standard toilet, but the fill mechanism is quite different.

The water level in such a toilet is regulated by a float ball and rod, rather than a float cup. When the tank empties during flushing, the ball drops with the falling water level. This lowers the rod, which in turn opens the ball cock, allowing water into the tank. The float ball is then buoyed upward as the tank refills. At the correct water level, the float rod turns off the ball cock.

If the water level is too high in a toilet that contains this mechanism, first check the float ball. A cracked or worn ball can partially fill with water, preventing it from rising enough to shut off the ball cock. Replace a float ball by grasping the float rod firmly with a pair of pliers and unscrewing the ball. Attach a new ball in the same way.

If the float ball is in good order, try adjusting the float rod slightly downward—about $\frac{1}{2}$ inch. Some plastic versions have a dial that can be turned to correct the height of the arm. Bend a metal float rod; if doing so proves difficult inside the tank, unscrew the rod and bend it over a rounded surface.

You can also replace a float-ball assembly and ball cock with a float-cup ball cock; it is less likely to need repairs *(pages 180–181).*

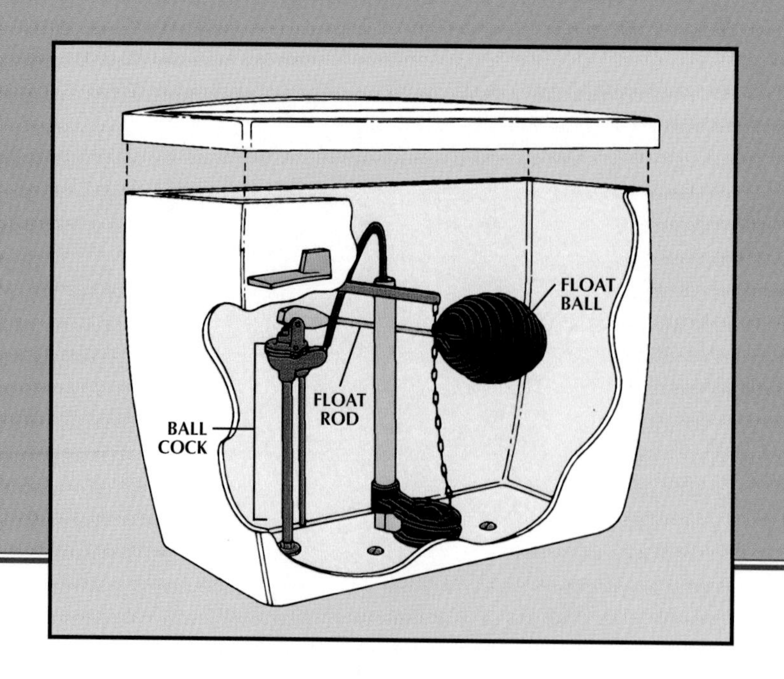

REPLACING A TOILET SEAT

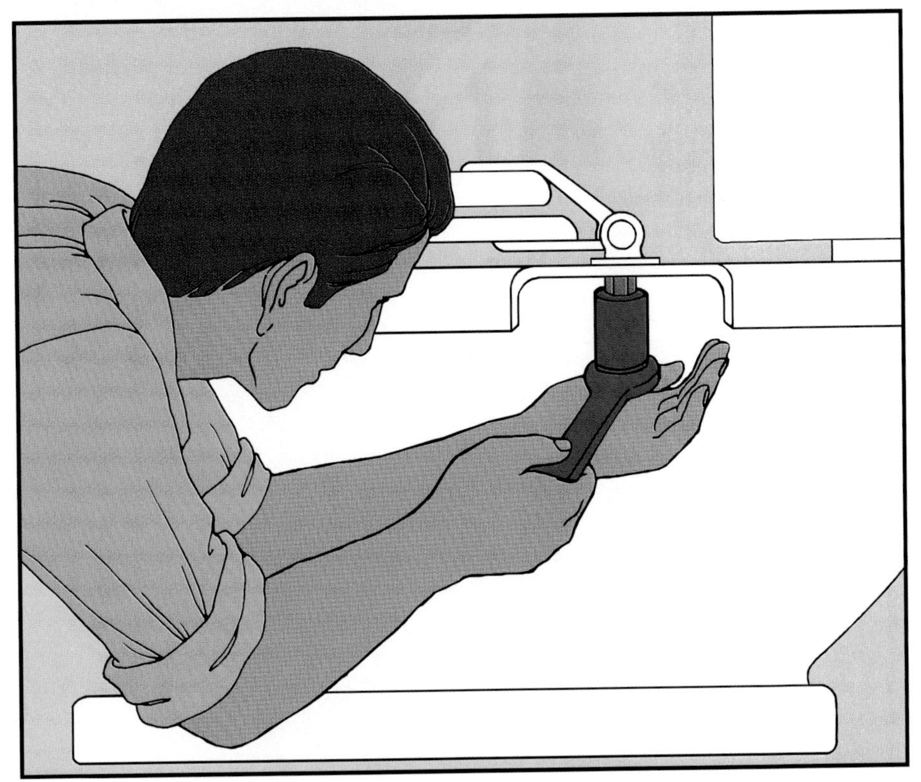

Removing the seat bolts.
To take off an old toilet seat, unscrew the nuts underneath the bowl. First try to turn the nuts with long-nose pliers. Should that fail, twist gently using a socket wrench with a deep socket. If the seat bolts are too corroded to loosen, apply the methods below.

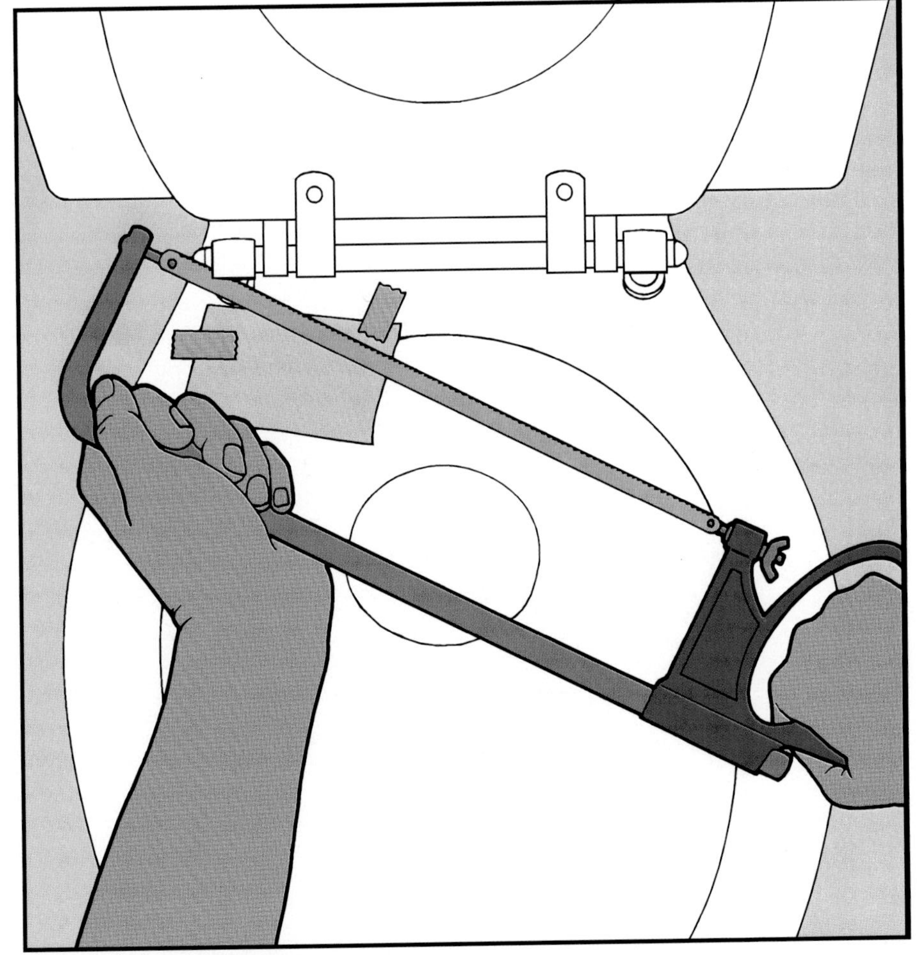

Freeing corroded bolts.

◆ Soak the bolts with penetrating oil for at least 30 minutes—overnight is better still. Then try loosening the nuts once more.

◆ If penetrating oil does not free the nuts, tape thin cardboard on top of the bowl next to the heads of the bolts to protect the china. Then, with a hacksaw, cut off the boltheads, sawing through the attached washers *(left)*.

6

CHAPTER

WIRING AND LIGHTING

When old houses were built, no one could anticipate the electrical requirements of life today. We need places to plug in television sets and home entertainment equipment, computers, power tools, kitchen appliances large and small, laundry equipment, and many other electrically operated items that were uncommon or even unknown a few decades ago. We also demand more extensive and more versatile lighting. So it is no wonder that you may need to make electrical improvements.

To perform the work safely, you first need to know about electrical safeguards and how to test a circuit to determine whether it is live, or "hot." Then you need to know how to connect wires and devices to lead the electricity to the desired areas of your house.

This chapter shows you the basics of electrical work and how to apply these skills in hanging light fixtures, replacing and adding switches and receptacles, putting in protective ground-fault circuit interrupters (GFCIs) where needed or required by electrical code, and installing a ceiling fan, track lights, or recessed lighting.

◁ *Left:* A single hanging fixture can light a specific area effectively and attractively. A chandelier, for more general illumination, is installed in the same way.

▷ *Right:* You can use a ceiling fan for air circulation in almost any room in a house. Many different styles are available, some with lights. Installation is similar to putting up a hanging light fixture.

△ *Above:* Electrical codes require GFCI outlets within six feet of all basins, sinks, tubs, and other damp locations. They provide instant life-saving protection against shock and are easy to install in place of existing outlets. Wall-mounted light fixtures and sconces are also easy to install.

△ *Above:* Recessed lights are unobtrusive and highly versatile. Interchangeable hoods and bulbs can adjust their output for reading or lighting a specific work area, for "wall washing," for spotlighting objects, or for general illumination.

▷ *Right:* Track lights can be mounted almost anywhere, on walls as well as ceilings. There is a variety of fixtures for adjustable direct and indirect illumination.

THE ELECTRICAL SYSTEM

Evaluating the electrical system of your house involves determining whether the power supply is adequate, checking the condition of the wiring and whether it is safe for rated loads, and testing receptacles to see if they work.

How Much Power: The amount of electricity entering the house is measured in amperes (amps). Older houses may have a service capable of supplying only 60 or 100 amps—too little to operate a collection of power-hungry appliances such as clothes dryers and ranges, which require 150- or 200-amp service.

Check the amperage rating on the service panel; it is commonly printed on the inside of the door on panels with fuses, or on the main breaker in a panel with circuit breakers. If you see no rating, look for it inside the glass housing on the electric meter, which can reveal service capacity even if it isn't marked there *(opposite, bottom)*.

Older houses tend to have fewer circuits than newer ones, but an electrician can add additional circuits up to the limit of the service. For example, 150-amp service can supply as many as 30 circuits; 200 amps support up to 40 circuits. Note also the number and positions of electrical receptacles in each room. If some walls have no receptacles, it's a good idea to add some.

Examine the Wiring: Since most wiring is hidden inside walls, a complete inspection is never possible, but you can get a general idea of its condition by scrutinizing wires in the attic and basement *(opposite, top)* and near fixtures.

Turn off power to a circuit at the service panel and remove the cover of a receptacle or switch on the dead circuit to check the condition of wires inside the box; frayed or cracked insulation around the wires there indicates that new wiring is probably needed in places, though not necessarily throughout the house.

In some cases improvements in the electrical system must meet the requirements of modern building codes. And if you rewire part of the house, there is a possibility in some locales that the inspector may require you to bring the entire house up to electrical-code minimums.

TOOLS
- Screwdriver
- Voltage tester
- Receptacle analyzer
- Three-prong receptacle adapter

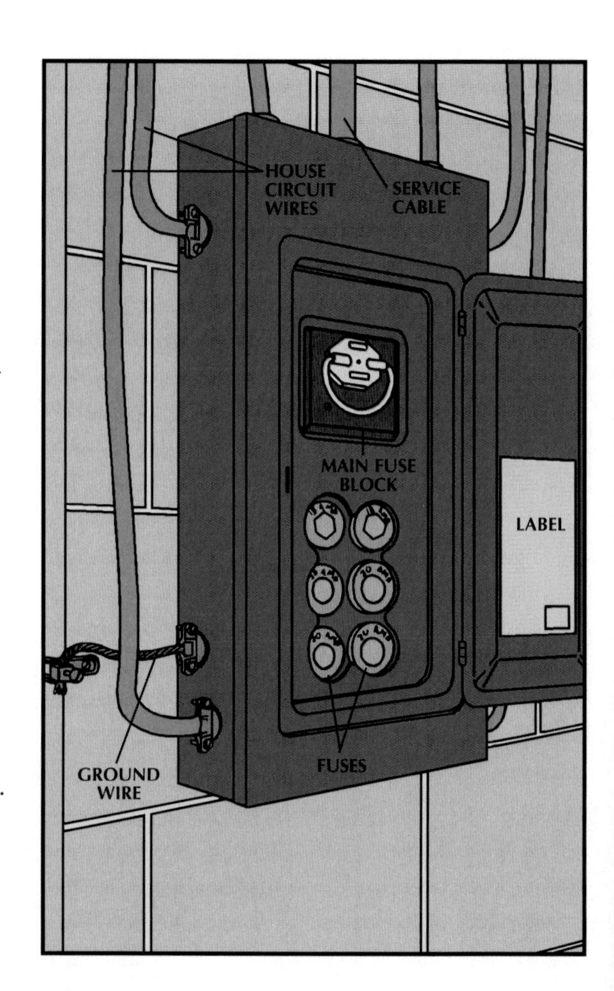

Evaluating a service panel. Power enters the house through a service-entrance cable located at the top of the main service panel. In a fuse-protected panel of the type shown here or on page 193, the electricity passes through the main fuse block—which cuts off power to the entire house when it is removed—and to the fuses to house circuits that exit from the sides of the box. The system is grounded by means of a bare copper wire that is clamped either to a nearby cold-water pipe at least $\frac{3}{4}$ inch in diameter or to a copper rod driven several feet into the ground outside. In a panel that contains circuit breakers *(page 192)*, a main breaker takes the place of a fuse block, and individual breakers control the circuits.

An old panel may be overloaded by modern appliances; if so, it poses a fire hazard and should be replaced as soon as possible. Signs of overloading include the presence of many 20- and 30-ampere fuses or circuit breakers, a burning smell near the panel, fuses that are warm to the touch, or darkened and discolored copper contact points under the fuses.

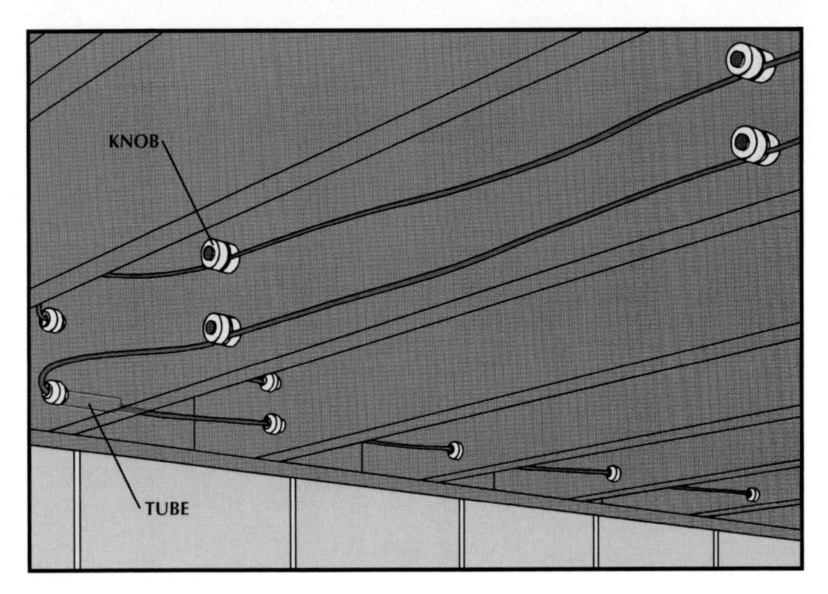

Evaluating the wiring.

If the basement or attic joists are exposed, check the wiring. Outdated knob-and-tube wiring, illustrated here and identified by its paper insulation and the porcelain insulators from which it gets its name, must be entirely replaced. This old system is ungrounded and therefore unsafe.

With other types of electrical wiring, check the insulation for fraying or cracking. Insulation problems indicate that rewiring is probably needed, although minor repairs are possible in some instances.

Evaluating receptacles.

Test all receptacles with a plug-in receptacle analyzer as shown on page 195. To adapt a two-slot outlet, remove the center screw from the cover plate, attach the adapter's ground contact to this screw, then plug in the analyzer and retighten the screw. Depending on the type of tester used, one or more test lights will glow if the outlet is functioning and safely grounded—check the manufacturer's instructions. If you find ungrounded outlets, consider replacing the first receptacle on the circuit with one containing a ground-fault circuit interrupter (GFCI). This tactic is just as safe as a grounded circuit and protects all receptacles downstream on the circuit. Bathroom receptacles and those within 6 feet of a kitchen sink should also be protected by a GFCI.

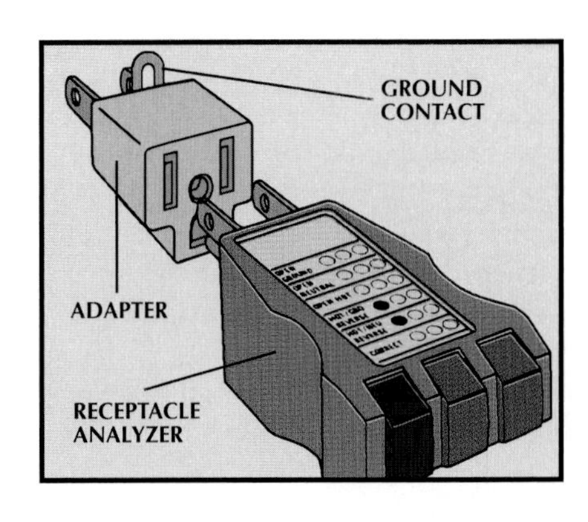

A Clue to Incoming Power

When all else fails, compare the electric meter outside a house with the photographs shown here to gauge how many amps the electric service provides. An old, 60-amp meter *(far left, top)* sits on a round socket that is barely larger than the glass housing. A 100-amp meter *(far left, bottom)* is fastened to a rectangular box little wider than the meter's glass bubble, while a 150- or 200-amp meter *(left)* is fastened to a box that is much larger.

TRICKS OF THE TRADE

Never break the seal on an electric meter or otherwise disturb it; the meter belongs to the electric utility, and tampering with it is a criminal offense in some jurisdictions.

A TOOL KIT FOR BASIC WIRING

The electrical repairs and improvements described in this chapter require a wide variety of tools, from hammers and screwdrivers to a stud finder and a star drill. If you have built or fixed things around the house, you probably already own some of these items.

When undertaking electrical work, consider the dozen tools shown here as potential additions to your tool kit. Not only do they speed the task and improve results, but the majority have no satisfactory substitute.

Even so, few jobs require all these devices. Buy them as you need them. In short order, you will assemble an electrical tool kit tailored to the kind of work that appeals to you.

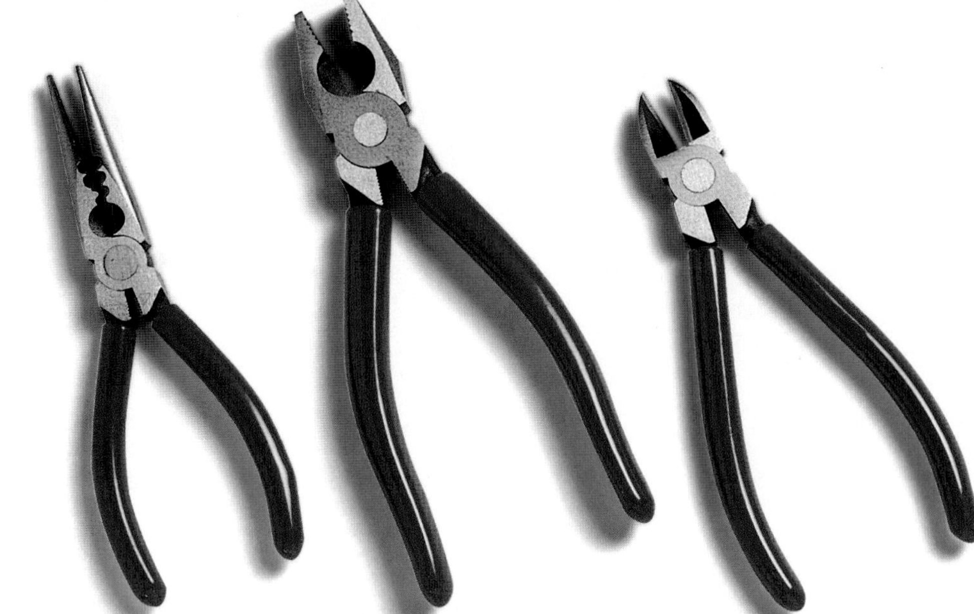

Long-nose pliers. Handy in tight spaces, this tool has rounded jaws to aid in bending wires to fit around screw terminals.

Lineman's pliers. This heavy-duty tool is used for pulling cable into fixture boxes, bending wire, and twisting knockouts from metal boxes.

Diagonal-cutting pliers. The narrow tip and angled jaws of this tool let you snip wires in tight spaces such as small fixture boxes.

Receptacle analyzer. Plugged into a receptacle, this device tests for electrical faults in the circuit. Three lights at the bottom of the tester glow in different combinations to diagnose several problems.

Conduit bender. Fitted with a long pipe handle for leverage *(not shown)*, a conduit bender turns metal conduit around a corner without crimping. This model has built-in spirit levels. They indicate 45-degree and 90-degree bends.

Voltage tester. A neon bulb glows when the two probes are touched to a live circuit. Voltage testers are used to check that the current is off inside an electrical box before you begin a job and to determine which is the incoming hot wire in a circuit.

Continuity tester. This device, used only when the power is turned off, detects interruptions in the path of current. Connected to a switch in the on position, for example, the tester lights if the switch is good.

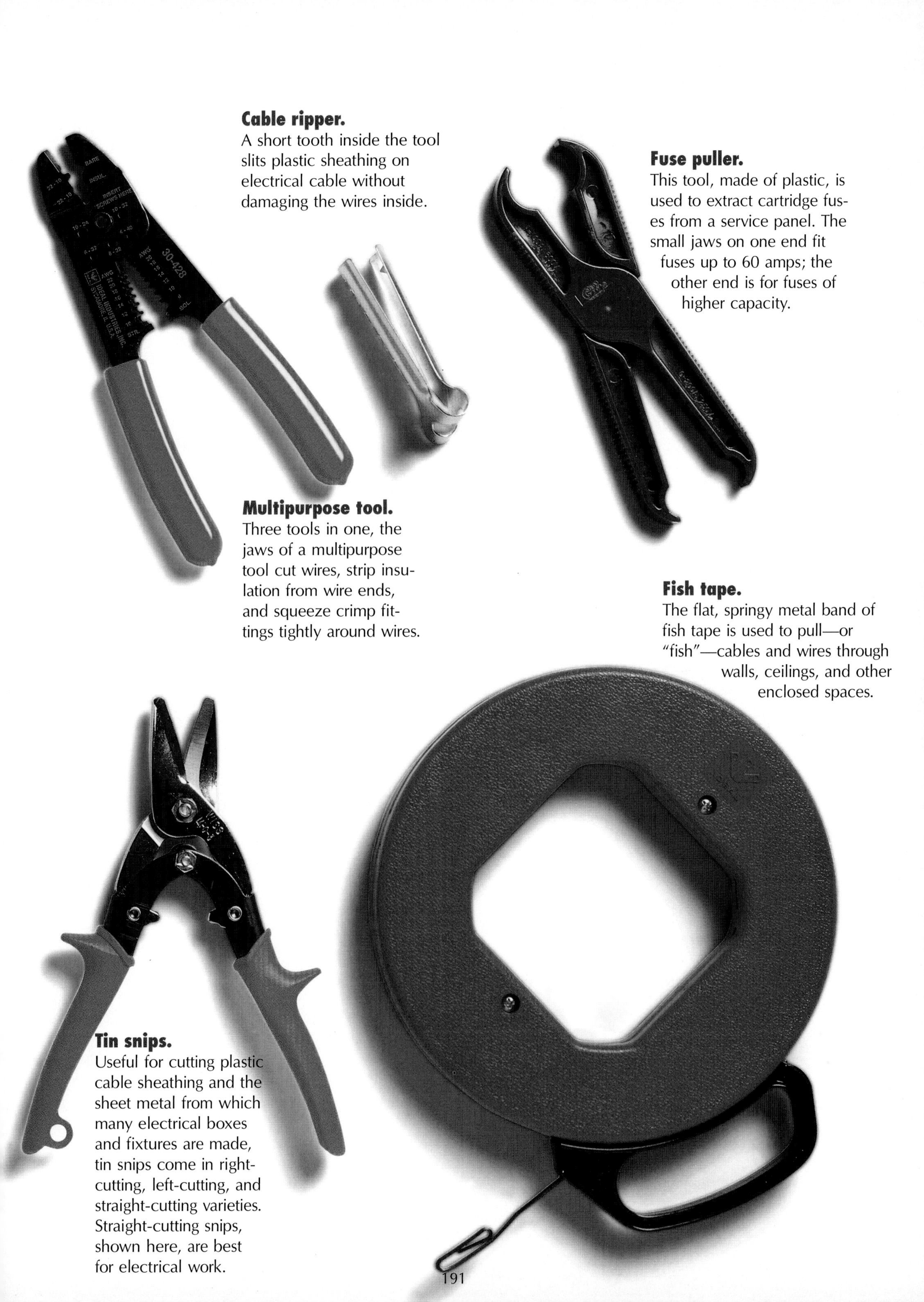

Cable ripper.
A short tooth inside the tool slits plastic sheathing on electrical cable without damaging the wires inside.

Fuse puller.
This tool, made of plastic, is used to extract cartridge fuses from a service panel. The small jaws on one end fit fuses up to 60 amps; the other end is for fuses of higher capacity.

Multipurpose tool.
Three tools in one, the jaws of a multipurpose tool cut wires, strip insulation from wire ends, and squeeze crimp fittings tightly around wires.

Fish tape.
The flat, springy metal band of fish tape is used to pull—or "fish"—cables and wires through walls, ceilings, and other enclosed spaces.

Tin snips.
Useful for cutting plastic cable sheathing and the sheet metal from which many electrical boxes and fixtures are made, tin snips come in right-cutting, left-cutting, and straight-cutting varieties. Straight-cutting snips, shown here, are best for electrical work.

THE SERVICE PANEL AND CIRCUIT TESTING

Each branch circuit from the main service panel is protected against overloads by an individual circuit breaker or fuse. These safety devices cut off power to defective circuits at the service panel. By preventing the flow of excessive current, they reduce the risk of fires resulting from overheated wires.

A circuit breaker is a sort of switch that "trips," turning itself off, when current exceeds the breaker's maximum amperage. In a fuse, too-high amperage causes a metal element to melt or to break, cutting off the current.

Causes and Cures: A tripped breaker or blown fuse always indicates a problem in its circuit, which must be fixed as soon as possible. The most common cause, and the easiest to remedy, is that the various devices on the circuit draw too much current. Reduce the load by turning off or unplugging some things on the circuit before replacing the fuse or resetting the breaker. If there appears to be no overload, check for malfunctioning appliances, which may draw more power than normal.

A circuit overload is more dangerous when it results from a short circuit—for example, when one bare wire touches another or touches a metal electrical box that allows the current to flow to ground. In such cases, the current meets almost no resistance, because it does not pass through an appliance or a light. The result is a surge of amperage that quickly overloads the circuit.

Circuit breakers and fuses protect only wires, not you. If you cause a short circuit by touching a wire (hot or neutral; both carry current) while you are grounded, a potentially fatal current can flow through your body in the split second before the breaker or fuse detects the overload. Only a GFCI circuit breaker *(pages 213–215)* can respond quickly enough to protect both you and the wires.

Safety While Working: Breakers and fuses serve another important safety function, allowing you to turn off power to an individual circuit while you work on it. You can also shut off power to the entire house from the service panel, by switching one or more breakers or by pulling out a block of fuses.

CAUTION *Tripping the main breaker or pulling the main fuse block turns off power throughout the house, but these actions do not completely kill power within the service panel. Only the power company can completely shut off power to the panel. Always exercise extreme caution when working around the service panel.*

SAFEGUARDS OF THE ELECTRICAL SYSTEM

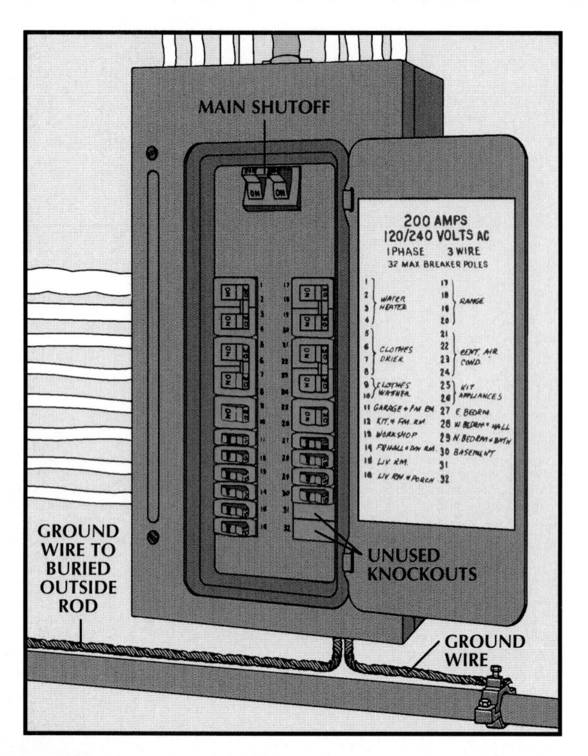

A straight-bus circuit breaker panel.
One large breaker on this panel serves as a main shutoff as well as limiting the total amperage of current flowing into the house. The panel shown at left has a 200-amp main breaker; similar panels in older houses may have a lower amperage rating.

◆ Circuits that carry 240 volts to appliances such as a water heater or a clothes dryer are protected by two linked breakers. Single breakers or small, space-saving breakers control the 120-volt circuits. The amperage rating is marked on each breaker.

◆ The unused space at the bottom right of the panel contains knockouts that allow later installation of more circuits and breakers.

◆ When a circuit breaker trips, it is reset by flipping the switch back to the on position. Some models require that the switch be pushed firmly to the off position before resetting.

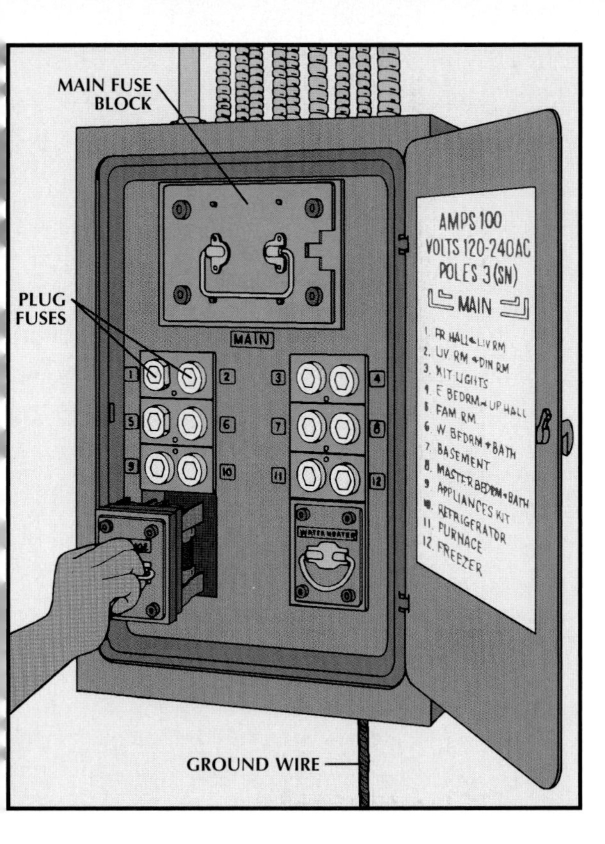

A straight-bus fuse panel. This type of panel contains a main fuse block with knife-blade fuses *(page 194)* that each control power to the circuits. Turning off all power to the house requires pulling the entire block out of the panel.

◆ Below the main block are screw-in plug fuses *(below, bottom),* rated for 15 amps or 20 amps, which protect the individual 120-volt circuits.

◆ Blocks at the bottom of the panel each contain two cartridge fuses *(page 194),* which protect 240-volt circuits.

◆ Before removing a fuse for any reason, ensure that no current is flowing through it by turning off all electrical devices on that circuit.

◆ To change a cartridge fuse, pull its block completely out of the panel *(left).*

◆ To change a plug fuse, unscrew it while touching only the insulated rim. Do not stand on damp ground and do not touch any other object while you are removing or replacing the fuse.

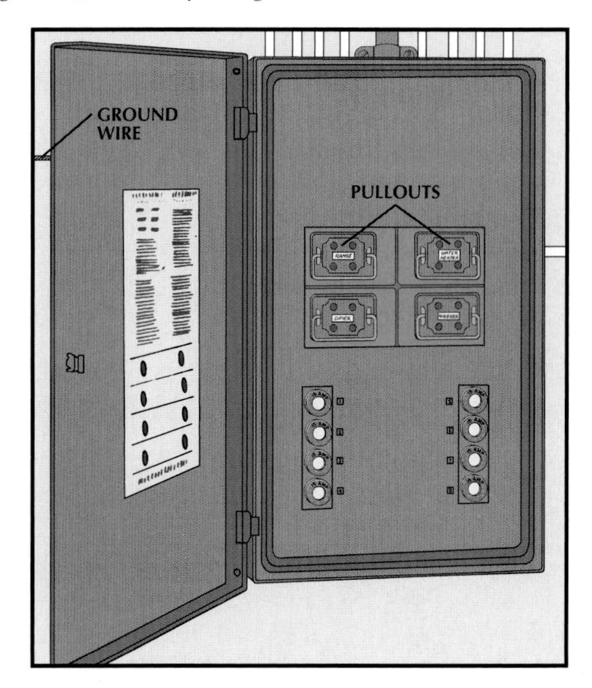

A split-bus panel. This type of panel, found in some houses built before the early 1980s, has no main shutoff. Instead, blocks of high-amp breakers or fuses control different groups of circuits; all must be tripped or removed to shut off power in the house.

◆ The split-bus fuse panel shown at right has four pullout blocks to control all power to the house. A split-bus breaker panel may have as many as six heavy-duty circuit breakers to do the job.

◆ Split-bus panels have been banned in construction since 1984.

TYPES OF FUSES

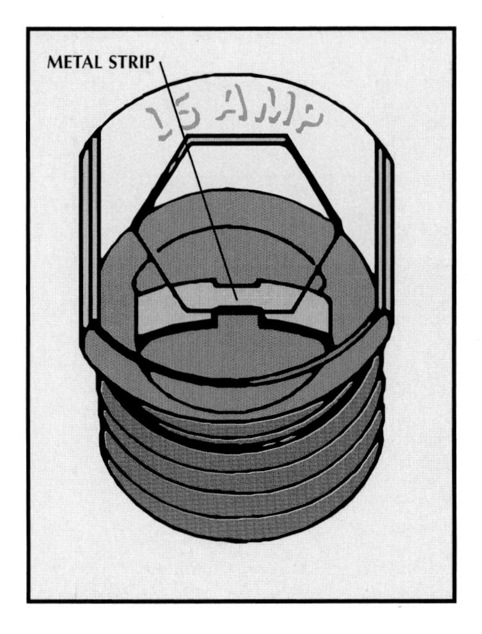

CAUTION *Never try to solve a continuing overload problem by replacing a fuse with one of a higher amperage rating. It will allow the wires to overheat and create a fire hazard.*

Plug fuse.
The plug fuse is the most common type. It screws into the panel in the same way that a light bulb screws into a socket. Current flows through a narrow metal strip—zinc in the United States—which melts through when overloaded, breaking the circuit. In Canada, the strip is made of copper, which melts at a lower temperature, making the fuse more sensitive.

Time-delay fuse.
Similar in shape to a plug fuse, this type also screws into the service panel. Its design allows it to withstand the momentary surge of current caused by the starting of a motor in an appliance such as a power tool or a refrigerator compressor. The zinc strip softens but does not melt through unless the surge continues. The larger current typical of a short circuit, however, melts the zinc immediately. The plug-type time-delay fuse cannot be used in Canada.

Type S fuse.
Also known as a tamperproof fuse, a Type S provides time-delay protection and prevents the use of fuses of the wrong amperage rating for a given circuit. A Type S fuse cannot be screwed directly into the service panel; instead, it fits an adapter that locks into the panel socket. Each adapter is sized for only one amperage rating. A fuse rated for 20 amps, for example, will not fit into an adapter for a 15-amp fuse. In Canada, this kind of fuse is designated Type D. A similar Canadian tamperproof fuse, Type P, does not have a time-delay function.

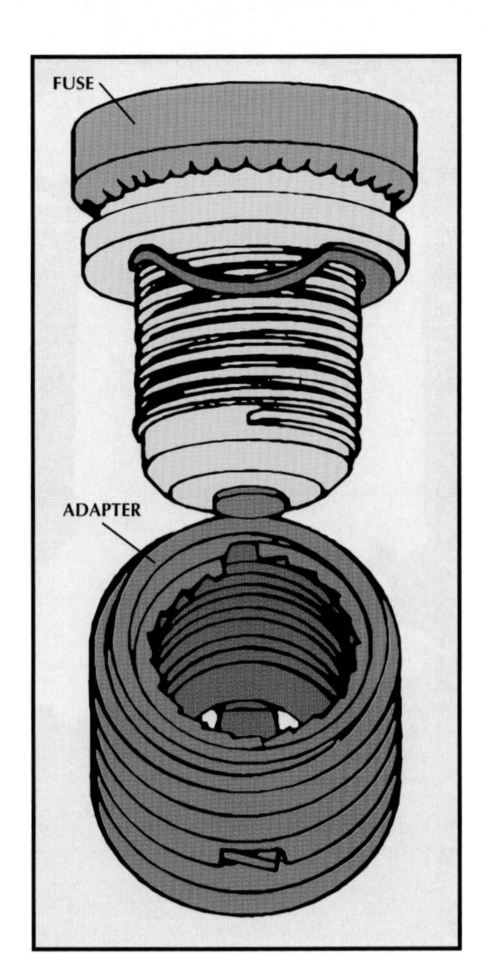

Cartridge fuse.
The metal-capped ends of a cartridge fuse, called ferrules, snap into metal spring-clip contacts. Often found in auxiliary fuse boxes, cartridge fuses are rated from 10 to 60 amps. They are generally used to protect circuits that are dedicated to large appliances such as ranges, dryers, or central air conditioners.

CAUTION

Use only an all-plastic, plierslike fuse puller (page 191) to remove a cartridge fuse. Grasp the fuse in the center with the puller and pull it straight out of the retaining clips.

Knife-blade fuse.
Another type of cartridge fuse, a knife-blade fuse is distinguished by metal blades at each end that snap into spring clips within a fuse block. Knife-blade fuses are rated for more than 60 amps and may be used in the main fuse block of the service panel.

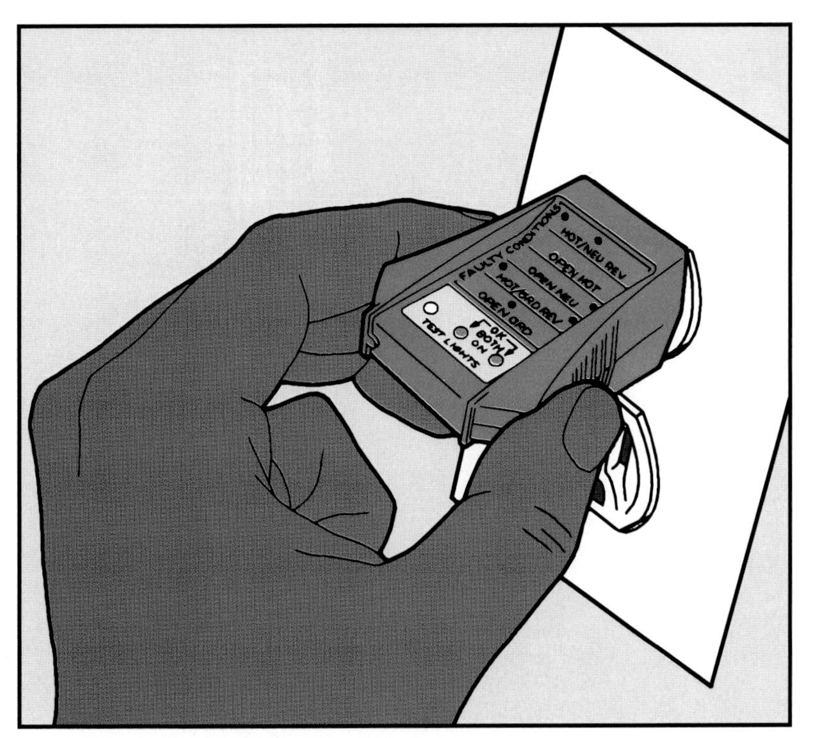

Verifying receptacle wiring.
A receptacle analyzer *(page 190)* detects several wiring problems when plugged into a live circuit, identifying the difficulty with different combinations of three glowing lights. Typically, wiring is correct when all three lights glow. No lights means that power is not reaching the receptacle. A guide printed on the analyzer explains other combinations of lights.

Testing a receptacle for power.
Before working, turn off power to the circuit at the service panel and make the following checks with a voltage tester. If the tester's neon bulb glows at any stage of the process, the circuit still has power; stop and try a different fuse or circuit breaker at the service panel.

◆ Before removing the cover plate, check that power is off by inserting the probes of a voltage tester into the receptacle's vertical slots.

◆ Remove the cover plate. Touch the probes to the terminal screws where the black and white wires attach to the receptacle *(left)*. On a dual receptacle, test both pairs of terminals.

◆ Test from each black wire to the ground wire to check for defects or improper wiring in the neutral circuit.

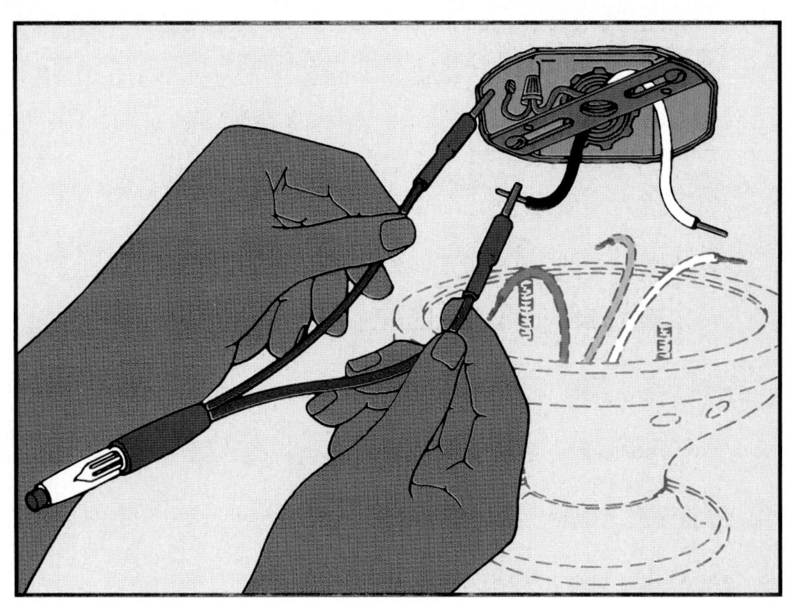

Checking a light fixture.

◆ Turn off power to the fixture at the service panel. Flip the wall switch to OFF.
◆ Unscrew the fixture and pull it away from the box to expose the wires.
◆ Hold the fixture in one hand and remove wire caps with the other. Keep black and white wires away from each other and the box if it is metal.
◆ Gently loosen each fixture wire from the corresponding house wire. Set the fixture aside.
◆ In the following checks, a voltage tester will not glow if the power is off. Touch one probe of the tester to the black wire in the box and the other to ground—the box if it is metal *(left),* or the ground wire in a plastic box. Check also for voltage between the black wire and the white wire and between the white wire and ground.

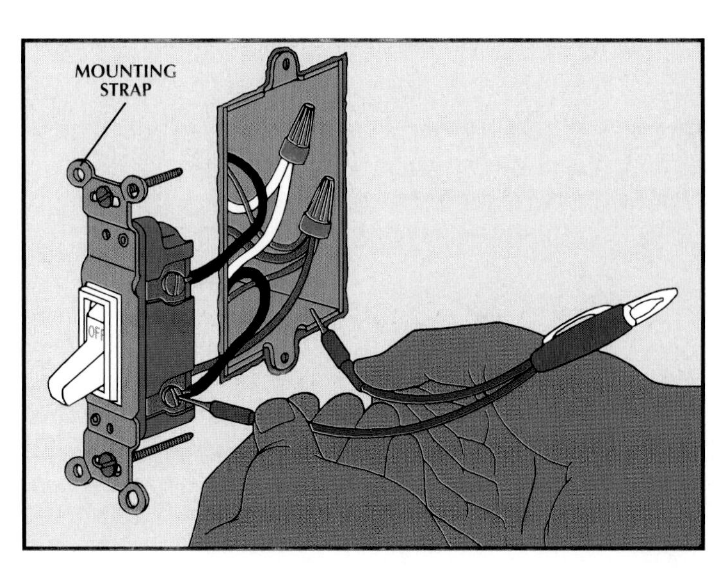

Testing a switch for power.

◆ To verify that electricity to a switch has been shut off, unscrew the cover plate, then the switch. Pull the switch from the box by the mounting strap.
◆ While touching one probe of a voltage tester to the outlet box if it is metal—or to the ground wire if the box is plastic—touch the other probe to each of the brass terminals on the switch. If the switch has push-in terminals *(page 200),* insert the probe into the release slots. The tester's bulb will not glow if electricity to the switch has been turned off.

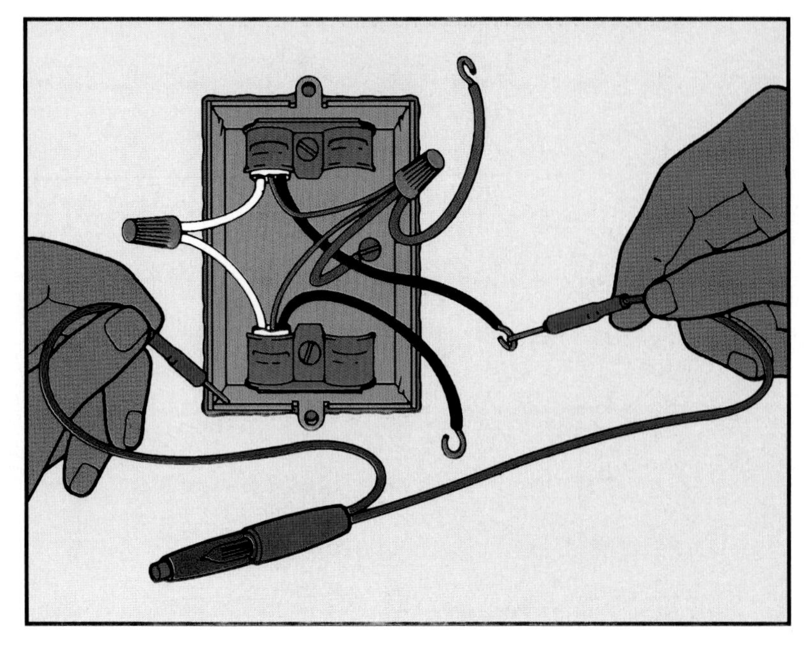

Identifying a feed wire.

◆ To find out which of the black wires in a box supplies current from the service panel, first cut power to the box.
◆ Pull the fixture or other device from the box, and confirm with a voltage tester that the electricity is off.
◆ Disconnect all black wires and arrange them so they are not touching each other, the fixture, or the box.
◆ Have a helper restore power to the circuit.
◆ Touching nothing but the insulated leads of a voltage tester, hold one probe against the box or ground wire, and the other against each black wire in turn. The tester will glow when the probe touches the feed wire.
◆ Have your helper turn off the power. After verifying that the feed wire is no longer hot, mark it with tape.

BASIC SKILLS

Almost every household wiring job entails a few basic tasks such as stripping cable sheathing and wire insulation, joining wires with wire caps, and connecting wires to switches and receptacles. Once you have become familiar with these easily learned skills, your home wiring projects will proceed more quickly and easily.

Taking Care with Cable: It is critical when stripping cable sheathing that you avoid damaging the insulation on the wires inside. Even a small nick on a wire's insulation can become an electrocution or fire hazard.

Likewise, avoid excessive marring of bare wires as you work with them. Minor scratches and nicks from tools are unavoidable, but badly damaged wires increase resistance, which can cause overheating.

Leave Enough Slack: When extending or adding a circuit, don't stint on cable. Two or three extra feet of cable provide a margin for error when stripping sheathing from cable or insulation from the wires inside. If you damage a wire or make some other mistake, you can cut off the error and proceed. Excess cable remains hidden inside the wall or ceiling.

Leave No Bare Wire Exposed: Strip $\frac{3}{4}$ inch of insulation or less from the ends of wires. Following this rule will, in most cases, ensure bare wire ends long enough for making connections to fixtures or to other wires, yet short enough that no bare wire can be seen after the connection is made. If the shine of copper is visible, undo the connection and trim the ends of the wires.

The Remarkable Wire Cap

Wires are connected to each other with a conical plastic fastener called a wire cap. Hollow at its base, a wire cap contains a copper coil. When the wire cap is tightened like a nut onto two or more wires, the coil binds them securely together.

Wire caps used in house wiring come in a variety of sizes. A wire cap that is too large or too small will result in an unreliable connection. The one to use depends on the number of wires in the connection and their gauge. Keep several sizes on hand; the best way to find the right one is to experiment.

WORKING WITH CABLE AND WIRE

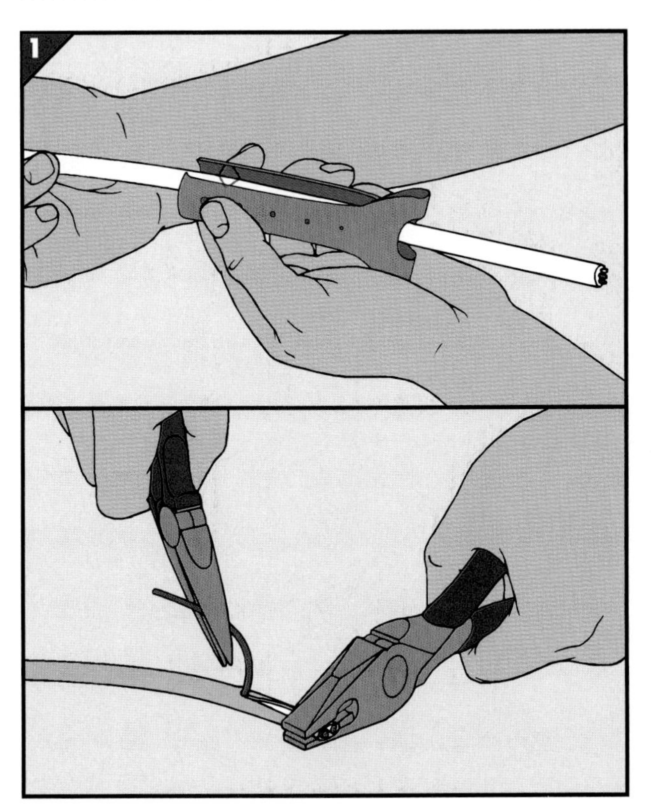

1. Exposing the wires in cable.

◆ With NM-B cable, the plastic-sheathed type most widely used for indoor wiring, insert 10 to 12 inches of cable into a cable ripper and squeeze the tool to force a tooth inside the tool through the sheathing. Pull the ripper toward the end of the cable *(left, top).*

◆ When stripping UF cable, used only for underground and outdoor wiring, cut a 3-inch slit alongside the ground wire with diagonal cutters. Grasp the wire with long-nose pliers and the end of the cable with lineman's pliers. Pull the ground wire through the sheathing to expose 10 to 12 inches of bare copper *(left, bottom).* Repeat for the insulated wires if necessary.

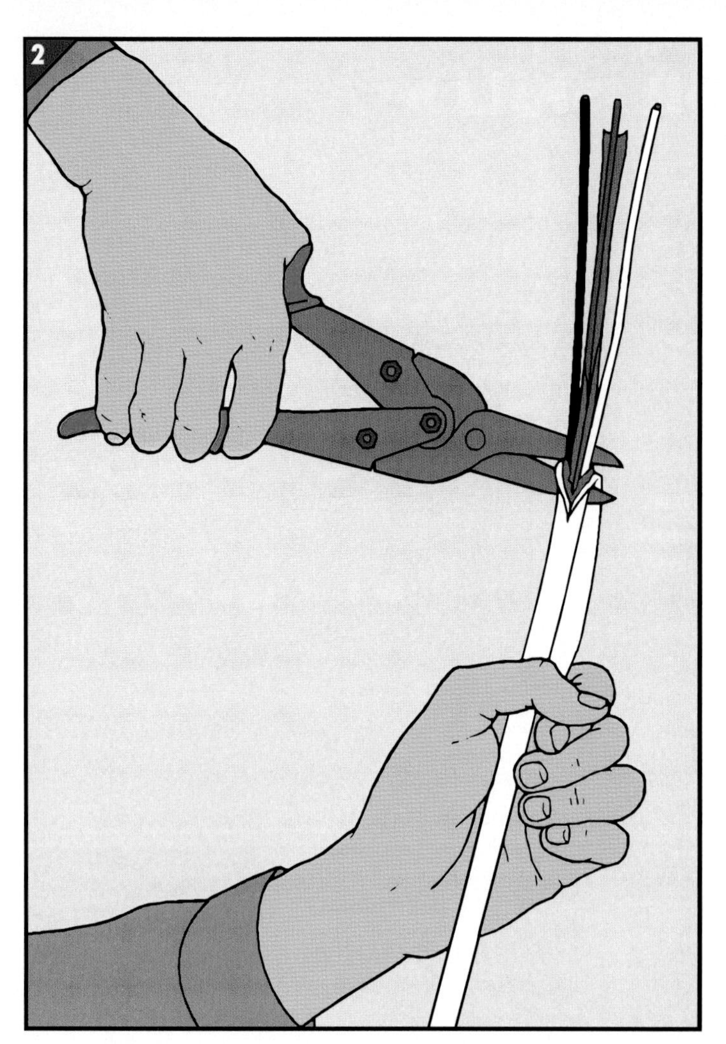

2. Removing cable sheathing.
With both types of cable, bend back the sheathing—and in the case of NM-B cable, its paper liner—then cut off the insulation with tin snips. Also tear off the brown paper wrapped around the ground wire in NM-B cable.

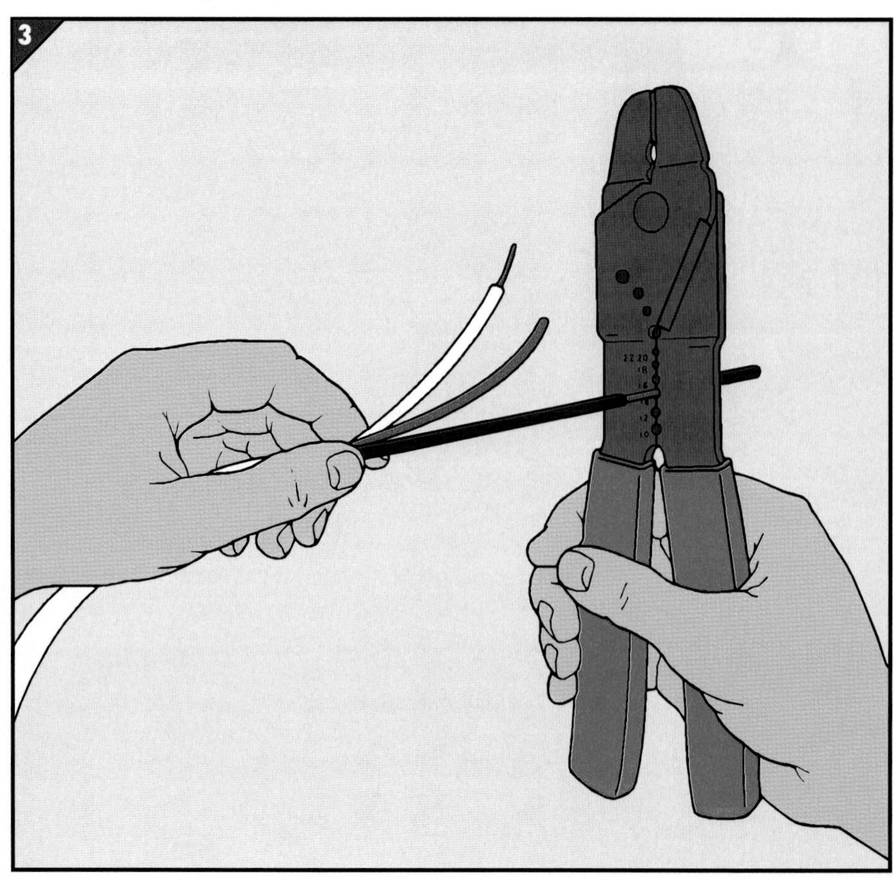

3. Stripping insulation.

◆ Match the gauge of wire you are working with—it is embossed on the plastic sheathing of the cable—to the corresponding wire stripping hole in a multipurpose tool *(left)*.

◆ Close the multipurpose tool over the wire $\frac{1}{2}$ inch to $\frac{3}{4}$ inch from the end and rotate the tool a quarter-turn in each direction.

◆ Without opening the tool, pull the severed insulation off the wire to expose the bare metal.

MAKING CONNECTIONS WITH WIRE CAPS

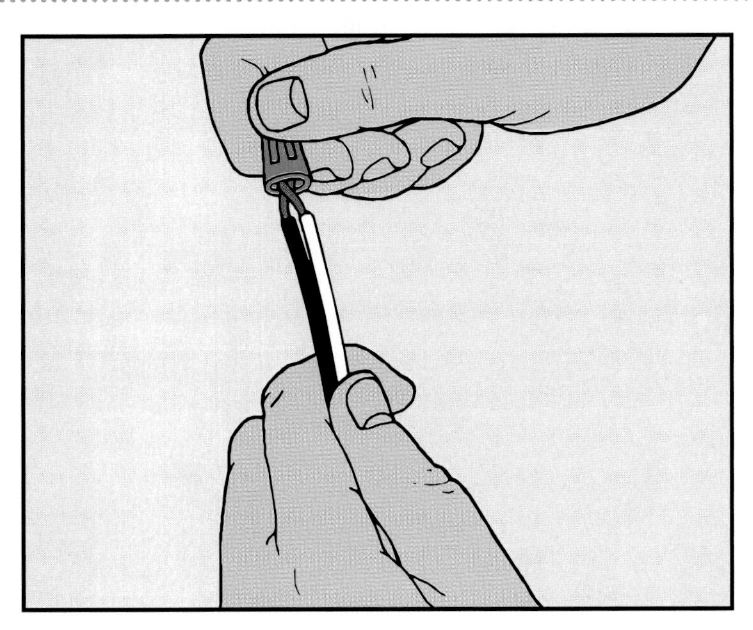

Making solid-wire connections.

◆ After stripping the insulation from the wires, hold them next to each other with long-nose pliers and twist the exposed metal ends together clockwise with lineman's pliers.

◆ Place a wire cap over the wires. If bare metal is visible *(left),* trim the ends of the wires without untwisting them.

◆ Push the wires firmly into the base of the cap as you twist the cap clockwise until the connection is tight.

Making stranded-wire connections.

◆ When connecting stranded wire to solid wire, strip about $\frac{1}{8}$ inch more insulation from the stranded wire than from the solid wire. Do not twist together the individual strands.

◆ Hold the two wires side by side as shown at right, then check the fit of a wire cap, making sure that it encloses every filament of the stranded wire.

◆ While pushing the wires firmly into the wire cap, twist it clockwise until the connection is tight.

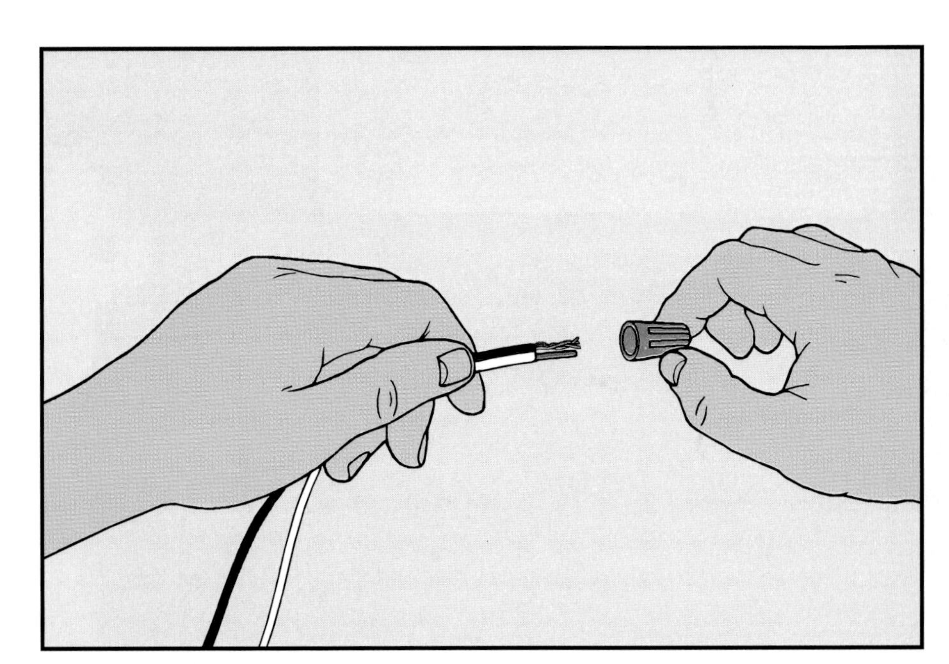

TRICKS OF THE TRADE

INCOMING GROUND

JUMPER TO BOX

JUMPER TO FIXTURE

CRIMPING BARREL

OUTGOING GROUND

An Alternative for Ground Wires

Wire caps are fast and easy to use, but some types of hookups require more ground wires than a wire cap can handle. In such cases, crimping barrels make ground connections easier and more secure. Because you can use crimping barrels only with bare copper wires, avoid jumper ground wires having green insulation.

To use a crimping barrel, first twist all the ground wires and ground jumpers together as close to the cable sheathing as possible. Slide a crimping barrel over the braid as far as it will go, then squeeze the barrel tightly against the wires with lineman's pliers. Snip off excess wire about an inch beyond the barrel.

TWO KINDS OF TERMINALS

The connection points for wires on switches, receptacles *(page 209)*, and other electrical devices are called terminals. There are two basic types, screw terminals and push-in terminals. Make connections as shown below.

Screw terminals.

◆ With long-nose pliers, form a partial hook in the stripped end of the wire.

◆ Loosen the terminal and fit the hook under the screwhead in the direction shown above.

◆ Bend the wire around the screw with long-nose pliers, then tighten the screw.

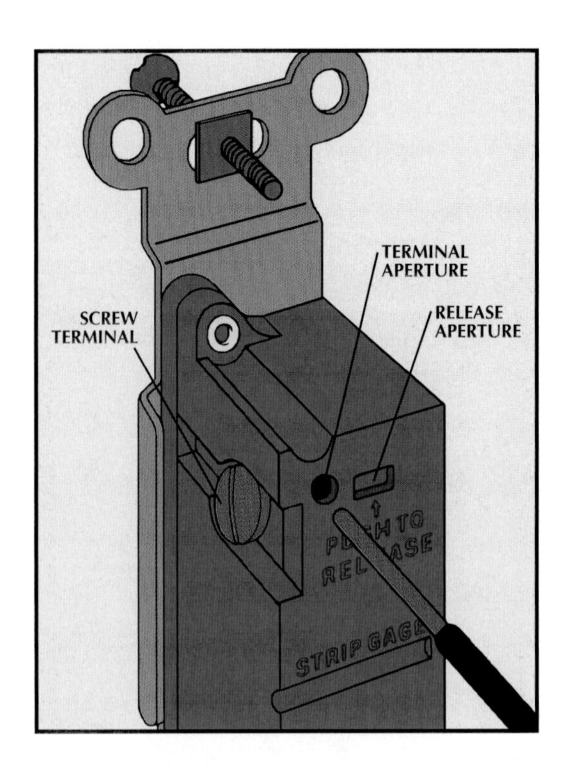

Push-in terminals.

Some fixtures offer the alternative of a push-in terminal.

◆ Trim the wire or remove additional insulation as necessary to make the bare end of the wire fit the strip gauge on the back of the fixture.

◆ Push the wire into the terminal aperture as far as it will go, leaving no bare wire exposed.

◆ To disconnect a wire, push the blade of a small screwdriver into the release aperture while pulling on the wire.

LIGHT FIXTURES

TOOLS

Utility knife
Screwdriver
Wire stripper
Adjustable wrench

MATERIALS

Coat hanger wire
Light fixture
Wire caps
Crossbar
Nipple
Reducing nut
Hickey

A new light fixture can both enhance a room's look and save energy. While incandescent bulbs produce softer and more natural light, fluorescents *(page 203)* use less wattage, give off less heat, and last far longer. The following procedures apply to almost any incandescent fixture mounted on a wall or ceiling. You can use them to replace an old fixture with a new one, or to hang a fixture on a properly installed and wired box in a new location.

Removing the Old Fixture: With the power turned off, remove the bulbs or tubes. Free a fixture stuck to the wall or ceiling with paint or caulk by cutting around the decorative cover, or canopy, with a utility knife. Unscrew any mounting screws or cap nuts, then pull the fixture away from the box and hang it from the box with a hook that is made of coat hanger wire. Disconnect the wiring.

If the exposed ends of house wires have cracked insulation, cut them back and strip off $\frac{1}{2}$ inch of insulation to reveal bright, clean wire. If necessary, strip the new fixture wires to the same length.

Mounting a Fixture: Most new fixtures come with mounting hardware and instructions. If not, and if the new fixture is similar in size and weight to the old one, you may be able to reuse some of the old hardware.

Every light fixture must be fastened securely to a ceiling or wall box. Moreover, heavy fixtures such as chandeliers must have additional support and should be attached to a box stud *(page 202)*.

HANGING LIGHTWEIGHT FIXTURES

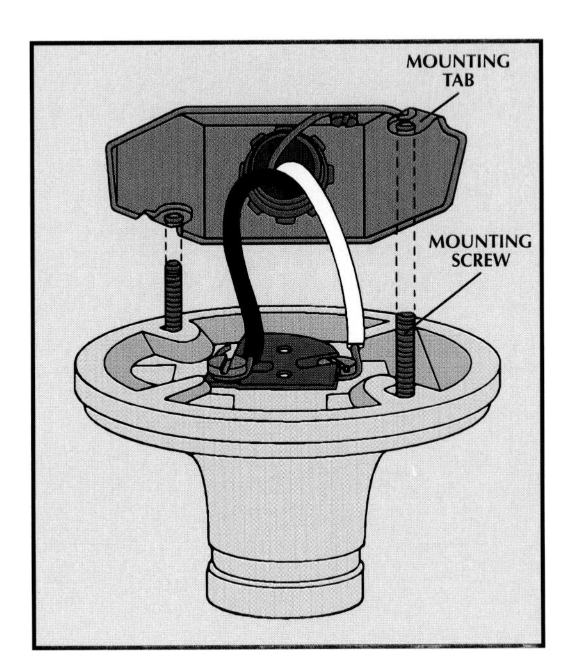

Connecting a simple fixture.
A single-bulb porcelain fixture, typically used in garages and basements, connects to house wiring by means of terminals.

◆ To install this type of fixture, connect the black house wire to the brass-colored terminal and the white house wire to the silver-colored terminal.

◆ Secure the fixture to the threaded mounting tabs of the box with screws. Tighten the mounting screws gingerly; overtightening can crack the ceramic.

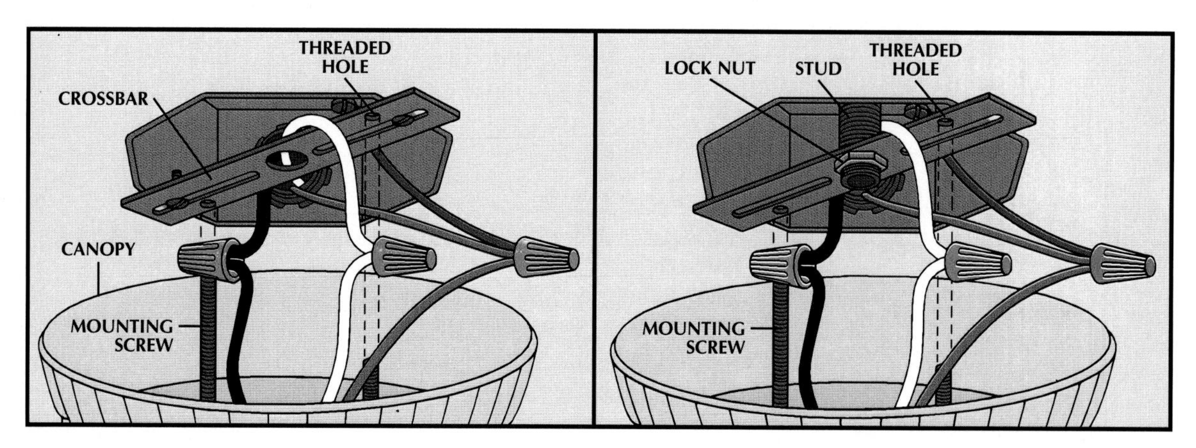

Attaching a fixture with an adapter.

Light fixtures are often fastened to outlet box mounting tabs with screws, typically through holes in the canopy.

◆ Where canopy holes do not align with the tabs, adapt the box with a slotted crossbar. Screw the crossbar to the tabs *(above, left),* or for box with a stud in the center, slip the crossbar onto the stud and secure it with a lock nut *(above, right).*

◆ Fasten the canopy to the threaded holes in the crossbar with screws trimmed, if necessary, so they do not press against the back of the box.

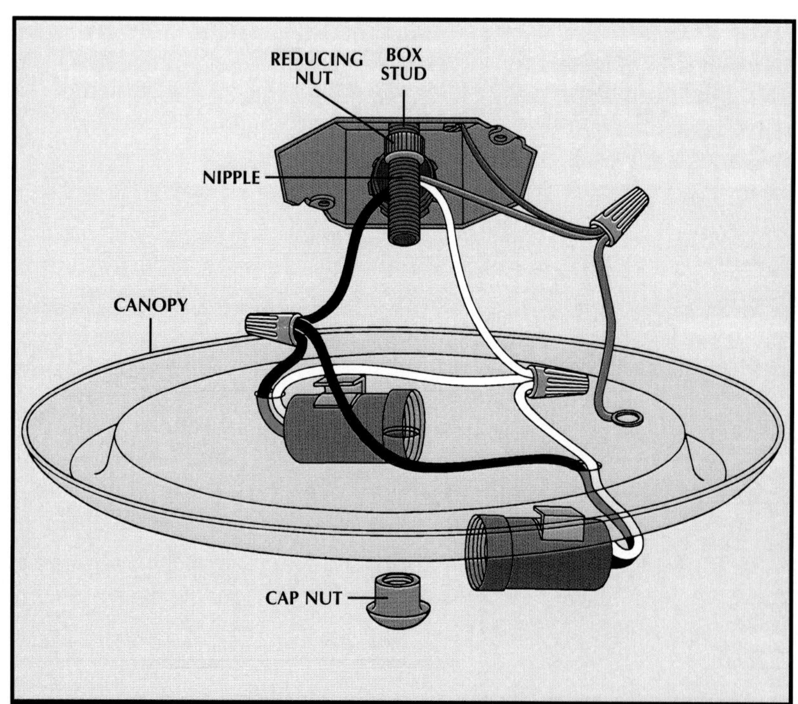

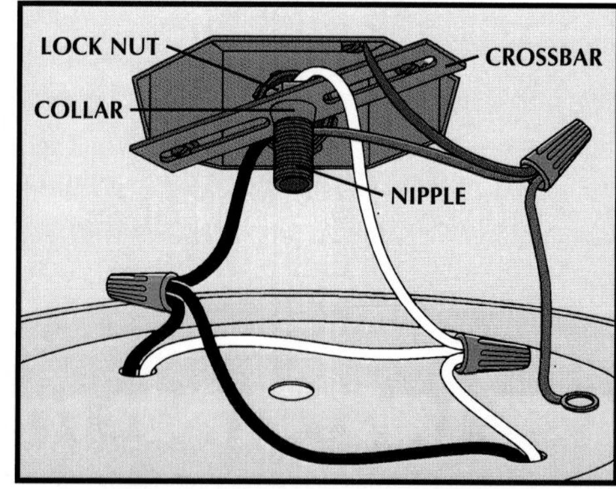

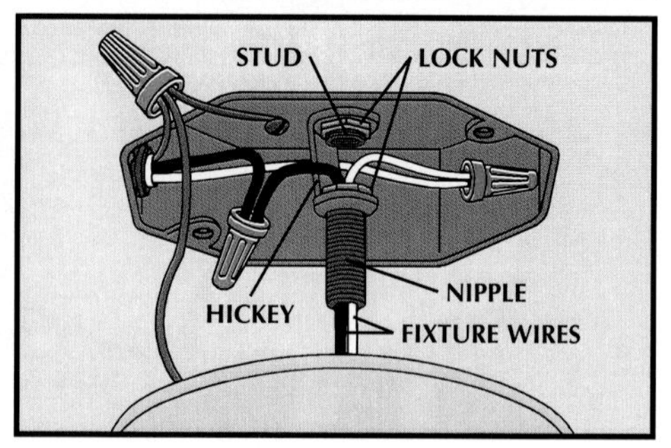

Securing center-mounted fixtures.

If the box has a built-in stud, extend it with a smaller-diameter nipple held to the stud by a reducing nut *(above, left).*

If the box has no stud, use a crossbar with a threaded collar in the center *(above right, top).* Screw a nipple into the collar and secure it with a lock nut so the nipple protrudes through the canopy just far enough to engage the cap nut. Fasten the crossbar to the box tabs.

To hang chandeliers or other fixtures whose wires pass through the canopy *(above right, bottom),* attach a nipple to the stud with a C-shaped adapter called a hickey. Secure both nipple and hickey with lock nuts. Pass the fixture wires through the nipple into the box.

◆ With the nipple in place, connect the fixture's white, black, and ground wires to the house circuit's corresponding wires. Fold the wires into the box or under the canopy.

◆ Fasten the fixture to the nipple with the cap nut, drawing the canopy against the wall or ceiling.

INSTALLING FLUORESCENT FIXTURES

Although the cost of bulbs and installation may be greater, fluorescent lighting gives more uniform illumination than incandescent lighting and is more energy efficient. Using the hardware that comes with a new fixture, you can mount fluorescents quite easily with an electric drill and spade bit. Follow the procedures on page 201 to remove old incandescent or fluorescent fixtures.

The heart of every fluorescent fixture is the ballast, a device that provides a quick surge of voltage to start the tube, then limits the current while the tube is lit. After 10 or more years, a ballast will wear out, but often it is more economical to install a new fixture than to replace a ballast.

Types of Fixtures: Fluorescents come in a variety of shapes and sizes, but most of them fall into three categories:

Rapid-start fixtures, which light after a few seconds' delay, often are used in home workshops and laundry rooms. These fixtures may malfunction if turned on and off frequently in a brief period of time.

Instant-start fixtures turn on at the flick of a switch but wear out quickly because of the high-voltage surge when switched on.

Compact fluorescent bulbs are self-contained fixtures that have the ballast or an adapter in the base. More efficient and versatile than fluorescent tubes, compact fluorescents screw into ordinary incandescent bulb sockets.

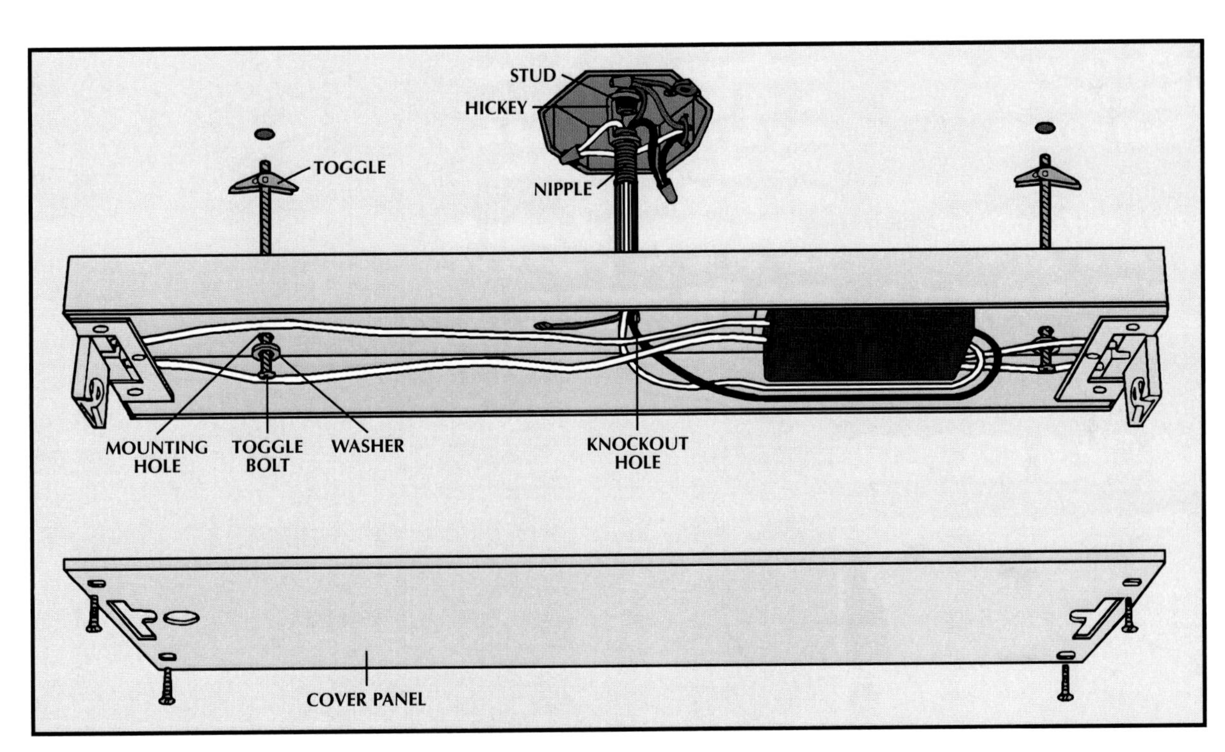

Mounting a ceiling fixture.

◆ Position the fixture with the knockout hole for the wires centered on the ceiling box, and mark the ceiling through the fixture-mounting holes. Lower the fixture and, with a spade bit, drill $\frac{5}{8}$-inch holes at the marks.

◆ Slip a toggle bolt and washer through the fixture-mounting holes and screw a toggle onto the end of each of the bolts. If you are installing a circular fixture, bolt holes are not needed. It attaches to a nipple connected by a reducing nut to the stud in the box.

◆ Thread a hickey to the stud and a nipple to the hickey; if there is no stud, attach a crossbar to the box tabs and a nipple to the crossbar *(opposite)*.

◆ Have a helper support the fixture or hang it from the box with a wire hanger, then lead the fixture wires through the nipple and connect them to those that are in the box, black to black and white to white. Connect the ground wires from the fixture and the house circuit to each other and to the grounding jumper in the box if it is metal.

◆ Raise the fixture. While folding the wires into the box, push the toggles through the ceiling holes and guide the fixture onto the nipple. Tighten the toggle bolts.

◆ Finally, install the cover panel and the tube.

REPLACING A SWITCH

Electrical switches are inexpensive and easy to replace. First, check the circuit breaker or fuse that protects the circuit, then test the switch itself *(opposite and page 206)*. If the switch passes the tests, the problem is elsewhere in the circuit and it is best to call in an electrician to diagnose the cause of the failure.

Type and Location: No matter what type of new switch you are putting in, you must first know the type you are replacing and where in the circuit it is located.

You can tell the type of switch by examining it. The arrangement of wires within the box tells whether the switch is located in the middle or at the end of a circuit.

Keep Track of the Wires: When replacing a simple single-pole switch, there are only two hot wires, and they can be hooked up in any order. But installing other kinds of switches can be more complicated. If you fail to identify or lose track of the wires for a three-way or pilot-light switch, for example, you can wind up with a device that does not work and a tedious chore making things right.

Switch Swapping Basics: As with any other electrical work, turn off power to the circuit at the service panel and then test to make sure it is off *(page 196)*. Remove the switch cover plate and loosen the two screws that hold the switch in the box. These screws will not fall free of the mounting strap; small fiber washers hold them in place. After loosening the screws, gently pull the switch out of the box until the wires are fully extended.

Many switches made before the 1980s will not have grounding terminals. When replacing one, always use a grounded switch.

TOOLS

- Long-nose pliers
- Lineman's pliers
- Screwdriver
- Wire stripper
- Voltage tester
- Continuity tester

CAUTION

Three-Way Wiring in Older Houses

Changes in electrical codes mean that three-way switches in some older homes were wired differently than those here. Working with them can be frustrating and even hazardous. In such a situation it is best to run new cable for the circuit and rewire all the switches according to modern code.

SINGLE-POLE SWITCHES

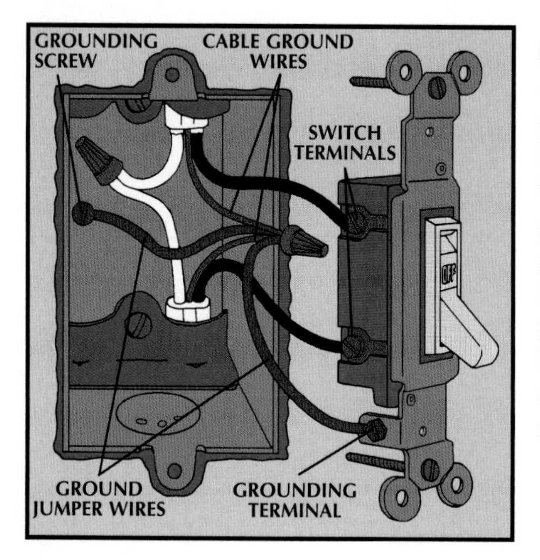

Middle-of-the-run switch.
Found anywhere between the beginning and the end of a circuit, a middle-of-the-run switch can be identified by the two or more cables that enter the box. In a metal box, as shown here, the ground wires are joined with jumper wires to the grounding terminal on the switch and the grounding screw in the box. A plastic box requires no grounding jumper to the box. The switch shown has two black wires, both hot, attached to its terminals. In some hookups, you might find a black and a red hot wire.

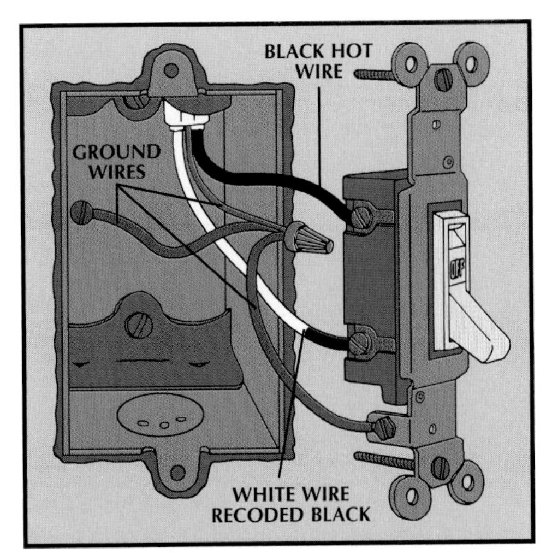

Switch loop.
One cable enters the box in a switch loop. The cable runs between a fixture and the controlling switch. The white wire carries current from fixture to switch; therefore it is a hot wire, and the end of the wire is recoded black by wrapping it with black tape or using an indelible black marker. Although codes do not require this, electricians consider it good practice that will help avoid confusion. The black wire carries current back to the fixture when the switch is on. Electricians use an expression to remember this scheme: "White down, black back."

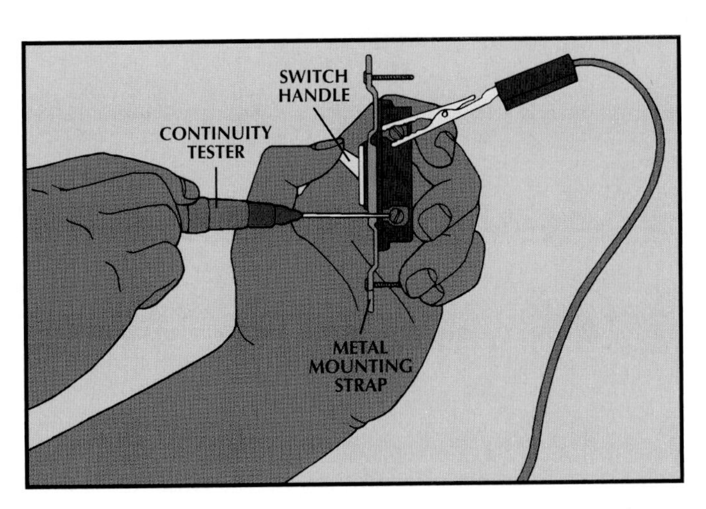

Testing a single-pole switch.
There are two tests you can perform on a suspect switch. If the switch fails either test, it is defective.

◆ Apply the clip of a continuity tester to one switch terminal and touch the other terminal with the probe *(left)*. Operate the switch handle; the tester should light when the switch is on but not when it is off.

◆ Fasten the clip to the metal mounting strap of the switch. Touch the probe to each terminal and operate the switch as you do. The tester's bulb should not light in either position.

Mounting a single-pole switch.

◆ Connect the two hot wires to the switch terminals, in either order.

◆ With the handle in the off position, push the switch into the box, carefully tucking in the wires.

◆ Fasten the mounting strap to the box with its screws. Maneuver the switch within the box so that it is perfectly vertical, even if the box is not, before tightening the screws. If the box is flush with the wall but the plaster ears get in the way, twist them off with lineman's pliers.

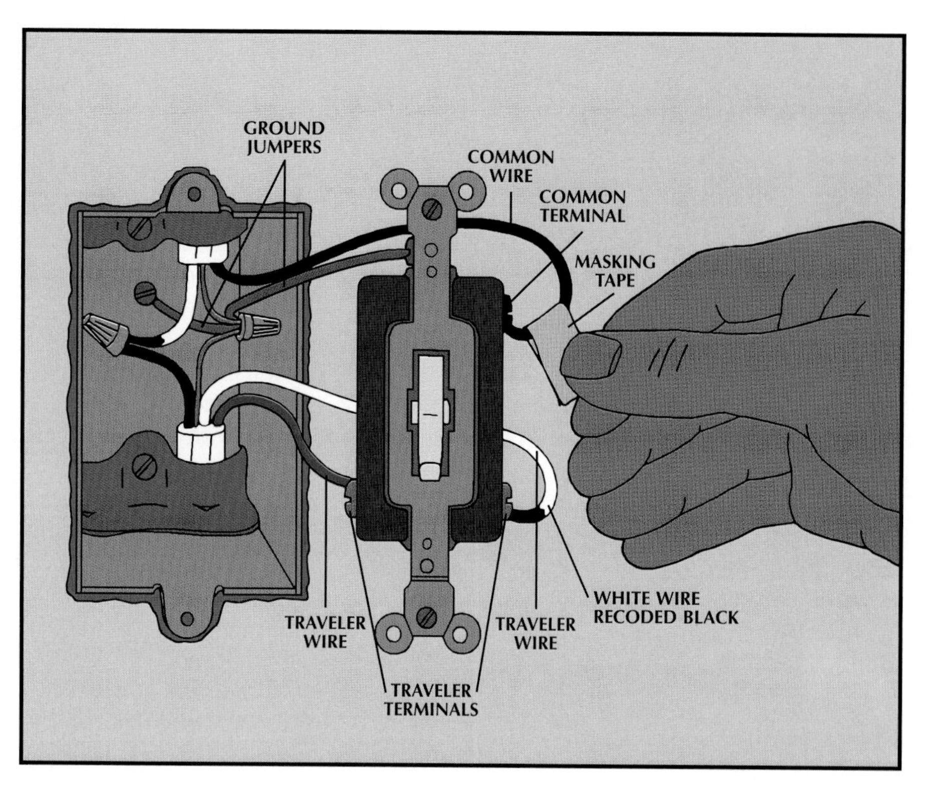

Replacing a three-way switch.

◆ Turn off the power at the service panel and test to see that the power is off at the switch *(page 196)*.

◆ Pull the old switch out of the box, but before you disconnect any wires, mark the common wire with masking tape *(left)*. The common wire is connected to a terminal that is black or otherwise darker than the two brass traveler terminals.

◆ Once the common wire is marked, disconnect all wires and remove the old switch. Connect the common wire to the dark common terminal on the new switch, then fasten the two other wires, called travelers, to the brass traveler terminals, in either order. Recode the white wire to indicate that it is hot. Mount the switch in the box.

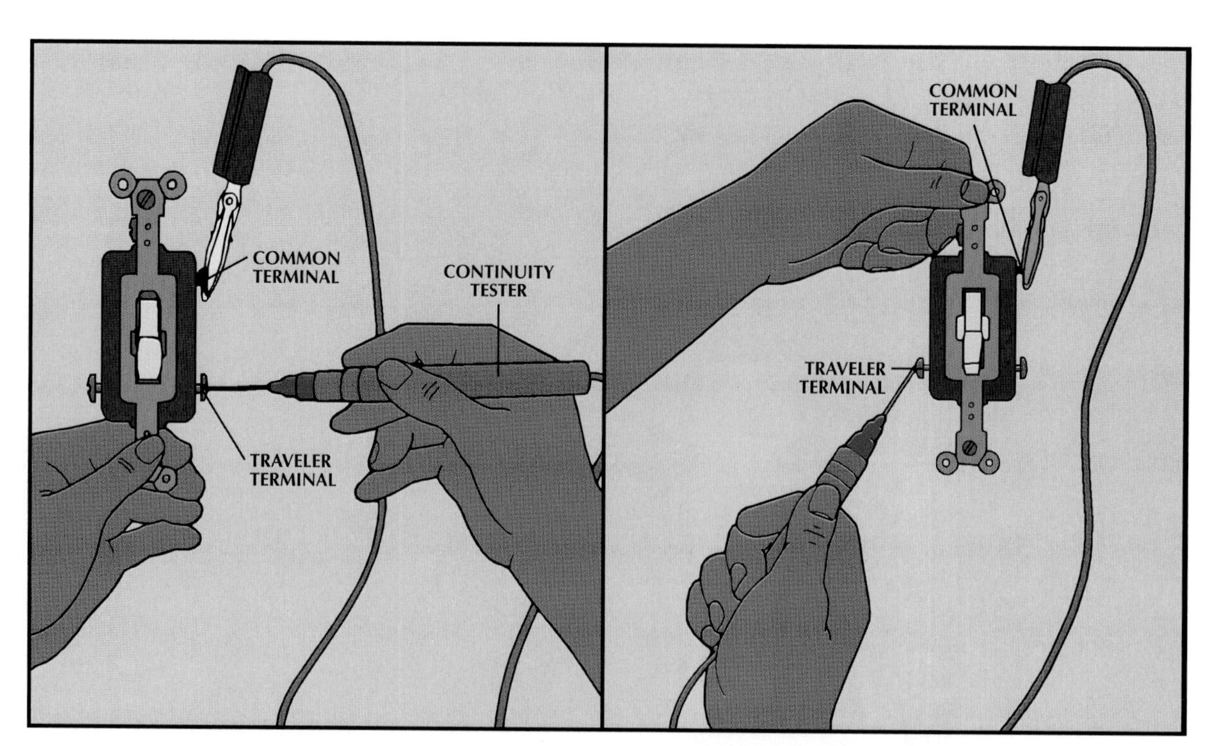

Testing a three-way switch.

◆ Once the circuit is turned off and the switch is removed, place the clip of a continuity tester on the common terminal.

◆ Place the tester's probe on one traveler terminal *(above, left)* and flip the switch up and down. The tester should light when the switch is in one position only.

◆ When the tester lights, leave the switch there and touch the probe to the other traveler terminal. The tester should not light.

◆ Without moving the probe, now flip the switch to the opposite position. The tester should light *(above, right)*. If the switch passes both tests, it is good. Remove the other switch in the circuit and test it.

REPLACING PLUGS AND RECEPTACLES

Swapping a new receptacle for a defective one is an inexpensive and easy home repair. It also may be necessary in some older houses. Before the early 1960s it was common practice to install ungrounded receptacles. Modern electrical codes require that ungrounded receptacles be replaced with grounded ones, the only exception being in a two-conductor system, where there is no separate ground wire. In such a case, you can obtain an extra measure of protection by replacing an old, ungrounded receptacle with a GFCI receptacle *(box below, and pages 213–215)*.

When you replace any receptacle, make sure the new one is rated for the correct voltage and amperage *(page 210)*.

Double Duty: Receptacle installations can do more than provide electricity. A switch-controlled receptacle offers easy control of plug-in fixtures; a light-receptacle fixture *(page 212)* provides light and a handy place to plug in an appliance.

Special Situations: Other receptacles are available for special locations. One recessed unit provides room for the cord of a plug-in wall clock and even a hook on which to hang the clock.

Floor receptacles are designed for large rooms so you can plug in a lamp or appliance that will not reach a wall receptacle.

A locking receptacle prevents a plug from being pulled out accidentally, and several varieties of safety receptacles prevent toddlers from inserting objects into them.

Replacing a Plug: This is even easier than installing a new receptacle. A new three-prong terminal plug is connected by attaching the black appliance cord wire to the brass screw, the white wire to the silver screw, and the green wire to the green screw. Lamps and many small appliances use cords with molded plugs permanently attached. If one of these is damaged, do not splice a cord to a molded plug. Instead, snip off the plug and replace it with a terminal plug, which is attached to the wires by screw terminals, or with a quick-clamp plug.

CAUTION *Modern polarized plugs have one wide blade to ensure correct polarity for the light or appliance (page 208), and many appliances and tools use cords with plugs featuring a grounding prong. These are important safety features, even though they are a nuisance when they won't fit into an older receptacle.*

Do not try to do a quick fix by filing down the wide blade or snipping off the grounding prong. It's far safer to replace the receptacle instead.

Substituting GFCIs for Ungrounded Receptacles

The national electrical codes in both the United States and Canada forbid replacing a two-slot receptacle on an old ungrounded system with a new three-slot variety because, with no ground wire present, the receptacle cannot be grounded. But the codes provide an easy solution: the substitution of a ground-fault circuit interrupter (GFCI) receptacle for a two-slot receptacle. Although the GFCI is not itself grounded in this situation, it protects users by shutting off the current in the event of a ground fault *(box, page 214)*. In addition to providing safety, the device features a third, grounding slot so you can use three-prong plugs in it. Moreover, the GFCI protects all receptacles downstream. The codes allow you to replace downstream outlets with regular, three-slot non-GFCI receptacles, even though they are not individually grounded, thus giving you three-slot receptacles on the entire circuit.

GFCI manufacturers package several stickers reading "GFCI Protected" with each unit. The codes require that all downstream receptacles protected by the one GFCI be so marked.

TYPES OF SLOTS AND PRONGS

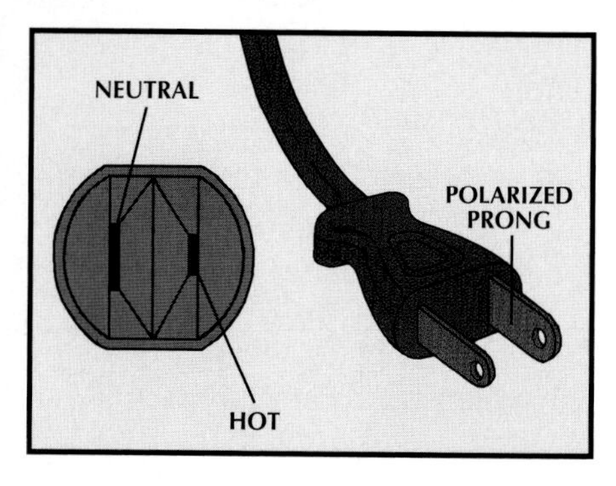

120-volt, 15-amp, ungrounded.
This receptacle is found only in older houses built before the mid-1960s. When it is wired correctly, the wide slot on the left is neutral, the narrow slot is hot.

An appliance or lamp with a polarized plug will fit only one way into this receptacle, ensuring correct polarity. In some two-slot receptacles, both slots are the same size, and polarized plugs will not fit them.

120/240-volt, 50-amp.
This receptacle and plug combination is used for an electric range. It supplies the oven and cooktop burners with 240 volts and the oven light, timer, and built-in receptacles with 120 volts. The Canadian-style receptacle *(inset)* and plug feature a fourth slot and prong for a ground.

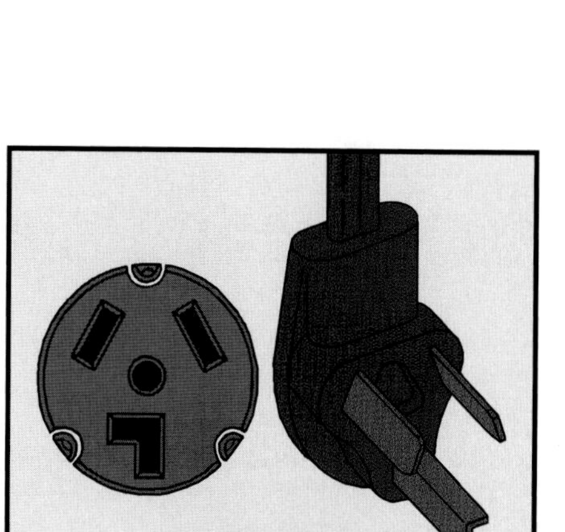

120/240-volt, 30-amp.
This receptacle and plug are designed especially for electric clothes dryers. They supply 240 volts for the heating coils and 120 volts for dryer accessories such as the timer and pilot light. The red and black wires in the plug and cord act as returns for each other as the electricity cycles 60 times a second. The white wire carries the 120 volts. The receptacle is grounded in its box with a ground wire. The Canadian receptacle *(inset)* and plug have a fourth slot that accommodates a separate ground besides the two hot and one neutral wire.

120-volt, grounded.
A modern 15-amp receptacle and a 20-amp one have a U-shaped slot for the grounding prong of the plug shown. They also have wide and narrow slots for correct polarity of two-prong plugs. The Canadian requirement for 20-amp receptacles is shown in the inset. In the United States, 20-amp receptacles require 20-amp circuits. Certain appliances have plugs that fit this shape receptacle only.

240-volt, 30-amp, grounded.
This receptacle supplies only 240 volts and is used for appliances such as window air conditioners. The black and white wires act as returns for each other as the electricity cycles 60 times a second, and the plug and receptacle have separate ground wires. The Canadian receptacle *(inset)* contains a fourth slot for a ground.

RECEPTACLE TERMINALS

Side-wired and back-wired receptacles.
A side-wired receptacle *(left)* features two brass-colored terminals on one side for the hot wires and two silver-colored terminals on the other side for the neutral wires. A small metal tab joins the upper and lower terminals. A back-wired receptacle *(right)* is connected by pushing the wires into spring-loaded grippers through holes in the back. A "strip gauge" molded into the back shows how much insulation must be removed to ensure proper wire contact. Both receptacles have green grounding terminals at one end. Back-wired receptacles often come with side-wiring terminals for versatility in installation.

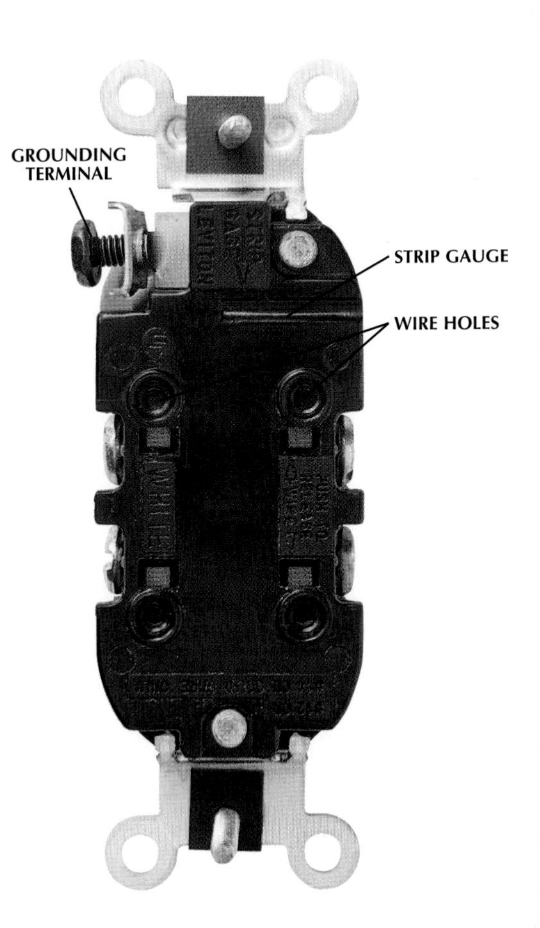

TWO SAFETY RECEPTACLES

Childproof outlets.
Safety receptacles have spring-loaded covers that keep small children from inserting objects, which is dangerous. One type *(right)* features a spring-loaded, slotted guard; a plug is inserted in the guard, then moved sideways to expose the receptacle slots. When the plug is removed, the guard face snaps back to cover the receptacle slots. Another type *(far right)* uses sliding plates to cover the entire receptacle. When you insert a plug, one or both plates slide vertically out of the way and are held open by the plug. When the plug is removed, the plate snaps back to cover the receptacle.

READING A RECEPTACLE

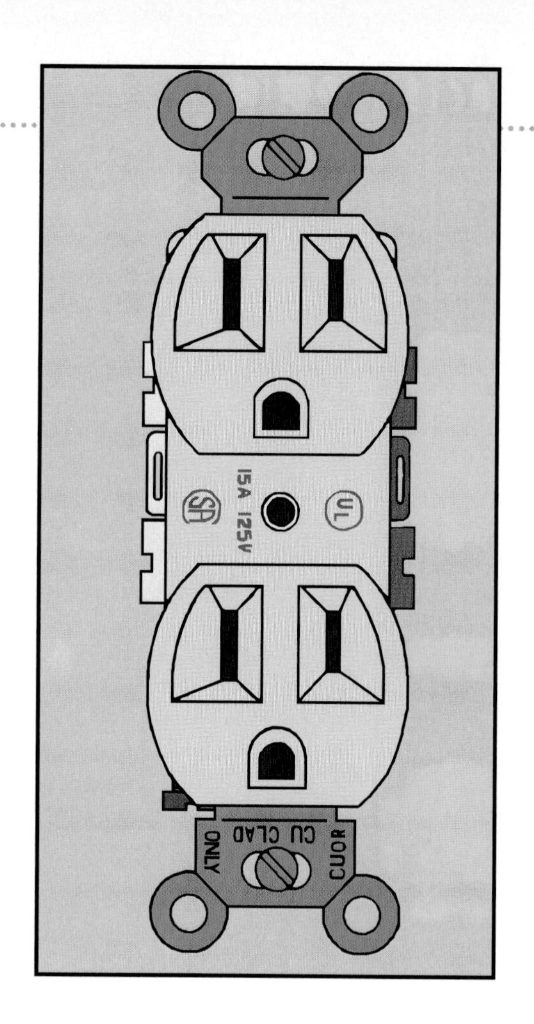

Facts to look for.
All receptacles must be marked with certain data to indicate their operating limitations and safety certifications. The receptacle at right is rated for 15 amps and 125 volts maximum. The "UL" mark indicates that it has been tested and certified by Underwriters Laboratories, an independent testing agency. The "CSA" logo shows the certification of the Canadian Standards Association. The statement "CU OR CU CLAD ONLY" on the metal strap indicates that only copper wire can be used with this receptacle. The abbreviation CO/ALR (sometimes "CU-AL" or "AL-CU" on older receptacles) would indicate that solid aluminum wire is also acceptable.

REPLACING 120-VOLT RECEPTACLES

Middle-of-the-run, plastic cable.
Two cables enter a box in the middle of a circuit run, each containing black, white, and bare copper wires.

◆ Connect each black wire to a brass-colored terminal in any order.
◆ Attach the white wires to the silver-colored terminals.
◆ In a metal box, attach a short jumper to the back of the box with a machine screw and attach another jumper to the green grounding terminal on the receptacle.
◆ Fasten these jumpers and the two bare copper wires from the cables with a wire cap *(right)*. For a plastic box, there will be no jumper needed to the box.

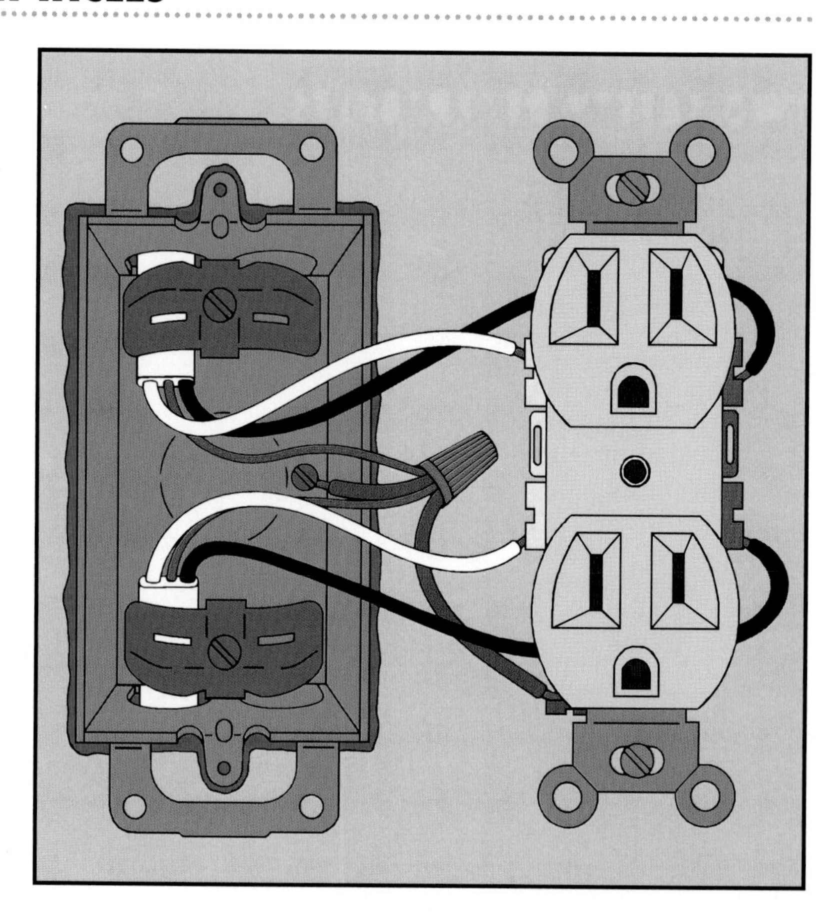

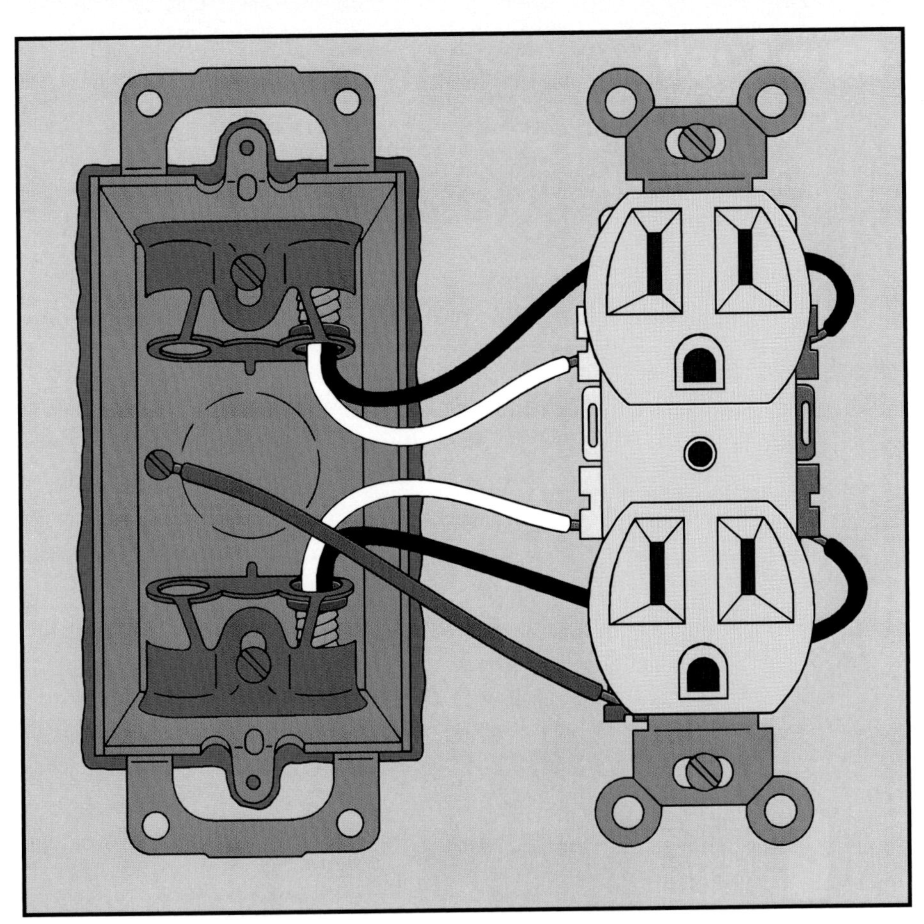

Middle-of-the-run, armored cable.
Wiring is the same as for plastic cable, with the exception of the grounding connections, because the metal cable jacket serves as the ground conductor.
◆ Connect each black wire to a brass-colored terminal and each white wire to a silver terminal.
◆ Run a jumper wire from the green grounding terminal on the receptacle to the back of the box and attach it with a machine screw.

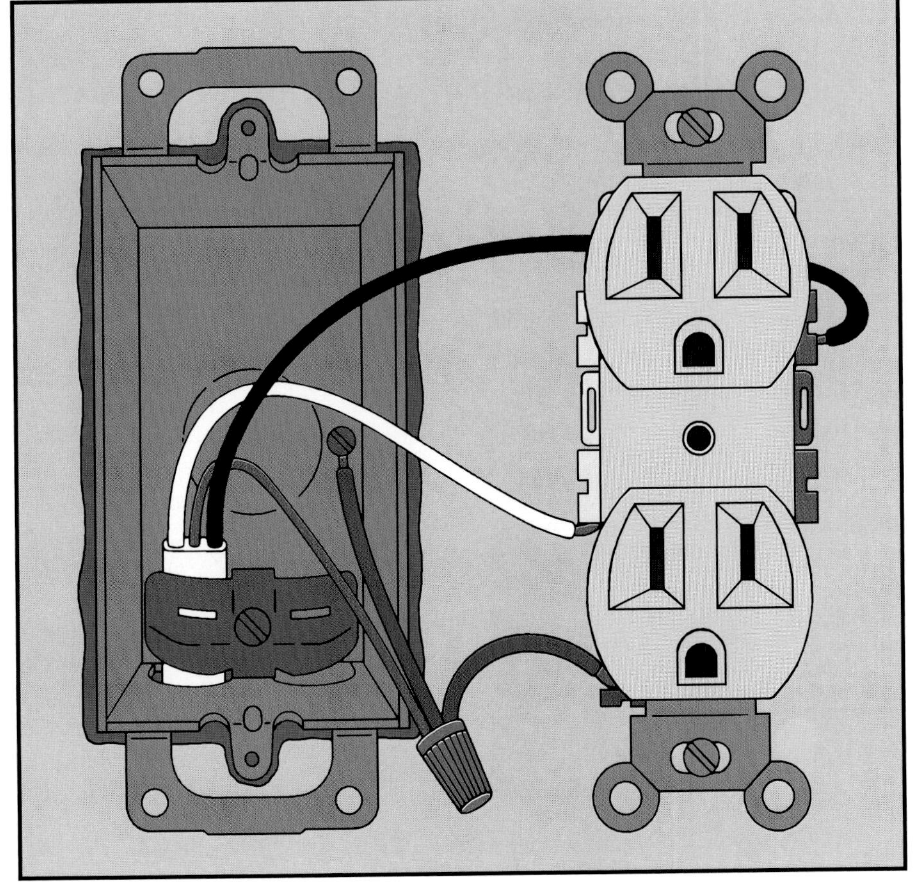

End-of-the-run, plastic cable.
Only one cable enters an end-of-the-run box.
◆ With plastic-sheathed NM-B cable, connect the one black wire to either brass-colored terminal and the white wire to either silver terminal.
◆ With a metal box, attach ground jumpers to the box and receptacle, and connect them to the bare copper wire with a wire cap. With a plastic box, there is no jumper to the box.
◆ Armored cable has no bare copper wire. Connect a jumper from the receptacle's grounding terminal to the back of the box.

A LIGHT-RECEPTACLE COMBINATION

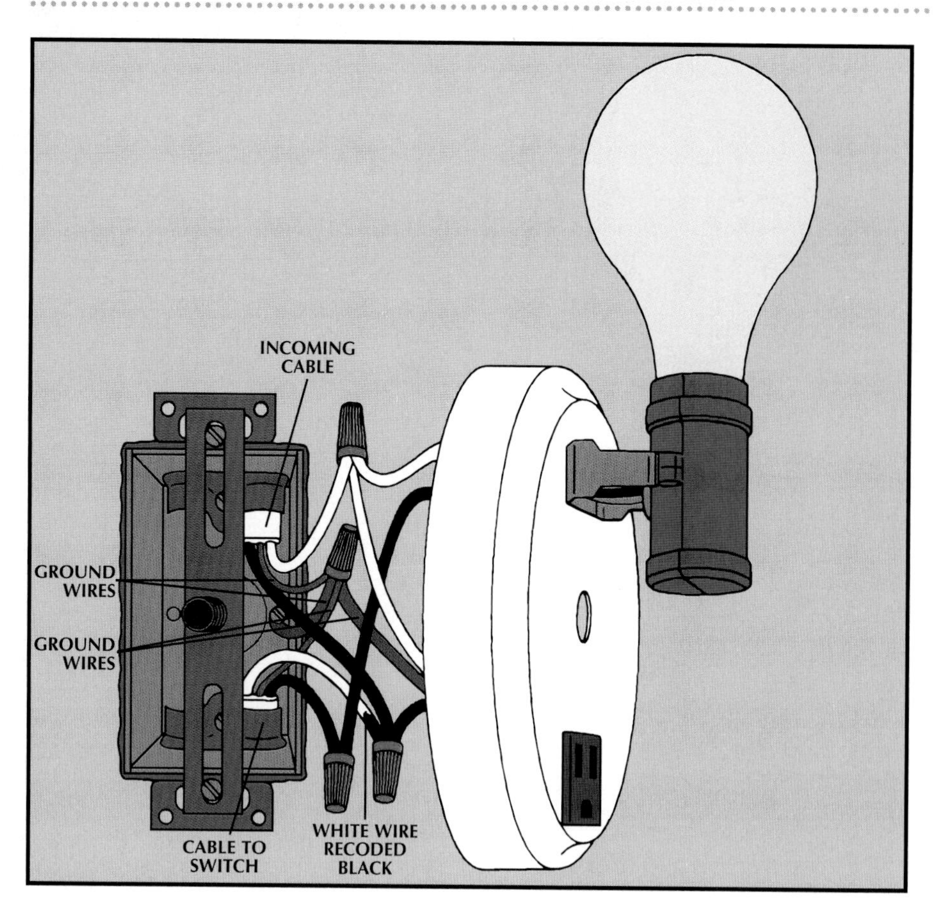

Middle-of-the-run installation. This is ideal for this fixture because, with two cables entering the box, you can wire the fixture so that the switch controls only the light while the receptacle remains always hot.

◆ The white wire in the switch cable should be recoded black to indicate that it will be hot *(page 205).*

◆ Using a wire cap *(page 199),* connect the black wire from the receptacle half of the fixture to the incoming black wire and white wire recoded black *(page 205).*

◆ Connect the black wire from the light half of the fixture to the black switch wire.

◆ Connect the two white wires from the fixture to the incoming white wire. Attach ground wires to the fixture, cables, and box as shown.

Note: If you are installing a sconce or other light-only wall fixture, the connections are the same as shown here *(above, below),* except that there will not be any leads from a receptacle to be connected.

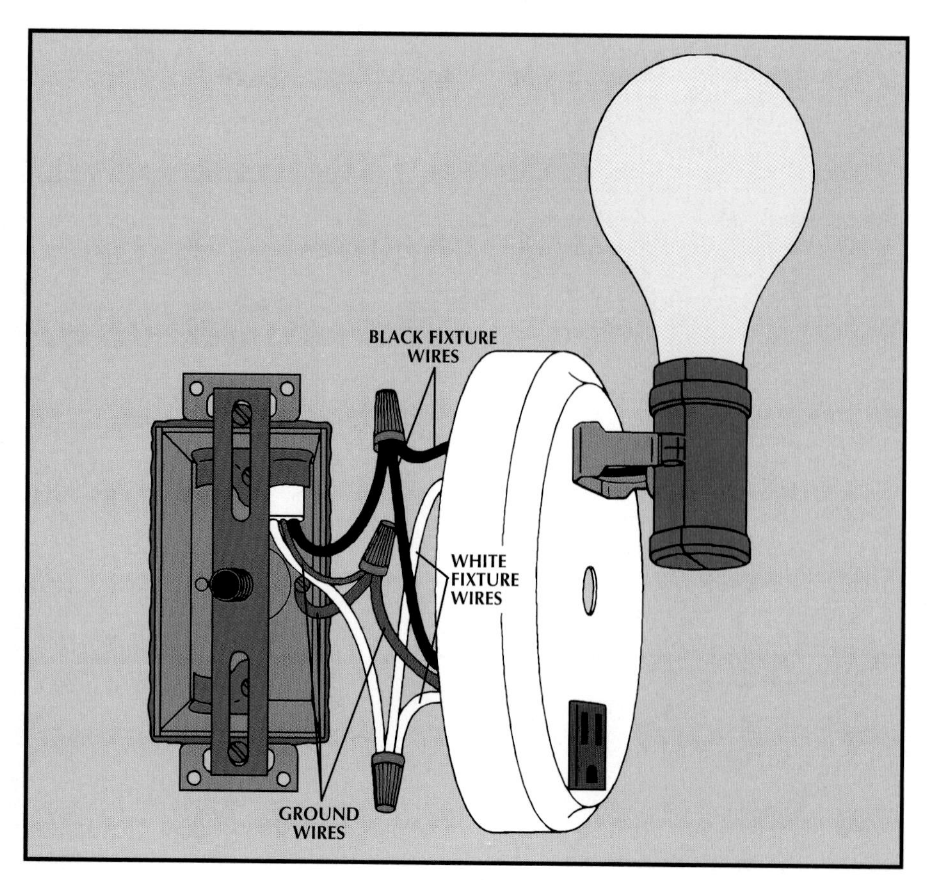

End-of-the-run installation. When only one cable enters the box, the switch will control both the receptacle and the light of the combination fixture.

◆ Connect the two black wires from the fixture to the incoming black wire with a wire cap, making sure no bare wire is exposed below the cap.

◆ Connect the two white fixture wires to the incoming white wire in the same way.

◆ Connect the green fixture wire and a jumper wire from the back of the box to the bare copper cable wire.

CAUTION *Electrical codes require that this type of combination fixture not be installed in a bathroom unless the incoming cable is protected by a GFCI upstream.*

GFCI: A SAFETY INNOVATION

Electricity can be deadly in very small doses. A current not much larger than 5 milliamps—$\frac{5}{1,000}$ ampere, or about $\frac{1}{3,000}$ the amperage required to trip a 15-amp circuit breaker—can fatally disrupt the rhythm of your heart.

Deviant Currents: The potential for danger arises when electricity leaks from a hot wire inside an electrical box or within an appliance or tool to a cover plate or casing. These accidentally energized elements may well pass unnoticed—unless you happen to touch one of them while working outdoors in bare feet or otherwise connected to ground.

Under such circumstances, your body can become a conductor for a minuscule but potentially deadly current. Such a shift from the current's usual path through the house wiring is called a ground fault.

An Electronic Sentinel: Since the middle of the 1970s, electrical codes have required safety devices called ground-fault circuit interrupters (GFCIs) in locations around the house where you might cause a ground fault *(box, next page)*.

A GFCI compares the amperage in a circuit's hot wire with that in the neutral wire. In a circuit without a ground fault, the two currents are identical. When a ground fault occurs, however, they differ by a small amount. A detector in the GFCI notes the discrepancy, and if the difference reaches 5 milliamps, the device will interrupt the circuit within $\frac{1}{40}$ second. Either style—receptacle or circuit breaker—will protect the circuits in most homes. In circuits containing more than 200 feet of cable, however, tiny leakages can add up to trip the device and make the circuit unnecessarily troublesome.

Two Types of Protection: GFCIs are available as receptacles that fit an ordinary outlet box and as circuit breakers for the service panel. A receptacle-style GFCI *(next page)*, in addition to offering protection where it is installed, also covers the circuit downstream from that point. The circuit breaker variety, installed in the service panel in place of an ordinary breaker, protects every outlet on the circuit.

A Monthly Checkup: GFCI receptacles and circuit breakers both have a test button that simulates a ground fault. Push the button monthly and replace any GFCI that fails to trip. Push the reset button to restore a good GFCI to operation.

Screwdriver
Long-nose pliers
Wire stripper
Voltage tester

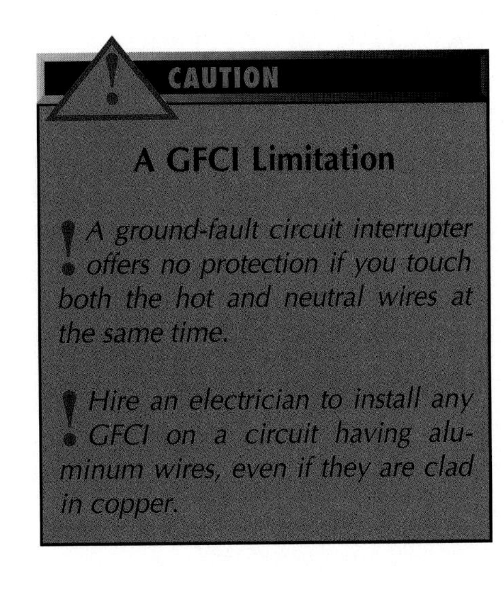

Where the Danger Lies

GFCI protection is required for new receptacles in the following locations:

✔ Bathrooms.
✔ Garages.
✔ Outdoors, when positioned less than 6 feet, 6 inches above ground level (8 feet, $2\frac{1}{2}$ inches in Canada).
✔ Crawlspaces.
✔ Unfinished basements.
✔ Within 6 feet of a kitchen sink or wet bar. The Canadian code does not require GFCIs in kitchens; instead it calls for split receptacles, which cannot be protected by a GFCI.
✔ Less than 20 feet from a swimming pool or similar installation, including underwater lighting. The Canadian code also requires GFCI protection in associated shower and locker areas.

In addition, all receptacles downstream of a GFCI must be marked as GFCI protected with stickers that come with the devices.

INSTALLING A GFCI RECEPTACLE

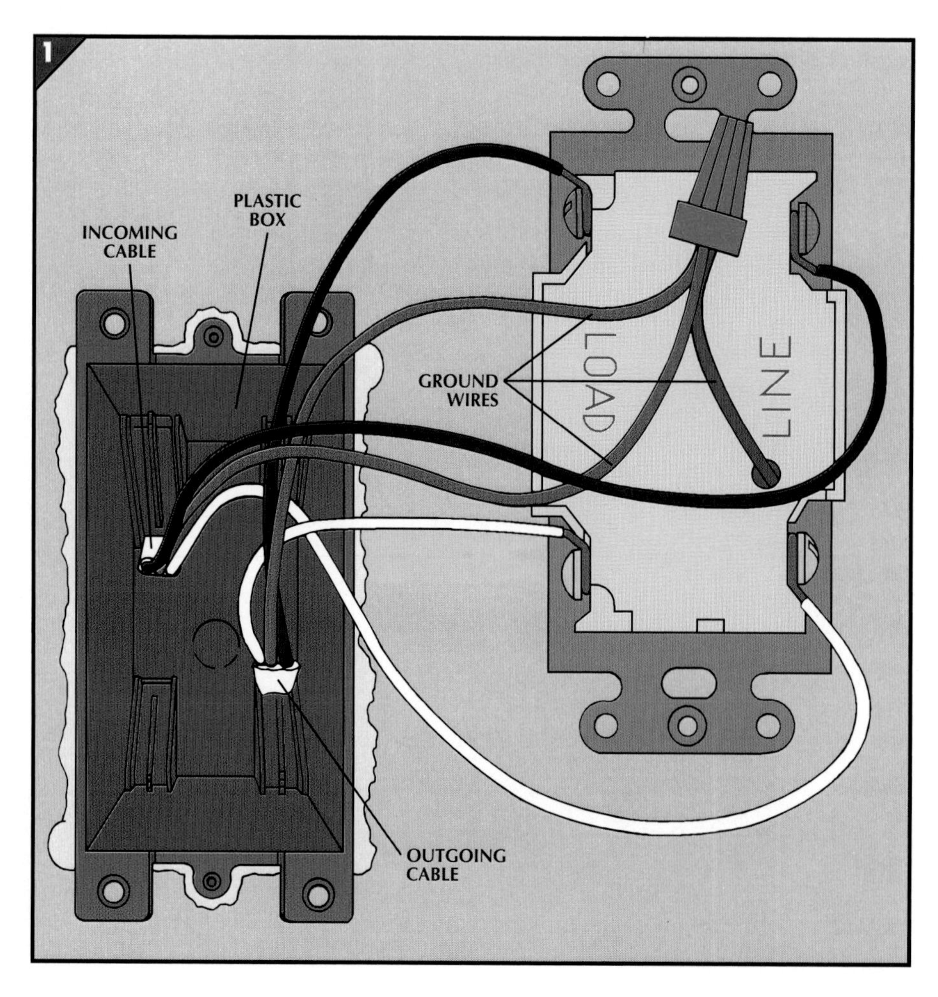

1. Wiring the receptacle.

◆ Determine which is the incoming cable or feed wire, using the procedure described on page 196, then turn off power to the circuit at the service panel.

◆ Connect the insulated wires of this cable to the "line" side of the receptacle, black wire to the receptacle's brass-colored screw as shown at left—or to the black wire that some GFCIs offer instead of a terminal—and the white wire to the silver-colored screw (or white wire).

◆ In the same manner, attach the wires of the outgoing cable to the "load" side. With no outgoing cable and a GFCI having wires instead of terminals, cover the bare ends of the unused wires with wire caps.

◆ In a plastic box, join the bare copper ground wires in the cables to the ground wire of the receptacle with a wire cap. If the box is metal, run a grounding jumper from the box to the wire cap.

2. Mounting the receptacle.

◆ After making all connections, tuck the wires into the outlet box, being careful not to loosen any connections.

◆ Push the receptacle into the box and secure it with mounting screws.

◆ Screw the cover plate in place.

3. Testing the receptacle.

◆ Restore power at the service panel and plug a radio into the first protected receptacle. Turn on the radio, then push the GFCI test button T *(right)*. If the reset button R pops out and the radio goes off, the GFCI is working correctly.

◆ Press the reset button and repeat the test with other receptacles downstream from the GFCI.

If you get other results, turn off power at the service panel and confirm that you have connected the incoming and outgoing wires correctly. Next, try a replacement GFCI. If the problem persists, call an electrician.

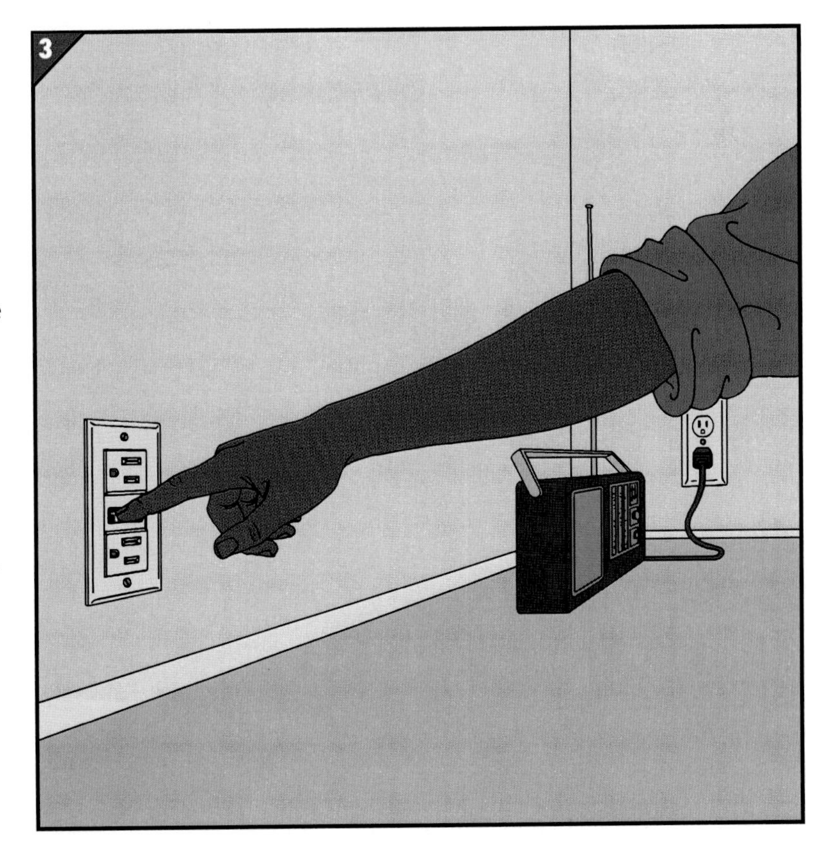

INSTALLING A CEILING FAN

Easy to install and modest in electricity consumption, a ceiling fan can be useful all year round. Most fans have reversible action to draw cool air upward in the summer and send warm air downward in the winter, abetting the work of your heating and cooling system. Some ceiling fans, such as the one shown here, can also accommodate a light fixture.

Proper Support: Because ceiling fans may weigh anywhere from 35 to 50 pounds, sturdy mounting is essential. The outlet box that the fan will be hung from must be metal—and it should be secured directly to a joist or suspended between joists by a crosspiece known as a bar hanger.

Placement Considerations: Fan blades must be at least 7 feet from the floor and 24 inches from the nearest obstruction. Where there is only a small amount of vertical room, choose a fan that mounts against the ceiling. For a higher ceiling or one that is angled or vaulted, hang the fan from an extension called a downpipe, available in several lengths. Never mount a fan where it may become wet—on an open porch, for example.

Installation: Fans are sold in kits, which include all the necessary parts. Before beginning work, turn off the electricity to the outlet at the service panel, and check that it is off with a voltage tester *(page 195, top)*. Although the fan is heavy, it can be installed by one person: A hook on the plate attached to the outlet box serves to support the fan while you connect the wires. Do not operate the fan motor until after the blades have been attached.

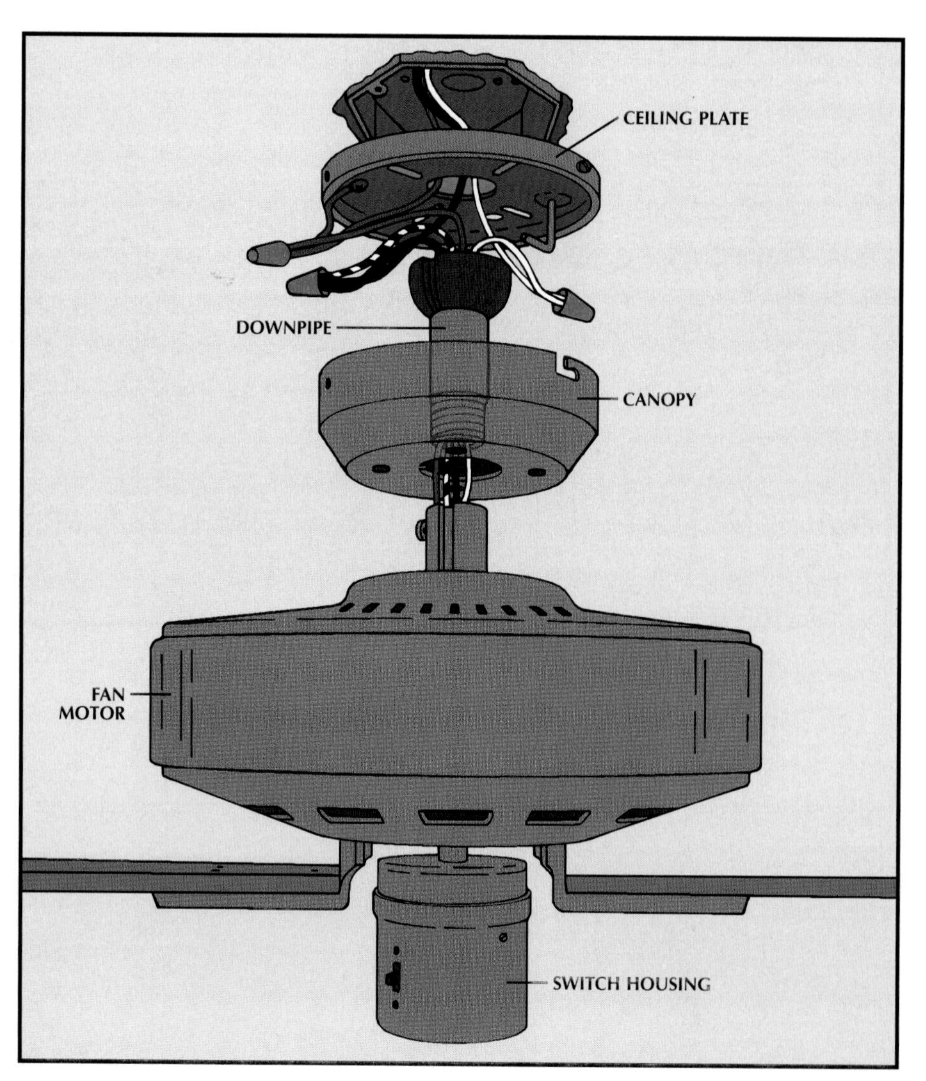

Anatomy of a ceiling fan. Electricity for the ceiling fan at left is supplied through an outlet box that is braced above the ceiling to support the weight of the fan motor. The fan hangs from a ceiling plate that is fastened to the outlet box. Often, a downpipe is used to lower a fan for better air circulation. A light kit *(next page)* that works independently of the fan motor can be attached to the switch housing so that a ceiling fan can double as a light source.

1. Assembling the fan.

◆ Insert the downpipe in the canopy, and feed the fan wires through the pipe.
◆ Screw the downpipe into the fan, and tighten the setscrew securing the fan to the pipe.

To omit the downpipe, feed the wires through the canopy and fasten it to the fan motor with the screws provided.

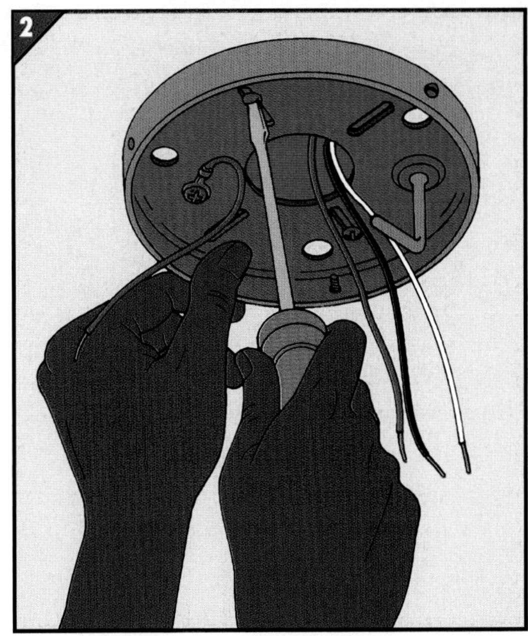

2. Attaching the ceiling plate.

◆ Feed the electrical wires from the outlet box through the ceiling plate.
◆ Position the plate on the outlet box and fasten it to the ears of the box with the screws that come with the box.

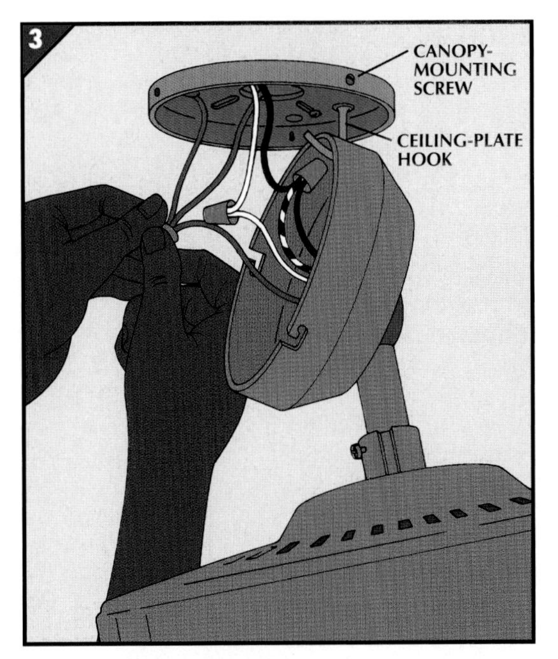

3. Connecting the wires.

◆ To support the fan, hang the canopy from the hook in the ceiling plate.
◆ Connect the black and black-and-white fan motor wires to the black ceiling-box wire.
◆ Join the two white wires, then connect the three ground wires *(above)*.
◆ Hook the canopy onto mounting screws in the ceiling plate and tighten them.

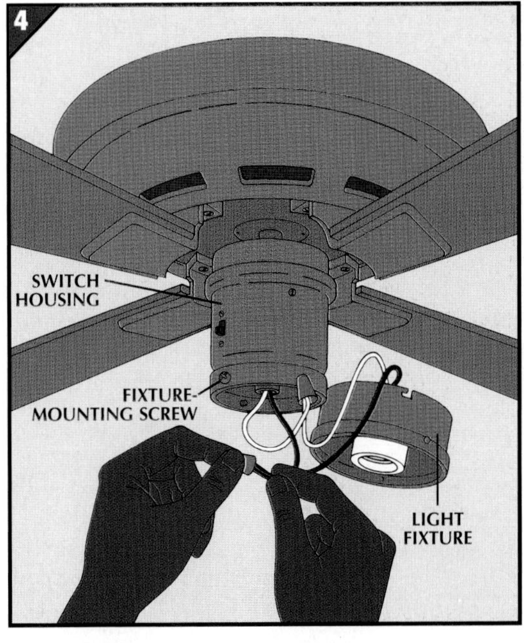

4. Attaching a light fixture.

◆ Remove the cover plate from the bottom of the switch housing.
◆ Connect the wires in the switch housing to those of the light fixture, black to black and white to white.
◆ Mount the fixture to the switch housing with the screws provided.

OVERHEAD LIGHTS WHERE YOU WANT THEM

For concentrated illumination from above, nothing surpasses a track light system and recessed fixtures. Track lighting, shown on these pages, is the more flexible of the two, but recessed units are a less obtrusive option.

Purchasing: Both types of equipment are sold in kits or as separate components. Track is available in 2-, 4-, and 8-foot sections that can be snapped together with connectors to form straight, right-angled, T-shaped, or X-shaped arrangements. Installation methods vary, and units from one manufacturer may not fit those of another.

Some recessed fixtures are designed specifically for finished or unfinished ceilings; others, like the unit shown on pages 220–221, can be adapted to either situation. For insulated ceilings, choose fixtures with an IC rating; these may be safely buried in insulation.

Wiring Requirements: A 15-amp circuit with a wall switch is adequate. A track system can be wired to a ceiling box at any point along its length by means of a special connector called a canopy. Recessed fixtures come with their own wiring boxes attached. When installing several such units on a single circuit, make sure that all but one are rated for "through-wiring" with two cables; the last fixture needs only a single cable.

TOOLS

- Nail set
- Hammer
- Screwdriver
- Drill with $\frac{3}{4}$-inch bit
- Tin snips
- Electronic stud finder
- Drywall saw
- Fish tape

MATERIALS

- Track lighting kit
- Canopy kit
- Light fixtures for track
- Electrician's tape
- Wire caps
- Bulbs
- Recessed lighting kits
- Cardboard
- Plastic-sheathed cable
- Patching materials for ceiling

WIRING TRACK LIGHTS TO A CEILING BOX

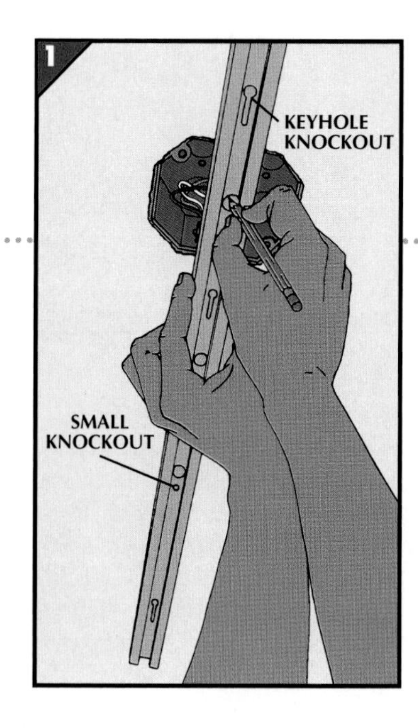

1. Removing the knockouts.

◆ Holding a length of track against the ceiling box, mark the large circular knockout nearest the center of the box *(right)*.

◆ Lay the track section upside down across two lengths of scrap lumber. With a nail set and hammer, remove the marked knockout and the small circular knockout next to it.

◆ In the same manner, remove a keyhole-shaped mounting knockout near each end of the track section.

◆ If you plan to install a single section, install the plastic end caps provided with the kit; otherwise, place caps on end sections before installing them.

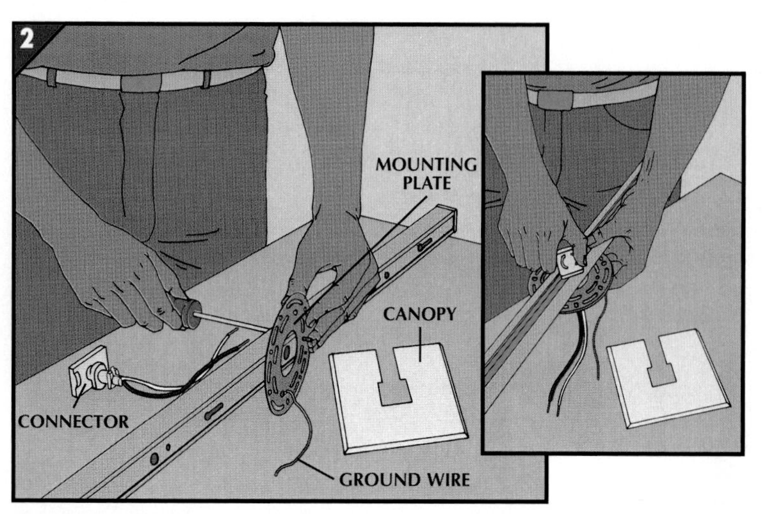

2. Attaching the mounting plate.

◆ Hold the plate against the ceiling side of the track, ground wire on top. Position the center hole at the large knockout opening, and align one of the threaded holes in the plate with the smaller knockout. Fasten the pieces together loosely with the screw provided *(far left)*, leaving a $\frac{1}{8}$-inch space between plate and track for the canopy.

◆ Thread the connector wires through the large track knockout and mounting plate. Lock the connector to the track by turning it clockwise *(inset)*.

3. Marking the ceiling.

◆ Fasten the plate to the ceiling-box mounting tabs temporarily, using the screws provided with the box.
◆ Pivot the track on the loosely fastened mounting plate screw to align the track parallel to a nearby wall, and mark the ceiling at the midpoint of each keyhole slot *(right)*.
◆ Unscrew the mounting plate from the ceiling box and drill holes for toggle bolts at the marks. Assemble two bolts and push their toggles into the holes.

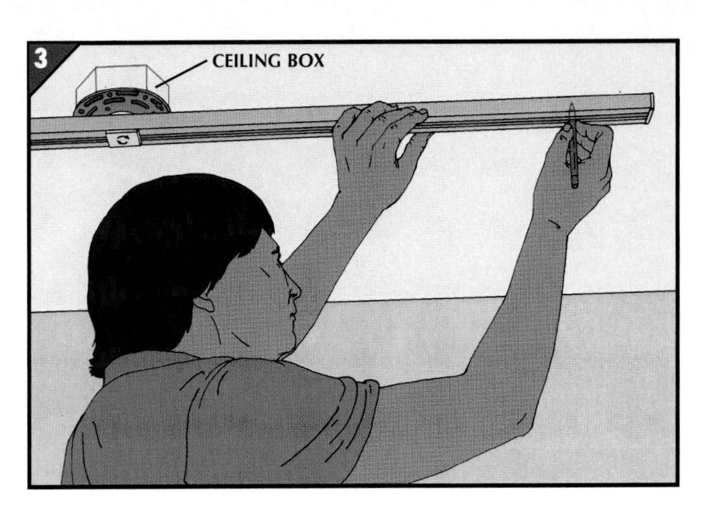

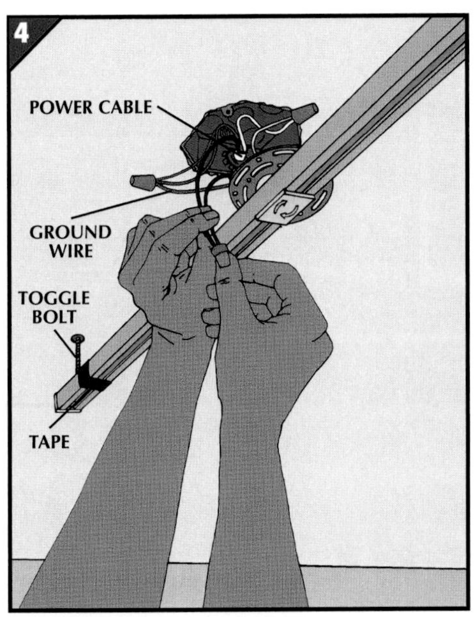

4. Wiring the track.

◆ Suspend the track from the toggle-bolt heads. Wrap tape around the track to prevent it from accidentally slipping off the bolt heads.
◆ Connect the connector wires to the wires of the cable entering the ceiling box, black to black and white to white *(left)*.
◆ Connect the ground wire from the mounting plate to the ground wire in the power cable and to the ceiling box, if it is metal.

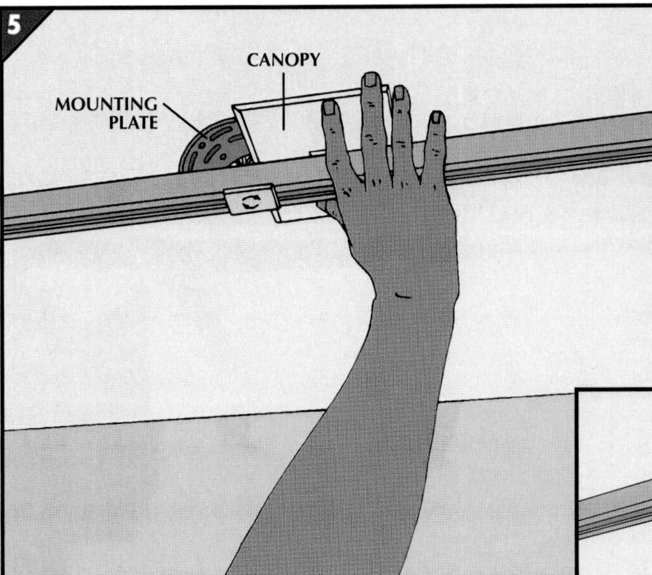

5. Adding the canopy.

◆ Tuck all wiring connections into the ceiling box, and screw the mounting plate securely to the box.
◆ Slide the canopy between the mounting plate and the track to conceal the plate and ceiling box *(left)*. Tighten the mounting plate screw.
◆ Unwrap the tape from the ends of the track and tighten the toggle bolts to hold the track against the ceiling.

◆ Extend the track as desired, using toggle bolts to secure each section of it to the ceiling.
◆ Fit light fixtures to the track *(inset)*, and then lock them in place.

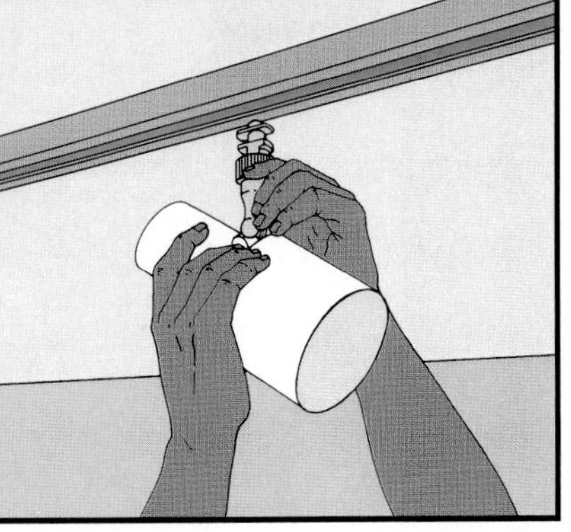

TECHNIQUES FOR RECESSED LIGHTING

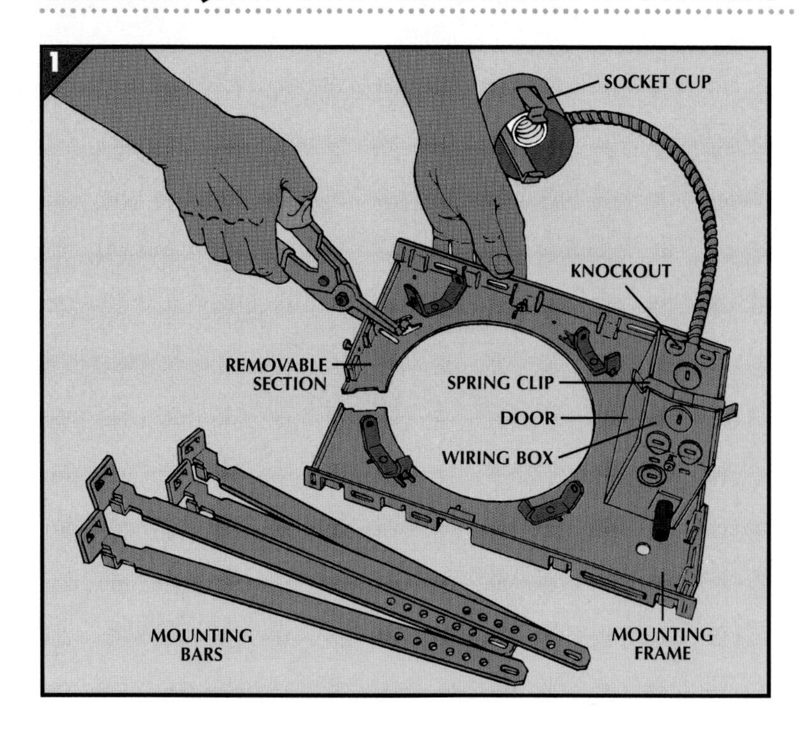

1. Preparing the mounting frame.

◆ Remove the frame's mounting bars and place the frame on a piece of cardboard. Outline the frame and circular opening with a pencil, then cut along the lines to create a template.

◆ With tin snips, cut out the removable section of the frame opposite the wiring box *(left)*.

◆ Lift the spring clip on top of the wiring box and remove one of its two detachable doors. If necessary, unscrew the two cable clamps that are inside and modify them for use with plastic-sheathed cable by clipping off the extra loops.

◆ Reinstall the clamps and remove one knockout above each clamp.

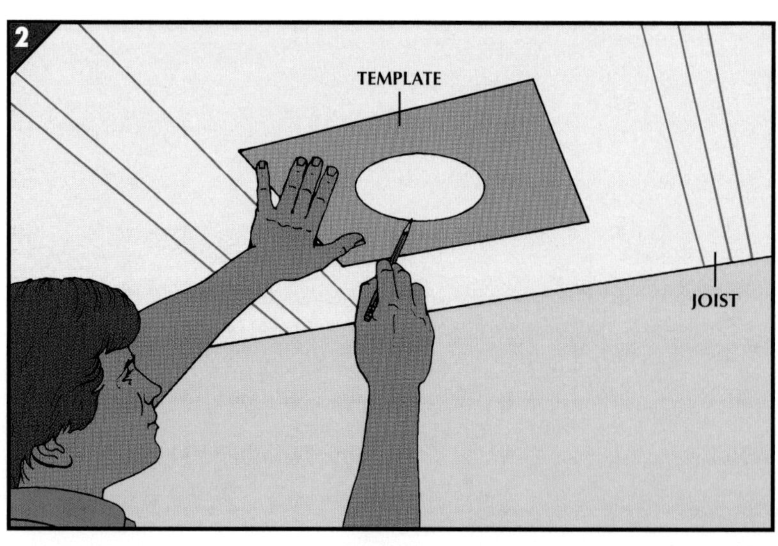

2. Cutting a ceiling opening.

◆ With a stud finder, locate the ceiling joists. Using the template, mark fixture locations on the ceiling between joists.

◆ Drill a small hole in the center of each circular mark. Bend hanger wire to a 90-degree angle, insert one end through the hole, and rotate the wire to check for obstructions. If you find any, relocate the fixtures. Otherwise, cut openings with a keyhole saw.

◆ At each joist running between fixtures, cut an access opening in the ceiling. Drill a $\frac{3}{4}$-inch hole through the center of each joist.

3. Wiring connections.

◆ Fish a two-conductor cable from a junction box to the first fixture opening, followed by another cable from the second fixture opening to the first—and so on downstream.

◆ At the first ceiling opening, rest a fixture-mounting frame atop a stepladder, and clamp the cable ends to opposite sides of the box.

◆ Red wire caps *(right)* indicate the connections to be made between the cable and fixture wires. Connect black to black, white to white, and the ground wires.

◆ Reattach the box door.

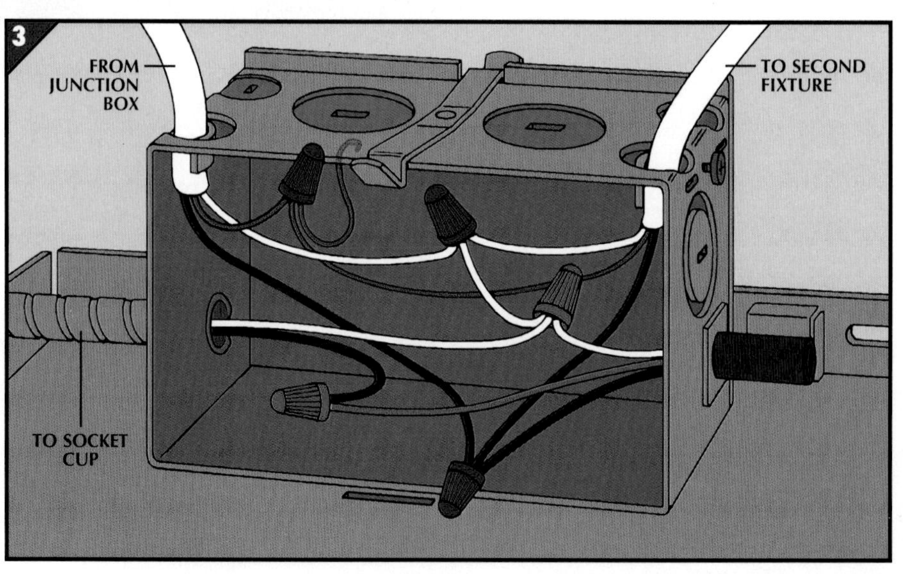

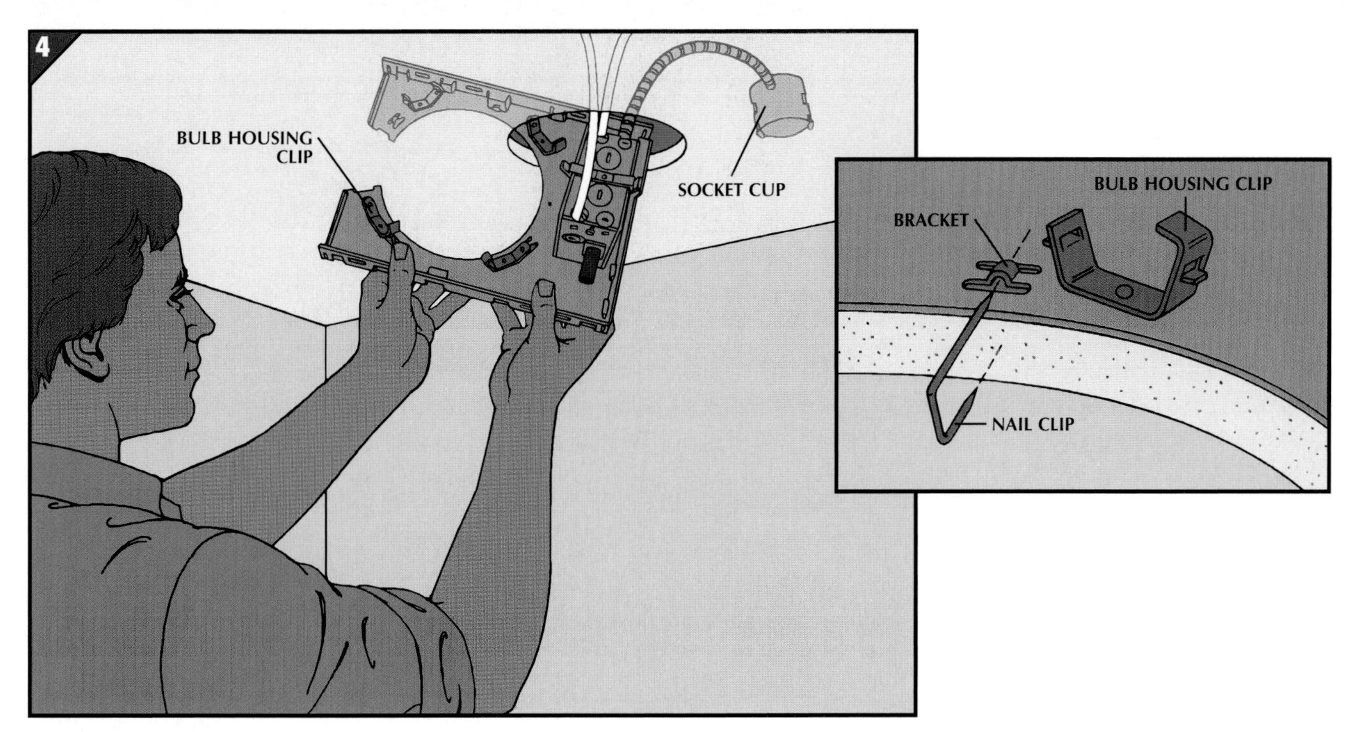

4. Securing the mounting frame.

◆ Push the socket cup through the ceiling opening and set it beside the lip of the hole.

◆ Beginning at the opening cut in the frame in Step 1, work the frame through the hole *(above),* and rest it on the ceiling with the opening in the frame aligned with the ceiling hole.

◆ Slide the long ends of the four nail clips provided with the fixture partway into the brackets at the frame's edge *(inset).* Align the short ends of the nail clips with the center of the ceiling material, then tap them into the ceiling with a hammer.

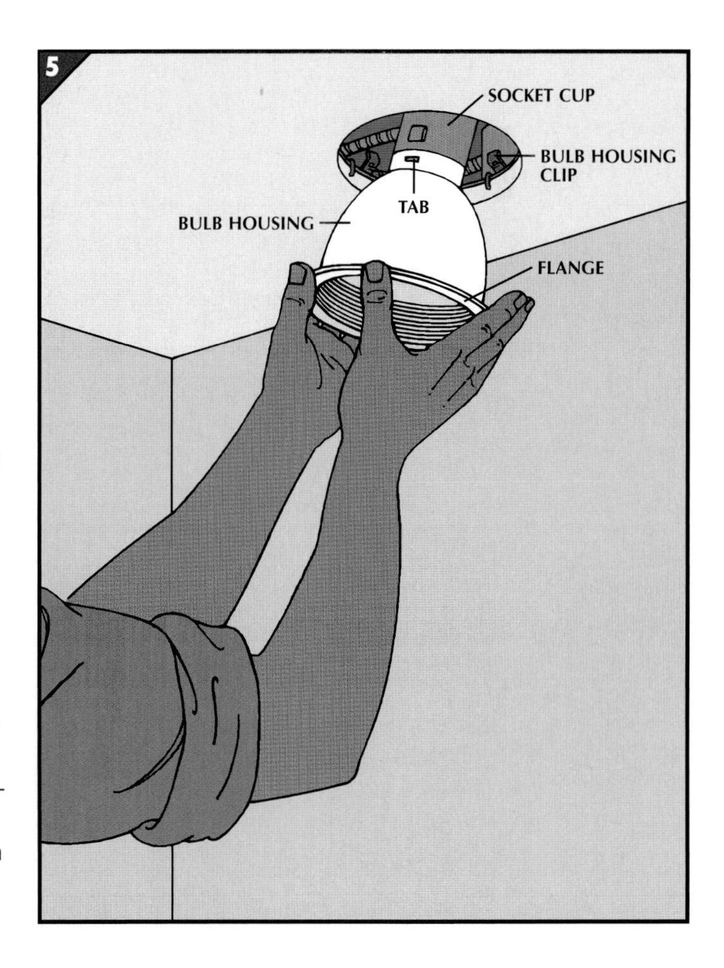

5. Installing the bulb housing.

◆ Bring the socket cup back through the opening. Rotate the bulb housing clips inward.

◆ Insert the socket cup into the top of the bulb housing so that tabs in the cup snap into slots in the housing.

◆ Push the assembly into the frame *(right)* until the bulb housing flange rests against the ceiling, completing the installation.

◆ At the second fixture opening, connect cables from the first and third fixture openings to the second fixture in its wiring box, and complete the installation as described above.

◆ When all fixtures are in place, patch the access holes at each joist as explained in Chapter 3.

ADDING RECEPTACLES AND SWITCHES

New electrical appliances, especially the rechargeable cordless variety, can easily outstrip the number of receptacles available, particularly in kitchens, bathrooms, and workshops. The solution is to add new receptacles.

Wiring Options: There are several ways to wire an electrical box for additional receptacles. If you are working on a 120-volt circuit, you can gang together boxes and add as many receptacles as you need, so long as you don't exceed the recommended number of outlets on the circuit.

A Switch for Convenience: As shown on the opposite page, you can control a receptacle by adding a switch to the circuit. Doing so lets you supply or interrupt power to the receptacle from wherever you choose to locate the switch.

The electrical connections between receptacle and switch depend on whether you wish to add a loop switch or a middle-of-the-run switch. The choice depends on whether you want to have the power cable run to the switch first or to the receptacle at the end of a run. If the circuit goes on to other outlets, they will also be controlled by the switch.

TWO WAYS TO MULTIPLY RECEPTACLES

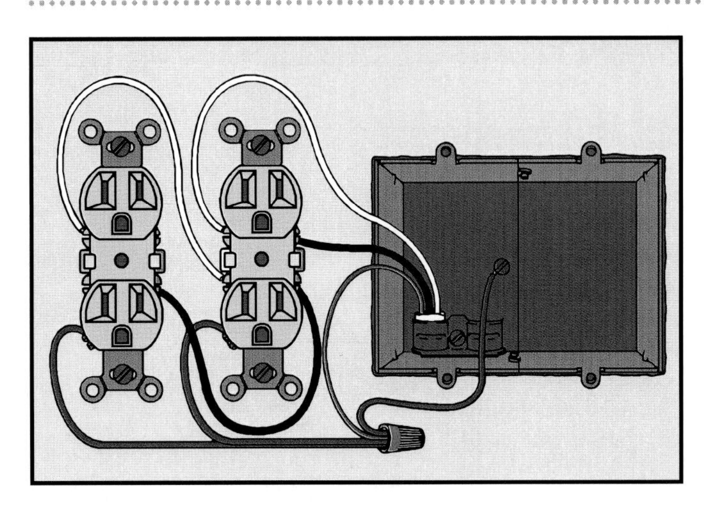

Adding a receptacle to a 120-volt box.

◆ Attach the black cable wire to either brass terminal on the first receptacle and the white wire to a silver terminal on the same receptacle.

◆ Next, run a black jumper wire from the remaining brass terminal of the first receptacle to either brass terminal on the second receptacle. Join silver terminals on the two receptacles in the same manner with a white jumper wire.

◆ Attach ground jumper wires to the green terminals of the receptacles and to the ganged boxes and join them to the cable ground with a wire cap.

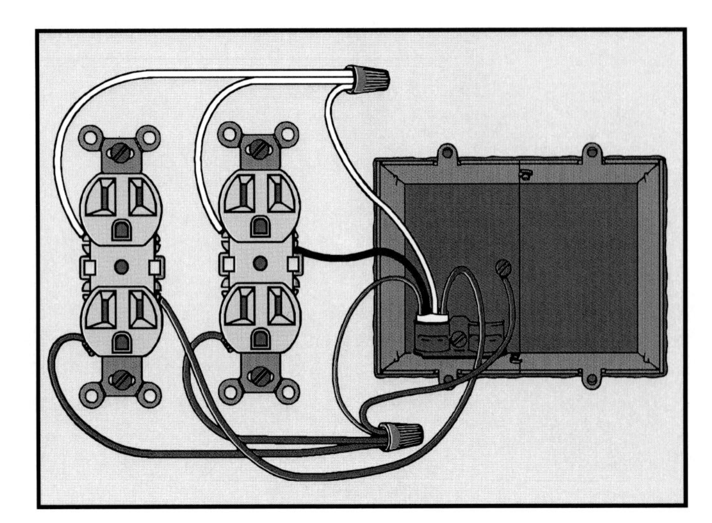

Two 120-volt receptacles in a 240-volt circuit.

◆ Run the black wire of the 240-volt, three-conductor cable to a brass terminal on the first receptacle and the red wire to a brass terminal on the second receptacle.

◆ Attach a white jumper wire to one silver terminal on each receptacle and connect these jumpers to the white cable with a wire cap.

◆ Ground by the method described above.

A SWITCH TO CONTROL A DUPLEX RECEPTACLE

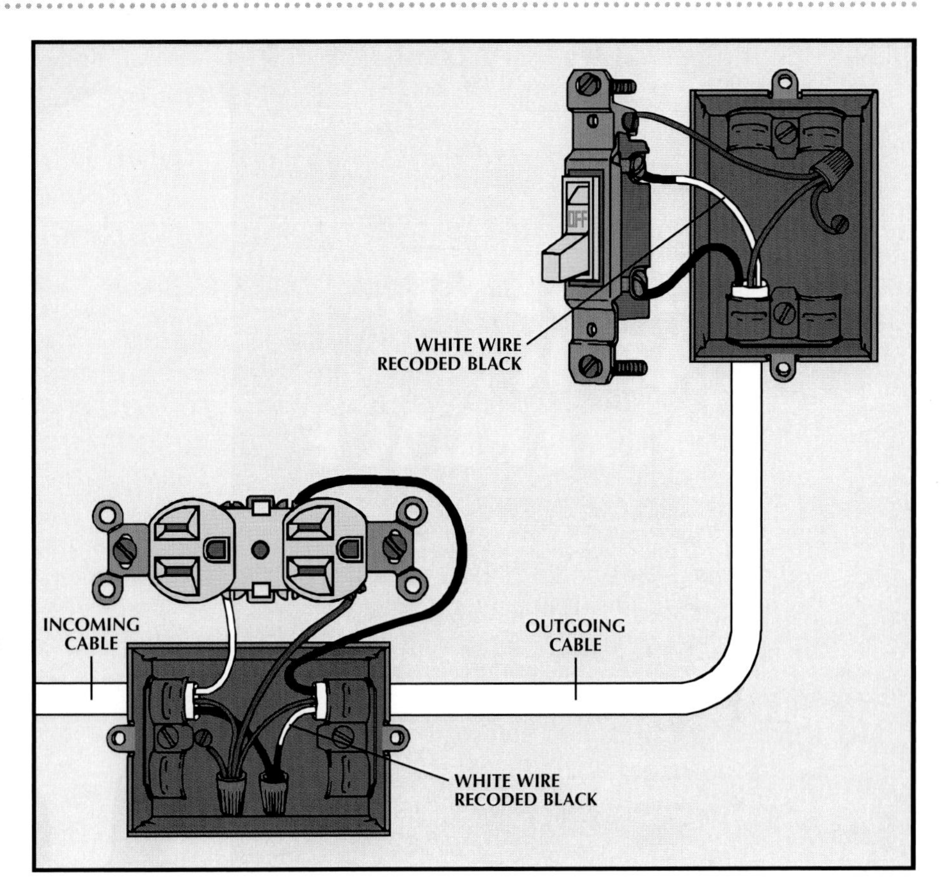

A switch loop.
This wiring scheme is used where it is convenient to have cable run first to the receptacle and then to the switch.
◆ At the receptacle, join the incoming black cable wire to the white wire of the outgoing cable. The white wire to the switch is now hot and should be recoded with a black mark *(page 205)*.
◆ Attach the incoming white wire to a silver terminal on the receptacle and the outgoing black wire to either of the brass terminals.
◆ Ground the receptacle with jumper wires from the box, if it is metal, and from the receptacle, connected to the cable ground wires with a wire cap.
◆ At the switch, attach both the black and the white wires to the brass switch terminals. Identify the white wire as hot with a black mark. Ground the switch with jumpers from the green grounding terminal and from the back of the box, if it is metal, both joined to the cable's ground wire.

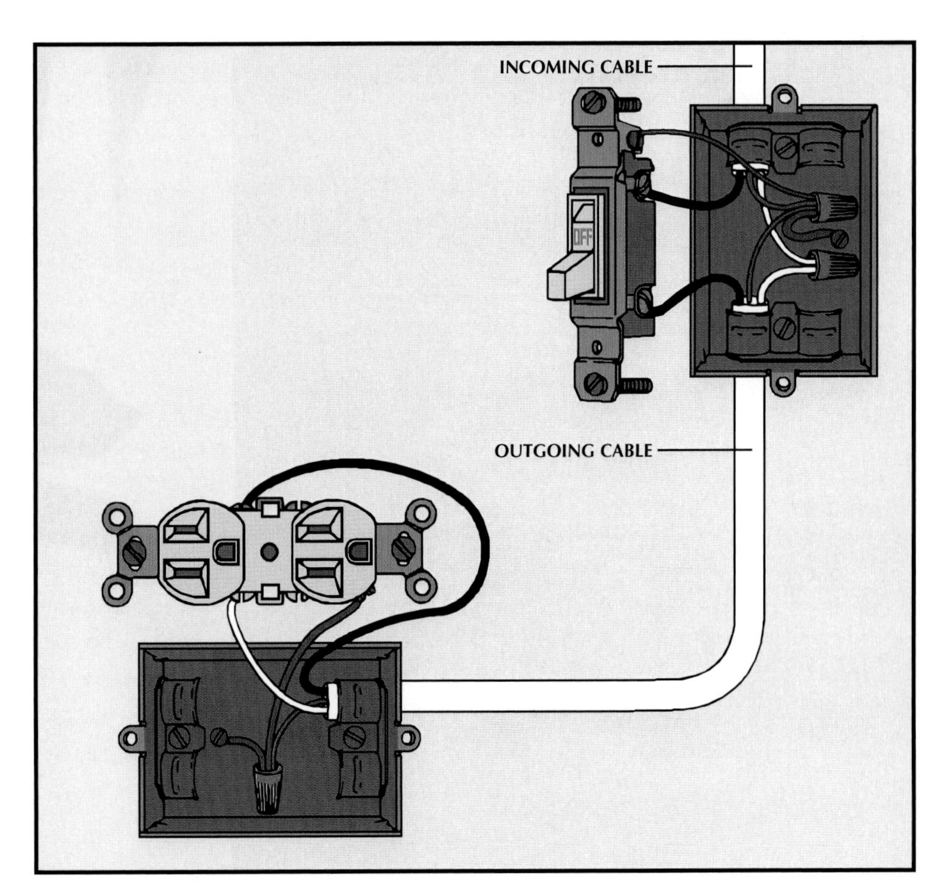

A middle-of-the-run switch.
Use this scheme when it is more convenient to run cable through a switch to the receptacle.
◆ At the switch, attach the black wires to the brass terminals and join the white wires of the incoming and outgoing cables with a wire cap. Ground the switch and box, if it is metal, with jumpers from the green grounding terminal and from the back of the box to the cable's ground wires.
◆ At the receptacle, connect the black wire to a brass terminal and the white wire to a silver terminal. Ground the receptacle and the box, if it is metal, with jumpers to the cable ground wire.

7

C H A P T E R

BASEMENT, ATTIC, AND FIREPLACE

The basement and attic are often the most "mysterious" parts of an old house. They also can be the most revealing, because they permit you to check the foundation and the supporting structure of the first floor, and the structure of the roof. Both places need periodic inspection to make sure that everything is dry and in good condition—and immediate attention if that is not the case. This chapter tells you what to do.

The basement and attic may also offer the potential for additional living space. There is basic information about finishing them for that purpose in this chapter, as well as directions for installing either of two attic fans for more comfort in hot weather.

A fireplace is a very attractive feature of many old houses. It, and its chimney, also require regular attention to make sure you can use the fireplace safely. In these pages you'll find out how to inspect, test, and clean them, make repairs, and install a glass fireplace screen.

▷ *Right:* Attic space is a real bonus in many older houses. Add insulation and install an exhaust fan for better heating and cooling; add racks and shelves for improved storage. You may even be able to finish the walls, floor, and ceiling for a playroom, study, or extra bedroom.

▽ *Below:* Making sure that downspouts direct water away from the foundation is the first step to a dry basement. The ground should slope away from the house for good drainage.

△ *Above:* Foundation walls support the house and block moisture penetration. They must be kept in good repair, and must stay absolutely dry if you want to finish the basement.

◁ *Left:* The condition of the chimney largely determines how well a fireplace works. For safety, efficiency, and economy you can inspect and clean the flue and make a number of exterior repairs yourself.

▽ *Below:* A glass fireplace screen provides maximum safety without hiding the beauty of the flames. Most screens are packaged as kits with everything you need to install them.

CHECKING THE TOP AND THE BOTTOM

Thorough inspection of the lowest and topmost levels of your house is as important as periodic evaluations of the exterior and the living spaces. Equally important is regular inspection and attention to a fireplace and its chimney, as well as the chimney that serves your furnace.

All you need to examine the basement and attic are a flashlight, some string, an awl, and a ruler. For fireplace and chimney inspection you'll need a flashlight, dust mask, eye protection, and work gloves. Major inspection points and improvements for basements are covered on pages 228–235. Information about attic structure, insulation, and fans for house cooling is on pages 236–244. Fireplaces and chimneys are covered on pages 245–249.

Assessing the Underpinnings: In an unfinished basement, structural soundness can be checked, since both the foundation and the framing members are visible. Some ways of dealing with structural matters such as sagging floor joists are covered in Chapter 2. You can apply the same techniques to brace up a sagging main beam (girder) or to help or replace a weak support post.

If drainage around the house is poor, large and small foundation cracks alike may allow ground water to seep in. A wet or excessively damp basement, or one that shows signs of flooding, may require modifications such as regrading the earth near the house, repairing gutters, or installing a sump pump *(pages 230–231)*.

Floor Repair: To fix a badly cracked floor area, break up the damaged concrete with a sledgehammer or electric jack hammer. Cut any reinforcing wire with metal shears and use a cold chisel to slope the hole toward the center. Dig out 4 inches of dirt, tamp the bottom of the hole, and pour in clean $\frac{3}{4}$-inch gravel up to the bottom of the slab. Cut reinforcing mesh to fit so the wire ends rest on the sloped edges of the hole; support the mesh with bricks. Slightly overfill the hole with patching concrete, to allow for settling. Level the surface by moving a 2-by-4 back and forth over the surface. Smooth the patch with a metal trowel. Follow the directions with the premix concrete for curing the patch.

A LOOK AT THE BASEMENT

Detecting signs of flooding.

◆ Examine basement floors and walls for water stains with a flashlight. Check for rust stains and mud on the floor at the base of the furnace—telltale evidence of flooding otherwise disguised by repainting *(right)*.

◆ Throughout the basement, inspect the walls for efflorescence (rough white deposits caused by water reacting with the minerals in mortar); look at any low-lying woodwork, such as baseboards, for dark spots of rot; and check tile floors for white, powdery deposits—efflorescence from the underlying concrete.

◆ Note how things are stored: Unused furniture and storage boxes kept on raised platforms sometimes imply flooding.

Analyzing cracks. Horizontal cracks in a bulging wall or vertical cracks in a corner of the basement that widen to $\frac{1}{4}$ inch or more at the top of the wall are cause for concern *(right)*. They are attributable either to water damage—which necessitates the correction of grading outside the wall *(page 231)*—or to foundation failure unrelated to flooding. Either of these types of cracking—which may be camouflaged with different shades of mortar from repeated patching—can threaten the integrity of an entire wall; consult a foundation engineer for a precise diagnosis. Smaller cracks—common in old houses—pose no threat to the structure but may be a source of leaks.

Examining wood framing.

◆ To check for sag in a girder or joist, tack a string taut between opposite bottom corners of the board *(left)*; if it droops below the string more than 1 inch in 12 feet, it needs additional support.

◆ Scrutinize all exposed framing members—joists, girders, sill plates, and the subfloor above (if any)—for rot or insect damage.

◆ Check for solid blocking or X-shaped bracing between joists, an indication of sturdy construction.

DEALING WITH FOUNDATION PROBLEMS

Whether built of stone, brick, block, or poured concrete, foundations can develop a multitude of flaws as they age. Small cracks, crumbling mortar, and broken pieces of masonry are structurally harmless. Larger cracks, caused by poor soil drainage or uneven settling of the house, pose a more serious problem.

Drainage Problems: If a high water table or some other unseen problem is causing a wet basement, drainage professionals will have to be called in—but first check to see if the situation is simply a result of faulty surface drainage. In a 10-foot-wide zone around the house, the grade should drop at least 1 vertical inch for every horizontal foot.

Correct any insufficiency in the grade *(opposite page, top)*, and at the same time use flexible plastic pipe to extend your gutter downspouts so that rainwater is channeled away from the house. Depending on the slope of your yard, the extension can end either in an underground dry well that traps and slowly disperses the water *(opposite page, bottom)* or in a simple culvert that drains it away.

Minor Flaws: Dry, stationary cracks in concrete walls can be filled with patching mortar or epoxy *(page 232, top)*. A seeping crack must be patched with hydraulic cement, which hardens even in the presence of water. Use masonry caulk to fill a crack that expands and contracts. If a crack is very large—or reaches the hollow core of a concrete block—pack in expansion-joint material before patching it.

Joints in brick foundation walls can be repointed *(page 232, middle)*. Where joints are damp, first remove the face bricks and check for damage in the layers behind them. Replace all cracked, flaking, or damaged bricks in each layer *(page 232, bottom)*.

TOOLS

- Line level
- Sod cutter
- Spade
- Tamper
- Cold chisel
- Maul (4-lb.)
- Wire brush
- Trowel
- Joint filler
- Ball-peen hammer
- Mason's hawk
- Jointer
- Tape measure
- Shovel

MATERIALS

- Wooden stakes and string
- Flexible nonperforated drainpipe
- Downspout adapter
- Splash block
- Topsoil
- Gravel
- Mortar mix
- Polyethylene sheeting (6-mil)
- 2 x 4s
- Brick

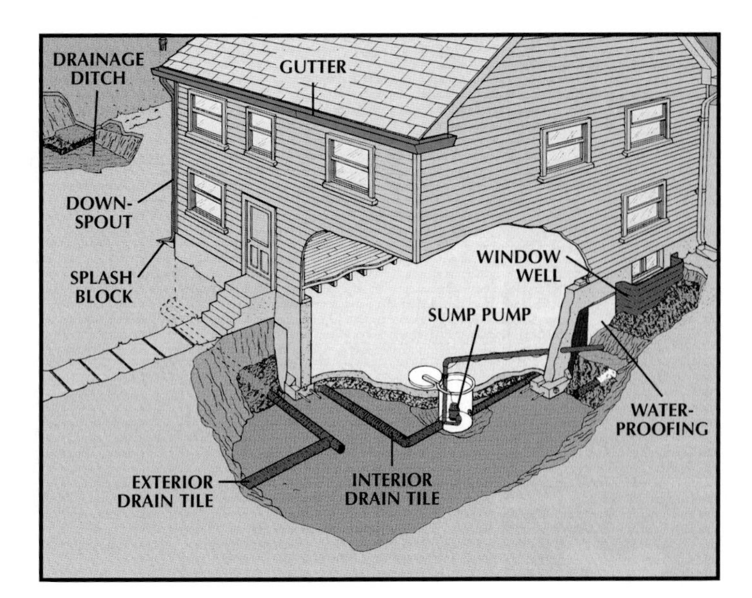

Combating water in the basement.
A system of gutters and downspouts carries water runoff from the roof away from the foundation. Sloped ground adjacent to the foundation also helps. Shored window wells keep water away from basement windows. On a hilly lot, a drainage ditch can divert runoff away from the house.

In some cases, more extensive measures may be required. An exterior drain-tile system installed along the footings prevents water buildup around the foundation, while an interior drain-tile system channels water from under the floor slab to a pit called a sump. A pump there expels the water outdoors. Exterior waterproofing protects against seepage through foundation walls. Consult a professional about the method appropriate for your site.

DIVERTING WATER FROM THE FOUNDATION

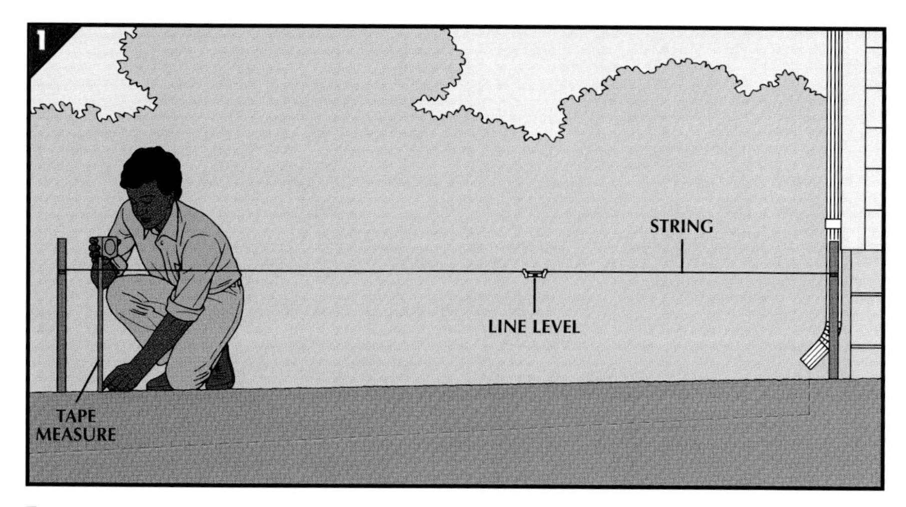

1. Checking the grade.

◆ Drive a stake next to the house and another one 10 feet away from the foundation. Tie a string between them and level it with a line level. Measure from the string to the ground at 1-foot intervals to calculate the grade. Move the stakes and repeat at other points along one side of the house.

◆ In any area where the grade drops less than 1 vertical inch for each horizontal foot, strip the sod and remove any shrubs.

◆ Dig a trench for the downspout extension; the trench should be 8 inches wide, a minimum of 10 feet long, and at least 6 inches deep at the downspout. It should also slope 1 inch per foot *(dashed lines, above).*

2. Extending the downspout.

◆ Attach an adapter to the end of the downspout.

◆ Lay flexible nonperforated drainpipe in the trench and connect it to the adapter. The pipe must lie flat along the bottom of the trench without any dips or humps. Remove or add dirt under the pipe as necessary.

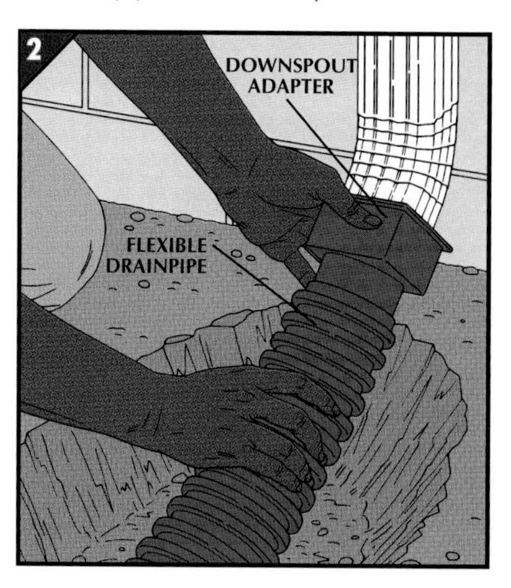

3. Making a dry well.

◆ At the end of the drainpipe trench, skim the sod from a $2\frac{1}{2}$-foot-square area and set it aside. Then dig a hole about 3 feet deep.

◆ Pull the flexible drainpipe so that the lip protrudes a few inches over the hole. Fill in the trench with topsoil and tamp it down.

◆ Fill the hole with gravel to a point about 1 inch above the top of the pipe. Add topsoil and replace the sod *(right).*

◆ If the trench ends on a slope, lead the pipe out of the hill and onto a splash block *(inset).* The block will prevent erosion at the outlet point.

◆ When the drainpipe extension is complete, correct any improper grade around the house. If you are piling dirt higher against the foundation, first treat the masonry with a waterproofing sealant. The soil level must remain at least 6 inches below wooden siding in order to keep termites out.

◆ Use a tamper to pack the soil firmly.

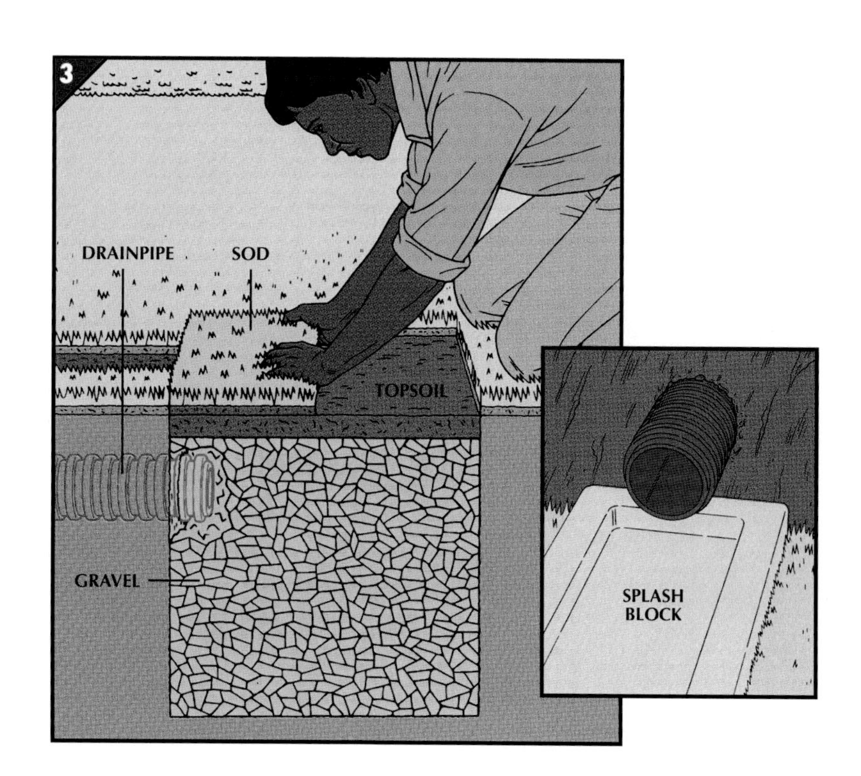

PATCHING AND POINTING BASEMENT WALLS

A dry, stationary crack in concrete.
◆ With a cold chisel and a maul, shape the crack into a groove about $\frac{1}{2}$ inch deep and $\frac{1}{2}$ inch wide. Chisel the sides to make the groove 1 inch wide at the back *(inset)*. Clean the groove with a wire brush.
◆ Spray the groove with water, then use a trowel to fill the crack halfway with patching mortar, mixed according to the manufacturer's instructions. Pack the mortar in tightly with a joint filler.
◆ Wait 1 minute, then fill the groove with mortar.
◆ Smooth the surface of the mortar with the trowel and rub it with a piece of damp burlap to give it a texture matching that of the wall.
◆ Cover the patch with a sheet of plastic propped up by 2-by-4s. Allow the mortar to cure for 3 days, misting it from time to time to keep it damp.

Repointing brick.
◆ Chisel out the old mortar to a depth of 1 inch.
◆ Mix new mortar according to the manufacturer's instructions—or colored to match the old mortar—and pile some on a mason's hawk.
◆ Spray the joints with water and press in mortar with a joint filler, holding the hawk just below the joint *(right)*. Scrape off any excess.
◆ When the mortar is firm to the touch, finish the joints to match the rest of the wall by running a jointer or its homemade equivalent along the joints. Use a convex jointer or a teaspoon for a concave shape, a V-jointer or the tip of a trowel for a V-shape, a trowel for flush joints.
◆ Moisten the work occasionally for 3 days while the mortar cures.

Replacing a broken brick.
◆ Chisel out the brick and mortar *(left)*, taking care not to damage nearby bricks.
◆ Cut 1 inch off the back of a new brick so it will have ample room.
◆ Moisten the pocket and mortar its back, top, and sides; then mortar the bottom of the pocket to match the thickness of the adjacent joints.
◆ Wet the brick and mortar its back, then place it on a mason's hawk or board and push it into the pocket.
◆ Tap it into position, using the butt of a trowel handle, and press mortar into the joints to fill any gaps.
◆ When the mortar is firm to the touch, finish the joints to match the rest of the wall *(above)*.

To replace a broken concrete block, chisel out the front half of the block, leaving the back half intact, and mortar a solid 4-by-8-by-16 block into the resulting pocket.

FINISHING A BASEMENT: THE BASICS

A basement with dry walls and a concrete floor in good condition can be finished to provide additional living space in a home—perhaps a recreation room, a home office, a study, a sewing room, or any of several other functions. What is called for is first a suitable base for a floor and then framing over the foundation walls and around obstructions.

Floor Preparation: Only in the driest climates is it possible to lay resilient tiles or sheet flooring or carpet directly on a concrete basement floor without eventual moisture and mildew problems. In most places you should first lay down support strips called sleepers, with a moisture barrier of polyethylene film sandwiched between them *(below)*. Then nail down a subfloor of 3/4-inch-thick plywood panels, with blocking under all joints that do not fall on sleepers. Lay the finish flooring on this base after the walls are done.

Wall Preparation: Foundation walls in older houses are likely to be irregular. To make an even support for finished walls, build frames of 2-by-4s on the floor and tip them up into place in front of but not touching the exterior walls *(page 234)*. Toenail the top and bottom plates into the ceiling joists and the subfloor. Build similar framework to enclose pipes, ducts, and other obstructions *(page 235)*. Then proceed as explained at the bottom of page 235.

A MOISTURE BARRIER

1. Laying bottom sleepers.

◆ Sweep the floor clean and apply a coat of masonry primer.

◆ When the primer dries, snap chalked lines 16 inches apart across the short dimension of the room.

◆ Cover each line with a 2-inch-wide ribbon of adhesive intended for bonding wood to concrete.

◆ Embed random lengths of pressure-treated 1-by-2s, or sleepers, in the adhesive, leaving a $\frac{1}{2}$-inch space between the ends of the boards.

◆ Use a 2-pound maul to secure the sleepers with $1\frac{1}{2}$-inch masonry nails about 24 inches apart.

2. Attaching the top sleepers.

◆ Lay sheets of 4-mil polyethylene film over the sleepers, overlapping joints 6 inches.

◆ Fasten a second course of 1-by-2s to each first course with ring underlay nails, sandwiching the film between the two layers.

A WALL FRAME OVER MASONRY

1. Making the frame.

◆ For the top and sole plates of a false wall, cut two 2-by-4s the length of the wall. On a concrete floor, make the sole plate from pressure-treated lumber.

◆ Lay the plates side by side on the floor, with their ends aligned. With the aid of a square, mark the stud positions across both plates simultaneously, beginning flush with one end of the plates *(left)*.

◆ Mark additional stud positions at 16-inch intervals. Finish with marks for studs flush with the other end of the plates.

◆ Turn the plates on edge, the marked faces toward each other, and position 2-by-4 studs cut $4\frac{1}{8}$ inches shorter than the height of the ceiling or joists.

◆ Fasten each stud with two $3\frac{1}{4}$-inch nails driven through the plate and into the stud, top and bottom.

2. Erecting the framing.

◆ Raise the wall framing into position about an inch away from the masonry wall. Plumb the framing at several points with a carpenter's level.

◆ Cut strips of $\frac{1}{2}$-inch wallboard $4\frac{1}{2}$ inches wide. Insert them between the top plate and the ceiling or joists; push them into position against the masonry wall and flush with the edge of the plate, to act as firestops. Shim as necessary for a snug fit.

◆ Nail the bottom and top plates to the floor and the ceiling with $3\frac{1}{2}$-inch nails.

◆ In cases where panels will be installed horizontally, toenail 2-by-4 supports *(inset)* between studs at 24-inch intervals to provide additional nailing surfaces for the paneling.

◆ Install similar nailing surfaces around electrical boxes or access doors.

ENCLOSURES TO CONCEAL PIPES AND DUCTS

A vertical enclosure.
Most pipes, ducts, and girders can be enclosed with smaller, modified versions of a false stud wall *(right)*. There is no need to add a drywall firestop above such a small enclosure.
◆ Construct two narrow vertical walls reinforced with horizontal supports.
◆ Nail the top plate of one wall to a ceiling joist; fasten the top plate of the adjoining wall to 2-by-4 blocking installed between joists.
◆ Nail adjoining end studs of the two walls together at the corner; secure the bottom plates of each wall to the floor.
◆ For three-sided enclosures, either vertical or horizontal *(below)*, first construct and install two stud walls for the parallel sides of the enclosure. Then install horizontal supports to form the third side.

A horizontal enclosure.
◆ Construct two stud assemblies, one to be hung vertically from the ceiling and the other to fit horizontally between it and the adjacent wall *(left)*.
◆ Nail the vertical assembly through the top plate to ceiling joists or to horizontal blocking between them.
◆ Fasten the other assembly to wall studs, then nail together the top plates of the two assemblies.

When the framing is complete, install insulation between the uprights (studs) of the wall frames. Ceiling insulation is not necessary. If the insulation has a foil face, make sure that it faces toward the room interior as you staple the flanges to the faces of the studs. If there is no foil facing, staple 4-mil plastic sheeting to the studs, overlapping edges between sheets, to prevent humid air in the room from reaching the cool outside walls, where it could condense. Alternatively, use foil-backed wallboard (drywall) panels with the foil facing the foundation walls.

Check that the ceiling joists provide a flat, even surface for wallboard by laying a straight 8-foot board across them or by stretching a string across at intervals. Add shims or thickness pieces where necessary. Install ceiling wallboard first, then cover the overhead pipe and duct enclosures. Do the walls next, and finally the enclosures around vertical pipes. Use the installation techniques shown on pages 102–110. Be sure all joints between panels fall on joists or studs or have blocking behind them, and use metal edging on all outside corners.

SURVEYING THE ATTIC

If there is no floor in your attic, tack-nail some boards or plywood across the joists. Do not attempt to walk on the joist edges themselves—one slip could seriously damage the plaster ceiling of the room below, or put your foot all the way through a wallboard ceiling. In surveying the attic, examine the condition of the roof framing, any signs of water damage, the amount of insulation, the need for ventilation, and the potential for improving the space.

Weak roof framing can be supported with braces and posts *(opposite page)*. Staining, or damp boards or insulation are sure signs of leaks. That probably means roof and flashing repair *(Chapter 1)*. Correlate any water paths you detect in the attic with signs of deterioration in walls or ceilings below.

Insulation is essential in all parts of the country, but needs differ considerably *(pages 238–239)*. The older a house, the more likely that you need to add insulation.

All vent stacks that enter the attic space must lead without interruption to the outside, either through the roof or a gable. Extend any improper vents you find.

Proper ventilation of the attic space with a gable fan *(page 241)* will significantly lower the cost of air conditioning the rest of the house in hot weather. A large ceiling fan that exhausts into a well-ventilated attic *(pages 242–244)* is an economical alternative to whole-house air conditioning.

For any significant use of an attic, first put down a floor of $\frac{3}{4}$-inch plywood, but only if the joists are spaced no more than 16 inches on center, to provide proper support. Finishing an attic calls for building wall frames adapted to the shape of the space, insulating them, and covering them with wallboard *(Chapter 3)*. You may need a building permit for this kind of work; be sure to check.

Roof framing.

◆ Examine all structural members for signs of rot, insects, or water damage, probing suspect areas with an awl *(right)*. If more than four consecutive rafters are rotted, rebuilding of the roof may be in order; consult a professional.

◆ Check that vent pipes—for plumbing or a kitchen fan—discharge outside.

◆ Look for rust streaks from nailheads, and for other water stains, on the roof sheathing and around chimneys and vent pipes.

Attic insulation.

◆ In an unfinished attic, insert a ruler alongside several joists to measure the thickness of any insulation present *(left)*. For energy efficiency, temperate climates require at least a 6-inch thickness of insulation.

◆ If there is new blanket or batt insulation laid between joists, make sure the vapor barrier—a shiny foil—faces down, toward the warmth of the house. New insulation laid atop old should have no vapor barrier, which would trap moisture in the lower layer.

To check the insulation in an attic with a floor, look for knotholes or missing floorboards near the bottoms of rafters.

REINFORCING THE ROOF FRAME

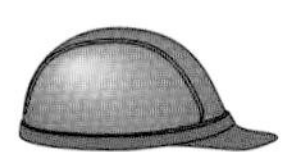

SAFETY TIP

When working in attics with low overhead space, a hard hat protects your head from sharp protruding nails.

Supporting sagging rafters.
One way to prevent a roof sag from worsening is to brace all of the rafters in the sagging area—plus an additional rafter to each side—against the joists below.
◆ Midway between the ridge and eave, nail a 2-by-6 brace at a right angle to each rafter *(right)*.
◆ Nail the other end to the side of the corresponding joist.

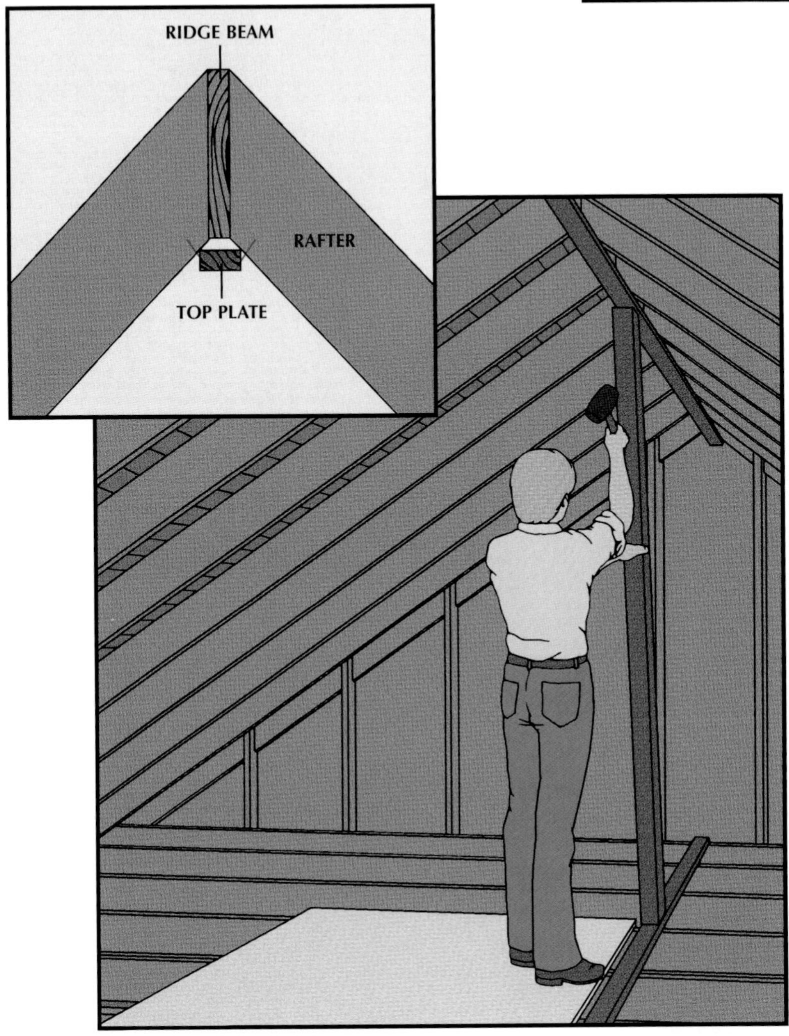

Strengthening the ridge beam.
You can brace a sagging ridge beam where there is a bearing wall under it on the floor below as follows:
◆ First, check that the wall is directly below the ridge beam by hanging a plumb bob from the beam to the attic floor; make sure the wall top plate is centered at the point indicated by the plumb bob. Also check that the wall runs the length of the ridge beam.
◆ Nail a 2-by-4 top plate to the underside of the ridge beam or, if necessary, to the undersides of the rafters *(inset)*. Directly below it, nail a 2-by-4 bottom plate across the joists.
◆ Measure the distance between the two plates and cut a 4-by-4 post that will fit tightly.
◆ Rest one end of the post on the bottom plate directly over a joist, angle the top end against the top plate, and tap the post into a vertical position with a heavy mallet *(left)*.
◆ Plumb the post with a carpenter's level, then toenail the post to the top and bottom plates.
◆ Install the remaining posts in the same way, spacing them every 8 to 10 feet along the length of the ridge.

PLANNING FOR COMFORT AND EFFICIENCY

When replacing a furnace, air conditioner, or heat pump, a new unit the same size as the old one can be a poor choice; it fails to take into account the aging of the house or improvements that may require different heating or cooling capacity.

A unit that is too small simply won't do the job, and one that is too large wastes money. In the case of an air conditioner, which dehumidifies the air in addition to cooling it, overcapacity can result in an uncomfortably clammy atmosphere: The unit cools the house before it has time to dry the air.

A Good Contractor: Buying the right size heating and cooling system is a complicated issue that is best left largely to a contractor. Find one who will agree to make a thorough assessment of your house and use the results to make a recommendation.

You can do some of the work yourself by filling in the house survey below. Using the map and charts at right, you can also assess insulation requirements, a factor that is as important to sizing a heating and cooling plant as it is to saving money on heating and cooling bills.

Other Factors: Even with this information, the contractor has many aspects of the house yet to investigate. Among them are the number of heating and cooling zones (or thermostats) in the house, and the condition of weather stripping and ducts. (Leaky ducts can rob a system of up to 30 percent of its capacity.) These factors and others, all influenced by the climate, indicate the total energy per hour required to heat or cool your house.

A Matter of Efficiency: No furnace, air conditioner, or heat pump is 100 percent efficient in using this energy. Yet the unit that wastes the least is not always the best choice. Often more expensive than a less efficient model, it may not pay for itself in fuel savings before you plan to sell the house. For this reason and others, your contractor may recommend something other than a unit with the highest efficiency rating.

Hiring a contractor.
Filling out this inventory will give a heating and cooling contractor a head start in evaluating your house for a new heating and cooling system. While most of the entries are unambiguous, a couple of them benefit from explanation. Under window types, for example, count storm windows as single pane, not double. If a ceiling or floor has no more than one-tenth the insulation recommended in the charts on the next page, count the area as uninsulated.

HOUSE INVENTORY

Window Area by Side of House

North: _____ sq. ft.
South: _____ sq. ft.
East: _____ sq. ft.
West: _____ sq. ft.

Window Types

Single pane: _____ sq. ft.
Double pane or glass block: _____ sq. ft.

Walls

Length of all exterior walls (southern exposure): _____ ft.
Length of all exterior walls (all other exposures): _____ ft.
Length of interior walls separating a garage or other unheated or uncooled space from the house: _____ ft.

Area of Roof or Ceiling

Roof, uninsulated: _____ sq. ft.
Roof with at least 1" of insulation: _____ sq. ft.
Ceiling with occupied space above: _____ sq. ft.
Ceiling below an insulated attic: _____ sq. ft.
Ceiling below an uninsulated attic: _____ sq. ft.

Floor (Disregard if house is on slab)

Insulated: _____ sq. ft.
Uninsulated: _____ sq. ft.

HOW MUCH INSULATION IS ENOUGH?

Insulation zones.
This map and accompanying chart reflect the U.S. Department of Energy's insulation recommendations, expressed as R-values, for each of three insulation zones in the United States. Irregular zone contours result in part from the generally lower temperatures found in mountainous regions. All of Canada lies in Zone 3, except for the west coast, which falls in Zone 2. If you live on the border between two zones, choose the zone with the higher number.

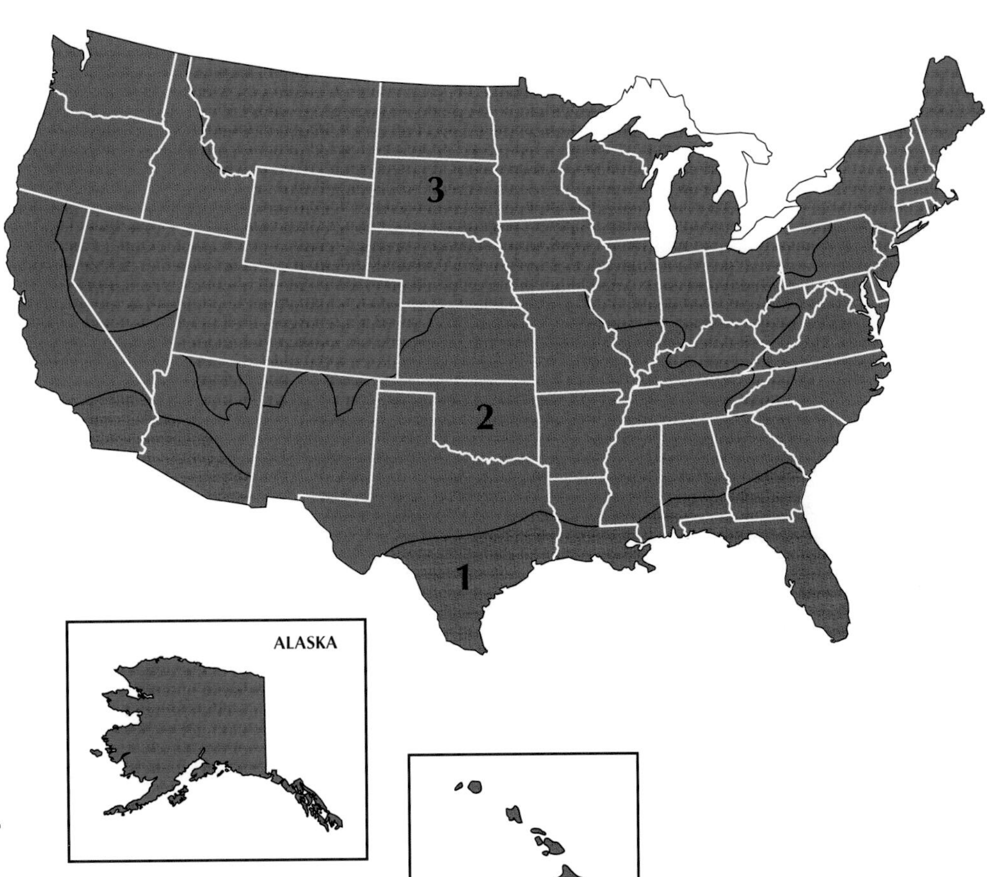

RECOMMENDED R-VALUES

Zone	Ceiling or roof	Exterior wall	Floor
1	R-30	R-11	0
2	R-38	R-11	R-19
3	R-49	R-11	R-19

R-VALUES BY THICKNESS OF INSULATION

R-Value	Mineral Fiber Batts or Blankets	Fiberglass Batts or Blankets	Cellulose Fiber Loose or Blown Fill
R-11	$3\frac{1}{2}$"	$4\frac{3}{4}$"	$3\frac{3}{4}$"
R-19	6"	8"	$6\frac{1}{2}$"
R-30	$9\frac{1}{4}$"	$12\frac{1}{2}$"	$10\frac{1}{2}$"
R-38	$11\frac{1}{2}$"	16"	13"
R-49	$15\frac{1}{4}$"	$20\frac{1}{2}$"	17"

Assessing your insulation.
Any house benefits from insulation installed in any partition—ceiling, roof, floor, or wall—that marks a boundary of the heated and air-conditioned parts of a house. To find out how much insulation you have, check unfinished attics, basements, or crawlspaces. Insulation batts and blankets usually have the R-value printed on the backing paper or foil. If not—or if you have loose, blown-in insulation—measure the thickness of the insulation and consult the chart to find the approximate R-value.

R-value can be increased in attics by laying new batts or blankets perpendicular to the existing material until the combined R-values equal the recommended number. In walls or floors, the cost of ripping out drywall or plaster must be factored against the benefit of lower energy costs over the period of time you expect to live in the house.

AN ATTIC FAN TO LOWER COOLING COSTS

When summer comes and the temperature rises, an attic fan can be a big money-saver. Air in an unvented attic may reach 150°F, making your home's air conditioner run continuously to hold the temperature in the living quarters at 78°F. A fan can reduce the attic temperature to 95°F and cut your air conditioning bill by as much as 30 percent.

Fan Choices: By far the easiest attic fan to install is one that mounts inside a vented gable *(opposite page)*. It creates a flow of air across the attic from a vent in the opposite gable. Be sure to get a unit with an adjustable thermostat that will turn the fan on and off at preset temperatures. If your house does not have central air conditioning, a whole-house ceiling fan *(pages 242–244)* is a better choice as long as your attic has or can be fitted with vents of sufficient area. An alternative choice for a house with masonry walls or where gable vents are not feasible, is a roof fan. It is more efficient, but requires cutting through the roof and doing some work from the outside. Installation of this kind of fan is not covered here, but most units come with adequate instructions.

Soffit Vents: Whatever kind of fan you install, you may need to add soffit vents *(opposite, bottom)* at regular intervals under the eaves on both sides of the house to replace the heated air expelled by the fan. Use the formula below to calculate the vent area required. Make sure attic insulation over the eaves does not block the air flow from the soffit vents. Install baffles to control loose-fill insulation if necessary.

TOOLS

- Extension ladder
- Ladder hooks
- Tape measure
- Hammer
- Linoleum knife
- Saber saw
- Electric drill with $\frac{3}{8}$" bit
- Spade bit ($\frac{3}{4}$")
- Pry bar
- Screwdriver
- Fish tape
- Wire cutter
- Wire stripper

MATERIALS

- Roofing cement
- Galvanized common nails ($2\frac{1}{2}$")
- Lumber (2 x 4)
- Fan thermostat
- 2-wire grounded cable (No. 12)
- Screw-on wire caps
- Soffit vents with mounting screws

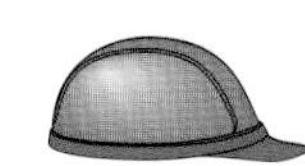

SAFETY TIPS

Wear rubber-soled shoes when on the roof, and use a ladder with ladder hooks over the ridge on a roof with a slope of more than 4 inches in 12. Use goggles, dust mask, and ear protectors when sawing, and goggles when nailing. Wear a hard hat in the attic for protection against projecting nails. Wear heavy work gloves when using a linoleum knife.

CALCULATIONS FOR FAN AND VENT CAPACITY

Attic floor area in square feet

_____________ x 0.7 = ____________ cfm

Fan capacity.

To determine the minimum capacity for a roof or gable fan, measured in cubic feet per minute (cfm) at "static air pressure," use the formula above. Add 15 percent for a dark roof, which absorbs more heat than a light one. If a fan is rated at "free air delivery," subtract 25 percent from its cfm rating to get its true capacity.

Attic floor area in square feet

_____________ ÷ 150 = ____________ sq. ft.

Estimating net vent area.

Use the formula above to determine the "net vent area" required for inlet vents. This formula is for vents that offer no more resistance to airflow than $\frac{1}{2}$-inch screening. Vents with metal louvers call for $1\frac{1}{2}$ times the net vent area; those with wood louvers call for twice as much. Most vents are 8 by 16 inches or smaller; install as many as needed to make up this area.

MOUNTING A FAN ON A GABLE VENT

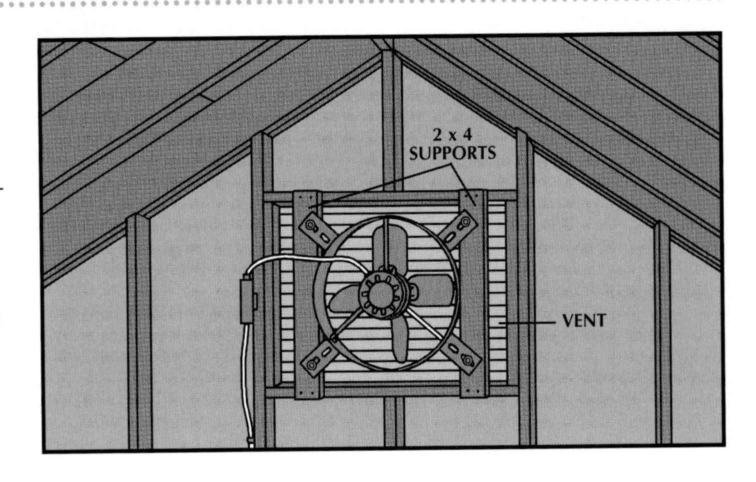

Over a rectangular vent.

◆ Position the fan at the center of the vent, and mark the width of the fan cylinder on the headers above and below.
◆ Cut two 2-by-4 supports to fit the vertical distance between the headers, and nail them in place with their inside edges flush with the marks.
◆ Screw the ventilator fan to these supports, and attach the thermostat to a convenient stud nearby. Connect the thermostat to a receptacle.
◆ If the gable vent at the other end of the attic is too small to serve the fan *(box, opposite page)*, add soffit vents *(below)*.

Over a triangular vent.

◆ If the fan flanges reach to the vent's wooden frame, screw the assembly directly to the frame.
◆ If the frame is larger than the flange, install vertical 2-by-4 supports *(above)* and attach the assembly to these supports.

Installing soffit vents.

◆ On the underside of the eave, locate the lookout beams by finding the rows of nails that secure the soffit to the beams.
◆ Hold the vent centered between the outside wall and the edge of the eave, and between two lookout beams. Outline the screened area of the vent on the soffit.
◆ Use a saber saw to cut out the vent opening, insert the vent into the hole from below, and secure it to the soffit with screws through the vent's flange holes.

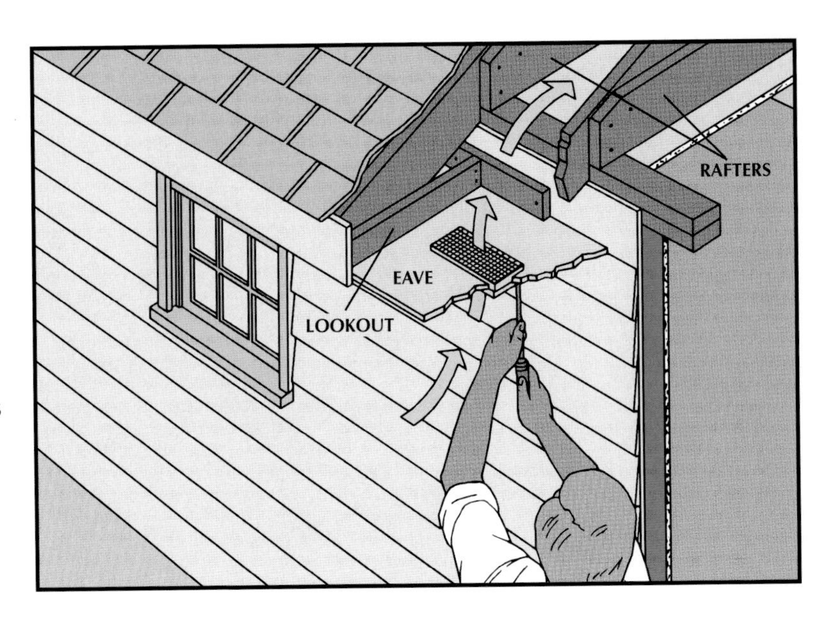

A KING-SIZE FAN TO COOL A HOUSE

A powerful fan, mounted on an attic's floor joists, can create a pleasant breeze throughout a house. Less expensive to install than central air conditioning, it also costs less to run.

Controlled by a switch downstairs, the fan pulls fresh air in through open windows and drives attic air out through gable and soffit vents. A louvered shutter below closes automatically when the fan is idle, sealing off hot summer air.

Installation Methods: Place the fan in a central location, or near a stairwell. Some models can be mounted directly on top of joists. Others require the construction of a supporting wood frame.

If the fan fits between joists, the frame consists of a square that is formed by two joists and two crosspieces nailed between them. More often, the frame must be built as shown opposite.

Buying a Fan: To determine how big a fan you need, use the formulas below. Look for a unit with an automatic shutoff for an overheated fan, and a control that shuts down the fan in a fire.

Ask the dealer for the correct attic vent area for your fan and calculate the net area for metal- or wood-louvered vents. Some methods for installing soffit and gable vents are shown on page 241.

TOOLS

Utility knife
Hammer
Electric drill and bits
Keyhole saw
Circular saw or saber saw
Tape measure
Screwdriver

MATERIALS

Cardboard sheet
Joist lumber
Common nails (2", $3\frac{1}{2}$")
1 x 3s

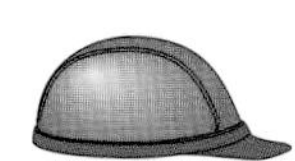

SAFETY TIPS

Safety goggles protect your eyes when you are hammering, working with power tools, and handling insulation. This material also requires a dust mask to prevent the inhalation of fibers, and work gloves to guard against skin irritation.

CALCULATING NET AIR VOLUME

Total floor area in square feet ________ x **Average ceiling height in feet** ________ = **Gross air volume** ________ **cubic feet**

Gross air volume ________ x 0.9 = **Net air volume** ________ **cubic feet**

The top formula gives the total volume of your house, which the second formula discounts for closets and other spaces that need no cooling. The result is net air volume. In the southern United States, buy a fan capable of moving this quantity of air each minute. Half that capacity is adequate in the North and Canada.

FRAMING AN OPENING

1. Making a template.

◆ Place the shutter, louvers up, on a sheet of cardboard and draw around it with a pencil. Cut along the line with a utility knife in order to make a template.

◆ Drive a nail through the ceiling at the location you have chosen for the fan.

◆ In the attic, remove any insulation that may be covering the nail and set it aside for use in cold-weather months to cover the fan.

◆ Set the template over the nail with one edge against a joist. Mark the corners of the edge on the surface below and drill two small holes at these points.

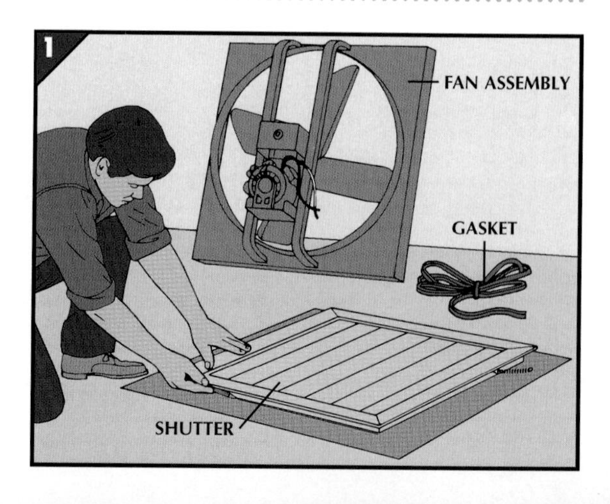

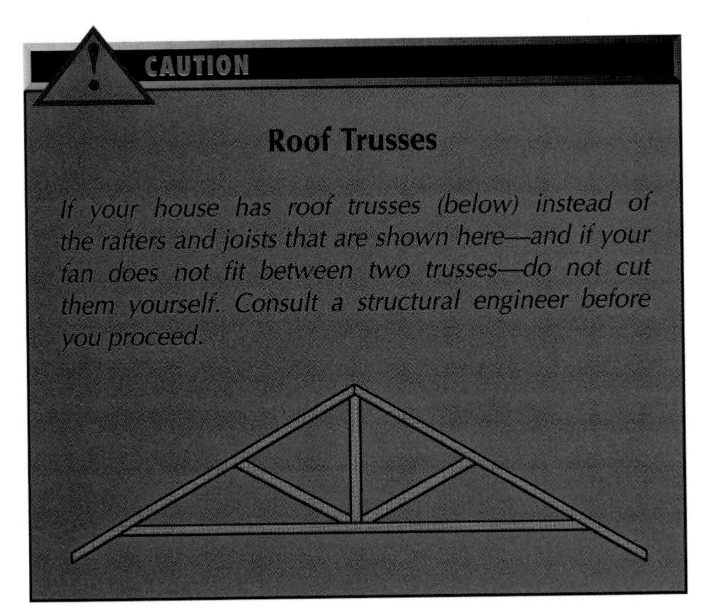

CAUTION

Roof Trusses

If your house has roof trusses (below) instead of the rafters and joists that are shown here—and if your fan does not fit between two trusses—do not cut them yourself. Consult a structural engineer before you proceed.

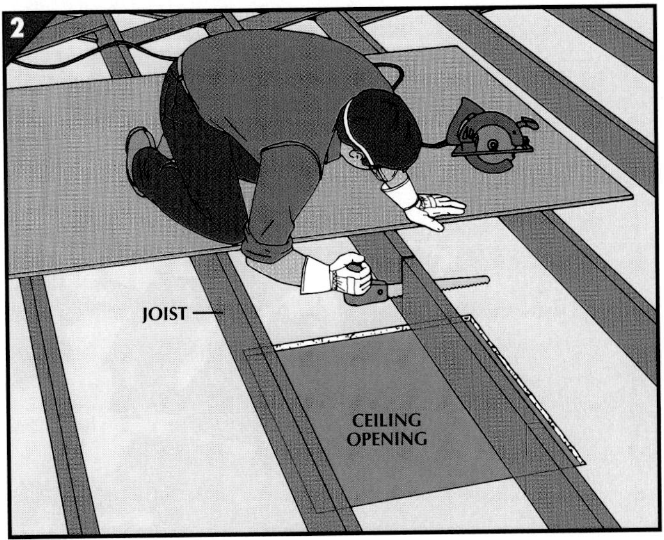

2. Cutting the opening.

◆ In the room below, align the template with the holes and mark the two other corners of the template on the ceiling. Drill small holes at these points.

◆ Join the four holes with straight lines to form a square and cut along the lines with a keyhole or saber saw. Skip over the ceiling joist when you come to it; after sawing, score the uncut segments of the outline with a utility knife.

◆ Break up the ceiling board under the joist with a hammer and tear it away with your hands.

◆ Working in the attic, remove a section of the exposed joist $1\frac{1}{2}$ inches outside the edges of the opening. Cut through most of the joist with a circular or saber saw. Then finish the cuts with a keyhole saw—reversing the handle to avoid damaging the ceiling below.

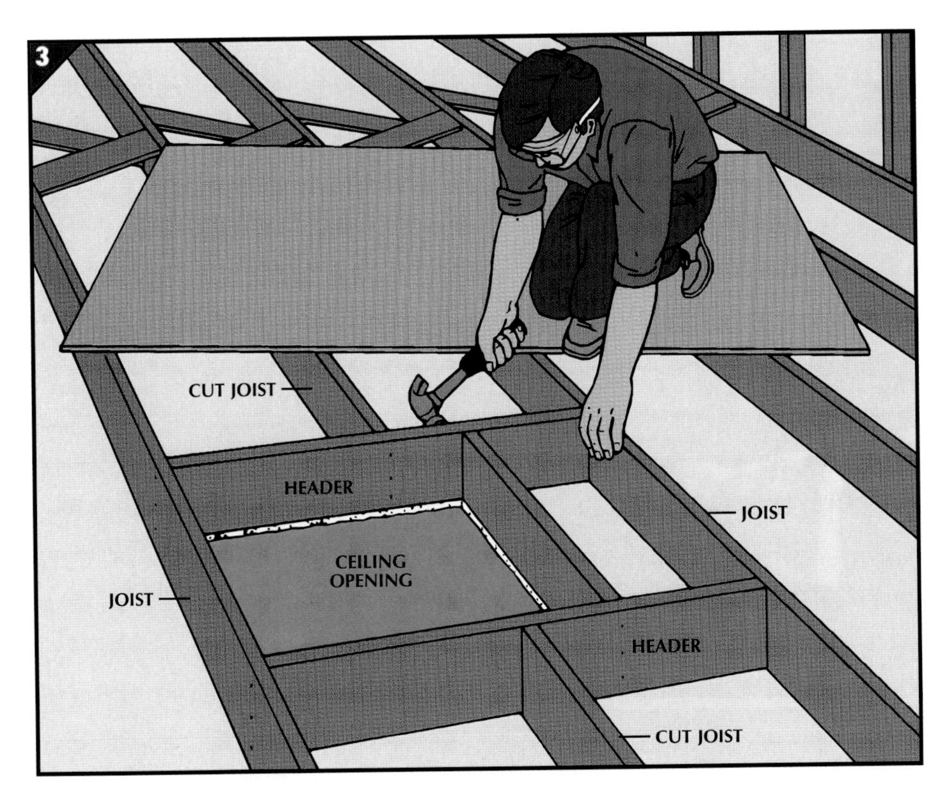

3. Making headers.

◆ Measure the distance between the uncut joists flanking the opening and cut two headers to this length, using wood the same size as the joists.

◆ Set the headers at the edges of the opening, and nail them to the sides of the uncut joists and the ends of the cut ones.

◆ To complete the frame, cut a third length of wood to fit between the headers, set it flush to the unframed edge of the opening, and nail it to the headers.

INSTALLING THE FAN

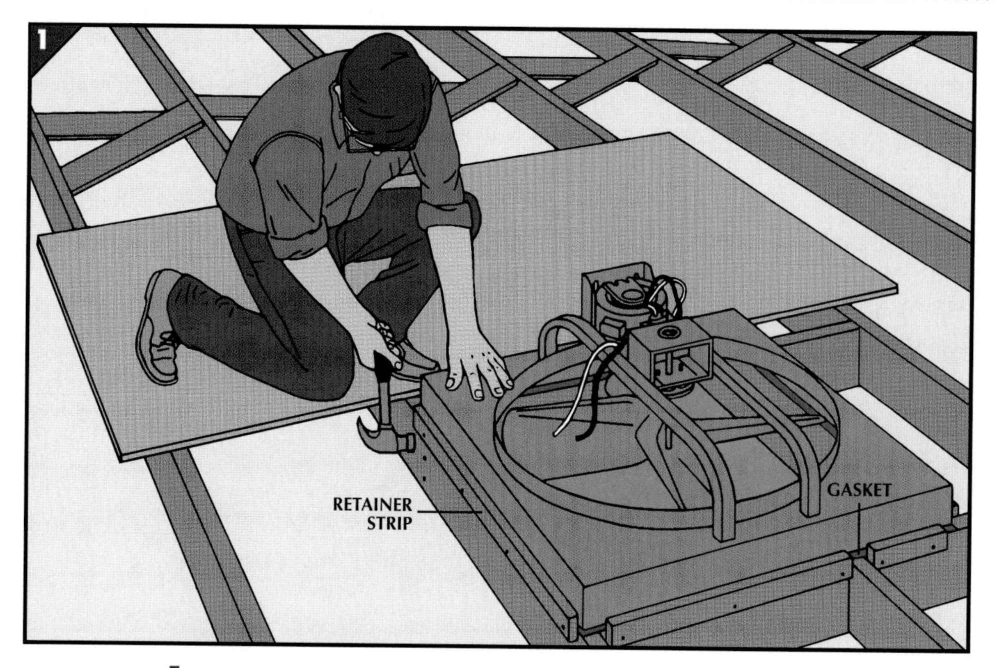

1. Positioning the fan assembly.

◆ Set the felt or rubber gasket on the wood frame (in some models this gasket is attached to the fan assembly at the factory) and then lower the fan onto the cushioned frame.

◆ Nail 1-by-3 retainer strips to the sides of the joists and headers around the fan assembly, with about an inch of each strip projecting above the frame.

2. Attaching the shutter.

◆ In the room below, adjust the spring at the side of the shutter to close the louvers gently when you hold them open and release them.

◆ Working from a stepladder, lift the vent into the ceiling opening and mark the positions of the screw holes in the shutter flange. Drill pilot holes at these points and screw the shutter through the ceiling to the frame above. If you are inexperienced with wiring, hire an electrician for the next two steps.

◆ In the attic, connect the black and white fan motor wires to a cable in an outlet box fastened to a nearby joist or header; from the box, run this cable to the basement service panel for a new 20-amp, 120-volt circuit connection.

◆ Install an on-off or a timer switch on a convenient wall in the living quarters.

SAFE AND EFFICIENT FIREPLACES

Fireplaces can be among the most attractive features of an old house, but their safety should not be taken for granted. Before using an old fireplace for the first time, check all its crucial parts. Particularly important is the flue liner *(below)*—a duct, normally of terra cotta, that serves as a protective seal for the chimney's interior, preventing leakage of the rising smoke and acting as a heat insulator. You can check for leaks in this lining by the method described at the bottom of the next page. If your chimney was built without a liner, or if the liner has misaligned tiles or other structural flaws, ask a chimney sweep for a safety evaluation. It may be necessary to have a liner installed or replaced—a major job.

Cleaning the Chimney: Make sure the flue is clean, and keep it that way: A buildup of soot and creosote in the flue could ignite and cause an intense fire within the chimney, spewing out flame and debris above and below. You can do routine cleaning with flexible rods and a properly fitted brush *(page 247)*, but if the deposits are thick, the services of a chimney sweep may be required.

Exterior Fixes: Check the chimney at its top for signs of deterioration or other problems. If the flashing is faulty and admitting rainwater, you may be able to seal it with roofing cement. Another trouble-prone area is the chimney crown, the mortar pyramid that sits atop the chimney; it can crack and allow water to leak in around the flue's edges. A cracked crown should be patched or rebuilt *(page 247)*.

You may also want to install a rain cap *(page 248)*. This simple addition will provide protection against puddles in the fireplace, keep out warmth-seeking animals, and prevent downdrafts into living spaces.

Fixing a Faulty Draft: If your fireplace smokes chronically, you can improve the draft by reducing the size of the fireplace opening. The interior dimensions of the flue should be roughly one-tenth the area of the fireplace. The easiest way to reduce the opening is to install a glass fire screen *(pages 248–249)*.

TOOLS

Droplight
Flashlight
Flexible rods and brush attachment
Hand-held brush
Vacuum with high-efficiency particulate air (HEPA) filter
Ball-peen hammer
Cold chisel
Trowel

MATERIALS

Refractory mortar
Plywood board
Wrap-on fiberglass insulation (3")
Silicone adhesive
Duct tape
Fiberglass patch
Sand mortar mix
Stainless-steel rain cap with setscrews
Glass screen set

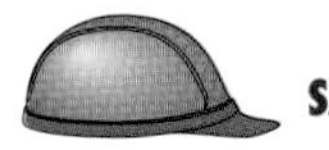

SAFETY TIPS

When cleaning the flue, wear goggles to protect against dust; add a respirator when working from below. Wear gloves and goggles to protect hands and eyes when chipping mortar.

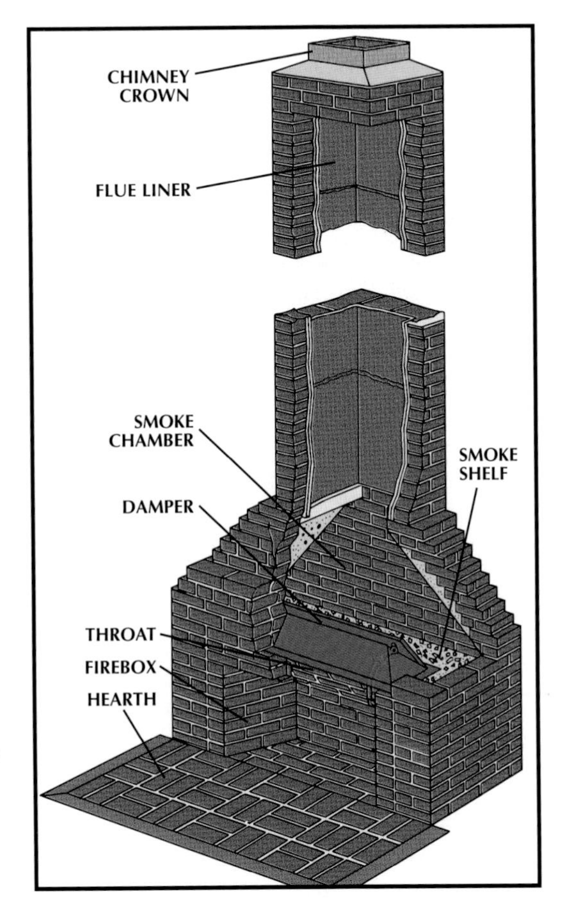

Flue check points.
◆ Working from the roof, lower a droplight into the flue liner. If soot and creosote obscure its surface, remove enough of these deposits to allow inspection.
◆ Examine the flue liner for cracks, misaligned tiles, and missing mortar in the joints between tiles.
◆ Make sure the chimney cap is solid and uncracked.
◆ Inside the house, check the joint between the firebox floor and the hearth. Loose or crumbling mortar in this area can be repaired with refractory mortar.
◆ Make sure that the damper works and that the smoke shelf is free of debris. Examine the smoke chamber, the throat, and the bottom of the flue liner; repoint any bad joints.

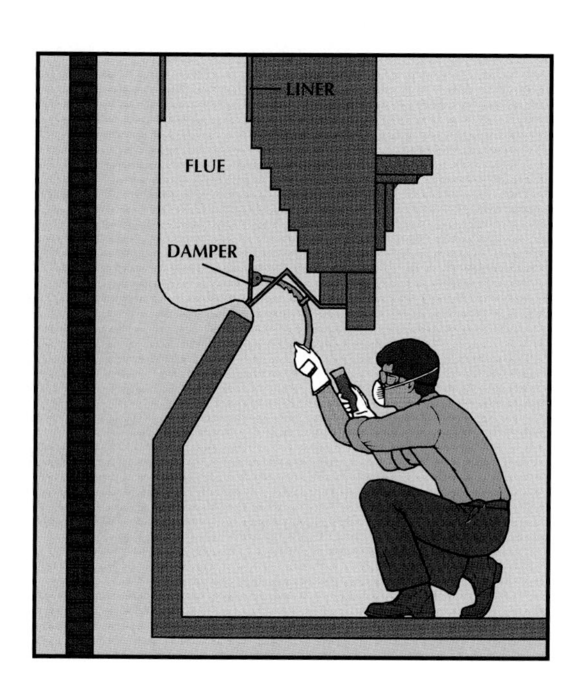

Inspecting fireplaces.
◆ Using a flashlight, make sure that the fireplace has a damper and that it operates easily and closes tightly.
◆ With the damper open, determine if the chimney has a liner and that it is in good condition, not crumbling. A chimney that lacks a liner is unsafe.
◆ Inspect the front of the fireplace and the wall above for smoke stains, which would indicate poor draw.
◆ Measure the flue; it should be about one-seventh the area of the fireplace opening, and at least 8 inches by 12 inches for wood fires. Fireplaces that were designed for burning coal and gas have flues too small for wood fires; rebuilding is impractical.

Checking for flue leaks.
◆ Make sure the flue liner and smoke chamber are clean.
◆ Cut a section of plywood board that is 3 inches taller and 6 inches wider than the fireplace opening.
◆ Line the outer perimeter of one side of the board with two layers of 3-inch-wide wrap-on fiberglass insulation, secured with a $1\frac{1}{2}$-inch bead of silicone adhesive.
◆ Prop some wet and dry twisted newspaper on the smoke shelf above the damper *(right)* and light it.
◆ Fit the board against the fireplace, insulation side facing the firebox.
◆ As soon as smoke begins to exit the flue, have a helper on the roof seal the chimney by taping a sturdy plastic bag to it with duct tape.
◆ Check the full length of the chimney for smoke leaks, indoors and out. Where the flue passes behind finished walls, look for leaks under baseboards or around frames of doors and windows; a leak will be easiest to spot if you do this inspection with a flashlight in the dark.
◆ Once the smoke test is done, uncover the chimney top and let the smoke clear for at least 15 minutes before slowly uncovering the fireplace opening.
◆ Clear off the smoke shelf.

CLEANING THE CHIMNEY

Cleaning the flue.

◆ Open the damper and tape two layers of plastic—from sturdy bags—over the fireplace opening.

◆ Remove any screen or cap that is covering the top of the flue.

◆ With flexible rods and a brush attachment sized to fit your flue opening *(left),* move the brush slowly up and down as you progress down the flue.

◆ As an alternate method, pour 2 to 3 pounds of sand into a cloth bag about half the size of a pillowcase. Tie a rope around the bag and lower it down the chimney several times, letting the bag rub against the sides of the flue.

◆ Wait an hour for the soot to settle, then unseal the opening and gently remove the debris with a HEPA filter-equipped vacuum. (Soot can ruin a household vacuum.)

◆ With a brush, sweep debris from the smoke shelf into a paper bag held at the fireplace throat.

REPAIRING THE CHIMNEY TOP

Renewing the chimney crown.

◆ If the crown mortar has just a small crack or two, fiberglass patches will be a sufficient seal.

◆ If the crown is mostly solid but has crumbled in a few places, remove any loose portions, fill the gaps, and cover with new mortar.

◆ For more serious deterioration, chip off the crown with a ball-peen hammer and a cold chisel *(right).* To avoid damaging the chimney, never direct the chisel toward the bricks.

◆ Brush away the debris and dust, and dampen the area.

◆ Trowel sand mortar on to form a sloping crown that extends from the edge of the brick to about halfway up the side of the top flue liner.

◆ Place the edge of a piece of cardboard—to serve as a spacer—between the mortar and the top of the flue liner, which should extend no more than 4 inches above the top of the crown.

◆ Cover the area with a large plastic bag secured to the side of the chimney with duct tape.

◆ Let the mortar dry for several days, then remove the plastic and the cardboard spacer. Fill the gap left by the spacer with silicone adhesive.

Adding a rain cap.

◆ At a hardware or hearth-products store, buy a stainless-steel rain cap to fit around the perimeter of the flue top.

◆ With a screwdriver, secure the cap to the top of the flue with the setscrews provided with the unit *(left).*

INSTALLING A GLASS FIREPLACE SCREEN

1. Positioning the frame.

◆ The frame for a glass screen may come with the doors attached; remove them according to the manufacturer's instructions.

◆ Attach fireproof insulation and the mounting-bracket and lintel-clamp assemblies to the back of the screen frame. (The insulation will keep air from flowing in from the sides of the frame.)

◆ Place the frame for the screen over the fireplace opening *(right).*

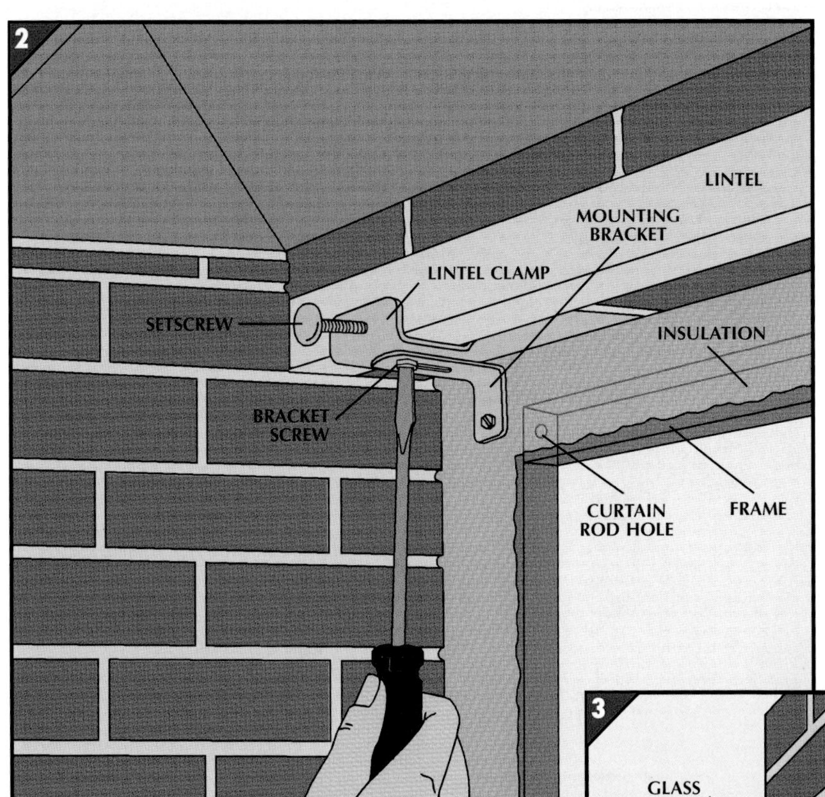

2. Fastening the clamps.

◆ Squatting or lying inside the fireplace, fit each lintel clamp over the lintel and tighten the clamp's setscrew.

◆ Holding the frame firmly against the fireplace opening so that the insulation forms a good seal, tighten the bracket screw that joins the mounting bracket to the lintel clamp *(left)*.

3. Fitting the mesh curtain and doors.

Methods of securing screens—either curtain or rigid types—and glass doors vary. For the unit shown at right, first slip the rod and curtain through the prefabricated holes at the top of the frame. Then slip the two door pins on the side of one door into the pin holes on the side of the frame. Fit on the other door in the same way.

CAUTION *Check the instructions for your glass screen carefully to see whether it is safe to close the doors when a fire is burning. The glass in some units cannot withstand high temperatures.*

APPENDIX: FINDING THE RIGHT SPECIALIST

There are few improvements that a homeowner cannot accomplish with patience and careful planning. Although a professional generally can work faster, homeowners possess the greatest incentive to do a job well: They have to live with the results.

Nonetheless, few homeowners have the time, the inclination, or the tools to tackle every job, and some tasks should be left to a professional for the sake of safety—changing an electric meter, for instance, or connecting natural-gas piping. In these situations, turning to a specialist makes sense.

Before you do, consult the directory below. It lists the most common building trades and services, describes what these professionals do, and offers tips on what to look for in a contract with them.

Evaluating Subcontractors: Successful subcontracting depends on careful planning and thorough research. In considering potential subcontractors, first see that they are reliable. Find out how long they have been in business. If they are new to the trade, try to determine their current credit rating. Check for any complaints with a local consumer-protection agency or ask suppliers whether they pay bills promptly. A bankrupt subcontractor can mean heavy losses for you.

Equally important are quality of work and the ability to finish it on time. Ask previous clients for references and, if possible, inspect the workmanship of past jobs. In many cases you can get sound referrals in your neighborhood, as it is a sign of good performance when a builder can rely on word of mouth to make a business prosper.

Whenever possible, secure more than one bid, but make sure you are comparing apples with apples. To do this, you may need to provide each bidder with a written list of materials and a description of the scope of work, as well as with copies of any sketches or plans.

Defining the Work: Once you have settled on a subcontractor, draw up a contract. Include your drawings and spell out—in writing—exactly what work is to be done, specifying the quantities, brand names, grades, and model numbers for any materials. Include a timetable for work and payments and stipulate that the workers clean up after the job. Finally, make certain that your subcontractor carries general liability insurance and provides workers' compensation for everyone employed on the project.

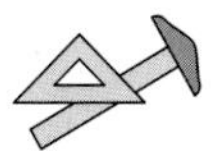

Architect

Traditional contracts with architects give them full responsibility for projects and pay them a percentage of the total cost, but for renovation projects you may be able to find someone who will work at an hourly rate. On this basis, the architect can serve largely in an advisory capacity, helping you decide what to do, providing you with drawings, and recommending other specialists. But make sure that the architect's tastes and ideas are compatible with your own.

Bricklayer

These specialists will repoint mortar joints, clean brickwork, repair stucco, and perform the heavier jobs involved in building or rebuilding masonry walls, fireplaces, and chimneys. Contact bricklayers early, because they may be hard to find during times when the weather is good.

Carpenter

The versatility of carpenters makes their skills essential for any renovation work. Some specialize in rough carpentry: framing new walls and floors, reinforcing old, and building forms for concrete. Others do finish carpentry: laying wood floors, hanging doors, and installing cabinets and decorative trim. Experienced carpenters are often competent at both. Carpenters can often recommend other specialists and give scheduling advice. Most will use the materials you supply, but many get discounts at lumberyards and are willing to pass on the savings.

Cement Mason

Check with these concrete or paving contractors when you want a professional to pour cement or to repair a driveway or sidewalk. You may have to make several calls; many companies are reluctant to do small jobs or give estimates.

Contractor

Generally, you will save time and money dealing directly with subcontractors. But if you have a large number of complicated or interrelated jobs, a coordinator may be essential. General contractors will digest the plans, assemble a team of specialists, schedule their work, and see that it is executed properly. Some, particularly those who operate small companies, will allow you to do portions of the work yourself to save money. If you take on an intermediate part of a long job, plan to conform to the contractor's schedule.

Drywall Installer

Any careful amateur can fasten small pieces of drywall to studs, but large sheets are unwieldy, and unless you have a helper, subcontracting may be the best way to guarantee a neat job. Many general carpenters will also do this work.

Electrician
Whenever you call in an electrician, you can reasonably expect the job to be done to professional standards. In most areas an electrician must pass a licensing examination, and electrical work must be inspected after the rough wiring is in and again after the job is completed. Most electricians will take small jobs or completely rewire an old house.

Excavating Contractor
This subcontractor has the heavy equipment to do grading, trenching, or backfilling around a house, or even to excavate a basement or swimming pool. Many excavating contractors may be reluctant to take a small grading job, so checking with paving and landscape contractors may prove worthwhile. The latter prefer jobs in which they can sell you some trees, plants, or sod, but they are equipped to do grading around houses.

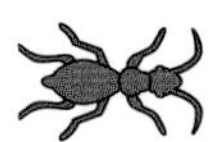

Exterminator
Most exterminators will contract for a single job or for ongoing services with a renewable guarantee. The market is competitive; shop for the best price.

Floor Layer
Professional floor layers work with carpeting, linoleum, and tile floor coverings and may specialize in one of these. Usually floor layers supply materials and labor; check the quality and price of materials as well as workmanship. This service is sometimes available through department stores.

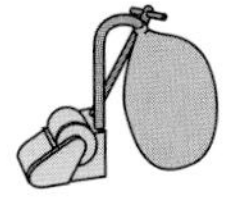

Floor Sander and Refinisher
This specialty is also performed by some floor layers and carpenters. Be sure to hire someone who does such work frequently, and always postpone floor refinishing until all other messy interior jobs have been finished.

Glazier
You can easily replace small panes of glass yourself, but contract with a glazier to cut, fit, and install insulating glass or plate-glass windows, mirrors, and glass doors. Glaziers will generally provide both materials and labor.

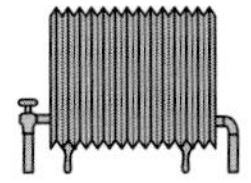

Heating and Cooling Contractor
Most heating and cooling companies feature a specific brand of furnace or air conditioner, so first determine the most appropriate appliance for your needs. Generally, the contractor provides all the equipment and oversees a crew of specialists—sheet-metal workers for air ducts, licensed plumbers or electricians for final connections. For repair jobs, ascertain the minimum charge for a service call as well as the hourly rates.

Insulation Worker
Insulation materials come in a variety of forms—rolls, sheets, pellets, blocks, and pastes—and some contractors specialize in only one or two. In many areas the home-insulation business has become very competitive. Get several bids and familiarize yourself with the type, insulating value, and fire rating of the material each contractor is promoting.

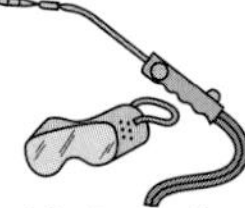

Ornamental-Iron Worker
Listings for ornamental-iron workers are usually mixed with those for heavy industry under "Iron Works." These specialists can fabricate and install, or repair, metal balconies, gates, fences, stairways, window grilles, and the like.

Painter and Paperhanger
Some professionals do both, but painting and paperhanging are often considered separate trades. Most of the cost of either goes for labor, so shop for the best rate you can get for quality work. A recommendation from your neighbors is often the best bet—whether you are looking to hire a small subcontractor or a large firm that may be better equipped for exterior projects requiring scaffolding.

Plasterer and Lather
Because most interior-wall finishing is now done with gypsum wallboard, locating a plasterer for interior walls, exterior stucco, or ornamental moldings may call for some detective work on your part. Ask local carpenters, general contractors, or the managers of old apartment buildings to make recommendations. Call a plasterer as far in advance as possible.

Plumber
Like electrical work, plumbing work is regulated by code and licensing requirements. The plumber assembles and maintains any piping that carries water, steam, or gas, and installs and connects such household appliances as water heaters or dishwashers.

Roofer
Roofers resurface or repair the outer layer of a roof to ensure that it is watertight. Some will work on the underlying structure, while others employ carpenters to replace sheathing or rafters. Select a recommended roofer specializing in your type of surface—asphalt, slate, tile, wood shingles, tin. Insist on a guarantee for a new roof; try to get one for any repair work as well. Many roofers repair gutters and will waterproof walls and basements. Some department stores contract for roofing and gutter work.

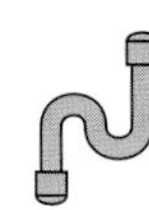

Septic Tank Servicer
These specialists pump out and clean septic tanks. They frequently offer sewer- and drain-cleaning services as well. Septic tank servicing is available in most areas, for a single job or as a continuing service.

Stonemason
A stonemason works with stone as a structural material in walls and chimneys and as a decorative surface for floors, patios, and stairs. You may have to make several calls to find a stonemason willing to do a small repair job.

A

B

C

D

E

F

Time-Life Books is a division of
TIME LIFE INC.

Time-Life Custom Publishing
Vice President and Publisher: Terry Newell
Project Manager: Christopher M. Register
Director of Sales: Neil Levin
Sales Manager: Liz Ziehl
Director of New Product Development: Regina Hall
Managing Editor: Donia Ann Steele
Production Manager: Carolyn Bounds
Quality Assurance Manager: James D. King

Produced by Roundtable Press, Inc.
Directors: Marsha Melnick, Susan E. Meyer
Senior Editor: William L. Broecker
Assistant Editor: Abigail A. Anderson
Photo Research: Ede Rothaus Associates
Production: Steven Rosen

First printing. Printed in U.S.A.
Published simultaneously in Canada.

Time-Life is a trademark
of Time Warner Inc. U.S.A.

Library of Congress Cataloging-in-Publication Data
YOUR OLD HOUSE: give new life to your older home
/by the editors of Time-Life Books.
p. cm.—
Includes index.
ISBN 0-7835-4829-X
1. Dwellings—Maintenance and repair—Amateurs' manuals.
I. Time-Life Books.
TH4817.3.Y683 1996 96-19374
643'.7 — dc20 CIP

Photography Credits:

Cover Photo: James Massey
William Abranowicz: 59, bottom right
Diana Adams: 40
Doug Adams/Unicorn Stock Photos: 43
Otto Baitz/ESTO: 184—185
Bob Barrett/Unicorn Stock Photos: 9, top right
BHP Steel Products USA, Inc.: 12
Alan Briere: 41
Bruce Hardwood Floors: 59, top left
Chicago Faucets: 143, top right
Clark Industries, Inc.: 70
Renée Comet: 14(2) prop courtesy Murray-Black Company, 19, 22–23, 47, 54, 83, 89, 98, 107, 109, 110, 122–23, 127, 135, 146–47, 148–49, 153, 181, 190–91, 209
Robert Finken/The Picture Cube: 41; 120, bottom
Georgia Pacific: 12
Jeff Greenberg: 187, top left
John M. Hall: 6—7; 8, top; 9, bottom right; 9, top left; 86 middle; 121, top left; 143, bottom right
Nancy Hutchinson: 189(3)
Ken Kay: 168
Alan Klehr: 12
Kohler: 142 top right
Michael Latil: 61, 73
Louisville Ladder Corporation: 24
Fred Lyon: 227, bottom
Lee Meyer: 226, bottom right
Bradley Olman: 58, top left; 59, middle; 87, middle; 143, top left; 226, bottom left
Peter Paige: 87, bottom left
PANELLIFT® brand drywall lift manufactured by Telpro Inc.: 104
Robert Perron: 58, top right; 86, bottom right; 224—225
Kenneth Rice: 40, 41, 42(2), 43
Eric Roth: 56—57; 87 top left; 118—119; 120, top; 140—141
Bill Rothschild: 86 top right; 121, middle
Jim Shippee/Unicorn Stock Photos: 227, top left
Southern Pine Council—Terry A. Smiley: 12(2)
Bonnie Sue Rauch: 226, top right
TYCOMM: 12(2)
Aneal Vohra/Unicorn Stock Photos: 42
Jessie Walker: 8, bottom; 58 bottom right; 84—85; 121, bottom right; 186, top; 186, bottom; 187, top right; page 187, bottom right
Werner Ladder Company: 26
George White Jr.: 43
Terry Wild Studio: 142, bottom